ENTREPRENEURSHIP

Starting and Operating a Small Business

SECOND EDITION

Steve Mariotti
Caroline Glackin

Prentice Hall
Upper Saddle River, New Jersey
Columbus, Ohio

Library of Congress Cataloging-in-Publication Data

Mariotti, Steve

   Entrepreneurship: starting and operating a small business.—2nd ed./Steve Mariotti, Caroline Glackin.
      p. cm.
   Includes bibliographical references and index.
   ISBN 978-0-13-236600-7 (alk. paper)
   1. New business enterprises—Management. 2. Entrepreneurship. I. Glackin, Caroline. II. Title.
   HD62.5.M3567 2010
   658.1'1—dc22   2008036698

Editor in Chief: Vernon Anthony
Senior Acquisitions Editor: Gary Bauer
Development Editor: Brooke Wilson, Ohlinger
Publishing Services
Editorial Assistant: Megan Heintz
Production Coordination: Roxanne Klaas,
S4Carlisle Publishing Services
Project Manager: Holly Shufeldt

Senior Operations Supervisor: Pat Tonneman
Art Director: Diane Ernsberger
Interior and Cover Designer: Candace Rowley
Manager, Rights and Permissions: Zina Arabia
Image Permission Coordinator: Vicki Menanteaux
Director of Marketing: David Gesell
Marketing Manager: Thomas Hayward
Marketing Assistant: Les Roberts

This book was set in New Aster by S4Carlisle Publishing Services and was printed and bound by Courier. The cover was printed by Phoenix Color Corp.

Photo Credits: Page 1: Tom Merton, Getty Images/Digital Vision, Page 2: Digital Vision, Ltd., Superstock Royalty Free, Page 3: *Arizona Daily Star,* Page 7: Frank Moore Studio, Corbis/Bettmann, Page 16: Apple Computer, Inc., Page 17: Matthew Simmons, Getty Images, Page 26: Landon Nordeman, Getty Images, Inc—Liaison, Page 28: Brand X, Superstock Royalty Free, Page 29: Tim Pannell, Corbis Royalty Free, Page 36: Courtesy of Harlan Tytus Beverly/Bigfoot Networks Inc., Page 74: Scott Barrow, Corbis Royalty Free, Page 75: Erik Snyder, Getty Images/Digital Vision, Page 82: AP Wide World Photos, Page 105: Getty Images Inc—Stockbyte Royalty Free, Page 106: Blend Images, Alamy Images Royalty Free, Page 107: Image 100, Corbis Royalty Free, Page 119: Michael L. Ambramson, Getty Images/Time Life Pictures, Page 128: Ray Tamarra, Getty Images, Page 130: Sam Roberts, Getty Images, Inc.—Photodisc., Page 131: Niall McDiarmid, Alamy Images Royalty Free, Page 135: Nick Ruechel, Eyesoar Inc., Page 148: Chris Buck, Corbis/Outline, Page 157: Andre Perlstein, Getty Images Inc.—Stone Allstock, Page 160: Todd Wright, Getty Images, Inc.—Blend Images, Page 161: Terry Vacha, Alamy Images Royalty Free, Page 170: Courtesy of T. Scott Gross, author *Postively Putrageous Services,* Page 191: Blend Images, Alamy Images Royalty Free, Page 192: Adam Crowley, Getty Images, Inc— Stockbyte Royalty Free, Page 193: Jupiter Images/Creatas, Alamy Images Royalty Free, Page 202: Bob Kaufman, Page 204: Getty Images Inc.—Hulton Archive Photos, Page 220: Mel Yates, Getty Images, Inc.—Photodisc., Page 221: Photodisc, Alamy Images Royalty Free, Page 234: Stinger/Time Life Pictures, Getty Images/Time Life Pictures, Page 244: Getty Images, Inc./Photodisc, Page 254: UpperCut Images, Superstock Royalty Free, Page 255: UpperCut Images, Getty Images Inc.—Punchstock, Page 256: Keystone, Getty Images Inc.—Hulton Archive Photos, Page 272: SuperStock, Inc., Page 273: Alan King, Alamy.com, Page 278: AP Wide World Photos, Page 279: AFP PHOTO John G. MaBango, Getty Images, Inc.—Agence France Presse, Page 294: David Young-Wolff, PhotoEdit Inc., Page 309: Getty Images Inc—Image Source Royalty Free, Page 310: Corbis RF, Page 311: John Van Hasselt, Corbis/Sygma, Page 332: Old Dartmouth Historical Society/New Bedford Whaling Museum, Page 332: Keith Philpott, Getty Images, Page 334: Digital Vision, Alamy Images Royalty Free, Page 335: Sean Justice, Corbis Royalty Free, Page 341: Flying Colours Ltd, Getty Images—Digital Vision, Page 351: Cultura, CORBIS-NY, Page 360: Tom Grill, © Corbis Permium RF/Alamy, Page 361: Courtesy of the Library of Congress, Page 366: John Todd, AP Wide World Photos, Page 377: Ed Quinn, Corbis/SABA Press Photos, Inc., Page 389: Tom Grill/ Corbis Royalty Free, Page 390: Getty Images—Digital Vision, Page 391: Bernard Gotfryd, Hulton Archive/Getty Images Inc., Page 394: Keystone, Getty Images Inc.—Hulton Archive Photos, Page 404: Chris O'Meara, AP Wide World Photos, Page 405: AP Wide World Photos.

Pearson Education Ltd., London
Pearson Education Singapore Pte. Ltd.
Pearson Education Canada, Inc.
Pearson Education—Japan

Pearson Education Australia Pty. Ltd
Pearson Education North Asia Ltd., Hong Kong
Pearson Educación de Mexico, S.A. de C.V.
Pearson Education Malaysia Pte. Ltd.

Prentice Hall
is an imprint of

www.pearsonhighered.com

10 9 8 7 6 5 4 3 2
ISBN-13: 978-0-13-236600-7
ISBN-10:   0-13-236600-2

Special thanks to Shelby Cullom Davis.
Also thanks to Kathryn Davis, Shelby M.C. Davis,
Kimberly La Manna, Abby Moffat, and
Diana Davis Spencer.

—Steve Mariotti

To my children, Elise and Spencer, whose support and love
are essential parts of this book.
To my parents, Howard and Maria Wiedenman,
who truly understood the importance
of education. My love and gratitude.

—Caroline Glackin

Brief Contents

Contents

> *The discussion of what it takes to be an entrepreneur is excellent. I think the examples that deal with entrepreneurs and their ideas are excellent.*
>
> —Marsha Wender Timmerman, LaSalle University, Philadelphia, PA

Excellent coverage of introductory entrepreneurial concepts written in a style that whets the student appetite for further exploration.

—Pamela Shackelford, Stephens College

My students and I thoroughly enjoy the case studies. They're fresh, insightful, and thought provoking.

—Don Ajene Wilcoxson, Riverside City College

" Very good coverage of marketing concepts and establishing a marketing strategy. "
—Larry Weaver, Navarro College, Corsicana, TX

" There are some great ideas that young entrepreneurs can incorporate into their businesses. This text is filled with practical information that many texts leave out. "
—Rusty Juban, Southern Louisiana University

"
Great discussion of the sales process and how to actually sell.
—Dr. Laura Portolese Dias, Shoreline Community College, Seattle, WA
"

Having taught this course for many years and being involved in a small business, I feel that Mariotti does a great job of covering the relevant topics that students should know.

—Michael Discello, Pittsburgh Technical Institute

I am very pleased with the depth and treatment of the material.

—Larry McDaniel, Alabama A&M

Chapter 9   Cash Flow and Taxes   254

I have just started two new businesses and find that the information in Chapter 9 is right on target.

—Emily Martin, Faulkner Community College, Bay Minette, AL

Chapter 10   Financing Strategy: Debt, Equity, or Both?   272

"The overall text is terrific. It is one of the best in this field that I have used in the last decade.
—Richard Benedetto, Merrimack College

Chapter 13 **Management, Leadership, and Ethics** 360

This is the most clearly written and concise text I have reviewed on this topic.
—Wayne Keene, Stephens College

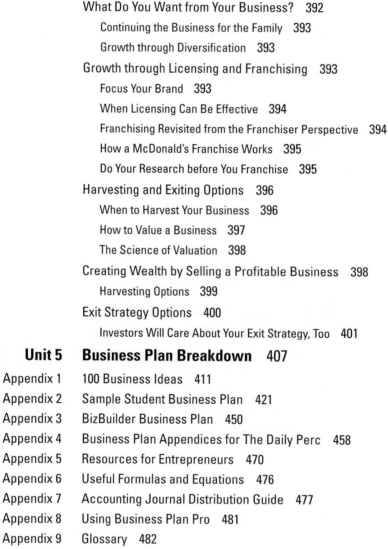

Help Your Students Build a Future

Why Use Entrepreneurship: Starting and Operating a Small Business?

Because It Works!

Entrepreneurship: Starting and Operating a Small Business is based on the National Foundation for Teaching Entrepreneurship (NFTE) academic programs developed by Steve Mariotti, founder of NFTE. Since 1987, the NFTE organization has reached over 180,000 students and professionals, and certified over 3,500 instructors to teach an innovative entrepreneurship curriculum. NFTE is widely viewed as a world leader in promoting entrepreneurial literacy and has a proven track record of helping students start a great variety of successful new ventures. For this second edition Steve Mariotti is joined by a coauthor, Caroline Glackin, from Delaware State University.

Combining Street Smarts and Academic Smarts

This textbook unites Steve Mariotti's experience as an entrepreneur with relevant academic theory and practice, supported by a rich variety of examples and stories that include experiences from NFTE program graduates who have started their own businesses. Caroline Glackin brings years of experience in the university classroom, as a lender to small and microbusinesses, and as an entrepreneur and former small business owner. This combination of authors yields a text that is practical, useful, and academically solid.

Never underestimate the power of a simple idea executed with a lot of energy and persistence. This book will enable college students to execute their ideas, grow their businesses, and tap into a greater power—the ability to use their ideas and energies to then achieve social and political goals that will empower their communities.

—Russell Simmons,
Chairman & CEO, Rush Communications

Chapter Learning System

Chapter 2

The Business Plan: Road Map to Success

"If you don't know where you are going, any road will get you there."

—Lewis Carroll, English author

Great business ideas can grow into great businesses or they can wither away from neglect or unfavorable environments. One thing that successful businesses have in common is a sound idea and an entrepreneur who has a plan for turning the idea into reality.

Many people dream about opening a retail store. Some people dream about owning *several* retail stores. Still others start with a single store and grow the enterprise into thousands of stores. That is what happened with Donald and Doris Fisher, the founders of Gap Inc. In 1969, the Fishers, in the midst of Woodstock, Vietnam, and landing on the moon, started a retail store in San Francisco. Don Fisher has stated, "I created Gap with a simple idea: to make it easier to find a pair of jeans. We remain committed to that basic principle."[1]

Gap Inc. continues providing store experiences that are easy for the customer and offer a broad selection of fits and styles. The company has expanded to include the Old Navy, Banana Republic, and Piperlime brands. There are more than 150,000 employees worldwide in over 3,100 stores. In 2006, Gap Inc. had revenues of $15.9 billion. The Fishers and their son Bob continue to serve on the Gap board of directors. The company has come a long way from its origins, while maintaining a strong focus.

Performance Objectives

1. Know what a business plan is and how to describe it.
2. Explain the various purposes for a business plan and the audiences for it.
3. Understand the components of a business plan.
4. Be able to demonstrate proper development and formatting of a business plan.

▲ Chapter Openers Set the Stage

Each chapter starts with an inspirational quote, introduction, and then Performance Objectives that provide a "road map" so readers know where they are headed. Readers connect with a real company story in the opening vignette that sets the stage for upcoming material.

Step into the Shoes...

Crushing the Competition

Bigfoot Networks, Inc
2005 Global Champion, MOOT Corp

Harlan Beverly describes himself as an extreme hardcore PC gamer since he was a child. He is also a person who was frustrated by the in-game lag experienced when playing online PC games. Harlan obtained an MBA at the University of Texas at Austin so that he could start a company that used Network Acceleration technology, a field in which he had filed over 19 patents while working at Intel. Along the way, he partnered with Michael Cubbage and Robert Grim to start Bigfoot Networks.

Bigfoot has won numerous awards, including the 2005 Global Championship in the MOOT Corp competition, and the 2005 Fortune Small Business Startup Competition. They have developed both software and hardware products to reduce lag in game servers and PCs. Their flagship product is Killer NIC (network interface card) that is powered by LLR Technology (patent pending). They received $4 million in venture capital funding in 2006.

The management team was formed at UT Austin and competed in numerous business plan competitions before launching the business from an incubator. The company has since created innovative technology to provide solutions to online gamers and the makers of online games. Bigfoot Networks has created an innovative, exciting venture from their business plan.

Sources: "Bigfoot Networks Receives $4 Million Investment from Venio Capital Partners to Accelerate Online Games." See *http://www.mootcorp.org/Bigfoot%20Funding. asp.* Dated February 2006. Accessed December 2007.
John Callahan, Bigfoot Networks Interview, *FiringSquad*, March 21, 2006. See *http://www. firingsquad.com/features/bigfoot_networks_interview/.*
Bigfoot Networks, Inc. Web site at *http://www.killerinc.com.*

▲ "Step into the Shoes" of the Experts

"Step into the Shoes" features appear in all chapters and give insights into the business practices of successful entrepreneurs.

BizFacts

BizFacts impart useful information regarding a company practice or a business application.

Entrepreneurial Wisdom

Entrepreneurial Wisdom features contain insights or advice that will help students in the preparation of a business plan.

Entrepreneurial Wisdom...

A useful way to evaluate a business idea is to look at its **S**trengths, **W**eaknesses, **O**pportunities, and **T**hreats (**SWOT**). This is called **SWOT Analysis**.

- *Strengths*—All the capabilities and positive points that the entrepreneur has, from experience to contacts. These are internal to the organization.
- *Weaknesses*—All of the negatives that the entrepreneur faces, such as lack of capital or training, or failure to set up a workable accounting system. These are internal to the organization.
- *Opportunities*—Any positive external event or circumstance (including lucky breaks) that can help the entrepreneur get ahead of the competition.
- *Threats*—Any external factor, event, or circumstance that can harm the business, such as competitors, legal issues, and declining economies.

Global Impact

Global Impact features, in all chapters, illustrate areas entrepreneurs should consider when doing business in other countries.

Global Impact...
Fashion and Fair Trade

Tarsian & Blinkley
2003 Winner, Global Social Venture Competition

Sarah Takesh was inspired to work in economic development by what she saw during a jeep trek in the Northern Territories of Pakistan in 2000. Her original plan was to start a handicrafts business in Peshawar, where the population of Afghan refugees was quite large. She believed that the best way to fight poverty was to create a cash-generating economic engine to break the cycle. Her plans changed with the events of September 11, 2001. Rather than starting in Pakistan, she was able to found her business in Kabul, Afghanistan.

From its start in 2002, Tarsian & Blinkley has worked with a nonprofit organization, Maharat (formerly the Afghan Women's Vocational Skills Learning Center), and has been committed to a social mission with international impact. The company's philosophy is to create beautiful garments that are sold in the United States, generating cash income for people of low social standing and limited education—properly compensating the art of the local female embroiderers.

Tarsian & Blinkley was incubated at the University of California at Berkeley as a social entrepreneurship venture. Sarah entered the National Social Venture Competition (now a global competition) in 2003 and won for the Best Blended Plan. The company is a for-profit that produces about 15 different styles at any given time, and estimates that it has benefited more than a thousand people as of 2006. Yet they have more goals, including training a hundred women to become "factory-ready tailors" for the company's new garment facility, adding day care, creating an emergency fund for workers, and supporting literacy.

Source: Tarsian & Blinkley Web site at *http://www.tarsian.com*. Accessed December 2007.

End-of-Chapter Learning Portfolio

End-of-chapter materials help students develop a working understanding of key concepts and develop critical thinking skills.

All chapters include the following:

- **Key Terms** list.
- **Critical Thinking Exercises** that require readers to ponder important issues and support a thoughtful response.
- **Key Concept Questions** that review core topics.
- **Application Exercises** that give readers a chance to apply what they have learned.
- **Exploring Your Community** and **Exploring Online** assignments that invite readers to go into the business community or search online material for information.
- **Cases for Analysis** include one short and one long case with analytical questions. Cases cover a variety of issues and draw on real and realistic business scenarios. Business examples include David Neeleman (JetBlue Airlines), Seth Goldman (Honest Tea Company), Russell Simmons (Rush Communications), and more. This second edition includes 11 new cases: Dr. Farrah Gray—Young Entrepreneur and Philanthropist; Dogfish Head Brewery; Sew What? Inc.; Daniel Uribe—Lazer Bearings; The Cajun Grill; Extreme Entrepreneurship Education; Warren Brown (CakeLove, Love Café); Portable on Demand Storage (PODS); Sumaya Kaza (The CulturalConnect); Small Parts Manufacturing; and Metal Recycling Services. These cases reflect a diverse set of entrepreneurs, industries, and geographic locations.

Entrepreneurship Portfolio

Critical Thinking Exercises

1. Shawn is creating a business that provides advertisi̶n̶g̶ ̶o̶n̶ ̶b̶a̶t̶h̶r̶o̶o̶m̶ stall doors. He is funding the project from his perso̶n̶ $5,000 and does not expect to use any outside financ̶ create a business plan? Why or why not?
2. Charity and Devon are planning to license technolog̶ that makes it impossible to accidentally lock a child̶ technology is complex and the market analysis and f̶ tions take up a lot of pages. Charity and Devon have̶ 80-page business plan. Explain your concerns about̶ plan in light of the chapter text.
3. What factors make the difference between a good bu̶ and an excellent one? (Hint: Use the chapter data an̶ competitions.)
4. Visit an Internet shopping site such as the Home Sh̶o̶ (http://www.HSN.com) or QVC (http://www.QVC.co̶m̶ products that are being sold that you find interesting̶ Make a list of the products and your explanation of t̶ opportunities they reflect.
5. *Errors of omission can sometimes be greater than erro̶r̶* How does this statement apply to business plans?

Key Concept Questions

1. Explain why the executive summary is the most impo̶ any business plan.
2. One mistake entrepreneurs make in their business pl̶a̶ only including an income statement. What other fina̶ should be included and why?

3. Print your assignment with 1-inch margins, double spaced, using 12-point Times New Roman. Then, print the same document with 0.8-inch margins, single spaced, using 10-point Arial type. Which is easier to read? Why? How does this relate to business plans?
4. Name three categories of investors/lenders that might have an interest in your business plan.
5. How can spending time researching and writing a business plan save an entrepreneur time and money in the short run and long run?
6. Why is it important to identify an organization's "culture" from the beginning?

Application Exercises

Visit or call (visit after calling) an entrepreneur in your community to discuss business plans.

a. Ask whether he or she wrote a business plan before starting the business. Since then?
b. If he or she did write a plan, for what has it been used?
c. If he or she did not write a plan, why not?
d. Did the owner have any assistance in writing or reviewing the plan?
e. If so, what was the source of assistance?

Exploring Online

Find a business plan on the Internet (not on the Business Plan Pro disk). Examine it to see whether it follows the guidelines provided in this text. Use a highlighter to mark the sections of the plan that are present. Then, make a list of missing or incomplete sections. Indicate how it does/does not follow the "rules" for formatting and content. Is the plan viable? Why or why not? Would you invest in it? Why or why not?

In Your Opinion

If an entrepreneur presents a business plan that an investor believes is deliberately vague and has provided inflated financial statements, what should that investor do?

New to the Second Edition

New! The Business Plan: Road Map to Business Success (Chapter 2)

The second edition includes a complete chapter devoted to the business plan. It encompasses a comprehensive outline, summaries of business plan contents, and a complete business plan from Business Plan Pro. Students learn the purposes of business plans and obtain useful information on both form and content. This chapter was added to conveniently provide a quick, comprehensive resource early in the course, so that students could envision the concept of a business plan from the start. In many cases, they have never seen a comprehensive business plan. In some cases, they may have been exposed to rudimentary plans or marketing or strategic plans that are called business plans. By learning about the topic early on, students will be "on the same page" with respect to the topic. This can save considerable challenges later in the course.

New! Daily Perc

Sample Business Plan

The Daily Perc sample business plan is a complete plan from Business Plan Pro which appears following Chapter 2. It includes a comprehensive market analysis and detailed financial projections, two of the sections that students often find the most challenging to create. While not a "perfect" plan, The Daily Perc is a solid example for students and one that many of them understand, to some extent, as customers of coffee shops. This plan is used throughout the text to illustrate the topics of each unit in practical form through the Business Plan Breakdown feature. Supporting financials are included in Appendix 4.

New! Business Plan Breakdown Sections

The Business Plan Breakdown, at the end of each unit, is a new feature that takes apart The Daily Perc sample business plan provided in Chapter 2 and relates the component parts to each unit's topics. Sections of the plan are excerpted and comments regarding their content are included in the margins. This breakdown of the business plan illustrates for students how the entrepreneurship topics relate to a business plan. For courses that require students to submit a business plan in stages, these examples provide tips and guidelines at each step of the way. The examples and callouts also offer an opportunity for class discussion and review at the conclusion of each unit. In essence, the Business Plan Breakdown operationalizes the concepts described in each unit.

BUSINESS PLAN

New! Chapter on Operating for Success

Chapter 12 covers important operations topics, including inventory management, quality assurance, supply chain management, cost control methods, product designs and costs, the making-versus-buying decision, and physical location and layout.

Other Important Changes

- The text has been reorganized to eliminate redundancy.

- Each chapter has a Step into the Shoes and Global Impact feature to illustrate chapter concepts and incorporate global opportunities.

- Terminology throughout the text has been broadened from a business-to-consumer focus to include business-to-business and business-to-government, as well as not-for-profit organizations.

- A discussion of the monetary and nonmonetary definitions of success has been added. (Chapter 1)

- Social entrepreneurship, venture philanthropy, and green entrepreneurship are introduced and discussed. (Chapter 1)

- Paths to small business ownership, including buying an existing business, securing franchise rights, and licensing technology, have been added. (Chapter 1)

- Core values and company vision and culture are introduced as critical components of a business definition and mission statement, and examples are provided. (Chapter 3)

- The iterative processes for identifying and sifting through business ideas are explained and illustrated. (Chapter 3)

- Methods for performing competitive analysis and comparisons with simple table examples have been added. (Chapter 3)

- The marketing research section has been rewritten to provide greater clarity and accessibility. (Chapter 4)

- The product life cycle discussion has been revised and an illustration added to enhance its effectiveness. (Chapter 4)

- The "Five P's" of marketing, including philanthropy, are combined into a single chapter. (Chapter 5)

- The discussion of electronic communications options has been updated, is was the use of technology. (Chapter 6)

- The accounting section includes updated information about software for small business accounting. (Chapter 7)

- The creation of financial statements has been moved to appear directly after the creation of journals. These topics are written as though students were using manual recordkeeping to ensure that they understand the underlying principles, although they are likely to use accounting software. (Chapter 7)

- The use of income statements and balance sheets for financial analysis and business operation is combined in a single chapter. The topic of balance sheets is thus addressed earlier in the text. (Chapter 8)

- The key ratios for financial analysis are explained and demonstrated in a well-organized manner in one chapter. (Chapter 8)

- The concepts of the time value of money, net present value, and future value are introduced with the discussion of cash flows and cash management. (Chapter 9)

- Financing options are articulated more clearly and discussed in terms of "fit" for entrepreneurs and their businesses. (Chapter 10)

- Debt options are identified in a chart providing the debt category, description of the category, the most common types of financing in each category, and duration of the term. (Chapter 10)

- A comprehensive section about Community Development Financial Institutions (CDFIs) has been added, as have ones on insurance companies, vendor financing, and agricultural finance. (Chapter 10)

- Trademark, service mark, copyright, and patent information is expanded and updated. (Chapter 11)

- The significance and contents of a disaster recovery plan is new. (Chapter 11)

- New materials and reorganized sections facilitate the discussion of growth and exit strategies. (Chapter 14)

- The chapter entitled "Investing for a Secure Future" has been deleted, with portions of it being incorporated into appropriate sections of the present text.

- The Sample Student Business Plan has been replaced by an award-winning undergraduate business plan, University Parent, Inc., by a team of students at the University of Colorado. (Appendix 2)

- The Advanced Business Plan appendix has been replaced by the BizBuilder Business Plan, which enhances the outline and materials from Chapter 2 and throughout the book with specific questions and exercises to guide students through the creation of their business plans. Instructors can break these topics into discrete assignments, to culminate in the creation of a comprehensive business plan. (Appendix 3)

- The Resources for Entrepreneurs include new books, Web sites, and other resources. (Appendix 5)

Building a Business Plan Step-by-Step

Students begin thinking about and planning a new business start-up from Chapter 1 onward. A new chapter on the Business Plan and inclusion of the complete *The Daily Perc* business plan in Chapter 2 introduces the process early.

Business Plan Breakdown

Sections at the end of each Unit tie the chapter materials to the sample plan.

BizBuilder Business Plan Worksheets and Templates

Students progressively build an effective Business Plan utilizing the BizBuilder Business Plan Worksheets included on the Companion Web site. Students follow a three-step process:

- **Step 1:** Students use the BizBuilder Business Plan Worksheets to work through every aspect of a business plan.
- **Step 2:** Students use the BizBuilder Business Plan Template to create a professional-looking business plan from their worksheets.
- **Step 3:** Students use the BizBuilder Business Plan Presentation Template to create a PowerPoint presentation of their business plan.

The Business Plan Worksheets, Template, and Presentation Template are located on the Companion Web site. Appendix 8 includes instructions on how to create a business plan using Business Plan Pro software.

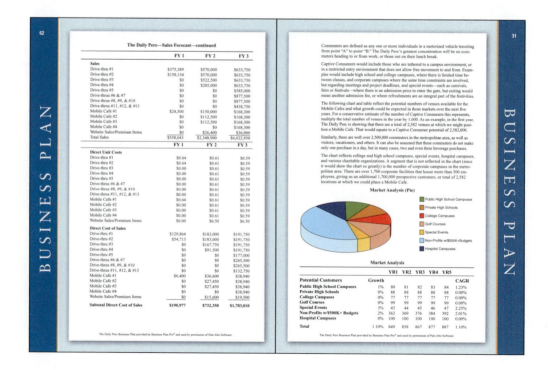

Business Planning Software Package

Step-by-Step Guidance to Build and Present Your Business Plan!

BizBuilder Business Plan Worksheets and Templates Online

Go to www.prenhall.com/mariotti to download business plan and presentation templates that will help you write your plan and present it.

- *BizBuilder Business Plan Worksheets* provide step-by-step instructions on building a business plan.
- *BizBuilder Business Plan Template* provides a professional-looking format for a business plan that ties in with assignments in the text.
- *BizBuilder Business Plan Presentation Template* guides you through the process of creating a PowerPoint presentation for your business plan.

Students build their business plans using the BizBuilder worksheets. Appendix 8 provides students with instructions on how to use the worksheets that mirror the planning process in the book and contains more questions in some areas than found in commercially available planning software. Once they have created a plan using the worksheets, they can generate a professional-looking document using the BizBuilder Business Plan Template or Business Plan Pro software.

BUSINESS PLAN PRO

Business Plan Pro Software CD

Business Plan Pro software, the most widely used professional business-planning software may be packaged packaged with a new text or may be purchased online at **www.pearsonhighered.com** (ISBN 0-13-195519-5). Once a student has created a business plan using the BizBuilder worksheet, it will be easy to cut and paste that information into Business Plan Pro. BPP includes a number of very useful features:

- 68 sample business plans students can study and compare with their own. Use the Sample Plan Browser to search the extensive library.
- Easy Plan Wizard that guides students through writing a plan.
- Spreadsheet tables with columns, rows, and formulas to automatically calculate totals.
- Pie and bar charts that can be automatically created from your spreadsheets.
- Financial statements that can be customized.
- Plan Review Wizard that reviews the plan for completeness, compares the financial statements to standard accounting practices, and checks for errors.
- Professional-looking printout of the business plan.
- Appendix 8 provides students with an overview of how to get started using Business Plan Pro.

Online Resources

Companion Website

The online Companion Website includes the following:

- **Test-Prep Quizzes** for each chapter, including true/false, multiple choice, and short essay. All questions include immediate feedback.
- **BizBuilder Business Plan Worksheets**
- **BizBuilder Business Plan Template**
- **BizBuilder Business Plan Presentation Template**
- **PowerPoint Chapter Review of Key Topics**
- **Links to Web-based Video Assignments at the Small Business School**
- **Web Links to Additional Resources**

courseconnect™ CourseConnect Distance Learning Course: Convenience, Simplicity, Success

Looking for robust online course content to reinforce and enhance your student learning? We have the solution: CourseConnect! CourseConnect courses contain customizable modules of content mapped to major learning outcomes. Each learning object contains interactive tutorials, rich media, discussion questions, MP3 downloadable lectures, assessments, and interactive activities that address different learning styles. When you buy a CourseConnect course, you purchase a complete package that provides you with detailed documentation you can use for your accreditation reviews. CourseConnect courses can be delivered in any commercial platform such as **WebCT, BlackBoard, Angel, Moodle,** or **eCollege** platforms. For more information, contact your representative or call 800-635-1579.

Instructor Resources

All instructor resources can be downloaded from the Prentice Hall Instructor's Resources website located at **www.pearsonhighered.com**

TestGen computerized Test Generator

PowerPoint Lecture Presentation Package

The **Instructor's Manual** includes the following:

- Answers to all end-of-chapter material, including teaching notes for short and long case studies
- Additional instructional material on how to teach writing a business plan and to supplement end-of-unit business plan sections
- Course outlines for 8-week term (short course), 12-week term (3 hours/week), and 15-week term (3 hours/week)
- Additional resources (print and Websites) for each chapter
- Test Item File

Entrepreneurship Videos on DVD

SmallBusinessSchool
Television for PBS and the Voice of America

The following four videos produced by the Small Business School are available to qualified adopters of the textbook. Please contact your local representative to place an order.

Modern Postcard

Steve Hoffman, founder of Modern Postcard, was smitten by process control and the theory of constraints. How can you get 32 postcards on one sheet of paper and maintain quality? Before the Internet was accessible to all, he was committed to winning and pleasing customers with a digital-only supply chain. Steve is an artist turned businessman, a deep thinker, a strategist, and a tactician. He grew from supplying high-quality photos for a few dozen real estate agents to use for promoting their listings to producing 100 million postcards a year for some 150,000 customers. At the time this story was recorded, Modern Postcard had 250 employees and had moved into its own state-of-the-art facility. You'll now see what happens when one person gets everybody thinking about how they can do things faster, cheaper, and better.

Wahoo's Fish Taco

Meet surfers who are building a chain of surfer food joints. They started from nothing and now have over 40 profitable locations, each generating about $1 million in sales. Wahoo's is famous for serving up clean food, piled high and priced low. Wherever they go, they have an instant family, an immediate bond with anyone who owns a surfboard, skateboard, or snowboard. Brothers Wing Lam Lee, Ed Lee, and Mingo Lee launched the business in 1988 with a $30,000 loan from their parents—which they paid back quickly. They discovered that they didn't know how to grow so they adopted a fourth partner as a brother. He is systems guru Steve Karfaridis, a Greek immigrant who managed five-star restaurants in his homeland. Learn how the four partners divide the work, market their products, and keep customers coming back.

Nicole Miller

Since childhood, Nicole Miller dreamed of doing exactly what she is doing now. After graduating from Parson's School of Design, she took a job in a New York City fashion house, where she met the man who became her business partner. It was 1986; at the time the well-made dress was frumpy and the fashionable dress was flimsy. The pair had a hunch that there was a need for well-made fashionable dresses and they were right. Today their company earns $300 million in revenue. Go to the heart of the fashion industry and behind the scenes of Nicole Miller, a fashion house on Seventh Avenue, to meet the founders, Nicole Miller and Bud Konheim. In an industry where even top designers have taken production overseas, Nicole Miller pieces all proudly bear the label "Made in New York."

Ziba Design

If you have ever wondered how those gizmos, gadgets, keyboards, printers, and other tools we use every day come to be, in this episode you will see for yourself. Ziba Design is an industrial design firm that has won its own industry's top awards, and creative perfectionists have come from all over the world to work side by side with founder Sohrab Vossoughi. Top brands—Procter & Gamble, McDonald's, FedEx, Hewlett-Packard, Microsoft, Nike, and Ford—ask Ziba to try to make their products just a little bit better. And then they do.

Sohrab says, "We strive for simplicity, innovation, human-centered interaction, visual interest, and efficiency." We also learn from the founder that to grow the business he had to give up his drawing board, hire people who challenged him, and put systems in place to deliver on time and on budget for his customers.

Small Business School is the television series made for PBS stations and Voice of America. On the Web at *http://smallBusinessSchool.org*, students will discover the largest video library in the world about small business.

About the Authors

STEVE MARIOTTI, founder of the National Foundation for Teaching Entrepreneurship (NFTE), is an expert in education for at-risk youth. He has been helping young people develop marketable skills by learning about entrepreneurship for more than 25 years.

Mariotti received an M.B.A. from the University of Michigan and has studied at Harvard University, Stanford University, and Brooklyn College. His professional career began as a Treasury Analyst for Ford Motor Co. (1976–1979). He then founded Mason Import/Export Services in New York, eventually acting as sales representative and purchasing agent for 32 overseas firms. In 1982, he made a significant career change and became a Special Education/Business Teacher in the New York City school system, choosing to teach in such inner-city neighborhoods as Bedford-Stuyvesant in Brooklyn and the "Fort Apache" section of the South Bronx. It was at Jane Addams Vocational High School in the Bronx that he developed the insight and inspiration to bring entrepreneurial education to low-income youth. This led to founding NFTE in 1987.

Steve Mariotti and NFTE have received numerous awards, including the 2004 Ernst & Young National Entrepreneur of the Year Award; the Golden Lamp Award from the Association of Educational Publishers (2002); and the National Federation of Independent Businesses—Best Business Teacher, 1988, as well as major media exposure that includes pieces in *The New York Times* and other prominent publications, and profiles on ABC News and CNN. Mariotti has co-authored some two dozen books and manuals that have sold over half a million copies.

CAROLINE GLACKIN, Doctorate. is a "pracademic" who has successfully worked as a microenterprise and small business owner and manager, as an executive director of a community-development financial institution, and as an academic in the areas of community-development finance, entrepreneurship, and management. She has been assisting entrepreneurs in achieving their dreams for over 25 years.

Glackin earned a Ph.D. from the University of Delaware, where her research emphasis was on the barriers, boosters, costs, and constraints for microentrepreneurs accessing financing. She received an M.B.A. from The Wharton School at the University of Pennsylvania and an A.B. from Bryn Mawr College. Her professional career began with the DuPont Company, American Bell, Bell Atlantic, and American Management Systems. Dr. Glackin then spent over 10 years working in or with small businesses, microenterprise, and not-for-profit agencies in turnaround and high-growth situations. After exiting a family business, she became the executive director of the First State Community Loan Fund, a community-development institution serving businesses, not-for-profits, and developers of affordable housing. With the completion of her doctoral work, she joined Delaware State University, a Historically Black College and University (HBCU) as the director of the Entrepreneurship Center.

Caroline Glackin has succeeded in leading change in the practical fields of her research and has received numerous honors and awards. They include the first Gloeckner Business Plan Award at The Wharton School (1983), the Minority Business Advocate of the Year for Delaware from the U.S. Small Business Administration (2000), and the She Knows Where She's Going Award from Girls Inc. (2000). Dr. Glackin co-chaired the Delaware Governor's Task Force for Financial Independence and has participated in the Cornell University Emerging Markets Think Tank Series.

Acknowledgments

First, sincere thanks to the team of reviewers who provided insightful feedback to this book and to the ninth and tenth editions of *How to Start and Operate a Small Business* by Steve Mariotti with Tony Towle, on which the first editor was based.

Consultants and Reviewers

Elaine Allen, *National Director Not-for-Profit Services Group, Ernst & Young*

Larry Bennett, *Johnson & Wales University—Providence, RI*

Sunne Brandmeyer, *Retired Lecturer/Advisor, Center for Economic Education, University of South Florida*

Stanlee Brimberg, *Teacher, Bank Street School for Children*

Howard W. Buffett, Jr.

John D. Christesen, *SUNY Westchester Community College, Valhalla, NY*

Steve Colyer, *Adjunct Professor, School of Business, Miami Dade College*

Laura Portolese Dias, *Shoreline Community College, Seattle, WA*

Alex Dontoh, *New York University*

Alan Dlugash, *CPA Partner, Dlugash & Kevelson*

Thomas Emrick, Ed.D.

George Gannage, Jr., *West Central Technical College—Carrollton, GA*

Thomas Goodrow, *Springfield Technical Community College—Springfield, MA*

Janet P. Graham, E. Craig Wall, Sr., *College of Business Administration, Coastal Carolina University*

John Harris, *Teacher of Business, Eastern High School, Bristol, CT*

Deborah Hoffman, *Audit Manager, Ernst & Young*

Donald Hoy, *Benedictine College—Atchison, KS*

Samira Hussein, *Johnson County Community College, Overland Park, KS*

Eileen M. Kearney, *Montgomery County Community College, Blue Bell, PA*

Sanford Krieger, Esq., *Partner, Fried, Frank, Harris, Shriver & Jacobson*

Dr. Jawanza Kunjufu, *President, African American Images*

Corey Kupfer, Esq., *Founding Partner, Kupfer, Rosen & Herz, LLP*

Emily H. Martin, *Faulkner Community College, Bay Minette, AL*

Alaire Mitchell, *Former Assistant Director of Curriculum Research, New York City Board of Education*

Timothy R. Mittan, *Southeast Community College, Lincoln, NE*

Eric Mulkowsky, *Engagement Manager, McKinsey and Company, Inc.*

Raffiq Nathoo, *Senior Managing Director, The Blackstone Group, LLP*

Ray E. Newton, III, *Managing Director, Perseus Capital, LLC*

Arnold Ng, *Pepperdine University—Rancho Palos Verdes, CA*

William H. Painter, *Retired Professor of Law, George Washington University*

Peter Patch, *Patch and Associates*

Alan Patricof, *Founder and Chairman, Apax Partners*

Carolyn J. Christensen Perricone, CPA, *Associate Professor and Curriculum Chair, Accounting, SUNY*

Robert Plain, *Guilford Technical Community College—Jamestown, NC*

Christopher P. Puto, *Dean and Professor of Marketing, Georgetown University, McDonough School of Business*

Richard Relyea, *NY Penn*

Ira Sacks, Esq., *Partner, Fried, Frank, Harris, Shriver & Jacbobson*

Dr. William Sahlman, *Professor of Business Administration, Harvard Business School*

Dr. Arnold Scheibel, *Professor of Neurobiology, University of California at Los Angeles*

Sandra Sowell-Scott, *State Director, Youth Entrepreneurship Education, Fox School of Business & Management, Temple University*

LaVerne Tilley, *Gwinnett Technical College—Lawrenceville, GA*

Marsha Wender Timmerman, *LaSalle University, Philadelphia, PA*

Liza Vertinsky, J.D., Ph.D., *Attorney, Hill & Barlow*

Peter Walker, *Managing Director, McKinsey and Company, Inc.*

Walter Lara, *Florida Community College—Jacksonville, FL*

Larry Weaver, *Navarro College—Corsicana, TX*

Dr. Donald Wells, *Professor of Economics, University of Arizona*

First, I would like to thank my co-author, Caroline Glackin, without whose talent and expertise this second edition would not have been possible; and Tony Towle, who from NFTE's inception has helped me organize my thoughts and experiences. I must single out the help of two outstanding educators: John Harris and Peter Patch, and would like to acknowledge the significant contributions of NFTE executives Michael J. Caslin, III, J. David Nelson, Julie Silard Kantor, Leslie Pechman Koch, Jane Walsh, Neelam Patel, Daniel Rabuzzi, Victor Salama, Del Daniels, Jonathan Weininger, Deirdre Lee, Rupa Mohan, Christine Poorman, Joel Warren, and Essye Klempner.

Special thanks as well to Gary Bauer, Brandon Elliott, Peter McCarthy, and Holly Shufeldt and the team at Pearson Prentice Hall, for their professionalism, and to Brooke Wilson at Ohlinger Publishing Services and Roxanne Klaas at S4Carlisle Publishing Services, for their editorial assistance. Also to Tom Goodrow of the Springfield Enterprise Center and the National Association of Community College Entrepreneurship (NACCE), and to John Christesen of SUNY Westchester Community College.

Thanks also to Howard Stevenson, Jeffry Timmons, William Bygrave, Bob Pritzker and NFTE Board Member Stephen Spinelli, for imparting their wisdom and to Richard Fink of Koch Industries, Carl Schramm of the Ewing Marion Kauffman Foundation, and Mike Hennessy and John Hughes of the Coleman Foundation. Special thanks to Eddy Bayardelle and Melanie Mortimer of Merrill Lynch Global Philanthropy, and Kim Davis of the JPMorganChase Foundation.

In addition, I would like to recognize the efforts and contributions of members of NFTE's National Board of Directors: Albert Abney, Patty Alper, William Daugherty, Philip A. Falcone, Michael L. Fetters, Lawrence N. Field, John B. Fullerton, Tom Hartocollis, Landon Hilliard, Consuelo Mack, James Lyle, Kevin Murphy, Alan Patricof, Marsha Ralls, Donna Redel, Robert Reffkin, Arthur J. Samberg, Diana Davis Spencer, Peter B. Walker, and Tucker York; and I would like to acknowledge the inspired guidance provided by our National Executive Committee: Bart Breighner,

Stephen Brenninkmeijer, Kathryn Davis, Lewis M. Eisenberg, Theodore J. Forstmann, Sir Paul Judge, Mary Myers Kauppila, the Hon. Jack Kemp, Elizabeth B. Koch, Abby Moffat, Jeffrey S. Raikes, Kenneth I. Starr, and the Hon. John C. Whitehead. I am deeply grateful as well to the many philanthropists who have supported our work, including Raymond Chambers, Charles G. and David H. Koch, Joanne Beyer of the Scaife Family Foundation, Barbara Bell Coleman of the Newark Boys' and Girls' Clubs, Chris Podoll of the William Zimmerman Foundation, Stephanie Bell-Rose of the Goldman Sachs Foundation, The Shelby Cullom Davis Foundation, Jeff Raikes and the Microsoft Corporation, The Nasdaq Educational Foundation, and Ronald McDonald House Children's Charities.

Further, I would like to acknowledge Steve Alcock, Harsh and Aruna Bhargava, Lena Bondue, Dawn Bowlus, Shelly Chenoweth, Janet McKinstry Cort, Erik Dauwen, Clara Del Villar, Christine Chambers Gilfillan, Andrew Hahn, Kathleen Kirkwood, Michael Simmons, Sheena Lindahl, Cynthia Miree, Henry To, Carol Tully, Dilia Wood, and Elizabeth Wright, as well as Peter Cowie, Joseph Dominic, Paul DeF. Hicks, Jr., Ann Mahoney, David Roodberg, Phyllis Ross Schless, and Remi Vermeir, who have provided countless insights into providing entrepreneurial opportunities to young people.

In addition, I would like to thank my brother, Jack, the best CPA I know, and my father, John, for financing much of NFTE's early work, and for their continuing love and guidance. Thanks are due to all the other teachers, students, experts, and friends who were kind enough to look over this book and help me improve it. Finally, I want to thank my mother, Nancy, a wonderful special education instructor who showed me that one great teacher can affect eternity. Any errors are mine alone.

Steve Mariotti

What Business Do You Want to Start?

Chapter 1

Entrepreneurs Recognize Opportunities

"Everyone lives by selling something."

—Robert Louis Stevenson, Scottish author

Debbi Fields was a young mother with no business experience when she started selling her chocolate chip cookies. In 2007, Mrs. Fields Original Cookies had a network of approximately 1700 retail concept stores in the United States and in over 24 foreign countries under the Mrs. Fields, Great American Cookies, and TCBY brands. Steven Jobs and Stephen Wozniak were barely out of college when they invented the personal computer in a garage in Cupertino, California. Now Apple sells millions of iBooks, iPods, iPhones, and other innovative products each year. Russell Simmons used his own passion for hip-hop to turn rap artists like Run DMC and LL Kool J into international pop stars. Simmons and his businesses—Def Jam Records, Rush Communications, and others—have come to be worth over $500 million.

Performance Objectives

1. Explain what entrepreneurs do.
2. Describe how free-enterprise economies work and how entrepreneurs fit into them.
3. Find and evaluate opportunities to start your own business.
4. Explain how profit works as a signal to the entrepreneur.

Entrepreneurship Defined[1]

Have you ever eaten a Mrs. Fields cookie? Used an Apple computer? Listened to a hip-hop CD? Entrepreneurs brought these products into your world.

What Is an Entrepreneur?

Performance Objective 1

Explain what entrepreneurs do.

Most Americans earn money by working in **business**. Business is the buying and selling of products or services in order to make money.

- A **product** is something that exists in nature or is made by human beings. It is *tangible*, meaning that it can be touched.
- A **service** is work that provides time, skills, or expertise in exchange for money. It is *intangible*. You cannot actually touch it.

America's small business owners and their employees represent more than half of the private workforce. These entrepreneurs, who create more than 75 percent of net new jobs nationwide and generate more than 50 percent of the nation's Gross Domestic Product, and the employees who work in small businesses, deserve our thanks. We salute them.

—*President George W. Bush, from speech celebrating Small Business Week*

Someone who earns a living by working for someone else's business is an **employee** of that business. There are many kinds of employees. At Ford Motor Company, for instance, some employees build the cars, some sell the cars, and some manage the company. But employees all have one thing in common—they do not own the business; they work for others who do. They know how much money they can earn, and that amount is limited to salary, plus bonuses and any stock options they may receive.

Some people start their own businesses and work for themselves. They are called **entrepreneurs**. Entrepreneurs are often both owners and employees. For an entrepreneur, the sky is the limit as far as earnings are concerned. Unlike an employee, an entrepreneur owns the profit that his or her business earns and may choose whether to reinvest it in the business or use it as payment.

An entrepreneur is someone who recognizes an opportunity to start a business that other people may not have noticed—and jumps on it. As economist Jeffry Timmons writes in the preface of *New Venture Creation: Entrepreneurship for the 21st Century*, "A skillful entrepreneur can shape and create an opportunity where others see little or nothing—or see it too early or too late."

The word *entrepreneur* first surfaced in France in the seventeenth century. It was used to describe someone who undertook a project, but after awhile it came to mean someone who started a new business—often a new kind of business or a new (and improved) way of doing business. French economist Jean Baptiste Say wrote at the turn of the nineteenth century: "The entrepreneur shifts economic resources [like wood or coal] out of an area of lower and into an area of higher productivity and greater yield." By doing this, Say argued, entrepreneurs added value to **scarce resources**. Oil is a resource because it is used as fuel. Wood is a resource because it can be used to make a house or a table or paper. Economists consider all resources that are worth money "scarce."

Debbi Fields took resources—eggs, butter, flour, sugar, and chocolate chips—and turned them into cookies. People liked what she did with those resources so much that they were willing to pay her more for the cookies than it cost her to buy the resources to make them. She added value to the resources she purchased by what she did with them—and created a multi-million-dollar business in the process.

---

[1] Many of the ideas and concepts in this chapter are adapted from the works of Jeffry A. Timmons, Howard W. Stevenson, and William Bygrave.

The Economic Questions[2]

Since time began, people have had to answer the same basic questions:

- What should be produced?
- When will it be produced?
- How will it be produced?
- Who will produce it?
- Who gets to have what is produced?

Families and individuals—as well as businesspeople, charitable organizations, corporations, and governments—all have had to answer these questions. The system a group of people creates through making these decisions is called an **economy**. The study of how these different groups answer these questions is called **economics**.

An economy is a country's financial structure. It is the system that produces and distributes wealth in a country. The United States economy is called a **free-enterprise system** because anyone is free to start a business. You do not have to get permission from the government to start a business, although you are expected to obey laws and regulations.

This economic system is also called **capitalism**, because the money used to start a business is called **capital**. Anyone who can raise the capital is free to start a business.

◀ **Performance Objective 2**

Describe how free-enterprise economies work and how entrepreneurs fit into them.

Voluntary Exchange

The free-enterprise system is also sometimes referred to as a "free-trade system" because it is based on **voluntary exchange**. Voluntary exchange is a trade between two parties who agree to trade money for a product or service. Each is excited by the opportunity the trade offers. Both parties agree to the exchange because each benefits.

Let's say you have a contracting business and your busy neighbors hire you to renovate their kitchen. You need money and are willing to use your skills and time to earn it. They want their kitchen renovated and are willing to give up money to get it done. You each have something the other wants, so you are willing to trade. Trading only takes place when both parties believe they will benefit. Robbery, in contrast, is an *involuntary* trade.

Global Impact...

Free Trade

For centuries, international trade was very difficult. To sell products in another country required long and dangerous journeys overland or by ship. Many countries were closed to outside trade. Governments also used their power to give their own businesspeople a competitive advantage over those from other countries by imposing trade barriers, such as taxes on foreign goods that made them too expensive to buy. Governments could also enforce restrictions on how many imports or exports could cross a country's borders.

Today, trade barriers have fallen in most parts of the world. The North American Free Trade Agreement (NAFTA) of 1994 ended trade barriers between the United States, Mexico, and Canada. This turned the entire continent into a free-trade zone. The General Agreement on Tariffs and Trade (GATT) cut or eliminated tariffs between 117 countries. Where people are free to trade voluntarily to as large a market as possible, their ability to find someone to buy their goods or services increases. So does their ability to meet consumer needs.

Meanwhile, the Internet has made it much easier for entrepreneurs to sell to customers all over the world. Shipping, too, has become much faster and less expensive. It is an exciting time to be in business!

---

[2] Source of definitions: United States Small Business Administration (SBA): *http://www.sba.gov.*

Benefits of Free Enterprise

We all benefit from living in a free-enterprise system because it discourages entrepreneurs who waste resources—by driving them out of business. It encourages entrepreneurs who use resources efficiently to satisfy consumer needs—by rewarding them with profit.

We also benefit because free enterprise encourages competition between entrepreneurs. Someone who can make cookies that taste as good as Mrs. Fields Original Cookies, and sells them at a lower price, will eventually attract Mrs. Fields' customers. This will force Mrs. Fields to lower prices to stay competitive. Consumers benefit because they get to buy the same quality cookies at a lower price.

What Is a "Small" Business?

The public often thinks of business only in terms of "big" business—companies such as General Electric, Ford, Microsoft, McDonald's, and Nike. A big business is defined by the SBA Office of Advocacy as having more than 500 employees and selling more than $5 million worth of products or services in a year.

Most of the world's businesses are small businesses. A neighborhood restaurant or a clothing boutique is each an example of a small business. A small business may have up to 500 full-time employees and annual sales of less than $5 million.

Surprisingly, the principles involved in running a large company, like MTV, and a corner deli are the same. However, the operation of a small business is not the same as that of a large one. Most multimillion-dollar businesses in this country started out as small, entrepreneurial ventures. This is why entrepreneurship is often called the "engine" of our economy. It "drives" the economy, creating wealth and jobs and improving our standard of living. It is no coincidence that the United States is one of the most entrepreneurial countries in the world and the richest.

Why Be an Entrepreneur?

When starting a business, it is a good rule of thumb to expect to lose money for the first 3 to 18 months. It usually takes at least that long for a business to start selling enough to earn a profit.

Entrepreneurs put a great deal of time and effort into launching their own businesses. While establishing a business, an entrepreneur may also pour all his or her money into it. He or she may not be able to buy new clothes or a fancy car, or go on vacation, or spend much time with family until the business becomes profitable and starts generating cash.

If so much work and sacrifice are involved, why be an entrepreneur? The entrepreneur is working for the following rewards:

1. *Control over Time:* Do you work better at midnight than at 8 A.M.? If you start your own business, you will have control over how you spend

---

BizFacts

- There are 26.8 million businesses in the United States with approximately 99.9 percent of them being small firms with fewer than 500 employees, according to 2006 data (SBA, December 2007).
- The small businesses in America employ about half of the country's private workforce, and create 60 to 80 percent of net new jobs annually (SBA, December 2007).
- Home-based businesses make up 52 percent and franchises 2 percent of small firms (SBA, December 2007).
- Small businesses represent 99.7 percent of all firms with employees (SBA, December 2007).

your time by the type of business it is. Are you the type of person who would rather work really hard for two weeks nonstop and then take a break? If you are an entrepreneur, you can. You can also choose to hire other people to perform tasks that you do not like to do or are not good at, so you can stay focused on what you do best. Bill Gates liked to spend his time designing software. He hired other people to manage Microsoft's operations and market and sell its products.

2. **Fulfillment:** Successful entrepreneurs are passionate about their businesses. They are excited and fulfilled by their work. Entrepreneurs are almost never bored. If something about running the business is boring to them and they have the income to support it, they can hire someone else for that task.

3. **Creation/Ownership:** Entrepreneurship is a creative endeavor. Entrepreneurs put their time into creating something that they expect will survive and become profitable. Entrepreneurs own the businesses that they create and the profits that the businesses earn. Ownership is the key to wealth. Your goal is to create a business that will create a continuing stream of earnings. Eventually, you may be able to sell that business for a multiple of those earnings. That is how entrepreneurs create wealth.

Real estate tycoon Donald Trump was asked on his national TV series The Apprentice *if he ran his many ventures for the money. He replied: "No, I do it for the challenge."*

4. **Control over Compensation:** Entrepreneurs choose how and when they are paid. As owner of your company you can decide to
   - Pay yourself a **salary**—a fixed payment made at regular intervals, such as every week or every month. No matter how much time you put in, the salary remains the same.
   - Pay yourself a **wage**—a fixed payment per hour.
   - Take a share of the company's profit—as the owner you can pay yourself a portion of the business's profit. This payment is called a **dividend**.
   - Take a **commission** on every sale you make. A commission is a percentage of the value of a sale. If you decide to pay yourself 10 percent commission and you sell one of your products for $120, your commission on the sale would be $12.

5. **Control over Working Conditions:** As an entrepreneur, you can create a work environment that reflects your values. If you support recycling, you can make sure your company recycles. You also evaluate your own performance. No one else has the power to fire you.

Some of the greatest entrepreneurs in the world have dealt with problems growing up, such as extreme poverty, abuse, learning disabilities, and other issues. Sir Richard Branson, for example, had such severe dyslexia that he dropped out of high school. He became a successful entrepreneur, however,

Step into the Shoes...
Henry Ford's Vision

Henry Ford dreamed of a "horseless carriage" that the average American could afford. Ford needed this strong vision to sustain him through years of business failure. By the time he was almost 40, Ford had been trying to realize his vision for many years. Several of his attempts to produce and sell automobiles had failed. His neighbors considered him a daydreaming mechanic. He continued to direct all his efforts toward making his vision real, and eventually created the Ford Motor Company. By the time he was 50, Ford was one of the richest and most famous men in the world. After a hundred years, Ford Motor Company is still a major American business.

The dream provides the motivation to succeed. What vision will sustain you?

creating Virgin Airlines and Virgin Records. Today he oversees more than 360 companies and has a net worth between $3.8 billion[3] and $7.8 billion.[4] As an entrepreneur, he was able to create an environment in which he could succeed.

The Desire to Make Money Is Not the Only Reason to Start a Business

Starting a business is an opportunity, and like any opportunity it should be evaluated by taking a careful look at the costs and benefits it offers. One thing is for certain, though, *the desire to make money, alone, is not a good enough reason to start one's own business.*

The financial rewards of owning your own business may not happen until you put in years of hard work. The desire to make money may not be enough to keep you going through the difficult early period. Most successful companies have been founded by an entrepreneur with a powerful and motivating dream.

Entrepreneurs say they are not in business for the money so often that it has almost become a cliché, but, like all clichés, it is based on a degree of truth.

Definitions of Success—Monetary and Other

Today, the Millennial Generation (born between 1977 and 1995) has redefined success. It is much more individualized and based upon factors beyond those of income and wealth. Business owners may start an enterprise to create a more environmentally friendly approach to a product or process, to provide jobs for a disadvantaged population, or to improve their mental or physical health. For these entrepreneurs, success may be determined by their ability to have an impact on the population they serve. Or, success may mean working to provide a lifestyle that permits a shortened workweek or telecommuting. Recognition from peers and others may also be a goal. Financial success may be just one of many measures of achievement for an entrepreneur.

Costs and Benefits of Becoming an Entrepreneur

Even if you do have a strong dream that you believe will motivate you through the ups and downs of running a business, look closely at the costs and benefits of being an entrepreneur before you decide whether this is the life for you.

Benefits include

- *Independence:* Business owners do not have to follow orders or observe working hours set by someone else.
- *Satisfaction:* Doing what you love to do, or turning a skill, hobby, or other interest into your own business can be highly satisfying.
- *Financial Reward:* Although income potential is generally capped for employees, entrepreneurs are limited only by their own imagination and tenacity. Entrepreneurs built most of our country's great fortunes.
- *Self-Esteem:* Knowing you created something valuable can give you a strong sense of accomplishment. It can help you feel good about yourself.

---

[3] "The World's Billionaires," *Forbes*, March 8, 2007.
[4] "The Sunday Times Rich List," *The Sunday Times*, April 2006.

Costs include the following

- ***Business Failure:*** About one in five new businesses fails in the first 8 years, although this is largely due to entrepreneurs not getting proper training.[5] Another third close because the entrepreneurs become discouraged and give up. Entrepreneurs risk losing not only their own money but also financial investment by others.
- ***Obstacles:*** You will run into problems that you will have to solve by yourself. Your family and friends may discourage you or not support your vision.
- ***Loneliness:*** It can be lonely and even a little scary to be completely responsible for the success or failure of your business.
- ***Financial Insecurity:*** You are not guaranteed a set salary or benefits. You may not always have enough money to pay yourself, particularly in the first 18 months of a new enterprise. You will have to set up and fund your own retirement fund.
- ***Long Hours/Hard Work:*** You will have to work long hours to get your business off the ground. Many entrepreneurs work 6 or even 7 days a week, often for 12 to 14 hours per day. Also, do not forget to look at the opportunities you will give up to start your own business. What are the "next-best opportunities" for your money and time? Some might include going to college or graduate school, or working for someone else.

Not everyone is cut out to be an entrepreneur. Entrepreneurs have to be able to tolerate a higher degree of risk and uncertainty than people who work steady jobs for established employers. With higher risk, however, comes the possibility of higher rewards.

Cost/Benefit Analysis

Using a comparison of costs and benefits to make a decision is called **cost/benefit analysis**. It is a helpful tool because we tend to make decisions with our emotions, not by using our intellect to evaluate the pros and cons. Strong emotions may overwhelm you to the point where you see only the benefits and not the costs of an action (or vice versa).

Say you plan to buy a car. You might be overwhelmed by the idea of making such a large purchase, even if the benefits are greater than the costs. On the other hand, you might decide to buy a car at a cost that outweighs the benefits it will bring because you are temporarily blinded by a desire to own a really impressive vehicle. Making a list that includes the dollars and cents of the costs and benefits of your purchase is a concrete way to take the emotion out of the decision.

To turn an opportunity into a business you will have to invest both time and money. Before making this investment, look carefully at two factors:

Costs. The money and time you will have to invest, as well as the opportunities you will give up to operate the business

Benefits. The money you will earn and the knowledge and experience you will gain

Opportunity Cost

Cost/benefit analysis is inaccurate without including **opportunity cost**. This is the cost of your "next-best investment." Perhaps your goal is to become a composer who writes scores for movies. You get a full-time job at a local store

[5] "Self-Employment on Rise," by Linda Yu, *Metro* magazine, June 2004.

Figure 1-1 *The "Do You Have What It Takes?" quiz.*

Take the following quiz to learn more about yourself and whether you have what it takes to be an entrepreneur. Circle the answer that best represents how you feel.

1. You are at a party and a friend tells you that the guy in the expensive-looking suit recently invested in another friend's business. What do you do?
   a. Race over to him, introduce yourself, and tell him every detail of your business idea while asking if he would be interested in investing in it.
   b. Ask your friend to introduce you. Once introduced, you hand the potential investor your business card and politely ask whether you might be able to call on him sometime to present him with your business plan.
   c. Decide that it is probably not a good idea to bother the man at a party. After all, he is here to relax. Maybe you will run into him again somewhere else.

2. Your boss puts you in charge of researching office supply stores and choosing the one that you think would be best for the company to use. What is your response?
   a. Yes! Finally, a chance to show the boss what you are made of—plus, you will be able to spirit a few of the supplies away for your own business.
   b. You are terrified; this is more responsibility than you really want. What if you make a mistake and cost the company money? You do not want to look bad.
   c. You are excited. This is a good opportunity to impress your boss and also learn how to compare and negotiate with suppliers . . . something you will need to do for your own business.

3. You are already going to school full-time when you are offered a part-time job that is in the same field as the business you want to start when you graduate next year.
   a. Take the job, after talking with your student advisor about how to juggle your schedule so it will fit, because you believe the experience and the contacts you will develop will be invaluable when you start your business.
   b. Take the job. In fact, you ask for extra hours so you can finally start making some real money. Who needs sleep?
   c. Turn down the job. School is hard enough without working, too. You do not want your grades to suffer.

4. You are offered a job as a survey-taker for a marketing firm. The job pays really well but will require you to talk to a great many people.
   a. Take the job. You like people and this job will be a good way to practice getting to know what consumers want.
   b. Turn down the job. Just the thought of approaching strangers makes you queasy.
   c. Take the job so you can conduct some market research of your own by also asking the people you survey what they think about your business idea.

5. Your last job paid well and was interesting, but it required you to put in long hours and sometimes work on the weekends. What is your response?
   a. You put in the extra hours without complaint, but mainly because you felt that the rewards were worth it.
   b. You went a little overboard and worked yourself into a state of exhaustion. Moderation is not your strong suit.
   c. You quit. You are strictly a 9-to-5 person. Work is definitely not your life!

6. You are such a good guitar player that friends keep offering to pay for you to give them lessons. What is your response?
   a. You spend some money to run a 6-week advertisement in the local paper, announcing that you are now available to teach at the same rate that established teachers in the area charge.
   b. You start teaching a few friends to see how it goes. You ask them what they are willing to pay and what they want to learn.
   c. You give a few friends some lessons but refuse to take any money.

7. Your best friend has started a business designing Web sites. He needs help because the business is really growing. He offers to make you a partner in the business even though you are computer illiterate. What is your response?
   a. You jump in, figuring that you will learn the ropes soon enough.
   b. You ask your friend to keep the partnership offer open but first to recommend a class you can take to get your skills up to speed.
   c. You pass. You do not see how you can work in a business you know nothing about.

Analysis of the "Do You Have What It Takes?" Quiz

Scoring

1. a = 2	b = 1	c = 0
2. a = 2	b = 0	c = 1
3. a = 1	b = 2	c = 0
4. a = 1	b = 0	c = 2
5. a = 1	b = 2	c = 0
6. a = 2	b = 1	c = 0
7. a = 2	b = 1	c = 0

Figure 1-1 *The "Do You Have What It Takes?" quiz.*

12 Points or More: You are a natural risk-taker and can handle a lot of stress. These are important characteristics for an entrepreneur to have to be successful. You are willing to work hard but have a tendency to throw caution to the wind a little too easily. Save yourself from that tendency by using cost/benefit analysis to carefully evaluate your business (and personal!) decisions. In your enthusiasm do not forget to look at the opportunity costs of any decision you make.

6 to 12 Points: You strike an excellent balance between being a risk-taker and someone who carefully evaluates decisions. An entrepreneur needs to be both. You are also not overly motivated by the desire to make money. You understand that a successful business requires hard work and sacrifice before you can reap the rewards. To make sure that you are applying your natural drive and discipline to the best possible business opportunity, use the cost/benefit analysis to evaluate the different businesses you are interested in starting.

6 Points or Fewer: You are a little too cautious for an entrepreneur, but that will probably change as you learn more about how to run a business. You are concerned with financial security and may not be eager to put in the long hours required to get a business off the ground. This does not mean that you will not succeed as an entrepreneur; just make sure that whatever business you decide to start is the business of your dreams, so that you will be motivated to make it a success. Use the cost/benefit analysis to evaluate your business opportunities. Choose a business that you believe has the best shot at providing you with both the financial security and the motivation you require.

for $400 a week to support yourself, so you can write and record music in the evenings that you hope to sell to producers, agents, or film companies.

You find, however, that whenever a producer or agent wants to meet with you, you cannot get out of work to go. You realize that, even though you are making $400 a week, you are missing some important opportunities. Perhaps it would be smarter to take a part-time job for $300 a week that would leave your mornings free for meetings. The opportunity cost of the $100 a week you will lose is made up for by the potential income from film-scoring jobs you are missing by not being free to see people in the business. If your first film-scoring job pays $5,000, for example, you definitely would have made the right decision to earn $100 a week less for a few months.

People often make decisions without considering opportunity costs and then wonder why they are not happy with the outcome. Each time you make a decision about what to do with your time, energy, or money, think about the cost of the opportunities that you are giving up. **Figure 1-1** presents a quiz to determine if you have what it takes to be an entrepreneur.

Entrepreneurship Options

Entrepreneurship extends beyond the traditional views of for-profit enterprises that are most commonly associated with it. There are many variations on entrepreneurship and the opportunities can only be limited by human imagination. Entrepreneurship may include for-profit enterprises that support the missions of not-for-profit organizations, businesses designed for social impact, and ventures that are environmentally oriented.

Social entrepreneurship is one type with multiple definitions and forms. It is commonly thought of as a for-profit enterprise that has the dual goals of achieving profitability and attaining social returns. Another view is that of taking an entrepreneurial perspective toward social problems.[6] Gregory Dees created the following definition:

Social entrepreneurs play the role of change agents in the social sector, by:

- Adopting a mission to create and sustain social value (not just private value),

---

[6] Gregory Dees, The Meaning of "Social Entrepreneurship," May 30, 2001. See *http://www.fuqua.duke.edu/centers/case/documents/dees_SE.pdf.* Accessed December 2007.

- Recognizing and relentlessly pursuing new opportunities to serve that mission,
- Engaging in a process of continuous innovation, adaptation, and learning,
- Acting boldly without being limited by resources currently in hand, and
- Exhibiting heightened accountability to the constituencies served and for the outcomes created.

In this view, social entrepreneurship is less about profit than it is about social impact.

In addition, **venture philanthropy** is a subset or segment of social entrepreneurship. Financial and human capital is invested in not-for-profits by individuals and for-profit enterprises with the intention of generating social rather than financial returns on their investments. In some cases, venture philanthropy may involve the investment of capital in the for-profit, commercial part of a not-for-profit. In others, it may mean investing in not-for-profits directly to encourage entrepreneurial approaches to achieve social impact.

Green Entrepreneurship is another form of entrepreneurship and can be defined as, "Enterprise activities that avoid harm to the environment or help to protect the environment in some way."[7] According to the Corporation for Enterprise Development (CFED), Green Entrepreneurship can:

- Create jobs and offer entrepreneurship opportunities.
- Increase energy efficiency, thus conserving natural resources and saving money.
- Decrease harm to workers' health.
- Enable businesses to tap into new sources of local, state, and federal funding.
- Take advantage of consumer preference for environmentally friendly goods.
- Preserve limited natural assets on which businesses and communities depend for business and quality of life.

Each of these alternative approaches offers opportunities for innovation and growth for the right entrepreneur. Is that you?

How Do Entrepreneurs Find Opportunities to Start New Businesses?

In the 1900s, Joseph Schumpeter expanded on Say's definition of entrepreneurship by adding that entrepreneurs create value "by exploiting an invention or, more generally, an untried technological possibility for producing a new commodity or producing an old one in a new way, by opening up a new source of supply of materials or a new outlet for products, by reorganizing an industry and so on."[8]

Schumpeter's definition describes five basic ways that entrepreneurs find opportunities to create new businesses:

1. Use a new technology to produce a new product.
2. Use an existing technology to produce a new product.
3. Use an existing technology to produce an old product in a new way.
4. Find a new source of resources (that might enable the entrepreneur to produce a product more cheaply).
5. Develop a new market for an existing product.

---

[7] Green Entrepreneurship. Corporation for Enterprise Development: Effective State Policy and Practice, Volume 5, Number 2, April 2004. Available at *http://www.cfed.org*.
[8] Joseph A. Schumpeter, *Capitalism, Socialism and Democracy* (New York: Harper & Row, 1942).

How Do Entrepreneurs Create Business Ideas?

1. **They listen.** By listening to others, entrepreneurs get ideas about improving a business or creating a new one.

   Create one business idea by listening. Describe how you got the idea:

2. **They observe.** By constantly keeping their eyes open, entrepreneurs get ideas about how to help society, about businesses to start, and about what customers need.

   Create a business idea by observing. Describe how you got the idea:

3. **They think.** When entrepreneurs analyze a problem, they think about solutions. What product or service could solve that problem?

   Create a business idea by thinking about a problem. Describe how you got the idea. Write your answers separately.

Entrepreneurs Creatively Exploit Changes in Our World

Today's economists and business experts have defined entrepreneurship even more sharply. Management expert Peter Drucker has pointed out that, for a business to be considered entrepreneurial, it should exploit changes in the world. These changes can be technological, like the explosion in computer technology that led Bill Gates and Paul Allen to start Microsoft, or cultural, like the collapse of Communism, which led to a great many new business opportunities in Eastern Europe.

Nothing changes faster than **technology**, which is defined as science that has been applied to industry or commerce. Several years ago, there were no bar codes, no electronic scanners, and hardly anyone used a fax or cell phone. Today, even the smallest of organizations needs to use current technologies to be competitive. Smart entrepreneurs multiply their efficiency by taking advantage of the latest breakthroughs in business technology. To learn about the latest in technology, read current business and trade magazines and visit Web sites, such as:

- The Business Technology Network, *http://www.techweb.com*.
- BusinessWeek Tech Supplement, *http://www.businessweek.com/technology*.

Peter Drucker defined an "entrepreneur" as someone who "always searches for change, responds to it, and exploits it as an opportunity."

Where Others See Problems, Entrepreneurs Recognize Opportunities

Here is a simple definition of "entrepreneur" that captures the essentials: *An entrepreneur recognizes opportunities where other people see only problems.*

Many famous businesses have been started because an entrepreneur turned a "problem" into a successful business. The entrepreneur recognized that the problem was actually an opportunity. Where there are dissatisfied customers, there are definitely opportunities for the entrepreneur.

Anita Roddick was an excellent example of an entrepreneur who started off as a dissatisfied customer. She started The Body Shop International because she was tired of paying for unnecessary perfume and fancy packaging when she bought makeup—and she thought other women might feel the same way. Bill Gates is another problem solver—before he cofounded Microsoft, most software was complicated and confusing to the average person. Gates decided to use his programming aptitude to create software that would be "user-friendly"—fun and easy for the average person to use.

Train Your Mind to Recognize Business Opportunities

The first step in becoming an entrepreneur is to train your mind to recognize business opportunities. The next step is to let your creativity fly. Roddick suggested that you develop your entrepreneurial instincts by asking yourself such questions as:

- What frustrates me the most when I try to buy something?
- What product or service would really make my life better?
- What makes me annoyed or angry?
- What product or service would take away my aggravation?

Entrepreneurs Use Their Imaginations

Businesses are also formed when entrepreneurs not only fume about products or services that annoy them but fantasize about products or services they would love to have in their lives. Jump-start your imagination by asking yourself such questions as:

- What is the one thing you would love to have more than anything else?
- What would it look like? Taste like?
- What would it do?

Consider posing these questions to friends and family members, as well. You might hear about an opportunity you had not yet recognized.

Figure 1-2 shows some simple business ideas to get your imagination jump-started.

An Idea Is Not Necessarily an Opportunity

Not every business idea you may have is an opportunity. In fact, most ideas are not viable business possibilities. An opportunity has a unique characteristic that distinguishes it from an ordinary idea. *An opportunity is an idea that is based on what consumers need or want and are willing to buy sufficiently often at a high enough price to sustain the business.* A successful business sells products or services that customers need, at prices they are willing to pay. Many a small business has failed because the entrepreneur did not understand this. It is critical that the idea "has legs" to go on to success.

In addition, according to Jeffry Timmons, "An opportunity has the qualities of being attractive, durable, and timely and is anchored in a product or service which creates or adds value for its buyer or end user."[9]

---

[9] *New Venture Creation: Entrepreneurship for the 21st Century*, 5th ed. (New York: Irwin/McGraw-Hill, 1999), p. 7.

Figure 1-2 *Sample low-investment business ideas.*

Advertising
Design flyers and posters
Distribute flyers, posters, and brochures
Image consultant
Publicist

Animals
Cat sitter
Dog walker
Pet grooming
Pet bowls

Art
Artist
Art gallery
Calligraphy
Pottery

Baking
Baked goods for people in need
Bake sales
Cookie delivery business

Bicycles
Bicycle repair
Messenger service
Bike design

Bilingual
Translation
Teach another language
Teach English as a second language

Birds
Birdcage service
Birdwatching guide
Raise birds for sale

Books
Book selling
Used book selling
Write a book

Children
Babysitting service
Mother's helper
Teach activities
Children's stories

Cleaning
Car washing
House/office cleaning
Laundry and ironing

Clothing
Clothing design
Vintage clothing
Buying wholesale for resale

Collecting
Vinyl records
Comics

Computers
Computer repair/software installation
Word-processing service
Desktop publishing
Web site design
Graphic arts

Cooking
Catering
Pasta
Organic baby food
Cookbook

Crafts
Candle-making
Greeting-card design
Handbags
Jewelry-making

Dancing
Dance lessons
Hip-hop dance troupe

Driving
Errand service
Meal delivery
Messenger service

Entertainment
Clown
Magician
Party DJ
Balloon decorating

Fish
Aquarium care
Fishing

Gardening
Fresh herbs and flowers
Yardwork
Plant care
Window boxes

Hair
Hairstyling
Hair clips
Hair wrapping

Holidays
Gift baskets
Seasonal sales

Internet
Genealogy
Web site design
eBay auctions

Music
Band
Music lessons
Stickers and buttons
String quartet

Painting
Housepainting
Furniture
Signage

People
Dating newsletter
Wake-up service

Photography
Wedding photography
Photo journalist

Sales
Candy
Jewelry, hats, pens

Silkscreening
T-shirts
Creative clothing

Teaching
Tutoring
Giving lessons

Video
Videotaping events
Videotaping concerts
Digital moviemaking

Woodworking
Carpentry
Bird cages
Decorative carving
Board games

Writing
Pennysaver newspaper
Fanzine

Entrepreneurial Wisdom...

A useful way to evaluate a business idea is to look at its **S**trengths, **W**eaknesses, **O**pportunities, and **T**hreats (**SWOT**). This is called **SWOT Analysis**.

- *Strengths*—All the capabilities and positive points that the entrepreneur has, from experience to contacts. These are internal to the organization.
- *Weaknesses*—All of the negatives that the entrepreneur faces, such as lack of capital or training, or failure to set

up a workable accounting system. These are internal to the organization.

- *Opportunities*—Any positive external event or circumstance (including lucky breaks) that can help the entrepreneur get ahead of the competition.
- *Threats*—Any external factor, event, or circumstance that can harm the business, such as competitors, legal issues, and declining economies.

Timmons defines a business opportunity as an idea, plus these four characteristics:

1. It is attractive to customers.
2. It will work in your business environment.
3. It can be executed in the window of opportunity that exists.
4. You have the resources and skills to create the business, or you know someone who does and who might want to form the business with you.

The "window of opportunity" is the amount of time you have to get your business idea to your market. You might have a great idea, but if several other competitors have it, too, and have already brought it to the marketplace, that window of opportunity has been closed.

Remember, not every idea is an opportunity. For an idea to be an opportunity, it must lead to the development of a product or service that is of value to the consumer.

Opportunity Is Situational

A problem is one example of an opportunity that entrepreneurs need to be able to recognize. A changing situation or trend is another. Opportunity is situational, meaning it is dependent on variable circumstances. There are no rules about when or where an opportunity might appear. Change and flux create opportunities.

Think about recent changes in computer technology. In the mid 1980s, the conventional wisdom was that only the biggest telecommunications companies were going to be in a position to exploit the Internet and all the opportunities that it had to offer. How could entrepreneurs compete with established, resource-loaded companies such as AT&T, for example? The opposite has been true, however. Entrepreneurs have penetrated and, indeed, dominated the market for Internet-based services. Think of AOL, EarthLink, Google, and Yahoo! Each one is an entrepreneurial venture that left the telecom giants scrambling to catch up.

As Timmons has pointed out, it can take a huge corporation (think dinosaur) over six years to develop and implement a new business strategy. Entrepreneurs, in contrast, can dart in and out of the market like roadrunners. They can "turn on a dime rather than a dollar bill."

The Five Roots of Opportunity in the Marketplace

There are "five roots of opportunity" in the marketplace that entrepreneurs can exploit.[10] Notice how similar these are to Schumpeter's definition of entrepreneurship!

Apple led the digital music revolution with its iPod portable music players. (Apple Computer, Inc.)

---

[10] Adapted from the *Master Curriculum Guide: Economics and Entrepreneurship*, ed. by John Clow et al. (New York: Joint Council on Economic Education, 1991).

Step into the Shoes...

Russell Simmons Makes Rap Happen

In the late 1980s, Russell Simmons was promoting rap concerts at the City University of New York. At the time, rap was considered a passing fad, but Simmons really loved it. Even though most record executives thought rap would be over in a year or two, Simmons truly believed it was a business opportunity. He formed Def Jam Records with fellow student Rick Rubin for $5,000. Within a year, they produced hit records by Run DMC and LL Cool J, and Simmons became a multimedia mogul.

Simmons took a chance on this opportunity because he felt that, if you personally know 10 people who are eager to buy your product or service, 10 million would be willing to buy it if they knew about it. Luckily for him, he was right about rap's popular potential, but he could have been wrong. That can be a problem with perceived opportunities—you may be passionate about something but there may not be enough consumer interest to sustain a business.

Simmons loved rap and hoped that other people would, too. That was the internal factor—he had the passion to sustain himself as he worked 24/7 to make his dream come true. As it turned out, music fans were a little bored with rock at that time, and looking for a fresh sound. Rap filled the bill. This was an external opportunity that happened to coincide with Simmons's internal commitment.

1. ***Problems*** that your business can solve.
2. ***Changes*** in laws, situations, or trends.
3. ***Inventions*** of totally new products or services.
4. ***Competition.*** If you can find a way to beat the competition on price, location, quality, reputation, reliability, or speed, you can create a very successful business with an existing product or service.
5. ***Technological Advances.*** Scientists may invent new technology, but entrepreneurs figure out how to use and sell it.

◀ **Performance Objective 3**

Find and evaluate opportunities to start your own business.

Internal Opportunities

It is helpful not only to be aware of the "five roots of opportunity" in the marketplace, but to think also about how we perceive opportunities ourselves. Opportunities fall into two classes: internal and external. An **internal opportunity** is one that comes from inside you or your organization—from a hobby, an interest, or even a passion. This may be the transformation of a strength into a business opportunity or it may be the resolution of a problem, such as creating a viable product from scrap material. An **external opportunity**, in contrast, is generated by a noticeable outside circumstance.

External Opportunities

External opportunities are circumstances you notice that make you say to yourself, "Hey! That would make a great business!" For example, you see that people in your neighborhood are complaining about the lack of available day care, so you start a day care center. But what if you find out very quickly that two-year-olds get on your nerves? That is a drawback of external opportunities. Your idea may fill a market need, but you may not have the skills or interest to make it a successful business.

The best business opportunities often combine both internal and external factors. Ideally, a business that you are passionate about fills a huge need in the marketplace.

Paths to Small Business Ownership

Not all business owners start their ventures from the ground up. Although the emphasis of this book is on starting and growing your own enterprise, the paths to business ownership are varied. You could buy an existing

Figure 1-3 *Selected business entry options.*

	Start a Business	Buy an Existing Business	Secure a Franchise or License	License Technology
Customers	None	Established	None—but may have name recognition	None
Location	Needed	In place	Assistance possible	Needed
Management Control	Owner	Owner	Owner within terms of license	Owner within terms of license
Operational Control	Owner	Owner	Owner within terms of license	Owner
Marketing	Needed	In place (+/−)	Assistance possible. Rules absolutely.	Needed
Reputation	None	In place (+/−)	Should be. If not, why license?	Possible
Royalties/Fees	Not usual	Maybe	Ongoing	Likely
Financing	Needed	Prior owner may provide	Assistance possible	Needed
Disclosures	None	Buyer beware	UFOC and contracts	Agreement

company, secure franchise rights, license critical technology or methods, inherit a company, or be hired to manage.[11] There are pros and cons to each approach and it is worthwhile to give thought to each option. Note the possibilities in **Figure 1-3**.

Buying an Existing Business

A business purchase, or **acquisition**, might be a good way to jump-start your entry into small business ownership. If you are purchasing a company with several years of history, you should perform **due diligence**, which is the process used to learn about its true financial condition (the current owners may have incentives to provide incomplete, misleading, or inaccurate information), its reputation, and its viability. There is both an art and a science involved in buying an existing business.

The challenge is to do a complete, in-depth analysis of the opportunity, just as you would for a start-up, with the added dimension of having an existing history, whether for better or for worse. Be wary of owners whose business seems to be too good to be true or who are overly eager to sell. Be thorough, whether you are buying a customer list, some or all assets, some or all debts, and the like. Done well, buying a business can be the starting point for business success. Done poorly, buying a business can be more challenging and problematic than starting a new venture.

Securing Franchise Rights

"A **franchise** is a legal and commercial relationship between the owner of a trademark, service mark, trade name or advertising symbol and an individual or group seeking to use that identification in a business."[12] The two primary forms of franchising are product/trade name franchising and business format franchising. The franchisers can provide assistance in marketing, site selection, securing financing, training, product supply, and business systems. McDonald's is an example of a business format franchise. Each franchise agreement is different and, while franchises fail less often than fully

---

[11] Jerome A. Katz and Richard P. Green, *Entrepreneurial Small Business* (New York: McGraw-Hill/Irwin, 2008).

[12] SBA Workshop, Is Franchising for Me? See *http://www.sba.gov/idc/groups/public/documents/sba_homepage/serv_slop_isfforme .pdf*. Accessed December 2007.

Figure 1-4 *Factors to consider before becoming a franchisee.*

1. **Franchiser success**—How many similar franchises are nearby? In total? How are they performing? What name recognition exists? What's its reputation? Ask franchisees and consumer protection agencies.
2. **Franchiser durability**—Determine the length of experience. Is this a long-term opportunity or a fad? Does the franchiser own any intellectual property?
3. **Franchiser financial health**—How healthy is the company? Financial statements should be in the disclosure documents. Be certain you understand them.
4. **Start-up investment**—What is the amount and what does it buy? Ask about all potential franchise costs. Be certain that ongoing costs and start-up costs are clear.
5. **Financing support**—Does the franchiser offer competitive financing? How much do you need until you reach positive cash flow? Do the financial projections under various conditions and know your options.
6. **Purchasing requirements**—Do you have to buy from the franchiser or their list of suppliers? Are there minimum purchases? Can you purchase from others? How does the pricing from the required suppliers compare?
7. **Term of the agreement**—What is it? What, if any, are the terms for selling the franchise rights to another operator? What are your renewal rights?
8. **Competition**—Are there any restrictions on how you can compete within your territory? Is there assistance to help you compete? What? What is the level of competition?
9. **Management fit**—Does the management style and level of control exerted by the franchiser fit for you? Is the loss of independence worth the gains?

independent businesses, they cannot guarantee success. **Figure 1-4** describes issues to address when considering becoming a franchisee.

Licensing Technology

One way to potentially shorten the product development cycle and to access innovative technology would be to identify and **license technology**, by entering into a contract to use the technology without purchasing the rights to own it. Whether you acquire rights through a university, state economic development office, federal agency such as NASA, or an individual scientist/inventor, you can create a business based on technology transfer. The MBA team of Bruce Black and Matt Ferris from the University of Georgia developed a business plan that garnered numerous competitive awards for the KidSmart Vocal Smoke Detector, which was created by an inventor and brought to market by them. The product is now available in major retail stores and on the Internet through the successor company, Signal One.

Before securing franchise rights, purchasing a business, or licensing technology, be certain to do your research thoroughly to understand what you are and are not buying and what your ongoing obligations (financial, operational, legal, and reporting) will be. For example, a franchiser is required to provide you with a copy of the Uniform Franchise Offering Circular (UFOC) as well as a copy of the franchise agreement, any other applicable contracts, and the company's financial statement. Because these transactions are complex and can have significant financial and personal implications for you, it is important to invest in qualified legal and financial counsel before signing any agreements of this kind.

Do Not Rip Off Someone Else's Creativity

You would be upset if someone made money from your invention or artistic creation, so resist the urge to base your business on someone else's creative work. Not only is it unethical, it is against the law. Be sure that any business you start respects the intellectual property of others.

- Do not sell counterfeit knockoffs of popular brands.
- Do not take graphics, music, or content from the Web without permission and/or payment.

- Always know the source of the goods you buy from suppliers, to avoid the risk of receiving stolen property.

Making the Business Work on Your Terms

What makes a business work is not solely profitability and cash flow, although they are of course necessary. Each entrepreneur has his or her own goals and objectives for the business. As an entrepreneur, it will be up to you to determine how you want your business to be and to make it happen.

A Business Must Make a Profit to Stay in Business

No matter how big or small, a business must make a **profit**; that is, the amount of money earned must be greater than the amount of money owed. Most businesses do lose money initially because entrepreneurs have to lay out cash to set up operations, and advertise to attract customers. If the business cannot make a profit and generate cash, eventually the entrepreneur will be unable to pay the bills and will have to close.

Closing a business is nothing to be ashamed of, if you operate ethically and learn from the experience. In fact, most successful entrepreneurs open and close more than one business during their lives. If your venture is not making a profit after you have gotten it up and running, that is a signal that you may be in the wrong business. Closing it may be the smartest decision.

An entrepreneur may change businesses many times over a lifetime in response to changing competition and consumer needs. Schumpeter called the process of constantly changing businesses "creative destruction."[13]

Profit Is the Sign That the Entrepreneur Is Adding Value

Performance Objective 4

Explain how profit works as a signal to the entrepreneur.

Profit is the sign that an entrepreneur has added value to the resources he or she is using. Debbi Fields added value to "scarce resources" by creating something that people were willing to buy for a price that gave her a profit. In contrast, not making a profit is a sign that the entrepreneur is not using resources very well and is not adding value to them.

Profit Results from the Entrepreneur's Choices

An entrepreneur's choices directly affect how much profit the business makes. For example, like Debbi Fields, you have a business selling home-made cookies. You might decide one week to buy margarine instead of butter because it is cheaper, even though your cookies may not taste as good made with margarine. This type of choice is called a **trade-off**. You are giving up one thing (taste) for another (money).

If your customers do not notice the change and continue to buy your cookies, you have made a good choice. You have conserved a resource (money) and increased your profit by lowering your costs. The increase in profit confirms that you have made the right choice.

If your customers notice the change and stop buying your cookies, your profit will decrease. The decrease in profit signals that you have made a bad choice. Next week you should probably buy butter again. The profit signal taught you that your consumers were dissatisfied and the trade-off was not worth it. Every choice an entrepreneur makes is a trade-off.

---

[13] Joseph Schumpeter, *Capitalism, Socialism and Democracy*, 1942.

Seven Rules for Building a Successful Business

Simmons and Rubin were also successful because they instinctively applied the seven basic rules of building a successful business:

1. *Recognize an Opportunity:* Simmons believed that rap music was an untapped business opportunity.
2. *Evaluate It with Critical Thinking:* He tested his idea by promoting concerts and observing consumer reaction.
3. *Build a Team:* Simmons formed a partnership with Rick Rubin.
4. *Write*—a realistic business plan.
5. *Gather Resources:* Simmons and Rubin pooled their $5,000.
6. *Decide Ownership:* Simmons and Rubin formed a legal partnership.
7. *Create Wealth.*

The Team Approach

Let's take a closer look at step 3: Build a Team. Alone, neither Simmons nor Rubin had enough money to launch a record label, but together they were able to do it. Their business was also helped by the fact that they each knew different artists and had different contacts in the recording industry.

Everyone you know is a potential business-formation opportunity. Your friends or family members may have skills, equipment, or contacts that would make them valuable business partners. Perhaps you truly want to start a Web site design business because you know of businesses in your community that want to put up Web sites. You are a graphic artist but you do not know how to use Web site development programs. If you have a friend who has that knowledge, you could start a business together. Or maybe you would like to start a DJ business, but you only have one turntable or laptop computer. If you form the business with a friend, you can pool equipment. (When forming a business team, organize the venture so that everyone involved shares in the ownership and profits. People work much better when they are working for themselves.)

Now carry this idea a step further—every person you meet is a potential contact for your business. Thinking this way will encourage you to **network**, or exchange valuable information and contacts with other businesspeople. Keep your business cards on you at all times and truly view every individual you meet as an opportunity for your business.

Entrepreneurial Wisdom...
Build Your Brain

Becoming a successful entrepreneur is all about making connections—those "Aha!" moments when you realize what your business opportunity is or when you figure out how to do something better than the competition. Research indicates that mental exercise will help your brain become better at making such connections. Even the most erudite scientists recognize the value of activities that encourage brain cells to make new connections. Robotics engineer Hugo De Garis, who is building an artificial brain for an artificial cat, plays classical piano every day before he sits down at the computer. "This helps to build my own brain," he told the *New York Times*.[14] Arnold Scheibel, head of the University of California–Los Angeles Brain Research Institute, suggests the following brain-builders:

- Solve puzzles.
- Play a musical instrument.
- Fix something—learn to repair cars or electrical equipment.
- Create art: write poetry, paint, or sculpt.
- Dance.
- Make friends with people who like to have interesting conversations.

[14] Nicholas D. Kristof, "Robokitty," *New York Times*, August 1, 1999.

Key Terms

advertising
assets
balance sheets
breakeven point
business plan
cash flow statement
competitive analysis
culture
direct marketing
elevator pitch
environmental analysis
exit strategy
income statement or profit and loss
  statement (P&L)
industry analysis
initial public offering (IPO)
inventory control systems

liabilities
management team
marketing mix
marketing plan
mission
mission statement
net worth/owner's equity
production methods
proof of market
public relations
publicity
quality assurance
ratio analysis
research and development
target market
vision

Entrepreneurship Portfolio

Critical Thinking Exercises

1. Shawn is creating a business that provides advertising on bathroom stall doors. He is funding the project from his personal savings of $5,000 and does not expect to use any outside financing. Should he create a business plan? Why or why not?

2. Charity and Devon are planning to license technology from NASA that makes it impossible to accidentally lock a child in a car. The technology is complex and the market analysis and financial assumptions take up a lot of pages. Charity and Devon have written an 80-page business plan. Explain your concerns about the length of the plan in light of the chapter text.

3. What factors make the difference between a good business plan and an excellent one? (Hint: Use the chapter data and rules from competitions.)

4. Visit an Internet shopping site such as the Home Shopping Network (*http://www.HSN.com*) or QVC (*http://www.QVC.com*). Select five products that are being sold that you find interesting or unusual. Make a list of the products and your explanation of the market opportunities they reflect.

5. *Errors of omission can sometimes be greater than errors of commission.* How does this statement apply to business plans?

Key Concept Questions

1. Explain why the executive summary is the most important section of any business plan.

2. One mistake entrepreneurs make in their business plans is that of only including an income statement. What other financial statements should be included and why?

3. Print your assignment with 1-inch margins, double spaced, using 12-point Times New Roman. Then, print the same document with 0.8-inch margins, single spaced, using 10-point Arial type. Which is easier to read? Why? How does this relate to business plans?

4. Name three categories of investors/lenders that might have an interest in your business plan.

5. How can spending time researching and writing a business plan save an entrepreneur time and money in the short run and long run?

6. Why is it important to identify an organization's "culture" from the beginning?

Application Exercises

Visit or call (visit after calling) an entrepreneur in your community to discuss business plans.

a. Ask whether he or she wrote a business plan before starting the business. Since then?

b. If he or she did write a plan, for what has it been used?

c. If he or she did not write a plan, why not?

d. Did the owner have any assistance in writing or reviewing the plan?

e. If so, what was the source of assistance?

Exploring Online

Find a business plan on the Internet (not on the Business Plan Pro® disk). Examine it to see whether it follows the guidelines provided in this text. Use a highlighter to mark the sections of the plan that are present. Then, make a list of missing or incomplete sections. Indicate how it does/does not follow the "rules" for formatting and content. Is the plan viable? Why or why not? Would you invest in it? Why or why not?

In Your Opinion

If an entrepreneur presents a business plan that an investor believes is deliberately vague and has provided inflated financial statements, what should that investor do?

The Daily Perc
Sample
Business Plan

Prepared by:

Bartholomew & Teresa Fisher
The Daily Perc, Inc.
P.O. Box 888
Coffee City, WA 99999-0888
777-777-7777

Fisher@TheDailyPerc.com

Table of Contents

Appendices

1. Executive Summary

The Daily Perc, Inc. (TDP) is a specialty beverage retailer. TDP uses a system that is new to the beverage and food service industry to provide hot and cold beverages in a convenient and time-efficient way. TDP provides its customers the ability to drive up and order (from a trained barista) their choice of a custom-blended espresso drink, freshly brewed coffee, or other beverage. TDP is offering a high-quality option to the fast-food, gas station, or institutional coffee.

The Daily Perc offers its patrons the finest hot and cold beverages, specializing in specialty coffees, blended teas, and other custom drinks. In addition, TDP will offer soft drinks, fresh-baked pastries and other confections. Seasonally, TDP will add beverages such as hot apple cider, hot chocolate, frozen coffees, and more.

The Daily Perc will focus on two markets:

The Daily Commuter—someone traveling to/from work, out shopping, delivering goods or services, or just out for a drive.

The Captive Consumer—someone who is in a restricted environment that does not allow convenient departure and return while searching for refreshments, or where refreshments stands are an integral part of the environment.

The Daily Perc will penetrate the commuter and captive consumer markets by deploying Drive-thru facilities and Mobile Cafés in the most logical and accessible locations. The Drive-thru facilities are designed to handle two-sided traffic and dispense customer-designed, specially ordered cups of premium coffees in less time than required for a visit to the locally owned café or one of the national chains.

In addition to providing a quality product and an extensive menu of delicious items, to ensure customer awareness and loyalty, as well as good publicity coverage and media support, we will be donating up to 7.5% of revenue to local charities based upon customer choices.

The Daily Perc's financial picture is quite promising. Since TDP is operating a cash business, the initial cost is significantly less than many start-ups these days. The process is labor intensive and TDP recognizes that a higher level of talent is required. The financial investment in its employees will be one of the greatest differentiators between it and TDP's competition. For the purpose of this pro-forma plan, the capital expenditures of facilities and equipment are financed. There will be minimum inventory on hand so as to keep the product fresh and to take advantage of price drops, when and if they should occur.

The Daily Perc anticipates the initial combination of investments and long-term financing of $515,000 to carry it without the need for any additional equity or debt investment, beyond the purchase of equipment or facilities. This will mean growing a bit more slowly than might be otherwise possible, but it will be a solid, financially sound growth based on customer request and product demand.

The Daily Perc chooses to become the Drive-thru version of Starbucks between the mountains, obtaining several million dollars through an initial public or private offering that would allow the company to open 20 to 30 facilities per year in all metropolitan communities in the North, Midwest, and South with a population of over 150,000. This is the preferred Exit Strategy of the Management Team. The danger in this is that competitors would rise up and establish a foothold on a community before—or in the midst of—the arrival of The Daily Perc, causing a potential for a drain on revenues and a dramatic increase in advertising expenditures to maintain market share. Knowing these risks—and planning for them—gives TDP the edge needed to make this scenario work.

The balance sheet estimates a Net Worth of $1,724,505 for the third year, cash balances of $1,097,010 and earnings of $1,294,371, based on 13 Drive-thrus and four Mobile Cafés, it is not unrealistic to put a market value of between $4 million and $9 million on the company. At present, such companies are trading in multiples of 4 to 10 times earnings, and it is simple mathematics to multiply the success of TDP by the number of major and smaller metropolitan areas between the mountain ranges of the United States.

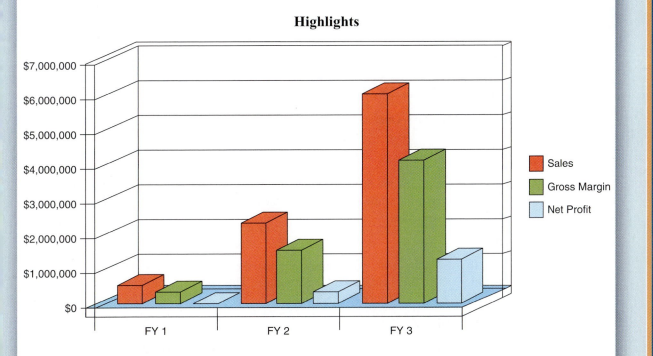

Highlights

1.1. Objectives

The Daily Perc has established three firm objectives it wishes to achieve in the next three years:

1. Thirteen Drive-thru locations and four fully booked Mobile Cafés by the end of the third year.

2. Gross Margin of 45% or more.

3. Net After-tax Profit above 15% of Sales.

1.2. Keys to Success

There are four keys to success in this business, three of which are virtually the same as any food service business. It is our fourth key—the Community Mission—that will give us that extra measure of respect in the public eye.

1. The greatest locations—visibility, high traffic pattern, convenient access.

2. The best products—freshest coffee beans, cleanest equipment, premium serving containers, consistent flavor.

3. The friendliest servers—cheerful, skilled, professional, articulate.

4. The finest reputation—word-of-mouth advertising, promotion of our community mission of charitable giving.

2. Mission, Vision, and Culture

The mission, vision, and culture of The Daily Perc are aligned for success. This is an organization that understands doing well by doing good and is designed to be profitable and an asset to the communities it serves.

2.1. Mission

The Daily Perc Mission is threefold, with each being as integral to our success as the next.

Product Mission—Provide customers the finest quality beverage in the most efficient time.

Community Mission—Provide community support through customer involvement.

Economic Mission—Operate and grow at a profitable rate through sound economic decisions.

2.2. Vision

The Daily Perc will be the purveyor of the finest quality beverages and baked goods in the most efficient time while sustaining our uncompromising principles and contributing to our communities.

2.3. Culture

The Daily Perc values teamwork; family and social responsibility; diversity; customer satisfaction, and a fun, healthy work environment. This creates a culture of collaboration and of high performance in small units.

3. Company Summary

The Daily Perc is a specialty beverage retailer. TDP uses a system that is new to the beverage and food service industry to provide hot and cold beverages in a convenient and time-efficient way. TDP provides its customers the ability to drive up and order from a trained barista their choice of a custom blended espresso drink, freshly brewed coffee, or other beverage. TDP is offering a high-quality option to the fast-food, gas station, and institutional coffee.

3.1. Company Ownership

The Daily Perc is a Limited Liability Corporation. All membership shares are currently owned by Bart and Teresa Fisher, with the intent of using a portion of the shares to raise capital.

The plan calls for the sale of 100 membership units in the company to family members, friends, and Angel Investors. Each membership unit in the company is priced at $4,250, with a minimum of five units per membership certificate, or a minimum investment of $21,250 per investor.

If all funds are raised, based on the pricing established in the financial section of this plan, Bart and Terri Fisher will maintain ownership of no less than 51% of the company.

3.2. Start-Up Summary

The Daily Perc's start-up expenses total just $365,670. The majority of these funds—roughly $300,000—will be used to build the first facility, pay deposits, and provide capital for six months of operating expenses. Another $35,000 will be used for the initial inventory and other one-time expenses. The Daily Perc anticipates the need for roughly $25,500 in operating capital for the first few months of operation.

4. Market Analysis Summary

The Daily Perc—Start-Up

Requirements	
Start-Up Expenses	
Legal	$3,500
Office Equipment	$4,950
Drive-thru Labor (6 months)	$65,000
Drive-thru Finance Payment (6 months)	$12,300
Drive-thru Expenses (6 months)	$8,520
Land Lease (6 months)	$7,200
Vehicle Finance (6 months)	$3,700
Administration Labor (6 months)	$54,000
Web site Development & Hosting	$5,600
Identity/Logos/Stationary	$4,000
Other	$5,000
Total Start-Up Expenses	$173,770
Start-up Assets	
Cash Required	$25,500
Start-Up Inventory	$35,000
Other Current Assets	$0
Long-term Assets	$131,400
Total Assets	$191,900
Total Requirements	**$365,670**

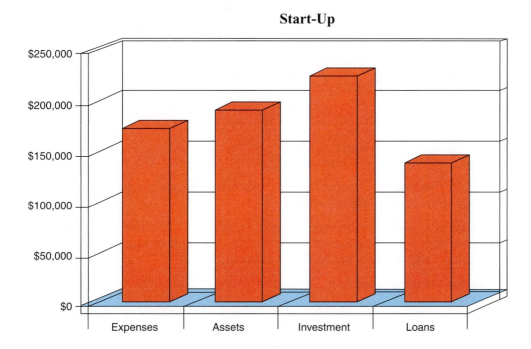

Start-Up

BUSINESS PLAN

The Daily Perc—Start-Up Funding

Start-Up Expenses to Fund	$173,770
Start-Up Assets to Fund	$191,900
Total Funding Required	**$365,670**
Assets	
Non-cash Assets from Start-Up	$166,400
Cash Requirements from Start-Up	$25,500
Additional Cash Raised	$0
Cash Balance on Starting Date	$25,500
Total Assets	**$191,900**
Liabilities and Capital	
Liabilities	
Current Borrowing	$9,000
Long-term Liabilities	$131,400
Accounts Payable (Outstanding Bills)	$0
Other Current Liabilities (Interest-free)	$0
Total Liabilities	**$140,400**
Capital	
Planned Investment	
Partner 1	$21,250
Partner 2	$21,250
Partner 3	$42,500
Partner 4	$25,500
Partner 5	$29,750
Other	$85,020
Additional Investment Requirement	$0
Total Planned Investment	**$225,270**
Loss at Start-Up (Start-Up Expenses)	($173,770)
Total Capital	$51,500
Total Capital and Liabilities	$191,900
Total Funding	$365,670

The Daily Perc will focus on two markets:

1. **The Daily Commuter**—someone traveling to or from work, out shopping, delivering goods or services, or just out for a drive.

2. **The Captive Consumer**—someone who is in a restricted environment that does not allow convenient departure and return while searching for refreshments, or where refreshments stands are an integral part of the environment.

4.1. Market Segmentation

The Daily Perc will focus on two different market segments: Daily Commuters and Captive Consumers. To access both of these markets, TDP has two different delivery systems. For the commuters, TDP has the Drive-thru coffee house. For the captive consumer, TDP has the Mobile Café.

Commuters are defined as any one or more individuals in a motorized vehicle traveling from point "A" to point "B." The Daily Perc's greatest concentration will be on commuters heading to or from work, or those out on their lunch break.

Captive Consumers would include those who are tethered to a campus environment, or in a restricted entry environment that does not allow free movement to and from. Examples would include high school and college campuses, where there is limited time between classes, and corporate campuses where the same time constraints are involved, but regarding meetings and project deadlines, and special events—such as carnivals, fairs, or festivals—where there is an admission price to enter the gate, but exiting would mean another admission fee, or where refreshments are an integral part of the festivities.

The following chart and table reflect the potential numbers of venues available for the Mobile Cafés and what growth could be expected in those markets over the next five years. For a conservative estimate of the number of Captive Consumers this represents, multiply the total number of venues in the year by 1,000. As an example, in the first year, The Daily Perc is showing that there are a total of 2,582 venues at which we might position a Mobile Café. That would equate to a Captive Consumer potential of 2,582,000.

Similarly, there are well over 2,500,000 commuters in the metropolitan area, as well as visitors, vacationers, and others. It can also be assumed that these commuters do not make only one purchase in a day, but in many cases, two and even three beverage purchases.

The chart reflects college and high school campuses, special events, hospital campuses, and various charitable organizations. A segment that is not reflected in the chart (since it would skew the chart so greatly) is the number of corporate campuses in the metropolitan area. There are over 1,700 corporate facilities that house more than 500 employees, giving us an additional 1,700,000 prospective customers, or total of 2,582 locations at which we could place a Mobile Café.

Market Analysis

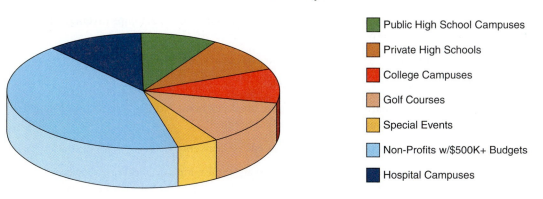

- Public High School Campuses
- Private High Schools
- College Campuses
- Golf Courses
- Special Events
- Non-Profits w/$500K+ Budgets
- Hospital Campuses

Market Analysis

Potential Customers	Growth	YR1	YR2	YR3	YR4	YR5	CAGR
Public High School Campuses	1%	80	81	82	83	84	1.23%
Private High Schools	0%	88	88	88	88	88	0.00%
College Campuses	0%	77	77	77	77	77	0.00%
Golf Courses	0%	99	99	99	99	99	0.00%
Special Events	3%	43	44	45	46	47	2.25%
Non-Profits w/$500K+ Budgets	2%	362	369	376	384	392	2.01%
Hospital Campuses	0%	100	100	100	100	100	0.00%
Total	1.10%	849	858	867	877	887	1.10%

The Daily Perc Business Plan provided by Business Plan Pro® and used by permission of Palo Alto Software.

4.2. Target Market Segment Strategy

TDP's target market is the mobile individual who has more money than time, and excellent taste in a choice of beverage, but no time to linger in a café. By locating the Drive-Thrus in high traffic/high visibility areas, this unique—and abundant—consumer will seek The Daily Perc out and become a regular guest.

To penetrate the target market for the Mobile Cafés, these units will do what they were designed to do. The Daily Perc will take the café to the customer! By using the community support program TDP is instituting, arrangements will be made to visit a high school, college campus, or a corporate campus once or twice a month (even visit these facilities for special games, tournaments, recruiting events, or corporate open houses). And, for every cup or baked good sold, a portion is returned to the high school or college. It becomes a tremendous, painless way for the institution to gain a financial reward while providing a pleasant and fulfilling benefit to their students or employees.

4.3. Industry Analysis

The coffee industry has grown by tremendous amounts in the United States. over the past five years. According to e-imports.com, "Specialty coffee sales are increasing by 20% per year and account for nearly 8% of the 18 billion dollar U.S. Coffee market." Starbucks, the national leader, had revenues in fiscal 2000 of $2.2 billion. That is an increase of 32% over fiscal 1999. Starbucks plans to increase revenues to over $6.6 billion from 10,000 retail outlets by 2005.

Even general coffee sales have increased with international brands such as Folgers, Maxwell House, and Safari coffee reporting higher sales and greater profits. According to data gathered by the Specialty Coffee Association of America (SCAA), "Nearly 52% of Americans over 18 years of age drink coffee every day. They represent over 100 million daily drinkers. 30 million American adults drink specialty coffee beverages daily." Other interesting statistics are available from e-imports.com on coffee consumption:

- Among those who drink coffee, average consumption is 3.1 cups (average of 9 ounces each) per day

- The price is $2.45 on average for an espresso-based drink

- Brewed coffee averages $1.38 each

- Coffee is primarily consumed during breakfast hours (65%), with 35% consumed between meals and the balance with other meals.

- Black coffee is preferred by 35% of coffee drinkers

- The average number of cups of espresso and coffee drinks sold per day at an espresso Drive-thru business with a great visible location is 250 with 500 cups being extraordinary.

- 69% of the coffee sold by independent coffee shops is brewed coffee and 31% is espresso-based.

America is definitely a coffee country and the coffee industry is reaping the rewards.

4.3.1 Competition and Buying Patterns

There are four general competitors in The Daily Perc's Drive-thru market. They are the national specialty beverage chains, such as Starbucks and Panera, local coffeehouses—or cafés—with an established clientele and a quality product, fast-food restaurants, and convenience stores. There is a dramatic distinction among the patrons of each of these outlets.

Patrons to a Starbucks, or to one of the local cafés, are looking for the "experience" of the coffeehouse. They want the ability to "design" their coffee, smell the fresh pastry, listen to the soothing Italian music, and read the local paper or visit with an acquaintance. It is a relaxing, slow paced environment.

Patrons of the fast-food restaurants or the convenience stores are just the opposite. They have no time for idle chatter and are willing to overpay for whatever beverage the machine can spit out, as long as it's quick. They pay for their gas and they are back on the road to work. Although they have the desire and good taste to know good from bad, time is more valuable to them.

Competitors to the Mobile Cafés on campuses would include fast-food restaurants—assuming they are close enough to the consumer that they can get there and back in the minimal allotted time, vending machines, and company or school cafeterias. The consumers in this environment are looking for quick, convenient, fairly priced, quality refreshment that will allow them to purchase the product and return to work, class, or other activity.

Competitors to the Mobile Cafés at events such as festivals and fairs would include all the other vendors who are licensed to sell refreshments. Attendees to such events expect to pay a premium price for a quality product.

5. Strategy and Implementation Summary

The Daily Perc will penetrate the commuter and captive consumer markets by deploying Drive-thru facilities and Mobile Cafés in the most logical and accessible locations. The Drive-thrus are designed to handle two-sided traffic and dispense customer-designed, specially ordered cups of specialty beverages in less time than required for a visit to the locally owned café or one of the national chains.

The Daily Perc has identified its market as busy, mobile people whose time is already at a premium, but desire a refreshing, high-quality beverage or baked item while commuting to or from work or school.

In addition to providing a quality product and an extensive menu of delicious items, to ensure customer awareness and loyalty, as well as positive public and media support, The Daily Perc could be donating up to 7.5% of revenue from each cup sold in individual Drive-thrus to the charities of the customers' choice.

5.1. Products

The Daily Perc provides its patrons the finest hot and cold beverages, specializing in specialty coffees and custom blended teas. In addition, TDP will offer select domestic soft drinks, Italian sodas, fresh-baked pastries, and other confections. Seasonally, TDP will add beverages such as hot apple cider, hot chocolate, frozen coffees, and more. The beverages come with a social mission, as up to 7.5% of revenues go to local charities selected by the customers. The precise list of products will be specific to the Drive-thru location selected.

5.2. Competitive Edge

The Daily Perc's competitive edge is simple. TDP provides a high-quality product at a competitive price in a Drive-thru environment that saves time.

5.3. Marketing Strategy

First and foremost, The Daily Perc will be placing its Drive-thru facilities in locations of very high visibility and great ease of access. They will be located on high traffic commuter routes and close to shopping facilities in order to catch customers going to or from work, or while they are out for lunch, or on a shopping expedition. The Drive-thrus are very unique and eye-catching, which will be a branding feature of its own.

The Daily Perc will be implementing a low cost advertising/promotion campaign, which could involve drive-time radio, but not much more.

The Daily Perc will rely on building relationships with schools, charities, and corporations to provide significant free publicity because of its community support program. By giving charitable contributions to these institutions, they will get the word out to their students/faculty/employees/partners about TDP. Word of mouth (or viral marketing) has always proven to be the greatest advertising program a company can instill. In addition, the media will be more than willing to promote the charitable aspects of TDP and provide the opportunity for more exposure every time TDP writes a check to another organization.

5.4. Sales Strategy

There will be several sales strategies put into place, including posting specials on high-profit items at the Drive-thru window. The baristas will also hand out free drink coupons to those who have purchased a certain number of cups or something similar. TDP will also develop window sales techniques such as the baristas asking if the customer would like a fresh-baked item with their coffee.

5.4.1. Sales Forecast

In the first year, The Daily Perc anticipates having two Drive-thru locations in operation. The first location will open in the third month of this plan and be fully operational beginning on the 1st day of September. The second Drive-thru will open six months later. TDP is building in a certain amount of ramp-up for each facility while commuters become familiar with its presence. The Drive-thrus will generate 288,000 tickets in the first year of operation, or approximately $558,000 in revenue. A detailed sales forecast for the first year appears in Appendix 4-A.

In the second year, The Daily Perc will add two more Drive-thrus and, in the third year, TDP will add an additional nine Drive-thru facilities. The addition of these facilities will increase the revenue from Drive-thrus to a total of over 1,000,000 tickets or $2.35 million in the second year and 2,675,000 tickets or just over $6 million in the third.

In addition to the Drive-thrus, The Daily Perc will deploy one mobile unit in the fourth quarter of the first fiscal year. TDP expects this mobile unit to generate 10,000 tickets each, at an average ticket price of $2.45, which will generate gross revenues of approximately $24,500.

In the second quarter of the second fiscal year, The Daily Perc will deploy a second and third mobile unit. TDP expects all three mobile units to generate

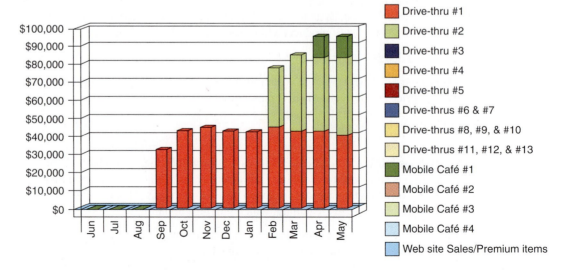

The Daily Perc—Sales Monthly

Legend:
- Drive-thru #1
- Drive-thru #2
- Drive-thru #3
- Drive-thru #4
- Drive-thru #5
- Drive-thrus #6 & #7
- Drive-thrus #8, #9, & #10
- Drive-thrus #11, #12, & #13
- Mobile Café #1
- Mobile Café #2
- Mobile Café #3
- Mobile Café #4
- Web site Sales/Premium items

The Daily Perc Business Plan provided by Business Plan Pro® and used by permission of Palo Alto Software.

150,000 tickets, or gross revenue of $375,00 in the second year. In the third fiscal year, with an additional fourth mobile unit deployed, TDP expects to see 264,000 mobile unit tickets, or $673,200 in gross revenue.

The Daily Perc is also showing revenue from the commerce portion of our Web site, where it will sell "The Daily Perc" T-shirts, sweatshirts, insulated coffee mugs, pre-packaged coffee beans, and other premium items. TDP is not expecting this to be a significant profit center, but it is an integral part of the marketing plan—as a function of developing our brand and building product awareness. TDP expects revenues from this portion, to begin in the second fiscal year, to reach $26,000 initially, and $36,000 in the third fiscal year.

Total first year unit sales should reach 298,402, equating to revenues of $558,043. The second year will see unit sales increase to 1,177,400, or $2,348,900. The third year, with the addition of such a significant number of outlets, we will see unit sales increase to 2,992,000, equating to gross sales revenue of $6,022,950.

The Daily Perc—Sales Forecast

	FY 1	FY 2	FY 3
Unit Sales			
Drive-thru #1	202,913	300,000	325,000
Drive-thru #2	85,489	300,000	325,000
Drive-thru #3	0	275,000	325,000
Drive-thru #4	0	150,000	325,000
Drive-thru #5	0	0	300,000
Drive-thrus #6 & #7	0	0	450,000
Drive-thrus #8, #9, & #10	0	0	450,000
Drive-thrus #11, #12, & #13	0	0	225,000
Mobile Café #1	10,000	60,000	66,000
Mobile Café #2	0	45,000	66,000
Mobile Café #3	0	45,000	66,000
Mobile Café #4	0	0	66,000
Web Site Sales/Premium Items	0	2,400	3,000
Total Unit Sales	298,402	1,177,400	2,992,000

	FY 1	FY 2	FY 3
Unit Prices			
Drive-thru #1	$1.85	$1.90	$1.95
Drive-thru #2	$1.85	$1.90	$1.95
Drive-thru #3	$0.00	$1.90	$1.95
Drive-thru #4	$0.00	$1.90	$1.95
Drive-thru #5	$0.00	$1.90	$1.95
Drive-thrus #6 & #7	$0.00	$1.90	$1.95
Drive-thrus #8, #9, & #10	$0.00	$1.90	$1.95
Drive-thrus #11, #12, & #13	$0.00	$1.90	$1.95
Mobile Café #1	$2.45	$2.50	$2.55
Mobile Café #2	$0.00	$2.50	$2.55
Mobile Café #3	$0.00	$2.50	$2.55
Mobile Café #4	$0.00	$2.50	$2.55
Web Site Sales/Premium Items	$0.00	$11.00	$12.00

(continued)

The Daily Perc—Sales Forecast—continued

	FY 1	FY 2	FY 3
Sales			
Drive-thru #1	$375,389	$570,000	$633,750
Drive-thru #2	$158,154	$570,000	$633,750
Drive-thru #3	$0	$522,500	$633,750
Drive-thru #4	$0	$285,000	$633,750
Drive-thru #5	$0	$0	$585,000
Drive-thrus #6 & #7	$0	$0	$877,500
Drive-thrus #8, #9, & #10	$0	$0	$877,500
Drive-thrus #11, #12, & #13	$0	$0	$438,750
Mobile Café #1	$24,500	$150,000	$168,300
Mobile Café #2	$0	$112,500	$168,300
Mobile Café #3	$0	$112,500	$168,300
Mobile Café #4	$0	$0	$168,300
Web Site Sales/Premium Items	$0	$26,400	$36,000
Total Sales	$558,043	$2,348,900	$6,022,950

	FY 1	FY 2	FY 3
Direct Unit Costs			
Drive-thru #1	$0.64	$0.61	$0.59
Drive-thru #2	$0.64	$0.61	$0.59
Drive-thru #3	$0.00	$0.61	$0.59
Drive-thru #4	$0.00	$0.61	$0.59
Drive-thru #5	$0.00	$0.61	$0.59
Drive-thrus #6 & #7	$0.00	$0.61	$0.59
Drive-thrus #8, #9, & #10	$0.00	$0.61	$0.59
Drive-thrus #11, #12, & #13	$0.00	$0.61	$0.59
Mobile Café #1	$0.64	$0.61	$0.59
Mobile Café #2	$0.00	$0.61	$0.59
Mobile Café #3	$0.00	$0.61	$0.59
Mobile Café #4	$0.00	$0.61	$0.59
Web Site Sales/Premium Items	$0.00	$6.50	$6.50
Direct Cost of Sales			
Drive-thru #1	$129,864	$183,000	$191,750
Drive-thru #2	$54,713	$183,000	$191,750
Drive-thru #3	$0	$167,750	$191,750
Drive-thru #4	$0	$91,500	$191,750
Drive-thru #5	$0	$0	$177,000
Drive-thrus #6 & #7	$0	$0	$265,500
Drive-thrus #8, #9, & #10	$0	$0	$265,500
Drive-thrus #11, #12, & #13	$0	$0	$132,750
Mobile Café #1	$6,400	$36,600	$38,940
Mobile Café #2	$0	$27,450	$38,940
Mobile Café #3	$0	$27,450	$38,940
Mobile Café #4	$0	$0	$38,940
Web Site Sales/Premium Items	$0	$15,600	$19,500
Subtotal Direct Cost of Sales	**$190,977**	**$732,350**	**$1,783,010**

6. Management and Operations Summary

The Daily Perc is a relatively flat organization. Overhead for management will be kept to a minimum and all senior managers will be "hands-on" workers. There is no intention of having a top-heavy organization that drains profits and complicates decisions.

Owners Bart and Teresa Fisher will be actively involved in the management and operations of the sites. The founders of TDP bring a strong management and technical foundation to TDP. Terri Fisher has approximately 15 years of progressive experience at Starbucks Coffee Company, starting out as a barista and moving through the ranks to senior financial management (see Appendix 4-G for her resume). Bart Fisher brings talents and experience in retail sales and marketing, having owned and operated an advertising agency and several Krispy Kreme franchises (see Appendix 4-G for his resume). They will initially divide the overall management responsibilities, with Terri emphasizing accounting and finance and Bart leading marketing and sales. They also will be part of the staff at the Drive-thru sites.

At the zenith of this three-year plan, there will be four "Executive" positions: chief operating officer, chief financial officer, chief information officer, and director of marketing. There will be other mid-management positions, such as district managers for every four Drive-thrus, and a facilities manager to oversee the maintenance and stocking of the Mobile Cafés, as well as overseeing the maintenance and replacement of equipment in the Drive-thru facilities.

6.1. Personnel Plan

The Daily Perc expects the first year to be rather lean, since there will only be two locations and one mobile unit—none of which will be deployed for the entire year. The total headcount for the first year, including management, administrative support, and customer service (production), will be 15, with a total payroll of $242,374, a payroll burden of $36,356, and a total expenditure of $278,730. The detailed first year personnel plan is in Appendix 4-B.

The second year, with the addition of two Drive-thrus and two mobile units, The Daily Perc will add customer service personnel, as well as a district manager and some additional support staff at headquarters, including an Inventory Clerk, Equipment Technician, and administrative support.

The headcount will increase by nearly 100% in the second year to 29, with a payroll of $846,050 and a payroll burden of $126,908.

The third year will see the most dramatic growth in headcount, due to the addition of nine Drive-thrus and another mobile unit. In the third year, there will also be an increase of 180% over the previous year. Total payroll for the third year will be $2,024,250, with a payroll burden of $303,638. A significant increase in the senior management team, with the addition of a chief financial officer, a chief information officer, and a director of marketing. There will also be a second and third district manager, and a corporate events sales executive. Total personnel will reach 81.

The chief financial officer will be brought on to oversee the increase in numbers of retail outlets and to manage a dramatically more detailed P&L statement and to manage the Balance Sheet. The chief information officer will be brought in to help us with the deployment of a point-of-sale computerized cash register system that will make tracking and managing receipts and charitable contributions more robust. Ideally, this individual will have a large amount of point-of-sale and Internet experience. Specifically, how to tie in POS systems to the Internet and inventory controls. Also, knowledge in establishing technology guidelines for the company and franchisees in the future. This individual will also be added in fiscal year three.

The director of marketing will be charged with managing the relationships with advertising agencies, public relations firms, the media, and our Web site.

The Daily Perc—Personnel Plan

	FY 1	FY 2	FY 3
Drive-thru Team	$135,474	$439,250	$1,098,650
Mobile Café Team	$9,400	$172,800	$225,600
Equipment Care Specialist (Headquarters)	$0	$22,000	$77,000
Other	$0	$12,000	$24,000
District Manager (Four Drive-thrus)	$0	$22,000	$77,000
Corporate Events Sales Exec	$0	$0	$36,000
Director of Marketing	$0	$0	$72,000
Other	$0	$0	$0
Bookkeeper/Office Administrator	$24,500	$46,000	$54,000
Warehouse/Site Manager	$7,000	$42,000	$48,000
Inventory Clerk	$0	$12,000	$42,000
Other	$0	$6,000	$12,000
Chief Operating Officer	$66,000	$72,000	$78,000
Chief Financial Officer	$0	$0	$96,000
Chief Information Officer	$0	$0	$84,000
Other	$0	$0	$0
Total People	15	29	81
Total Payroll	**$242,374**	**$846,050**	**$2,024,250**

6.2. Physical Locations/Facilities

One of the most exciting aspects of The Daily Perc is the flexibility in selecting locations. The Drive-thrus are relatively small and the Mobile Cafés are just that. Site selection is based upon population demographics and traffic patterns. With a focus on The Daily Commuter and The Captive Customers, locations are well-defined. Drive-thru espresso shops will be opened in metropolitan communities with a population greater than 150,000. These facilities will be located on accessible sites with high visibility, on high traffic commuter routes and close to shopping facilities. Each Drive-thru will be double sided and attractively decorated. According to the previously compiled market segmentation information, TDP has calculated 2,582 venues where Mobile Cafés might be positioned.

6.3. Inventory, Production, and Quality Assurance

The Daily Perc uses innovative coffee brewing technology and tight inventory controls with excellence in quality assurance. TDP has adopted a new type of coffee equipment that produces espresso drinks very rapidly with consistently excellent flavor. By having trained baristas personally take customer orders and produce hot and cold beverages, quality is increased and production errors are decreased. Because of this delivery system, customers can buy high-quality, freshly prepared beverages in less time than is required for a visit to a locally owned café or chain.

Because of the technology used and the delivery system, inventory can be controlled through economic order quantities with a computer-based reorder system. The product line is sufficiently broad to satisfy customer requests, but sufficiently narrow as to yield relatively straightforward inventory control. Coffees and teas served are all Fair Trade goods and the coffee beans are roasted locally. Bart Fisher manages the quality assurance with respect to the roasted beans. Each manager has a quality assurance manual and a test system for beverage production. Terri Fisher manages the quality assurance process for baked goods.

7. Financial Plan

The Daily Perc's financial picture is quite promising. Since TDP is operating a cash business, the initial cost is significantly less than many start-ups these days. The process is labor intensive and TDP recognizes that a higher level of talent is required. The financial investment in its employees will be one of the greatest differentiators between it and TDP's competition. For the purpose of this pro-forma plan, the facilities and equipment are financed. These items are capital expenditures and will be available for financing. There will be a minimum of inventory on hand so as to keep the product fresh and to take advantage of price drops, when and if they should occur.

The Daily Perc anticipates the initial combination of investments and long-term financing of $515,000 to carry it without the need for any additional equity or debt investment, beyond the purchase of equipment or facilities. This will mean growing a bit more slowly than might be otherwise possible, but it will be a solid, financially sound growth based on customer request and product demand.

7.1. Important Assumptions

The financial plan depends on important assumptions, most of which are shown in the following table. The key underlying assumptions are:

- The Daily Perc assumes a slow-growth economy, without major recession.
- The Daily Perc assumes, of course, that there are no unforeseen changes in public health perceptions of its general products.
- The Daily Perc assumes access to equity capital and financing sufficient to maintain its financial plan as shown in the tables.
- Assumptions for the first year appear in Appendix 4-C.

The Daily Perc—General Assumptions

	FY 1	FY 2	FY 3
Plan Month	1	2	3
Current Interest Rate	10.00%	10.00%	10.00%
Long-term Interest Rate	9.00%	9.00%	9.00%
Tax Rate	0.00%	0.00%	0.00%
Other	0	0	0

7.2. Break-even Analysis

To arrive at the average monthly fixed costs, The Daily Perc calculated the fixed costs for the Drive-thru to be $28,294. Using the average price per unit, less the average cost per unit, divided into the fixed costs of operation, TDP concludes that we will need at least 23,003 units per month to reach breakeven at $43,016 per month.

BUSINESS PLAN

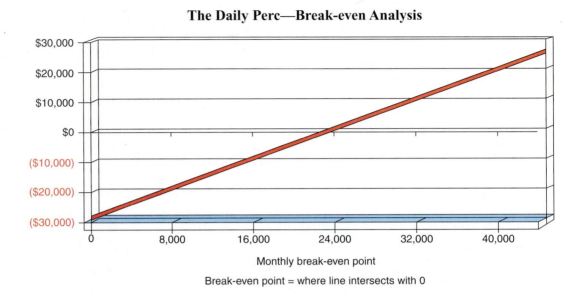

The Daily Perc—Break-even Analysis

Monthly break-even point

Break-even point = where line intersects with 0

The Daily Perc—Break-even Analysis

Monthly Units Break-even	23,001
Monthly Revenue Break-even	$43,014
Assumptions:	
Average Per-Unit Revenue	$1.87
Average Per-Unit Variable Cost	$0.64
Estimated Monthly Fixed Cost	$28,294

7.3. Projected Profit and Loss

The Daily Perc is expecting some dramatic growth in the next three years, reaching $558,043 in sales and a 65.5% Gross Profit Margin by the end of the first year. Expenses during the first year leave a Net After-tax profit of $9,960, or 1.8%. Detailed profit and loss information is included in Appendix 4-D.

Aside from production costs of 34.4%, which include actual production of product and commissions for sales efforts, the single largest expenditures in the first year are in the general and administrative (G&A) area, totaling 54.7% of sales. G&A includes expenses for rents, equipment leases, utilities, and the payroll burden for all employees.

Sales increase by nearly 400% in the second year, due to the addition of two more Drive-thrus and two more Mobile Cafés, reaching a total of $2,348,900. Although operating expenses double in the second year, The Daily Perc will be able to realize a Net After-tax profit of $368,675 or 15.7% of sales. In that same year, TDP will make charitable contributions of $70,000.

The third year is when The Daily Perc has the opportunity to break into markets outside the metropolitan area. TDP will see nine additional Drive-thru facilities open in the third year, which will drive sales to $6,022,950 and, even with a 200% increase in production costs, help reach a Gross Profit Margin of 68.9%. Several expenses take substantial jumps this year—advertising increasing from $36,000 to $72,000 and donations increasing from $72,000 to $180,000—and TDP will be adding several key management team members. These increases, as well as those for increased equipment leases and rents, raise our operating expenses to $2,772,993, leaving a Net After-tax profit of $1,294,371, or 21.5% of sales.

The Daily Perc—Profit Monthly

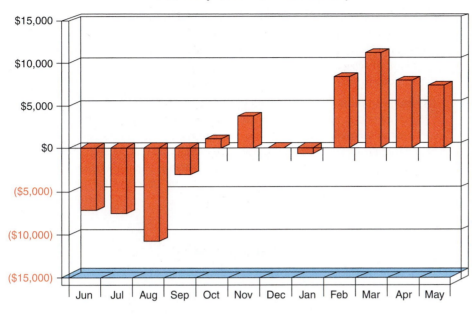

The Daily Perc—Pro Forma Profit and Loss

	FY 1	FY 2	FY 3
Sales	$558,043	$2,348,900	$6,022,950
Direct Costs of Goods	$190,977	$732,350	$1,783,010
Sales Commissions	$1,416	$35,234	$90,344
Cost of Goods Sold	$192,393	$767,584	$1,873,354
Gross Margin	$365,650	$1,581,317	$4,149,596
Gross Margin %	65.52%	67.32%	68.90%
Expenses			
Payroll	$242,374	$846,050	$2,024,250
Sales and Marketing and Other Expenses	$0	$0	$0
Depreciation	$21,785	$92,910	$196,095
Leased Offices and Equipment	$0	$6,000	$18,000
Utilities	$9,640	$19,800	$41,100
Insurance	$12,570	$32,620	$63,910
Rent	$16,800	$50,400	$126,000
Payroll Taxes	$36,356	$126,908	$303,638
Other General and Administrative Expenses	$0	$0	$0
Total Operating Expenses	$339,525	$1,174,688	$2,772,993
Profit before Interest and Taxes	$26,125	$406,629	$1,376,603
EBITDA	$47,910	$499,539	$1,572,698
Interest Expense	$16,165	$37,954	$82,232
Taxes Incurred	$0	$0	$0
Net Profit	$9,960	$368,675	$1,294,371
Net Profit/Sales	1.78%	15.70%	21.49%

7.4. Projected Cash Flow

Cash flow will have to be carefully monitored, as in any business, but The Daily Perc is also the beneficiary of operating a cash business. After the initial investment and start-up costs are covered, the business will become relatively self-sustaining. With the exception of seasonal dips, which TDP has attempted to account for, through changes in the menu items.

Assuming an initial investment and financing of $515,000, which would include $25,500 of operating capital, The Daily Perc anticipates no cash flow shortfalls for the first year or beyond. March and May are the greatest cash drains, since TDP will be experiencing the cost of a second Drive-thru and mobile unit start-up. Again, TDP sees heavier than normal drains of cash in December and January, as there will be certain accounts payable coming due. A detailed pro forma cash flow for the first year of operations is included in Appendix 4-E.

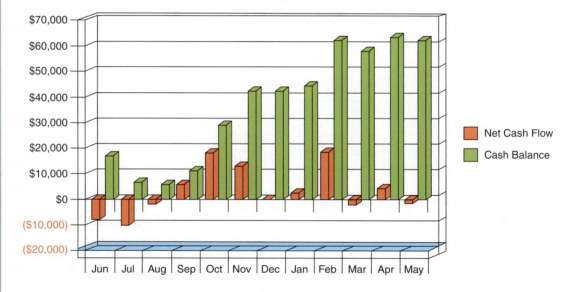

The Daily Perc—Cash

BUSINESS PLAN

The Daily Perc—Pro Forma Cash Flow

	FY 1	FY 2	FY 3
Cash Received			
Cash from Operations			
Cash Sales	$558,043	$2,348,900	$6,022,950
Subtotal Cash from Operations	$558,043	$2,348,900	$6,022,950
Additional Cash Received			
Sales Tax, VAT, HST/GST Received	$0	$0	$0
New Current Borrowing	$0	$0	$0
New Other Liabilities (Interest-free)	$0	$0	$0
New Long-term Liabilities	$181,463	$253,970	$729,992
Sales of Other Current Assets	$0	$0	$0
Sales of Long-term Assets	$0	$0	$0
New Investment Received	$0	$0	$0
Subtotal Cash Received	$739,506	$2,602,870	$6,752,942

	FY I	FY 2	FY 3
Expenditures			
Expenditures from Operations			
Cash Spending	$242,374	$846,050	$2,024,250
Bill Payments	$240,175	$1,091,066	$2,573,382
Subtotal Spent on Operations	$482,549	$1,937,116	$4,597,632
Additional Cash Spent			
Sales Tax, VAT, HST/GST Paid Out	$0	$0	$0
Principal Repayment of Current Borrowing	$1,500	$0	$0
Other Liabilities Principal Repayment	$0	$0	$0
Long-term Liabilities Principal Repayment	$26,469	$0	$0
Purchase Other Current Assets	$0	$0	$0
Purchase Long-term Assets	$191,850	$429,700	$1,356,993
Dividends	$0	$0	$0
Subtotal Cash Spent	$702,368	$2,366,816	$5,954,625
Net Cash Flow	$37,139	$236,054	$798,317
Cash Balance	$62,639	$298,693	$1,097,010

7.5. Projected Balance Sheet

The Daily Perc's projected balance sheet shows an increase in net worth to just over $1 million in FY 3, at which point it also expects to be making 21.5% after-tax profit on sales of $6.02 million. With the present financial projections, TDP expects to build a company with strong profit potential, and a solid balance sheet that will be asset heavy and flush with cash at the end of the third year. The Daily Perc has no intention of paying out dividends before the end of the third year, using the excess cash for continued growth. The first year projected balance sheet for TDP appears in Appendix 4-G.

The Daily Perc—Pro Forma Balance Sheet

	FY 1	FY 2	FY 3
Assets			
Current Assets			
Cash	$62,639	$298,693	$1,097,010
Inventory	$35,159	$134,826	$328,252
Other Current Assets	$0	$0	$0
Total Current Assets	$97,798	$433,519	$1,425,263
Long-term Assets			
Long-term Assets	$323,250	$752,950	$2,109,943
Accumulated Depreciation	$21,785	$114,695	$310,790
Total Long-term Assets	$301,465	$638,255	$1,799,153
Total Assets	$399,263	$1,071,774	$3,224,416

	FY 1	FY 2	FY 3
Liabilities and Capital			
Current Liabilities			
Accounts Payable	$43,909	$93,775	$222,054
Current Borrowing	$7,500	$7,500	$7,500
Other Current Liabilities	$0	$0	$0
Subtotal Current Liabilities	$51,409	$101,275	$229,554
Long-term Liabilities	$286,394	$540,364	$1,270,356
Total Liabilities	$337,803	$641,639	$1,499,910
Paid-in Capital	$225,270	$225,270	$225,270
Retained Earnings	($173,770)	($163,810)	$204,865
Earnings	$9,960	$368,675	$1,294,371
Total Capital	$61,460	$430,135	$1,724,505
Total Liabilities and Capital	$399,263	$1,071,774	$3,224,416
Net Worth	$61,460	$430,135	$1,724,505

7.6. Business Ratios

Standard business ratios are included in the following table. The ratios show a plan for balanced, healthy growth. The Daily Perc's position within the industry is typical for a heavy growth start-up company. Industry profile ratios based on the Standard Industrial Classification (SIC) code 5812, Eating Places, are shown for comparison.

Comparing the ratios in the third year with the industry, this pro forma plan appears to be within an acceptable difference margin.

TDP's return on net worth and net worth number differ from the Industry Profile due to the lack of overhead when compared to a typical walk-in café. The Drive-thru and Mobile business model is lean thus allowing for an increased return ratio and providing a lower Net Worth.

The Daily Perc—Ratio Analysis

	FY 1	FY 2	FY 3	Industry Profile
Sales Growth	0.00%	320.92%	156.42%	7.60%
Percent of Total Assets				
Inventory	8.81%	12.58%	10.18%	3.60%
Other Current Assets	0.00%	0.00%	0.00%	35.60%
Total Current Assets	24.49%	40.45%	44.20%	43.70%
Long-term Assets	75.51%	59.55%	55.80%	56.30%
Total Assets	100.00%	100.00%	100.00%	100.00%
Current Liabilities	12.88%	9.45%	7.12%	32.70%
Long-term Liabilities	71.73%	50.42%	39.40%	28.50%
Total Liabilities	84.61%	59.87%	46.52%	61.20%
Net Worth	15.39%	40.13%	53.48%	38.80%
Percent of Sales				
Sales	100.00%	100.00%	100.00%	100.00%
Gross Margin	65.52%	67.32%	68.90%	60.50%
Selling, General & Administrative Expenses	44.74%	30.63%	29.15%	39.80%
Advertising Expenses	3.23%	1.53%	1.20%	3.20%
Profit before Interest and Taxes	4.68%	17.31%	22.86%	0.70%
Main Ratios				
Current	1.90	4.28	6.21	0.98
Quick	1.22	2.95	4.78	0.65
Total Debt to Total Assets	84.61%	59.87%	46.52%	61.20%
Pre-tax Return on Net Worth	16.21%	85.71%	75.06%	1.70%
Pre-tax Return on Assets	2.49%	34.40%	40.14%	4.30%

	FY 1	FY 2	FY 3	
Additional Ratios				
Net Profit Margin	1.78%	15.70%	21.49%	n.a
Return on Equity	16.21%	85.71%	75.06%	n.a
Activity Ratios				
Inventory Turnover	7.02	8.62	7.70	n.a
Accounts Payable Turnover	6.47	12.17	12.17	n.a
Payment Days	27	22	21	n.a
Total Asset Turnover	1.40	2.19	1.87	n.a
Debt Ratios				
Debt to Net Worth	5.50	1.49	0.87	n.a
Current Liabilities to Liabilities	0.15	0.16	0.15	n.a
Liquidity Ratios				
Net Working Capital	$46,389	$332,244	$1,195,708	n.a
Interest Coverage	1.62	10.71	16.74	n.a
Additional Ratios				
Assets to Sales	0.72	0.46	0.54	n.a
Current Debt/Total Assets	13%	9%	7%	n.a
Acid Test	1.22	2.95	4.78	n.a
Sales/Net Worth	9.08	5.46	3.49	n.a
Dividend Payout	0.00	0.00	0.00	n.a

BUSINESS PLAN

BUSINESS PLAN

8. Funding Request and Exit Strategy

8.1. Funding Request

The Daily Perc, LLC requires initial financing of $515,000 for its start-up phase without any anticipated need for additional equity or debt except for as needed to complete the purchase of additional facilities and/or equipment.

The plan calls for the sale of 100 membership units in the company to family members, friends, and Angel Investors. Each membership unit in the company is priced at $4,250, with a minimum of five units per membership certificate, or a minimum investment of $21,250 per investor.

If all funds are raised, based on the pricing established in the financial section of this plan, Bart and Terri Fisher will maintain ownership of no less than 51% of the company.

8.2. Exit Strategy

There are three scenarios for the investors and management to recover their investment—two with significant returns on each dollar invested.

Scenario One:

The Daily Perc becomes extremely successful and has requests from other communities for Daily Perc operations to be opened there. This opens the door for franchising opportunity. When one looks at the wealth that has been created by the likes of McDonald's, Wendy's, Kentucky Fried Chicken, Burger King, and Taco Bell, the value of franchising a great idea cannot be dismissed. However, developing a franchise can be extremely costly, take years to develop, and be destroyed by one or two franchisees who fail to deliver the consistency or value on which the founding company had built its reputation.

Scenario Two:

The Daily Perc chooses to become the Drive-thru version of Starbucks, obtaining several million dollars through an initial public or private offering that would allow the company to open 20 to 30 facilities per year in the region of the country between the mountain ranges, in both major and small metropolitan communities. This is the preferred Exit Strategy of the Management Team. The danger in this is that competitors would rise up and establish a foothold on a community before—or in the midst of—the arrival of The Daily Perc, causing a potential for a drain on revenues and a dramatic increase in advertising expenditures to maintain market share. Knowing these risks—and planning for them—gives TDP the edge needed to make this scenario work.

Scenario Three:

By the third year, the growth and community support for The Daily Perc will have made the news in more than just the metropolitan area. It can be assumed that competitors, such as Starbucks or Quikava, will have seen the press and realized the value proposition in The Daily Perc's business plan. This will make TDP an attractive target for buyout. The company could be purchased by a much larger competitive concern by the end of the third year.

Taking a conservative approach to valuation and estimating that The Daily Perc would be valued at $7.5 million, and assuming that all 250 units of ownership in TDP are distributed to investors, a cash purchase of TDP would net each unit $30,000. With each unit selling at $4,250, that constitutes a Return on Investment of 705% over the three years. However, any buyout will most likely involve a cash/stock combination. A cash/stock buyout would be favorable, since the buying company would pay a higher price and the transaction would not have such severe tax consequences to the sellers.

Conclusion:

Of the three scenarios, the management team prefers Scenario #2. The same numbers would relate to a public or private offering as are used in Scenario #3, but to make an offering available, there would be a dilution of shares that would provide additional shares for sale to the new investors.

Assuming the capital acquisition described in this plan is completed, there will be 250 units of the company in the hands of investors, constituting 100% of the authorized and issued units. For purposes of future fund-raising, it will be necessary to authorize a stock split of, perhaps 5,000 to one, turning the current 250 units into 1,250,000 units.

Using the balance sheet for the third year, which estimates a Net Worth of just over $1.7 million, cash balances of $1.1 million and earnings of $1.3 million, based on 13 Drive-thrus and four Mobile Cafés, it is not unrealistic to put a market value of $15 million to $25 million on the company. At present, such companies are trading in multiples of 20 to 30 times earnings, and it is simple mathematics to multiply the success of TDP by the number of commuter-heavy metropolitan areas in the United States.

With a corporate valuation of $7,500,000, each of the new units would have a market value of $6/unit. By authorizing an additional 750,000 units, there would be a total of 2,000,000 units with a market value of $3.75 per share. By offering the 750,000 shares at the price of $3.75 per unit, TDP would raise an additional $2,812,500 in expansion capital, which would be sufficient to open locations in an additional three to five cities.

8.3. Milestones

The Milestone table reflects critical dates for occupying headquarters, launching the first Drive-thru and subsequent Drive-thrus, as well as deployment of the mobile units. The Daily Perc also defines our break-even month, our Web site launch and subsequent visitor interaction function, and other key markers that will help us measure our success in time and accomplishment.

The Daily Perc—Milestones

Milestone	Start Date	End Date	Budget	Manager	Department
Light Web Site	6/1/YR1	8/15/YR1	$5,600	COO	Mktg.
Open First Drive-thru	7/15/YR1	8/31/YR1	$105,400	COO	Admin.
First Break-even Month	12/1/YR1	12/31/YR1	$0	COO	Finance
Open Second Drive-thru	12/15/YR1	2/1/YR1	$105,400	COO	Admin.
Receive First Mobile Unit	3/1/YRI	3/30/YRl	$86,450	COO	Admin.
Launch Web Site Voting	5/1/YR1	6/1/YRI	$12,500	COO	Mktg.
Open Third Drive-thru	4/15/YR1	6/1/YR1	$105,400	COO	Admin.
Receive Second and Third Mobile Units	7/15/YR2	9/1/YR2	$172,900	COO	Admin.
Open Fourth Drive-thru	12/15/YR2	2/1/YR2	$105,400	COO	Admin.
Install Point-of-Sale System	12/1/YR2	2/1/YR2	$21,000	CIO	MIS
Occupy Headquarters	4/1/YR2	5/15/YR2	$45,000	COO	Admin.
Open Fifth Drive-thru	4/15/YR2	6/1/YR3	$105,400	COO	Admin.
Receive Fourth Mobile Unit	4/15/YR2	6/1/YR3	$86,450	Equip.	Admin.
Open Drive-thrus 6 and 7	7/15/YR3	9/15/YR3	$210,800	COO/Dir.	Mgmt.
Open Drive-thrus 8, 9, and 10	10/15/YR3	12/15/YR3	$316,200	COO/Dir.	Mgmt.
Open Drive-thrus 11, 12, and 13	1/15/YR3	3/1/YR3	$316,200	COO	Admin.
Expand to Kansas City	1/15/YR3	6/1/YR3	$176,943	COO	Mgmt.
Open First Franchise	10/31/YR3	9/1/YR4	$45,000	CFO	Finance
Initiate Exit Strategy	10/1/YR4	1/1/YR4	$100,000	CFO	Mgmt.

Totals

Appendices

The appendices for The Daily Perc business plan appear in Appendix 4 at the end of the book.

Chapter 3

Creating Business
from Opportunity

"Problems are only opportunities in work clothes."

—Henry J. Kaiser, American industrialist

Sometimes entrepreneurs see a customer need even before consumers do! When automobiles were invented, for example, they were considered playthings for the rich. Henry Ford, however, imagined an automobile in front of every American home—long before most Americans ever thought they would need their own cars. Similarly, Stephen Wozniak envisioned a computer in every American home at a time when computers were huge and unaffordable. His company, Apple Computer (cofounded with Steve Jobs), became a leader in the development of personal home and office computers. Both Ford Motor Company and Apple Computer were pioneers in their fields, meeting needs that people were not aware they had.

Performance Objectives

1. Define your business.
2. Articulate core beliefs, mission, and vision.
3. Analyze your competitive advantage.
4. Perform initial viability testing using the "Economics of One Unit."

Apple Creates the Personal Computer

Tom Watson, Jr., built IBM, his father's company, into a huge international success based on these core beliefs: respect for the individual, unparalleled customer service, and the pursuit of superiority in all that the company undertook.

In 1943, IBM's founder, Thomas Watson, said, "I think there is a world market for about five computers." A **market** is a group of people or organizations that may be interested in buying a given product or service, has the resources to purchase it, and is permitted by law and regulation to do so. When Watson made his statement, computers were forbiddingly large and expensive machines that only the government, universities, and a few giant corporations could afford. That was the market for computers at the time.

By the 1970s, however, a few people were talking about creating personal computers. These enthusiasts were considered dreamers. One such visionary was Stephen Wozniak, who had landed his first job at Hewlett-Packard, then as now a major company. He was also attending meetings of the Homebrew Club, a group of amateur computer enthusiasts. Wozniak was determined to build a small, "personal" computer to show the club. He believed that there was a much larger market for computers than IBM and Hewlett-Packard thought.

Wozniak offered Hewlett-Packard a chance to co-develop his small computer. The company did not recognize that this was an incredible opportunity, and they turned him down. To be fair to Hewlett-Packard, though, most everyone was unable to see the vast market for personal computers at that time. Wozniak's friend Steve Jobs also recognized this opportunity. Jobs and Wozniak started Apple Computer in Wozniak's parents' garage in Cupertino, California, with only $1,300. This is a classic demonstration of entrepreneurs recognizing opportunities that others do not see.

Wozniak worked on his design until he created the Apple II, now considered one of the great achievements in the computer industry. Jobs, meanwhile, searched for an investor. Finally, after being turned down by friends and family, he found Mike Markkula, who also saw the potential of the personal computer. Markkula agreed to back the company in return for a share of the profits. He also put together Apple's business plan.

By 1984, Apple had sales of $1.5 billion and, in 2007, of over $24 billion. Wozniak and Jobs recognized an opportunity that led to a product that

Apple cofounder Stephen Wozniak participating in a panel discussion of Mac OS X operating software at the Macworld Expo in downtown San Francisco.
(AP Wide World Photos)

satisfied the needs of an enormous market that the giants of the industry did not recognize.

Business Definition[1]

In order to operate a successful enterprise, you will need to be able to provide a complete company description. This description should include the need for your product or service that is either unsatisfied by the current players in the market or is something you can provide better, differently, or more economically.

◀ Performance Objective 1
Define your business.

Before you can start a business, you must define it in several dimensions. The *business definition* answers three questions: who, what, and how?

1. *Who* will the business serve? In other words, who are the potential qualified customers in the market for your product or service? They may not currently recognize a need for your specific product or service, but they are in the market for the products or services of your competition.

2. *What* will the business offer the customers? What is the complete bundle of products or services your enterprise will provide? This should address not only the tangible product or intangible service, but the benefits it provides. For example, a mattress store sells "comfortable sleep" rather than just "mattresses."

3. *How* will the business provide the products or services it offers? What are the primary actions and activities required to conduct this business? All businesses must produce a product or service, sell it to a customer, deliver it, and receive payment. This part of the business definition includes the primary activities of:
   - Buying or developing or manufacturing the product.
   - Identifying its potential qualified customers and selling the product to them.
   - Producing and delivering the product or service.
   - Receiving payment.

A solid business definition has three elements:

1. *The Offer:* What will you sell to your customers? That is called your *offer*, and includes exactly which products and services you will bring to the market and how you will price them. For example, you will provide online and telephone fitness consulting service for an initial 4-week period at $25 per week, or 8 weeks at $20 per week.

2. *Target Market:* Which segment of the consumer market are you aiming to serve? As discussed in Chapter 2, this is your *target market*. Defining your target market in a way that will help you identify potential customers is an important factor in achieving success. This definition must be precise enough so that you can identify a viable market for the business and focus your marketing efforts. A target market of "every adult in the United States" is clearly too broad and unfocused. A market of "every member of Congress from the State of Rhode Island" (three individuals) would be too narrow.

3. *Production and Delivery Capability:* How will you provide your offer to your targeted customers? This includes how to perform the key activities required to produce the product or service, deliver it to your customers, and ensure that they are satisfied.

---

[1] Special thanks to Peter Patch for providing many ideas for this chapter.

Apple began as a manufacturing business, making a product. There are four basic types of businesses:

1. **Manufacturing**—Produces a tangible product and sells it either through distributors or directly to end customers.
2. **Wholesale**—Buys in bulk from manufacturers and sells smaller quantities to retailers.
3. **Retail**—Sells individual items to consumers.
4. **Service**—Sells an intangible product to consumers.

Exercise

Imagine you are Stephen Wozniak. On a separate paper, define your business:

1. *Who* will the business serve?
2. *What* will the business offer? What are the products (or services) the business will sell?
3. *How* will the business provide the products or services it offers? What are the primary actions and activities required to conduct this business?

What Sort of Organization Do You Want?

Each organization has the opportunity to create a unique mission, vision, and culture that are supported by its core values. The founding team can determine how to use the company's competitive advantage to satisfy customers. Culture can be shaped according to the environment and how employees, customers, and other stakeholders are treated, a model that is set by the entrepreneur (owner).

Your Company's Core Values

Performance Objective 2 ▶

Articulate core beliefs, mission, and vision.

When you start your own company, what beliefs will you use to guide it? These are the **core values** of your business. Core values include the fundamental ethical and moral philosophy and beliefs that form the foundation of the organization and provide broad guidance for all decision making.

Examples of the core values of a business might be:

- "At Superior Printing, we believe in business practices that affect the environment as little as possible."
- "At Sheila's Restaurant, we believe in supporting local organic farmers."

Core values will affect business decisions. The owner of Superior Printing, for example, will choose ink that is less harmful to the environment over a cheaper ink that is more so. Superior Printing may also have a paper-recycling program to minimize its paper consumption. The owner of Sheila's Restaurant will only buy fruits and vegetables from local organic farmers. Your core beliefs will affect everything from the cost of materials to the prices you charge and how you treat customers. For additional examples of core values, see **Figure 3-1**.

Your Company's Mission Is to Satisfy Customers

The mission of your business, expressed in a mission statement, is a concise communication of your purpose, business definition, and values. The

Figure 3-1 *Core values.*

Tyson Foods Inc.

Based on our heritage of more than 65 years, these are the core values that we strongly believe in (listed in alphabetical order):
- *Brand Excellence*
- *Commitment, Fun and Opportunity*
- *Environmental, Food Safety and Team Member Safety Responsibility*
- *Family and Social Responsibility*
- *Innovation*
- *Integrity*
- *Market and Customer Focus*
- *Self-leadership and Learning*
- *Teamwork*

Dow AgroSciences

To ensure the prosperity and well-being of Dow AgroSciences employees, customers and shareholders, cumulative long-term profit growth is essential. How we achieve this objective is as important as the objective itself. Fundamental to our success are the core values we believe in and practice.
- *Employees are the source of Dow AgroSciences success. We communicate openly, treat each other with respect, promote teamwork, and encourage personal initiative and growth. Excellence in performance is rewarded.*
- *Customers receive our strongest commitment to meet their needs with high quality products and superior service.*
- *Products are based on innovative technology, continuous improvement, and added value for our customers and end users.*
- *Our conduct demonstrates a deep concern for human safety and environmental stewardship, while embracing the highest standards of ethics and citizenship.*

DuPont Company

Safety, concern and care for people, protection of the environment and personal and corporate integrity, are this company's highest values, and we will not compromise them.

---

function of a mission statement is to clarify what the business is trying to do in the present, but it can provide direction and motivation for future action through a clear and compelling message.

As noted in Chapter 2, a well-crafted mission statement will not only tell your customers and employees what your business is about, but can (and should) be a guide for every decision you make. It should capture your passion for the business and your commitment to satisfying your customers. A mission statement should be limited to 40 to 50 words to compel clarity in thinking and writing. The mission statement should address the following topics: target customers; products and services; markets served; use of technology; importance of public issues and employees; and focus on survival, profitability, and growth.

Here is an example of a mission statement for The Most Chocolate Cake Company:

> *The Most Chocolate Cake Company will create the richest, tastiest, most chocolaty cakes in our area. They will be made from the finest and freshest ingredients with our own special frostings and fillings. Baked to order and individually decorated for that special occasion, they will make any event as special as our cakes!*

The Most Chocolate Cake Company's mission statement defines the business and its competitive advantage, the core of its strategy. Examples of mission statements from a range of organizations appear in **Figure 3-2.**

Figure 3-2 *Mission statements.*

Nike—Crush Reebok.

Walt Disney—To make people happy.

W.L. Gore & Associates—Our products are designed to be the highest quality in their class and revolutionary in their effect.

Slumber Parties, Inc.—We seek to empower women at every stage of life through our products, demonstrations and careers. To achieve this goal, we offer women the opportunity to become more confident and satisfied in all aspects of their lives.

DuPont—Sustainable Growth: Increasing shareholder and societal value while reducing our environmental footprint

Dell Computers—With the power of direct and Dell's team of talented people, we are able to provide customers with superb value; high quality, relevant technology; customized systems; superior service and support; and products and services that are easy to buy and use.

Figure 3-3 *Vision statements.*

Caterpillar—Be a global leader in customer value.

McDonald's—Our vision is to be the world's best quick service restaurant experience. Being the best means providing outstanding quality, service, cleanliness, and value, so that we make every customer in every restaurant smile.

General Motors—GM's vision is to be the world leader in transportation products and related services. We will earn our customers' enthusiasm through continuous improvement driven by the integrity, teamwork, and innovation of GM people.

Bimbo Bakeries USA—To be the baking leader in the United States through quality, freshness, service and the building of our brands.

DuPont Company—Our vision is to be the world's most dynamic science company, creating sustainable solutions essential to a better, safer, healthier life for people everywhere.

Cargill—Our purpose is to be the global leader in nourishing people. We will harness our knowledge and energy to provide goods and services that are necessary for life, health and growth.

Your Company's Vision Is the Broader Perspective

The vision for your business is broader and more comprehensive, painting a picture of the overall view of what you want your organization to become in the future, not what it is in the present. It is built upon the core values and belief systems of the organization. It should energize your people and they should embrace it with enthusiasm and passion. This means that the vision has to be compelling across the organization. It has to matter. Employees have to be empowered to fulfill the vision. Examples of vision statements for various organizations appear in **Figure 3-3**.

Your Company's Culture Defines the Work Environment

The culture of an organization is largely shaped by its leadership. *Culture* is the core values of the organization in action. Leaders of an organization build a particular culture by making the beliefs, values, and behavioral norms explicit and intentional. Culture includes factors such as risk tolerance and innovation; orientation with respect to people, teams, and outcomes; attention to detail; and communication norms. Organizational culture is learned by members of the team in a number of ways, including anecdotes, ceremonies and events, material symbols, and particular use of language. For example, at General Electric, stories of Jack Welch are legendary. At Hewlett-Packard there was the "Hewlett-Packard Way," based on anecdotes passed down from employee to employee. Those who work in small enterprises often see the top management daily and take their cues directly—there are very few or no layers between them. As enterprises become larger, leaders frequently take on "larger than life" roles through stories.

Ceremonies can make a significant difference in company culture. Are there regular recognition events for innovation? Does the company invite family members to events throughout the year? Is there a birthday celebration for each employee? Are years of service recognized? Material symbols come in many shapes and forms. At the legacy MBNA America, the values of the company appeared on every archway, and handprints of the employees made colorful wall art in some buildings. Reserved parking spots and special privileges for certain employees send a message to everyone. Are these spaces for top executives? Expectant mothers? Are office sizes determined by pay grade? Finally, language tells a lot about the culture. Is everyone on a first-name basis with everyone else? Are some people addressed informally and others not? Is the language around the company in general formal or informal? Is communication respectful?

These and many other factors are all part of the *culture* of an organization. Culture should be crafted to follow core beliefs and support the mission and vision of the company.

The Decision Process

Translating opportunity into success can and has happened in literally millions of different ways. Each business has a different story. However, there are three primary routes to identifying opportunities:

- The entrepreneur searches for business opportunities through a process of identification and selection, beginning with self-developed (or group-developed) ideas:

- The entrepreneur uses essentially the same process, but starts with research on "hot" businesses or growth areas.

- The entrepreneur has an idea for a product or service and searches for a market.

In each case, a decision is made based on personal values and thinking. While each ultimately "funnels" the procedure down to a business concept, the processes are repeated, often with many ideas being considered before a viable idea emerges. The first two options listed previously are market driven and the third is product driven. Entrepreneurs do better looking to the market(s) of interest, rather than creating a product and then trying to find a customer base. You can do this all alone, but it is best to work with others who will provide honest, constructive feedback.

Your Competitive Advantage

Performance Objective 3 ▶

Analyze your competitive advantage.

For your business to be successful and to fulfill your mission and vision, you will need a strategy for beating the competition. This is your competitive advantage, or core competency. It is whatever you can do better than the competition that will attract sufficient customers to your business for it to succeed. Your competition is defined by your target market and can be *direct* competition (selling the same or similar products to the same market), or *indirect* (selling products that compete for the same share of customer spending but are not the same). For example, a children's museum may have to compete with rental movies or movie theaters, indoor or outdoor play areas, sports and recreation, and other family leisure-time activities to secure family entertainment time and money. Your competitive advantage is whatever meaningful benefit you can provide that puts you ahead of the competition.

- Can you attract more customers than your competitor by offering better quality or some special service?
- Can you supply your product at a lower price than other businesses serving your market?

If you are running a video-game rental business, perhaps you could deliver the games, along with snacks, so the customers would not have to come to the store. That would be your competitive advantage. If you can beat your competitors on price *and* service, you will be very strong in your market.

Find Your Competitive Advantage by Determining What Consumers Need and Want

Bill Gates did not invent computer software, but he did recognize that people were frustrated and intimidated by it. He created user-friendly software

---

Step into the Shoes...
Michael Dell Focuses on Benefits and Scores Big

Pretend you are Michael Dell, sitting in your Texas dorm room, figuring out how to convince your fellow students to let you build computers for them. You know you can build customized computers that are cheap and reliable. Those are the features of your product, but your friends might be only mildly interested. There is a better way to present your case, and that would be to focus on the benefits. These would include:

- If a purchaser has a problem with the computer, he or she can come see you personally.

- If a computer "crashes" (breaks), you will repair it immediately.
- Less money spent for a new computer means more money for other things.
- A customized computer is faster than a generic one, because it is not loaded down with software the student will never use.

Dell used this approach to create Dell Computer and, by age 38, he was earning $3.44 million a year as the CEO—because he understood that *benefits* sell products, not *features*—features are just facts.

applications that consumers wanted, and packaged them in bright, attractive cartons with easy-to-read manuals. That was his competitive advantage over other software companies. When you know your customers' wants and needs, and your competitors' capabilities, you should be able to find a competitive advantage.

You Have Unique Knowledge of Your Market

You may be wondering: "How do I figure out what customers need? I don't know anything about customers." Actually, you do. Your market may well be composed of your friends, neighbors, classmates, relatives, and colleagues. You already have the most important knowledge that you need to succeed. If you are starting a business to address a problem that you have encountered, chances are that you know your own market very well.

Sir Richard Branson, the CEO of Virgin Corporation, chose the name "Virgin" for his company because it reflected his total inexperience in business. His empire, which includes Virgin Megastores, Virgin Atlantic Airways, and Virgin Mobile, began as a tiny discount mail-order record company, which he started at age 19 after he had dropped out of high school. "I realized I'd be hopeless at studying," Branson told *Woman's Journal* magazine in 1985. "So I quit to do something I knew I could do and which interested me." Branson knew his market—other young people who were into music—very well. Then, he learned about the other markets that he entered.

How will you know if a business idea is going to be successful? You cannot have a guarantee, but your market will tell you a lot about your chances. The answer will come in the form of the signal called *profit*. You can learn a lot about your potential for success well ahead of starting your enterprise through customer and market research, in addition to competitive analysis.

The Six Factors of Competitive Advantage

Competitive advantage comes from one (or a combination) of six factors:

1. *Quality:* Can you provide higher quality than competing businesses?
2. *Price:* Can you offer a lower price on a sustained basis than your competition?
3. *Location:* Can you find a more convenient location for customers?
4. *Selection:* Can you provide a wider range of choices than your competitors?
5. *Service:* Can you provide better, more personalized customer service?
6. *Speed/Turnaround:* Can you deliver your product or service more quickly than the competition?

> *Failure is the opportunity to begin again more intelligently.*
>
> *—Henry Ford*

Entrepreneurial Wisdom...

A new business usually will require time before it can turn a profit. Federal Express, in fact, suffered initial losses of a million dollars a month! But if you are not making enough money to stay in business, that is the market speaking. It is telling you that your business is not satisfying consumer needs well enough. Do not take it personally. Many famous entrepreneurs opened and closed many businesses during their lifetimes.

Henry Ford went bankrupt twice before the Ford Motor Company was a success. If you want to be a successful entrepreneur, start growing a thick skin and decide right now that you intend to learn from failures and disappointments. Do not let them get you down. Most importantly, learn from them so that you do not make the same mistakes again.

Is Your Competitive Advantage Strong Enough?

When determining whether your business concept is viable, it is essential to determine your competitive advantage and whether it is strong enough. According to Jeffry Timmons,[2] a successful company needs the following:

- ***To sell to a market that is large and growing.*** The market for digital cameras is a good example. New products are being marketed to meet the demand, such as printers that turn digital photos into prints and digital photo frames.

- ***To sell to a market where the competition is able to make a profit.*** It will be interesting to observe what happens in the market for hybrid cars. Right now the jury is out as to whether the companies selling them can make a profit—so most automakers are not yet entering the market. There may not be a sufficiently large market to make entry worthwhile.

- ***To sell to a market where the competition is succeeding but is not so powerful as to make it impossible for a new entrepreneur to enter.*** Microsoft has been taken to court several times by competitors who argue that it is so big that new software companies cannot enter the market. **Barriers to entry** are the factors that contribute to the ease or difficulty for a new competitor to join an established market, and they cannot be so high that market entry and success are not possible for you.

- ***To sell a product or service that solves problems consumers may have with the competition (such as poor quality or slow delivery).*** This is how FedEx beat its competition—the U.S. Postal Service and United Parcel Service—when it entered the delivery market with its guaranteed overnight service.

- ***To sell a product or service at a competitive price that will attract customers.*** UPS fought back by offering a less-expensive overnight delivery service than that of FedEx.

If all of these are in place, you need to do the following:

- Understand the needs of your customers.
- Have a sustainable competitive advantage or multiple advantages.
- Deliver a product or service that meets your customers' needs at the right price.

If you do, you should be able to beat the competition and make a healthy profit.

Checking Out the Competition

One useful exercise is to learn everything you can about particular competitors—especially those that have earned the respect of the marketplace. Try to identify the sources of their competitive advantage. Look at their Web sites. Conduct Internet searches. Track their advertising and promotion, including print, broadcast, Internet, and sponsorships. If they are retailers, shop their stores or have your friends and family do so. Get to know them, but do not do anything unethical or illegal to obtain information. You will also need to keep an eye on your competition *after* you have started your business, because new factors might undermine your competitive advantage.

Today's entrepreneurs, even those starting very small ventures, may face competition from far beyond their neighborhoods because customers can go shopping on the Web. Most entrepreneurs are *optimistic*—optimism

Sometimes the best competitive strategy is to cooperate with the competition.

---

[2] Jeffry Timmons, *New Venture Creation*, 6th ed. (New York: McGraw-Hill/Irwin, 2003).

is a trait that goes with entrepreneurship—so they tend to get excited about the Web's potential customer base. What they often do not consider is that, "The world already is selling to their customers—aggressively and seamlessly."[3] Therefore, get online yourself and conduct a thorough search of your industry. You may find that there is literally a world of opportunity or, conversely, that the world is full of competitors.

To determine whether you have a competitive advantage that will enable you to outperform your closest and strongest competitors, ask these questions:

- *Competitive offers:* How does your offer compare with those of your leading competitors? What are the key features of each?
- *Unique selling proposition:* Based on that comparison, what is your **unique selling proposition (USP),** the distinctive feature and benefit that sets you apart from your competition? This will require a comparison of offers and identifying what is unique about yours. What is it about yours that your competitors cannot or will not match?
- *Cost structure:* What is different about your business activities and the cost of doing business from that of your competitors? Overall, are you at a cost advantage or disadvantage?

To be successful, you must have a USP that will attract customers to buy from you. Second, you must have a cost structure that is sufficiently advantageous so that, when all of your costs are deducted from your revenue, you will have sufficient profit left over. If you can achieve a cost advantage or, at least, minimize any cost disadvantage, this will help you achieve a profit. This profit is your reward for operating a successful business.

The Most Chocolate Cake Company

There are a number of ways to highlight your competitive advantage and to identify opportunities. In this example, Amy makes and sells chocolate cakes. She chose this product because she loves chocolate and she enjoys baking cakes. She decided to make the most *chocolate* cakes possible. From this decision, she came up with the concept for her product and the name of her business: The Most Chocolate Cake Company.

Amy's target market was the segment of the public that loved chocolate cakes but did not have the time or interest in baking them. Because cakes are usually purchased for special occasions, our entrepreneur believed she could charge a good price—at least as much as a bakery store cake.

She decided she would make the cakes "special" in three ways:

- By using the finest ingredients (quality)
- Through expert custom-decorating, to personalize each cake (selection)
- By baking the cakes to order, so they would be fresh for the event (quality)

She bakes her cakes at home, which makes them literally "homemade" and thus reduces the cost of making them—she is not renting commercial space or paying a staff. Of course, the flip side of baking at home is that her production is limited. Also, she may have to take time to deliver each cake, depending on local zoning regulations regarding retail trade.

---

[3] Fred Hapgood, "Foreign Exchange," *Inc.* magazine, June 1997.

The following chart shows how Amy answered the key questions about business definition.

Business Definition Question	The Most Chocolate Cake Company
1. *The Offer*—What products and services will be sold?	1. Chocolate cakes, for special events, at a price competitive with neighborhood stores.
2. *Target Market*—Which consumer segment will the business focus on?	2. People who love chocolate and those who want a special cake for a special event.
3. *Production Capability*—How will that offer be produced and delivered to those customers?	3. Homemade and baked to order to ensure freshness, using high-quality ingredients.

The chart below addresses competitive differences for the Most Chocolate Cake Company.

Competitive Advantage Question	Competitive Advantage
1. *The Offer*—What will be better and different about the products and services that will be sold?	1. Most Chocolate will use more and higher-grade chocolate; better ingredients in general, especially in frostings and fillings; will have personalized decorations; and will be freshly baked to order.
2. *Target Market*—What consumers should be the focus of the business to make it as successful as possible?	2. People who love chocolate and those who want a special cake for a special event.
3. *Production and Delivery Capability*—What will be better or different about the way that offer is produced and delivered to those customers?	3. Homemade and baked to order to ensure freshness; using highest-quality ingredients.

Our entrepreneur is betting that her more chocolaty cake, with its special frosting and decoration, as well as its freshly homemade quality, will be successful in the marketplace. This is her USP. She hopes this will be a source of competitive advantage, along with the cost advantage of baking the cakes at home. Based on this analysis, she has determined how she wants to make her offering better and different from those of her competitors.

Another approach to the analysis is to compare your business concept with the competitors that you have identified through your research. A simple comparative table is a good way to display this. The table should include each of the six factors of competitive advantage. Plus, if there are particular features that you want to highlight or specific aspects of the six factors, adding them to the table will make them more prominent. These ratings can be done solely by you, your team, through market research techniques, or however you think you can get the most unbiased responses.

There are many ways to construct this type of competitive analysis table. The table in **Figure 3-4** is one where ratings of excellent, good, moderate, fair, and poor describe each factor for each competitor. This makes competitive advantages and weaknesses readily apparent. However, it does not yield an overall rating.

The table in **Figure 3-5** is an example of a more quantitative approach to competitive analysis. First, based upon industry data or quality customer research, each factor is assigned a weight according to its importance to the company's target customers, with the total of all factors equaling 1.00. For

Figure 3-4 *Comparative analysis—qualitative—The Most Chocolate Cake Company.*

	Most Chocolate Company	Mega Super Market, Inc.	Average Bakery Co.	Fancy Bakery, LLC
Quality	Excellent	Fair	Fair	Excellent
Price	Fair	Good	Moderate	Poor
Location	Moderate	Excellent	Moderate	Good
Selection	Fair	Moderate	Good	Moderate
Service	Excellent	Fair	Moderate	Fair
Speed/Turnaround	Good	Excellent	Moderate	Fair
Specialization	Excellent	Poor	Fair	Moderate
Personalization	Excellent	Moderate	Good	Excellent

Figure 3-5 *Comparative analysis—quantitative—The Most Chocolate Cake Company.*

	Wt.	Most Chocolate Company		Mega Super Market, Inc.		Average Bakery Co.		Fancy Bakery, LLC	
		Rating	Wtd. Rating	Rating	Wtd. Rating	Rating	Wtd. Rating	Rating	Wtd. Rating
Quality	0.20	5	1.00	2	0.40	2	0.40	5	1.00
Price	0.10	2	0.20	4	0.40	3	0.30	1	0.10
Location	0.10	3	0.30	5	0.50	3	0.30	4	0.40
Selection	0.15	2	0.30	3	0.45	4	0.60	3	0.45
Service	0.10	5	0.50	2	0.20	3	0.30	2	0.20
Speed/Turnaround	0.05	4	0.20	5	0.25	3	0.15	2	0.10
Specialization	0.20	5	1.00	1	0.20	2	0.40	3	0.60
Personalization	0.10	5	0.50	3	0.30	4	0.40	5	0.50
Total	1.00	xxxxx	**4.00**	xxxxx	**2.70**	xxxxx	**2.85**	xxxxx	**3.35**

example, quality could be weighted 0.20 and location weighted 0.10, with other factors adding up to 0.70, if customers are very concerned about the quality of the product and they can buy it on the Internet. Second, each competitor should be rated on an odd-numbered scale, such as 1 to 5, with 1 being lowest and 5 being highest, on each factor. For example, the Most Chocolate Cake Company could rate a 5 on quality and 2 on selection while the supermarket could rate 2 on quality and 5 on location. Third, to calculate a weighted score, each rating should be multiplied by the associated weight to obtain a total. For example, if quality is rated 0.20 and Most Chocolate's quality is rated 5, the weighted value is 1.00. Looking across the competitors at weights on individual factors can yield insights into areas of strength or vulnerability. Finally, all the weighted values for each company should be totaled and an overall rating calculated. By looking at the ratings, it becomes apparent who the strongest and weakest competitors are, and the company can be effective in addressing the results of the analysis.

Competitive Strategy: Business Definition and Competitive Advantage

Your business will only succeed if you can offer the customers in your market something more, better, and/or different from what the competition does. Your competitive advantage (core competency) is essential and, once you establish it, your business decisions will start to fall into place. Every advertisement, every promotion, even the price of your product and the location of your business, should be designed to get customers excited about your competitive advantage.

Your **competitive strategy** combines your business definition with your competitive advantage. A competitive advantage must be *sustainable,* meaning that you can keep it going. If you decide to beat the competition by selling your product at a lower price, your advantage will not last long if you cannot afford to continue at that price. Small business owners should realize that price alone is not likely to work as an advantage for long. A larger business can almost always beat you on price because it can buy larger quantities from its suppliers, who will be more willing to give them lower wholesale prices.

Being able to temporarily undercut the competition's prices is not a competitive advantage. Being able to *permanently* sell at a lower price because you have discovered a cheaper supplier *is* a competitive advantage. Being able to develop and maintain proprietary product or service features and benefits is another approach to finding a sustainable advantage.

Strategy versus Tactics

Your **strategy** is the plan for outperforming the competition. Your **tactics** are the ways in which you will carry out your strategy.

If you plan to open a bookstore, how will you compete with the chain outlet in the neighborhood? This competitor buys more books and will receive higher discounts from wholesalers. So you probably will not be able to compete on price. How else could you attract customers? Perhaps you could make your bookstore a kind of community center so people will want to gather there. What tactics could you use to carry out this strategy?

- Hold poetry readings and one-person concerts to promote local poets and musicians.
- Create special-interest book discussion groups.
- Offer free tea and coffee.
- Provide comfortable seating areas for conversation and reading to encourage customers to spend time in your store.
- Set up a binder of personal ads as a dating service.

If your tactics attract enough customers to make a profit, you will have found a strategy for achieving a competitive advantage.

To find a competitive advantage, think about everything your business will offer. Examine your location, product, design, and price. What can you do to be different, and better in some way, than the competition?

Feasibility: The "Economics of One Unit" as a Litmus Test

Performance Objective 4 ▶

Perform initial viability testing using the "Economics of One Unit."

Once you have chosen a business idea and determined your competitive advantage, you should make a preliminary analysis to determine whether the business can be financially viable. In other words, can you provide your product or service at a price that will cover your costs and provide you with a profit? Wozniak and Jobs were able to move out of the garage once they had enough cash flow and profit to hire people to make the computers for Apple. This freed them to create new products and new strategies for their business. Before investing considerable time, effort, and money on your business concept, you can use what you learned from your competitive analysis to make a preliminary assessment of the financial opportunity. There is considerably more financial analysis to be done before "opening your doors," but this is a good point to do an evaluation.

Entrepreneurs use profits to pay themselves, to expand their businesses, and to start or invest in other businesses. Every entrepreneur, therefore, needs to know how much **gross profit** (price minus cost of goods sold) the business will earn on each item it sells. To do this, entrepreneurs calculate the **economics of one unit of sale (EOU)**, which will tell you how much gross profit is earned on each unit of your product or service that you sell.

Defining the Unit of Sale

Begin with the **unit of sale**, which is the basic unit of the product or service sold by the business. Entrepreneurs usually define their unit of sale according to the type of business. For example:

Manufacturing. One order (any quantity; e.g., 100 watches)

Wholesale. A dozen of an item (e.g., 12 watches)

Retail. One item (e.g., 1 watch)

Service. One hour of service time (e.g., one hour of lawn-mowing service) or a standard block of time devoted to a task (e.g., one mowed lawn)

If the business sells a combination of differently priced items (such as in a restaurant), the unit of sale is more complicated. The entrepreneur can use the average sale per customer minus the average cost of goods sold per customer for the economics of one unit of sale. The formula would be as follows:

$$\text{Average Sale per Customer} - \text{Average Cost of Sale per Customer} = \text{Average Gross Profit per Customer}$$

A business that sells a variety of items may choose to express one unit of sale as a combination of items that comprises the average sale per customer (see **Figure 3-6**).

Figure 3-6 *Unit of sale as a combination of different items.*

UNIT OF SALE AND ECONOMICS OF ONE UNIT OF SALE			
Type of Business	**Unit of Sale**	**Economics of One Unit of Sale**	**Gross Profit per Unit**
1. Retail & Manufacturing	One item (e.g., one tie)	$7 – $3 = $4	$4
2. Service	One hour (e.g., one hour of mowing a lawn)	$20 – $10 = $10	$10
3. Wholesale	Multiple of same item (e.g., one dozen roses)	$240 – $120 = $120	$120
4. Combination	Average sale per customer minus average cost of goods sold per customer (e.g., restaurant meals)	$20 – $10 = $10	$10 average gross profit

Cost of Goods Sold and Gross Profit

To get a closer look at one unit of sale, entrepreneurs analyze the **cost of goods sold (COGS)** of one unit. These are:

- The cost of materials used to make the product (or deliver the service).
- The cost of labor directly used to make the product (or deliver the service).

For a product, the cost of direct labor used to make the product plus the cost of materials used are the cost of goods sold (COGS). The equivalent for a service business, the **cost of services sold (COSS)**, are the cost of the **direct labor** used to deliver the service plus the costs of the delivery of the service.

The cost of goods sold can be thought of as the cost of selling "one additional unit." If you buy watches and then resell them, your COGS per unit is the price you paid for one watch. Once you know your COGS, you can calculate gross profit by subtracting COGS from revenue (see **Figure 3-7**).

Your Business and the Economics of One Unit

The economics of one unit of sale is a method for seeing whether your business idea might be profitable. If one unit of sale is profitable, the whole business is likely to be. On the other hand, if one unit of sale is not profitable, then no matter how many units you sell, the business will never be successful. Use Figure 3-7 as an example.

Say you have a simple business selling decorative hand-blown wineglasses that you buy from a local artist wholesale for $12 each, and resell them to friends for $20 each. The cost of goods sold for each wineglass is the wholesale price of $12 (gross profit: $8).

Assume you buy a dozen glasses for $12 each wholesale. Your unit of sale is one glass. Your cost of goods sold is $12 per unit, assuming you have no direct labor cost.

Assume you sell all the glasses at $20. Here is how you would calculate your gross profit.

Total Revenue = 12 Glasses × $20 Selling Price = $240
Total Cost of Goods Sold = 12 Glasses × $12 Purchase Price = $144
Total Gross Profit (Contribution Margin) = $96
$240 revenue – $144 COGS = $96

Total Revenue – Total Cost of Goods Sold = Total Gross Profit

You made a gross profit of $96.

For a manufacturing business, one unit might be one pair of sneakers. The costs would include **direct labor**, the money paid to the people who

Figure 3-7 *Economics of one unit of sale versus total gross profit.*

	Economics of One Unit (EOU)	Total Gross Profit for 12 Units (@$10 per Unit Sold)
Price Sold/Revenue	$20	$240 (12 × $20)
− Cost of Goods Sold	−$12	$144 (12 × 12)
Gross Profit	$8	$96 (12 × 8)

make the product (sneakers, in this example), and the supplies, such as fabric, rubber, and leather (see **Figure 3-8**).

The manufacturer makes a gross profit of $3 for every pair of sneakers sold. That may not seem like much, but manufacturers sell in *bulk*. In other words, a manufacturer might sell several million pairs of sneakers per year.

The economics of one unit also applies to wholesale, retail, and service businesses. Assume the wholesaler buys a set of one dozen sneakers from the manufacturer for $180 and can sell them to a retailer for $240 (see **Figure 3-9**).

The retailer pays the wholesaler $240 for one dozen sneakers. The retailer's COGS, therefore, is $20 ($240/12—shoes only—the retailer does not add direct labor). The store sells each pair to its customers for $35 (see **Figure 3-10**).

Figure 3-8 *Economics of one unit, manufacturing.*

ECONOMICS OF ONE UNIT (EOU)			
Manufacturing Business: Unit = 1 Pair of Sneakers			
Selling Price per Unit:			$15.00
Labor Cost per Hour:	$4.00		
No. of Hours per Unit:	2 hours	$ 8.00	
Materials per Unit:		4.00	
Cost of Goods Sold per Unit:		$12.00	12.00
Gross Profit per Unit:			$ 3.00

Figure 3-9 *Economics of one unit, wholesale.*

ECONOMICS OF ONE UNIT (EOU)	
Wholesale Business: Unit = 1 Dozen Pair of Sneakers	
Selling Price per Unit:	$240.00
Cost of Goods Sold per Unit:	180.00
Gross Profit per Unit:	$ 60.00

Figure 3-10 *Economics of one unit, retail.*

ECONOMICS OF ONE UNIT (EOU)	
Retail Business: Unit = 1 Pair of Sneakers	
Selling Price per Unit:	$35.00
Cost of Goods Sold per Unit:	20.00
Gross Profit per Unit:	$15.00

Here is the economics of one unit for a hair stylist who charges $50 per cut (see **Figure 3-11**).

Figure 3-11 *Economics of one unit, service.*

ECONOMICS OF ONE UNIT (EOU)		
Service Business: Unit = 1 Hour		
Selling Price per Unit:		$50.00
Supplies per Unit (hair gel, etc.):	$ 2.00	
Labor Costs per Hour:	25.00	
Cost of Goods Sold per Unit:	$27.00	27.00
Gross Profit per Unit:		$23.00

The Cost of Direct Labor in the EOU

Janet has a business designing handmade bookmarkers. Her unit of sale is one bookmarker. Below is additional information about Janet's business:

- She sells 40 bookmarkers per week to a bookstore in her neighborhood.
- Her selling price is $4.50 each, including an envelope.
- Her costs are 80¢ per card for materials (construction paper, glue, and paint) and 20¢ each for the envelopes, for a total of $1.00 each.
- On average, it takes her one hour to make six bookmarkers.
- Janet pays herself $9 an hour.

The direct labor for each bookmarker is $1.50 ($9/6). Janet wisely realizes that she must include the cost of her labor in the EOU. See how she did this in **Figure 3-12**.

Janet's gross profit was $2 per bookmarker sold. Assuming no other expenses, she will keep this as owner of the business. She also earned $1.50 per bookmarker by supplying the labor, thus ending up with a profit of $3.50 per bookmarker.

Now, think back to Amy of the Most Chocolate Cake Company and perform a similar analysis.

- Amy takes an average of two hours to bake a cake.
- It costs $5.00 for the ingredients for an average cake.
- Amy pays herself $15 an hour.
- The price of an average cake is $40.

This yields a gross profit of $5 per cake. With the gross profit of $5 and the $30 she paid herself, Amy ends up with $35 per cake. Assuming she does

Figure 3-12 *EOU example, Janet's company.*

ECONOMICS OF ONE UNIT (EOU)		
Manufacturing Business: Unit = 1 Bookmarker		
Selling Price per Unit:		$4.50
Materials:	$1.00	
Labor:	1.50	
Cost of Goods Sold per Unit:	$2.50	2.50
Gross Profit per Unit:		$2.00

not have to deliver the cakes, this may be sufficient for her. If she needs to earn more, she will have to charge more, work faster, work more hours, or decrease the costs. These may or may not be realistic options.

Hiring Others to Make the Unit of Sale

Janet realizes that, if the bookstore wants to order more bookmarkers or she can sell them to additional bookstores, she will not have enough time to make them all herself. To solve this issue, she hires a friend to make the bookmarkers for $9 per hour. Although the EOU stays the same, Janet will have more time to look for new opportunities for her business. Her income from the business will now come solely from the gross profit, which is currently $2 per unit.

Amy can produce about 20 cakes during a 40-hour workweek and 30 in 60 hours. That means she can earn $600 to $750 per week, or between $31,200 and $39,000 per year before taxes, without allowing for any vacation or sick days. There would be an additional $100 to $150 in gross profit per week before other expenses are paid. Assuming Amy can sell 20 to 30 cakes per week at $40 each, she will have a maximum income of about $46,800.

Amy knows that she will have other expenses, so $40,000 is more realistic. Like Janet, Amy wants to earn more than that per year so she, too, could add employees if the market would support greater volume. If she paid her employees $15 per hour (the minimum living wage in some areas in 2004), she would need to sell 8,000 cakes per year to make her $40,000. That is 154 cakes per week, requiring perhaps seven full-time bakers. This would not be possible in her home kitchen.

However, we have to be sure that Amy is not comparing apples to oranges when making the analysis. With more people, the tasks could be delegated so that it took only one hour per cake, bringing the gross profit to $20 each. If Amy could also get better pricing on ingredients due to increased volume, the gross profit would be even higher. At $20 per unit gross profit, Amy would need to sell only 2,000 cakes per year, or 39 per week. That could be accomplished with two full-time bakers. As a home-based business, that would be more realistic.

Amy, like any entrepreneur, has to decide what is realistic and achievable and what her goals are.

Going for Volume

Janet meets a bookstore supply wholesaler. He offers to buy 2,000 bookmarkers if Janet can deliver them in one month and sell them for $3.50 each, $1 less than she had been getting. This would reduce her gross profit but offer more revenue. Three questions immediately came to mind:

1. Can I produce the 2,000-unit order in the required time frame?

After doing some calculations, Janet realized that, if she hired 10 people each to work 35 hours a month, she could deliver the order in time. Janet convinces 10 people to take on the one-month commitment by offering $12 per hour.

2. If I lower the price to $3.50 for each bookmarker (instead of $4.50), will I still make an acceptable gross profit per unit?

To answer this question, Janet created a chart (see **Figure 3-13**) and realized that her new gross profit per unit would be $1.00. Let us look at the EOU if she factors in her labor at $12.00 per hour, or $2 per bookmarker.

3. How much in total gross profit will I make from the order?

To answer this question, Janet created another chart (see **Figure 3-14**) and realized that her total gross profit would be $1,000.

Figure 3-13 *EOU example, Janet's company with employees.*

ECONOMICS OF ONE UNIT (EOU)		
Manufacturing Business: Unit = 1 Bookmarker		
Selling Price per Unit:		$3.50
Materials:	$1.00	
Labor:	1.50	
Cost of Goods Sold per Unit:	$2.50	2.50
Gross Profit per Unit:		$1.00

Figure 3-14 *Gross profit projection, Janet's company with employees.*

GROSS PROFIT PROJECTION (BASED ON EOU)		
Janet's Total Gross Profit		
Revenue ($3.50 × 2,000 bookmarkers):		$7,000.00
Materials ($1 × 2,000):	$2,000.00	
Labor ($2.00 × 2,000):	4,000.00	
Cost of Goods Sold:	$5,000.00	6,000.00
Gross Profit:		$1,000.00

Janet concluded that $1,000 in gross profit was much better than earning $80 a week in gross profit and $60 a week for her labor (what she earned making the bookmarkers herself each week at a selling price of $4.50). Even though the wholesaler was asking for a lower selling price, her total revenue, and therefore her total gross profit, would be much higher. When Janet realized that she could deliver the order in the required time and make $1,000, she accepted the offer.

Five breakthrough steps entrepreneurs can take are:

1. Calculating the unit of sale
2. Determining the economics of one unit of sale
3. Substituting someone else's labor
4. Selling in volume
5. Creating jobs and operating at a profit

Global Impact...

Selling Your Product around the World

Through the Internet, even a very small business run by one person can reach customers internationally. What if a customer from Germany contacts you through your Web site and wants to buy your product—in euros, the currency of much of Europe? **Currency** is money that can be exchanged internationally. In the United States, the currency is the dollar. In Japan, it is the yen. In Mexico, it is the peso.

The **foreign exchange (FX) rate** is the relative value between one currency and another. It describes the buying power of a currency. The foreign exchange rate, or FX rate, is expressed as a ratio. If one dollar is worth 1.25 euros, to figure out how many euros a certain number of dollars is worth, multiply that number by 1.25.

$$\$5 = \$5 \times €1.25 = €6.25$$

How would you figure out how many dollars €6.25 is worth? Simply divide €6.25 by €1.25 to get $5.00.

TIP: There are currency converters available online, such as http://finance.yahoo.com/currency?u.

At first, an entrepreneur can be part of his or her own economics of one unit. If you start making (manufacturing) computers in your garage, like Steve Jobs and Stephen Wozniak did when they started Apple, you should include your labor on the EOU worksheet.

Over time, though, Jobs and Wozniak made enough profit to hire others to manufacture the computers. This left them free to develop new ideas for Apple that brought more business and profit to the company. Jobs and Wozniak took themselves out of the economics of one unit so they could be the creative leaders of the company. And by lowering prices they were able to sell millions of units.

Chapter Summary

Now that you have studied this chapter, you can do the following:

1. Define your business.
   - Identify the four basic types of business.
     - Manufacturing—makes a tangible product.
     - Wholesale—buys in quantity from the manufacturer and sells to the retailer.
     - Retail—sells to the consumer.
     - Service—sells an intangible product to the consumer.
2. Articulate your core beliefs, your mission, and vision.
3. Find and analyze your business's competitive advantage.
   - Your competitive advantage is whatever you can do better than the competition that will attract customers to your business.
   - Find your competitive advantage by thinking about what consumers in your market need. You have unique knowledge of your market.
4. Perform initial feasibility analysis by calculating the economics of one unit of sale.
   - The EOU is the basis of business profit.
   - Entrepreneurs use profits to pay themselves, expand the business, and start or invest in new businesses.
   - The entrepreneur chooses how the unit is defined:
     - One item (unit).
     - One hour of service time (if the business is a service business).
     - If the business sells differently priced items (such as in a restaurant), use the average sale per customer as the unit. The average would be total sales divided by the number of customers:

       Total Sales/Number of Customers = Average Unit of Sale
   - To get a closer look at the costs involved in figuring one unit, entrepreneurs analyze the cost of goods or services sold (COGS or COSS) of a unit.
     - The cost of materials used to make the product (or deliver the service)
     - The cost of labor used to make the product (or deliver the service)
   - Once you know your cost of goods sold, you can calculate gross profit. Subtract total COGS from your total revenue to get your gross profit.

       Revenue – COGS = Gross Profit

Key Terms

barriers to entry	manufacturing
competitive strategy	market
core values	retail
cost of goods sold (COGS)	service
cost of services sold (COSS)	strategy
currency	tactics
direct labor	unique selling proposition (USP)
economics of one unit (EOU)	unit of sale
foreign exchange (FX) rate	wholesale
gross profit	

Entrepreneurship Portfolio

Critical Thinking Exercises

1. Use the following charts to define a business you would like to start and analyze your competitive advantage.

Business Definition Question	Response
The Offer—What products and services will be sold by the business?	
Target Market—Which consumer segment will the business focus on?	
Production Capability—How will that offer be produced and delivered to those customers?	

Competitive Advantage Question	Competitive Difference (USP)
The Offer—What will be better and different about the products and services that will be sold?	
Target Market—Which segments of consumers should be the focus of the business to make it as successful as possible?	
Production and Delivery Capability—What will be better or different about the way the offer is produced and delivered to those customers?	

	Wt.	Your Company Rating	Your Company Wtd. Rating	Competitor #1 Rating	Competitor #1 Wtd. Rating	Competitor #2 Rating	Competitor #2 Wtd. Rating	Competitor #3 Rating	Competitor #3 Wtd. Rating
Quality									
Price									
Location									
Selection									
Service									
Speed/Turnaround									
Specialization									
Personalization			_____		_____		_____		_____
Total	1.00	xxxxx		xxxxx		xxxxx		xxxxx	

2. Are there customers for your business in other countries? How do you plan to reach them?

3. Describe any international competitors you have found who may be able to access your customers. How do you intend to compete?

4. Describe three core values you will use to run your own company.

5. What are three of the concepts that a mission statement should contain and why?

6. Write a mission statement for your business.

Key Concept Questions

1. Gross profit is the profit of a business before which other costs are subtracted?

2. What is the average unit of sale for the following businesses?
   - Business 1: A restaurant that serves $2,100 in meals to 115 customers per day.
   - Business 2: A record store that sells $1,500 worth of CDs to 75 customers per day.

3. For the following business, define the unit of sale and calculate the economics of one unit:

   Sue, of Sue's Sandwich Shoppe, sells sandwiches and soda from a sidewalk cart in a popular park near her house. She sets up her cart in the summers to earn money for college tuition. Last month she sold $1,240 worth of product (sandwiches and sodas) to 100 customers. She spent $210 on the sandwich ingredients and buying the sodas wholesale. Her unit is one sandwich ($4) plus one soda ($1).

4. When Stephen Wozniak and Steve Jobs envisioned a computer in every home, computers were large, expensive machines. They were only available to the government, universities, scientists, and large companies. What technology currently available today to only a few people can you envision meeting a need for many consumers in the future?

5. Is there a service presently available to only a few consumers? Or one that is not available yet? Write about a service that you can imagine eventually becoming very popular, and the need(s) it will meet.

6. If the FX rate between the U.S. dollar and the Japanese yen is 1:119, how many yen will it take to equal $20?

7. If the FX rate between the Japanese yen and the euro is 189.35:1, how many yen will equal 10 euros?

Application Exercises

You own a small record label. You sell CDs through your Web site for $15, including shipping and handling. You get an offer from someone who owns a record store in Germany who would like to sell your CDs. He wants to buy them at $10 each and sell them for $30. He says his profit from each sale would be $12 and he will split it with you. Assuming the exchange rate between the dollar and the euro is $1 = €2:

   a. How much profit would you get from the sale of each CD in the German store?

   b. How much is that profit in dollars?

   c. Is this a good business opportunity for you? Why or why not?

   d. If the FX rate between the dollar and the euro falls to $1 = €1 would this still be a good business idea for you? Why or why not?

Markets and Marketing Defined

Ray Kroc invented a new way of marketing hamburgers by realizing that customers cared more about fast service, consistent quality, and a low price than about the "ultimate hamburger."

Marketing is satisfying the customer at a profit.[1] A market, as defined in Chapter 3, is a group of people or organizations that may be interested in buying a given product or service, has the resources to purchase it, and is permitted by law and regulation to do so. Marketing is the business function that identifies these customers and their needs and wants.

Through marketing, the name of your business comes to mean something clear and concrete in the customer's mind. As an entrepreneur, your current and future customers should always be your top priority.[2] Above all, marketing is the way a business tells its customers that it is committed to meeting their needs. Marketing should constantly reinforce your competitive advantage.

Ray Kroc understood what the customers wanted from McDonald's and he did not tinker with it.

Nike sells sneakers. It puts them in stores where consumers can buy them. But Nike also *markets* sneakers. Nike creates advertisements and promotions designed to convince customers that Nike sneakers will inspire them to *Just Do It*. You can choose sneakers from many companies, but Nike hopes you will feel inspired by its marketing to seek out and buy its brand.

The Nike "swoosh"—A logo recognized worldwide. (Sandy Feisenthal, Corbis Bettmann)

A Business That Markets versus a Market-Driven Business

Do not make the mistake of treating marketing as an isolated business function, instead of the engine that drives all business decisions. Most experts agree that, to be successful, a business must develop its marketing vision first, and then use it as the basis for all subsequent decisions.

Market Research Prepares You for Success

Whether you have a product or service that you want to market, or are searching for a market opportunity and are creating a product or service to fill that need, research can help you succeed. Your research can be

---

[1] Adapted from Philip Kotler and Gary Armstrong, *Principles of Marketing*, 9th ed. (Upper Saddle River, NJ: Prentice Hall, 2001).
[2] Adapted from Kotler and Armstrong, *Principles of Marketing*.

Exercise

On a Separate Piece of Paper

1. Give an example of a company that you believe operates as a market-driven organization, and why.
2. Give an example of a company that functions as an organization that markets.

conducted at the level of the industry, the market segment, or the individual consumer. While the questions you ask will be very different at each level, the methods for answering them are similar.

Types and Methods of Research

How you conduct your research is very important to determining whether it is reliable and valid. Clearly, you do not want to make business decisions based upon partial or incorrect information. The quality of your research defines the quality of the answers to your research questions. You or a market research firm (or a student group) can do two types of research. **Primary research** is research conducted directly on a subject or subjects. **Secondary research** is research carried out indirectly, through existing resources. For example, if you conducted 100 interviews with students on campus, it would be primary research. If you found a study on those students conducted by someone else, it would be secondary. Often, primary research is expensive and time-consuming to conduct. However, if you want to test a product or idea, it can be your best option.

Bear in mind when you design a market-research survey that *the method you use may affect the answers you get*. A combination of primary and secondary research is generally best, and for each type of research there is a set of methods that you can select to fit your needs. These methods are tools that can aid you in determining the viability of your business concept and/or product. The number of options is seemingly endless. Which methods to use will depend upon your level of analysis (individual, market, industry, and the like), your research questions, and the time and money you can devote to them. Remember, it is better to do your research and discover that you should revamp your plans, than it would be to skip this step or ignore the results and find out through an expensive failure in the marketplace.

Getting Information Directly from the Source—Primary Research

When you need to ask questions specific to your product or service, or need to observe how people act or react, it is best to conduct primary research. Some methods of primary research include:

- *Personal interviews:* Interview individuals in person either using question guides with flexibility or structured step-by-step surveys. For example, you could interview students on campus or customers in a shopping area.

- *Telephone surveys:* Personal interviews but not conducted in person. When your customer base will not be strictly local, you can reach more people via telephone.
- *Written surveys:* These can be administered via the traditional mail service or through electronic mail. There are numerous survey programs available on the Internet to simplify this process. One example is Survey Monkey (*http://www.surveymonkey.com*), which creates neat, written surveys online. The survey questions should be clearly stated, easy to understand, and relatively short.
- *Focus groups:* If you want to get information that is generated through guided group discussion, you can use focus groups. There are facilities designed specifically for conducting focus groups, or you can simply find a quiet space with adequate facilities.
- *Observation:* By watching, you can observe patterns of interaction, traffic patterns, and volumes of purchases that will help you understand your prospective customers and your competition. Secret shoppers (people who are hired to "shop" a store) fall in this category. Also, attending an event such as a trade show or professional meeting is an opportunity to observe and learn. Make certain you do this ethically and legally.
- *Tracking:* It can be useful to track advertisements, prices, and other information through the media. You can compile this data to see pricing and promotion patterns, as well as the marketing strategies, of your competitors.
- *Review of books and records:* Although it is rare to have the opportunity, if you can examine records (or even journals or research notes) that are pertinent to your business, you may gain valuable insights. This is particularly true if you are buying a business and practicing due diligence.

Getting Information Indirectly—Secondary Research

When you want to learn about your industry, competition, or markets, secondary research may be your best option. Some methods of secondary research are:

- *Online searches:* By using search engines such as Google, Yahoo! Search, Dogpile, Ask.com, Live Search, and Excite, you can find stories, historical records, biographical information, and statistics. Be wary of sources for the Internet data, as the information may not always be reliable.
- *Article and book searches:* You can use proprietary databases at a college or public library to find articles and books on your market. Interestingly, much of the information available on businesses, populations, markets, and the like is not available through Internet search engines. Libraries sign up for databases that are available only by costly paid subscriptions. They also have services to provide certain journal and magazine articles for downloading or printing.
- *Trade associations, chambers of commerce, and public agencies:* These types of organizations frequently collect demographic and statistical data on and for their members or constituents. They issue publications that contain valuable data in such areas as pricing trends, productivity, cost structures, legal matters, economic and environmental topics, and statistics. This kind of information can be extremely expensive to gather and can be of great value to a start-up enterprise.

Developing a Marketing Plan

Now that you understand how marketing shou
you are ready to develop a plan for introducing
ket. The marketing plan, as discussed in Chap
alone document or be part of a complete bu
should be a functioning, evolving part of your b
tomer analysis because, before you can develop
need to know who your customers are and wh

*Q: Why does a customer go to a hardware s
A: Because she needs to make a hole.*

The *hole* is what the customer needs, not the
bought at the hardware store, the customer
drill.[9] If you are marketing drills, therefore, yo
tomer what good holes they make! If someone
drill manufacturers will soon be out of busines

Your marketing plan must include an u
customers and their wants, needs, and demand
analyze market segments. The plan should inc
and trend analysis. It will state your market-pos
a marketing plan looks at all aspects of the m
prise, from the broadest to the narrowest persp

Chapter Summary

Now that you have studied this chapter you ca

1. Explain how marketing differs from sellin
   - Marketing is the business function that id
     their needs and wants.
   - Through marketing, the name of your bus
     thing clear and concrete in the customer's
     is the way a business communicates its cc
     market.
2. Understand how market research prepare
   Market research is the process of finding o
   tomers are, where you can reach them, and
   - Getting the information directly from the
     - Personal interviews
     - Telephone surveys
     - Written surveys
     - Focus groups
     - Observations
     - Tracking
     - Review of books and records
   - Getting information indirectly: Secondary
     - Online searches
     - Books and articles
     - Trade associations, chambers of comme
   - Researching customers and industries

---
[9] Special thanks to Joe Mancuso for this concept.

consum
eral gov
census a
on the f
- Age
- Annua
- Ethnic
- Gende
- Geogr
- Intere
- Occup
- Type c
  apartn
- Spend

Market
given area. T
graphic locat
also delve int
their homes.
demographi
Many ki
ing Office. T
is sold onlin

Industry R

Industry re
ment of busi
trends, new
to start a rec
ing. Is it grov
the major cc
What kind o

To mak
tify your ind
tion (NAICS
generally us
digits), you
and SIC cod
*System: Uni
sification M*
NAICS code
epcd/naics02
tions until y

Once yo
find statistic
Standard an
.census.gov),
and *Bizmine*
number of f
cases there a
ous other so
tions as:

- What is
- What is
  or neigl

- **Competitor Web sites:** Look for annual reports, which are available to
  the public and reveal marketing and other information about a company. Annual reports provide information for benchmarking and include industry insights. In addition, check out their blogs and
  newsletters. It is amazing what you can find if you just look!

Market Research Helps You Know Your Customer

Before you can put a marketing plan in place and deliver your competitive
advantage to your customers, you will need to find out who your customers
are or *can be*. **Market research** is the process of finding out:

- Who your potential customers are
- Where you can reach them
- What they want and need
- How they behave
- What the size of your potential market is

Through market research, business owners ask prospective customers
questions. President Woodrow Wilson once stated proudly, "I not only use
all the brains that I have, but all that I can borrow."

Whether your customers are consumers or other businesses, you will
want to get into your current and potential customers' minds and find out
what they really think about topics such as:

- Your product or service
- The name of your business
- Your location
- Your logo and branding materials
- Your proposed prices
- Your promotional efforts

Market research helps you get a fix on who your customers are, including such information as:

- How old are they?
- What kind of income do they earn?
- What are their hobbies and interests?
- What is their family structure?
- What is their occupation?
- What is the benefit your product or service offers that would best at-
  tract them?

The ideal customer should be at the center of your marketing plan.
This profile will guide every marketing decision you make. If your target
customer is affluent, for example, you might decide to price your product
fairly high to reflect its quality. If your target market is more middle income, you might choose a strategy of lower prices to beat the competition.

Do You Know 10 People Who Love Your Product? You May Have a Winner!

Not everybody has to like your product. What's important is that some people love it—a lot.

Woman con...
about bankir...
ans at the Li...
Mall in Miar...
(© Jeffrey G...
Researchers...

sought U.S. Food
tional use.

For services,
ever, extending th
Starting a new cy

Is Your Marke

Figuring out whe
market is close to
in your market alr
has a 39 percent
phones.[7] But that
troduced its Shor
to be sent betwee
Finnish teenagers
the technology sp
ment ideas about
they sold cell pho

Market Pos
Competitiv

Performance Objective 4
Position your product or
service within your market.

After deciding whi
to decide what po
segments. *Position*
uct occupies relat
market **positionii**
from others being
can do that by focu
Burger King pron
Burger King you c
pared and garnish

As you can se
clearly communic
demonstrating ho
tion your product/
brand that provide
velop a positioning

(Your business
(provides thes
market.)

Here is an ex
bile maker) that (
can families).

By the time yo
you will know you
ket intimately. It is
let marketing driv
the odds that your

[7] Mark Landler, "Nokia Pushes t...
[8] Adapted from Kotler and Armst...

Window of Opportunity

Early on, Simmons decided that he wanted to make his own way in the world. His father had been a teacher and his mother worked as a recreation coordinator. Both enjoyed stable jobs, but Simmons was not driven by a need for security—he wanted to live a fast-paced life and call his own shots. In 1977, Simmons, who never liked school very much, enrolled at the City College of New York as a sociology major. That year, something happened that permanently changed the course of his life. He went to hear a rap artist named Eddie Cheeba perform and was amazed to see how the rapper had cast a spell over the audience with his freestyle rhymes. In Simmons's own words:

Just like that, I saw how I could turn my life in another, better way. . . . All the street entrepreneurship I'd learned, I decided to put into promoting music.[12]

At that time, "rap" and "hip-hop" were underground musical styles, but Simmons set out to change this. He believed that rap music had the potential to reach a larger audience and so he teamed up with another aspiring rap producer named Rick Rubin. Rubin had built a recording studio for rap artists in his New York University dorm room. Together, they decided to transform Rick's "studio" into a viable record label. By 1985, Def Jam Records was officially underway.

Def Jam experienced its first surge of success when it scored a hit with Run DMC's remake of the Aerosmith classic "Walk This Way." Bridging the worlds of rock and rap music turned out to be a stroke of genius. Simmons and Rubin single-handedly introduced a whole new market of mostly white, suburban heavy-metal music fans to hip-hop. Suddenly, Run DMC was being featured on MTV, and rap was no longer an "underground" fad.

Marketing Insight—Authenticity Matters

Simmons learned an important lesson from Run DMC's success. He realized that these rap artists had gone to the top of the charts because they had remained true to their street style and musical origins. While Run DMC may have popularized wearing gold chains, Adidas sneakers, and nameplate belts among suburban teenagers, these were the fashions that its core audience of urban youth had already embraced. Simmons understood that being perceived as *authentic* was key to making it in his segment of the music industry.

You have to tell the truth. It endears you to the community. The [people] can smell the truth, and they're a lot smarter than the people who put the records out.[13]

Simmons knew how to market his product, and his ability to promote rap music and the hip-hop lifestyle was influenced by how close he was to it.

Simmons has maintained this philosophy of "keeping it real" throughout his business career. It permeates everything he does and is even reflected in his preference for wearing Phat Farm sweatshirts instead of Brooks Brothers suits. Since those early days, Simmons has gone on to launch many other business ventures, which are all geared toward the same target market—urban teens and young adults. This market has the power to influence the tastes and preferences of other consumers.

Simmons's Empire Grows

In 1999, Simmons sold his stake in Def Jam records to Polygram Records for over $100 million. He has since focused his energies on developing the various entertainment, fashion, and multimedia companies that make up Rush Communications. Simmons's business goals have evolved from promoting hip-hop music to developing new products and services for the urban youth market. One of his recent pet projects is the "Rush Card"—a prepaid debit card that will compete with costly check-cashing services that target urban youths who do not have bank accounts.

These days, Simmons is also using his status as a taste-maker and hip-hop entrepreneur to influence public debate about political issues. In

[12] Russell Simmons, *Life and Def: Sex, Drugs, Money + God* (New York: Crown Publishing, 2002).
[13] Jennifer Reingold, "Rush Hour," *Fast Company* magazine, no. 76, November 2003.

2002, he organized a "youth summit" in New York featuring hip-hop artists such as Jay-Z and Alicia Keyes. When Simmons put out a call to action over the airwaves, over 20,000 students showed up at New York's City Hall to protest the mayor's proposed cuts to the education budget. Simmons has demonstrated that he has the skill and sophistication to market ideas as well as products and services. Rumor has it that he may even decide to run for public office at some point. But, for now, he continues to sit at the helm of Rush Communications where he keeps his radar attuned to new opportunities in the marketplace.

Case Study Analysis

1. Why do you think Russell Simmons has been successful?
2. Describe the target market that Simmons is trying to appeal to in all of his business ventures. What does this target market value?
3. Simmons grew up surrounded by hip-hop music and culture. In what ways did this give him an advantage in the marketplace? How might his "insider's knowledge" also function as a limitation?
4. Brainstorm a business idea that you could pitch to Russell Simmons that would be appropriate for Rush Communications. What market research would you need to conduct in advance to assess whether or not your idea has the potential to be successful?
5. Russell Simmons invested $5,000 to start Def Jam and then later sold his business to Polygram Records for $100 million. Calculate Simmons's return on investment (ROI).

Case Sources

Jennifer Reingold, "Rush Hour," *Fast Company* magazine, no. 76, November 2003.

Russell Simmons, *Life and Def: Sex, Drugs, Money + God* (New York: Crown Publishing, 2002).

Chapter 5
Developing the Right Marketing Mix

> *"I found that if you give the consumer a snapshot where he could see himself as he really is and the way he wants to be portrayed, people really respond to it."*
>
> —Thomas Burrell, founder, the Burrell Communications Group

All of BMW's marketing—from the price of the cars to the advertisements in magazines catering to people who buy expensive things—is designed to convince customers that it makes luxury automobiles. If BMW lowered the price of a sedan, would that damage the customer's belief in BMW's competitive advantage as a provider of luxury cars? This is the question that working through the next step of the marketing process will help answer. BMW illustrates the importance of getting the marketing mix—product, price, place, and promotion—right. Without an effective combination of these elements, your business is likely to fail.

Performance Objectives

1. Combine the "Four P's"—product, price, place, and promotion—into a marketing mix.
2. Choose the attributes of your product or service.
3. Choose your pricing strategically.
4. Decide on the location that is best for your customers.
5. Determine the mix of promotion to use for your business.
6. Find a way to add the fifth "P"—philanthropy—to your business.
7. Use breakeven analysis to evaluate your marketing plan.

The Four Marketing Factors

The four marketing factors, referred to as the "Four P's," which together will communicate your marketing vision and competitive advantage to your customer:

- Product
- Price
- Place
- Promotion

If you tweak one "P," you must pay attention to how it affects the others. If you raise your price, for example, are you now still selling the product in the right place? Or will you need to move to a location that will put you in contact with consumers willing to pay the new price? Where will you promote your product at the higher price? Will you have to take out ads in different magazines or newspapers to reach these more affluent consumers?

Your marketing goal is to bring the right product to the right place at the right price with the right promotion.

As you choose the elements of your marketing plan, always keep your vision in mind. What is the benefit your product or service is providing to consumers?

Performance Objective 1

Combine the "Four P's"—product, price, place, and promotion—into a marketing mix.

- *Product:* The product (or service) should meet or create a customer need. The product is the entire bundle, such that the packaging is also part of the product. Your customer might throw away your packaging but that does not mean it is unimportant. Starbucks revolutionized the coffee shop by creating different cup sizes and using Italian names.
- *Price:* Generally, a product has to be priced low enough so the public will buy it and high enough for the business to make a profit. Price should also reflect your marketing vision. If you are marketing a luxury item, a relatively low price might confuse the consumer, who will be led to wonder about its quality.
- *Place:* The location where you choose to market your product, whether a retail storefront, in a customer's home, on an online storefront, or from a cart on the street, must be where customers who will want or need it shop. Selling bathing suits on a beach in Alaska in February is not going to fill a customer need. Where should you go to bring your product or service to the attention of your market? If you are selling a luxury item, you will need to place it in stores that are visited by consumers who can afford it.
- *Promotion:* **Promotion** is the development of the popularity and sales of a product or service through advertising, publicity, and other promotional devices such as discount coupons or giveaways. **Publicity** is free, while advertising is purchased. If a newspaper writes an article about your business, it is publicity. If you buy an ad in that newspaper, you are advertising.

Product: What Are You Selling?

As we have seen, Steve Jobs and Stephen Wozniak were in their early twenties in California when Jobs sold his Volkswagen mini-bus, and Wozniak his Hewlett-Packard calculator, to raise $1,300 to start Apple Computer. They built the computers themselves in Wozniak's parents' garage.

Jobs and Wozniak made sales calls to every computer store in the area with their one sample computer and finally convinced a small store in Mountain View to order 50. The store agreed to pay Apple $548 for each machine.

Jobs and Wozniak had one month to build the 50 computers, but they did not have the money to buy the necessary parts. Using the order, though, the partners found a parts supplier that was willing to give them $25,000 worth of parts on 30-day credit. They started building the computers. By the end of the month, they had built 100, and delivered 50 to the store in Mountain View. They paid the supplier back for the parts on the 29th day. Apple has come a long way since then.

Your business, no matter how humble its beginnings, may have the potential to grow into a multimillion-dollar business, so it is important that you think through every step of its development. How you define and refine your product or service will have a tremendous impact on your ability to grow.

Select Your Product or Service Wisely

A *product* is something that exists in nature or is made by human industry, usually to be sold, while a service is *intangible*—work, skills, or expertise provided in exchange for a fee. Your product will be defined by its physical attributes (i.e., size, color, weight, shape), its performance characteristics (i.e., speed, strength, efficiency, durability), as well as its pricing, "branding," and delivery. It is the total "bundle" that people are buying. A dirty rock on a piece of cardboard with a scrawled, handwritten price is a much different product from one that has been cleaned, polished, placed in a nest of attractive packing material on an attractive display in an upscale retail store.

◀ Performance Objective 2
Choose the attributes of your product or service.

A parallel exists for services. Think about a one-person cleaning service where the individual arrives in an old, battered van and appears tired and unkempt, and compare it with neatly dressed, uniformed personnel that arrive in a new vehicle (with the name of the company on the side of the truck) to work as a team. Retail service businesses sell directly to the end consumer, but there are also service businesses that serve wholesale or manufacturing customers.

The selection of your product or service and its branding will be a critical part of your marketing mix.

Focus Your Brand

The key to building a successful brand is to focus tightly on the primary benefit you want customers to associate with your business. Marketing expert Al Ries explains that the most successful businesses focus their marketing so that they come to own a category in the customer's mind.[1] You want to own a benefit the way Volvo owns "safety," or Federal Express, with its guaranteed overnight delivery.

Even entertainers can become a brand. Oprah Winfrey is among the most recognized and wealthiest celebrities in the world today. She has become the head of a global media empire and philanthropist.[2] From her roots in Nashville radio, Winfrey has

Oprah Winfrey, philanthropist and media mogul.
(AP Wide World Photos)

[1] Al Ries, *Focus: The Future of Your Company Depends on It* (New York: Harper Collin, 2005).
[2] Information available at *http://www.oprah.com.*

become a media mogul with such well-recognized names as *The Oprah Winfrey Show; O, The Oprah Magazine; O at Home; Oprah & Friends Radio;* Harpo Films, and Oprah.com.[3]

Ford's Costly Failure—The Edsel

One of the most notorious examples of a product that failed due to lack of focus is the car Ford introduced in 1956, the Edsel.

Ford tried to include every kind of gadget and design element the company thought consumers might possibly want in a car. They also manufactured more than 20 different models, at varying prices that overlapped some Ford and Mercury models, thus confusing the public as to which brand was a step up from which. The goal seemed to be to try to appeal to everyone, but Ford soon learned that a car with something that appealed to almost everyone appealed to no one! The Edsel had no outstanding benefit that could be clearly marketed. When it was introduced on the market, it bombed completely.

Even millions of dollars of marketing will not make consumers buy a product they do not want. Ford spent more money on advertising the Edsel than had ever been spent before on one line of cars. Three years and $350 million later, Ford pulled the plug on the Edsel.

Ford's Focus on Success—The Mustang

Ford learned from the Edsel mistake, however. When it introduced the Mustang in 1964, it focused very clearly on a target market of people from 20 to 30 years old. Everything about the car—from its design to the colors it came in—was focused on appealing to young drivers. The marketing described the Mustang as "for the young at heart." Only one model was offered. The Mustang was a huge success.

Interestingly, Ford tried to offer some luxury and four-door versions of the Mustang a few years later. Sales dropped—probably because the brand had started to lose focus. Today, the Mustang remains one of Ford's stronger sellers.

How to Build Your Brand

You can build your own brand with these steps:

- *Choose a business name that is easy to remember, describes your business, and helps establish* **mindshare**: which is the degree to which *your* business comes to mind when a consumer needs something that your product or service could provide.
- *Create a logo that symbolizes your business to the customer:* A **logo** (short for *logotype*) is an identifying symbol for a product or business. A logo is printed on the business's stationery, business cards, and flyers. When a logo has been registered with the U.S. Patent and Trademark Office to protect it from being used by others, it is called a **trademark**, which is any word, name, symbol, or device used by a manufacturer or merchant to distinguish a product. The Nike "swoosh" is an example of a logo. So are McDonald's "golden arches."

A company uses a trademark so that people will recognize its product instantly, without having to read the company name or even having to think

---

[3] The Oprah Winfrey Show and Oprah & Friends are registered trademarks of Harpo, Inc. *O, The Oprah Magazine* and *O at Home* are registered trademarks of Harpo Print LLC.

The world's most well-known trademark—McDonald's golden arches.
(© James Leynse/CORBIS SABA)

about it. Rights to a trademark are reserved exclusively for its owner. To infringe on a trademark is illegal.

- *Develop a good reputation:* Make sure your product or service is of the quality you promise. Always treat your customers well. You want people to feel good when they think of your brand or hear it mentioned.

Global Impact...

Protecting Your Trademark Worldwide

If you plan to do business outside the United States, you will need to make sure your trademark is properly registered and protected. The International Trademark Association (*http://www.inta.org*) is an excellent resource. It can help you apply for a Community Trade Mark (CTM), for example, which provides protection for a trademark in the 25 current member countries of the European Union (Austria, Belgium, the Czech Republic, Cyprus, Denmark, Estonia, Finland, France, Germany, Greece, Hungary, Ireland, Italy, Latvia, Lithuania, Luxembourg, Malta, the Netherlands, Poland, Portugal, Slovakia, Slovenia, Spain, Sweden, and the United Kingdom).

Step into the Shoes...

Trademarking a Domain

In 1998, Laurel Touby purchased the domain name *www.hire-minds.com* for her online job listings network for New York City journalists and editors, but she failed to apply for a trademark. By 1999, Touby had a thriving site. She was charging publishers looking for writers and editors $100 per ad, and her clients included many national publications.

Soon, however, she got a phone call from a recruiter for Boston computer companies informing her that she had purchased all the domain names around Touby's and was applying for the trademark for her domain name, as well. As your business grows, or if you are starting an online business, you may want to purchase a domain name for your Web site(s).

The domain name is the first part of the URL; it ends in ".com," for a commercial business, ".org," for a not-for-profit, or ".net," for a network. Check out InterNIC, *http://www.internic.net,* where you can register a domain name. If you do purchase a domain name, seriously consider spending an additional $200 to have it trademarked. The U.S. Patent and Trade Office will award the trademark to whichever business can prove it used the domain name in trade first.

- ***Create a brand personality:*** Is your brand's "personality" youthful and casual, like the Gap? Safe and serious, like Volvo? Customers will respond to brand personality and develop a relationship with it. Personality will reinforce your name and logo.
- ***Communicate your brand personality to your target market:*** What type of advertising will best reach your target market? Where should you put flyers? Which newspapers or magazines does your target market read?

Always present yourself and your business in such a way that people will have confidence in your product or service. Anything that harms your reputation will damage your sales and profits. Anything that boosts your reputation will have a positive impact on your business.

Here are seven things you can do to build and maintain your brand and its reputation:

1. Provide a high-quality product or service.
2. Maintain the highest ethical standards.
3. Define your product or service clearly—focus!
4. Treat your employees well.
5. Make all your advertisements positive and informative.
6. Associate your company with a charity.
7. Become actively involved in your community.

Price: What It Says About Your Product

Performance Objective 3 ▶

Choose your pricing strategically.

According to *Guerrilla Marketing Attack* by Jay Conrad Levinson, a study of consumers in the furniture industry found that price came ninth, when consumers were asked to list factors affecting their decision to make a purchase.[4] Quality was the number two influence on buying patterns, and confidence in the product was number one. Service was third.

Although your business may not behave exactly like the furniture industry, the lesson here is that simply undercutting your competitors' prices will not necessarily win you the largest market share. For one thing, consumers tend to infer things about the quality or specialness of a product or service based on its price. It is important, therefore, for entrepreneurs to consider not only the economics but also the psychology of pricing. Studying the pricing strategies of your competitors will tell you a lot about the importance of psychological pricing in your market.

An increasingly popular strategy is "value" pricing, which began in the 1990s as a reaction to the "Glitzy Eighties," when marketers used high prices to pitch luxury and extravagance. Companies like Wal-Mart and Procter & Gamble shifted to value pricing—offering more for less by underscoring a product's quality, while at the same time featuring its price. Value pricing is not just price-cutting. It means finding the balance between quality and price that will give your target customers the value they seek.

Simply selling at a lower price will not necessarily win you a large market share.

New entrepreneurs often assume they should simply sell their product or service at the lowest price they can afford. Sometimes, however, consumers assume that a low price indicates low quality.

Keystoning: The Retailer's Rule of Thumb

Retailers who buy goods wholesale and resell them in stores sometimes **keystone**, or double, the cost of goods sold, as a rule of thumb for estimating

---

[4] Jay Conrad Levinson, *Guerrilla Marketing Attack* (Boston: Houghton Mifflin, 1989).

what price to charge. If you buy cell phones for $22 each from a wholesaler, for example, selling them for $44 each in your store will probably cover your costs and provide you with an acceptable profit.

Keystoning is a good way to estimate a price. If you are selling hacky-sack balls that cost $4, consider selling them for $8. When pricing, however, the entrepreneur must always be sensitive to the market and to what competitors are charging.

Other Pricing Strategies

Other pricing strategies include the following:

- *Cost-plus:* This method simply takes your cost and adds a desired profit margin. However, it fails to take marketing vision and market conditions into consideration.
- *Penetration:* This strategy uses a low price during the early stages of a product's life cycle to gain market share. Japanese companies employed this method to dominate the VCR market. However, it is often difficult to increase your price once you start at a low price point.
- *Skimming:* The opposite of penetration strategy, skimming seeks to charge a high price during the introductory stage of the PLC, when the product is novel and has few competitors. RCA used this strategy when it introduced color television.
- *Meet or Beat the Competition:* This is a common strategy for service businesses. Airlines tend to compete intensely by lowering their ticket prices. The more you can show that your business is different from your competition, however, the less you will have to compete with your price. When Sir Richard Branson started Virgin Atlantic Airways, he offered massages and individual videos at each seat. His marketing emphasized how much fun it was to fly on Virgin. This strategy was successful, even though Virgin did not always offer the lowest fares.

Pick a price that communicates your competitive advantage to your market segment. The same goes for the rest of the Four P's—make all your business decisions market-driven and you will be successful.

A Typical Markup

Depending upon whether you manufacture, distribute, or retail your products, or perform a combination of these steps, you will have to keep end price and industry markups in mind. A **markup** is an increase in the price of a product to cover expenses and create a profit for the seller. The manufacturer and retailer typically keystone the cost to determine a selling price. A wholesaler usually marks up by about 20 percent to figure the selling price, since the wholesaler is only providing a service (stocking the manufacturer's product) for the retailer. If the wholesaler were to charge too high a price, the retailer might try to buy directly from the manufacturer and "eliminate the middleman."

Here is how a dollar of manufacturing cost gets marked up:

Manufacturer
$1.00 Manufacturer's Cost
$2.00 Manufacturer's Price

  Wholesaler
  $2.00 Wholesaler's Cost
  $2.40 Wholesaler's Price

Retailer

$2.40 Retailer's Cost

$4.80 Retailer's Price

Consumer

$4.80 Consumer's Cost

There can be other links in this chain besides these four. A manufacturer may have to buy raw materials or manufactured parts to make the product. There may be other middlemen, such as agents, brokers, or other wholesalers, between manufacturer and wholesaler or between wholesaler and retailer.

Exercise

Using the markups described previously, calculate the price at each link in the distribution chain for a blouse that cost the manufacturer $4.75 to make:

Manufacturer's cost: $_____

Manufacturer's price: $_____

Wholesaler's cost: $_____

Wholesaler's price: $_____

Retailer's cost: $_____

Retailer's price: $_____

Because many entrepreneurs sell a variety of items at different retail prices with different wholesale costs, it would be time-consuming to try to figure an acceptable markup for each item. Instead, retailers use *percentage* markups. Every item in a gift shop, for instance, could be marked up 50 percent.

$$\text{Wholesale Cost} \times \text{Markup \%} = \text{Markup}$$

If you know the markup and wholesale cost of an item, you can figure the markup percentage using this formula:

$$\frac{\text{Markup}}{\text{Wholesale Cost}} \times 100 = \text{Markup \%}$$

Let's say the gift shop buys cards for $2 each from the wholesaler and sells them for $3 each.

$$\text{Markup} = \$3.00 - \$2.00 = \$1.00$$

If the gift shop owner finds, while doing her monthly income statement, that she is not generating enough profit, she can raise her markup percentage slightly to try to increase revenue. Or she can try to find a cheaper wholesale supplier to lower costs.

Place: Location, Location, Location!

Performance Objective 4

Decide on the location that is best for your customers.

Regarding place, the type of business you are running will influence your choice of location. For a retail business, location is the key to attracting customers. Ideally, you will want your store or business to be where your market is. Site location is one of the most important decisions for a retailer. This is why you did the work of consumer and market analysis to figure out who your customers were. You should know where they shop. Your goal is to find a location you can afford that is also convenient for your customers.

Wal-Mart has done an efficient job of choosing locations that were perfect for its customers yet underserved by similar retailers. Wal-Mart was the first mass-merchandise store to choose locations in rural and semirural markets. This strategy has been so successful that other stores now seek to be located next to a Wal-Mart!

Of course, the Internet has made it possible for an entrepreneur to start a retail business out of his or her home and reach customers all over the world. This has led to the belief that online stores can forgo the expense of renting a location that caters to foot traffic. As the old saying goes, however, you can lead a horse to water but you can't make him drink. How do you get your customers to your site, and then induce them to buy? If you are going to start a retail business online, you must figure out how you will attract customers to your Web site (*market* the site).

For nonretail businesses, the key to location might be cost or convenience, rather than proximity to the market. Wholesale businesses require a great deal of storage space and are best located in areas where rent or property costs are low. They look for low-rent, low-tax areas with warehouse space, and roads for trucks and vans.

The Internet is making it easier for people who provide services—such as graphic or Web site design, writing/editing, or accounting—to start businesses at home. Communication with clients is easy via e-mail, and the overhead costs are certainly minimal! On the other hand, working at home requires discipline and a tolerance for isolation. If you are the sort of person who would be miserable spending your workday alone, it is probably not for you.

Promotion: Advertising + Publicity

Promotion is the use of advertising and publicity to get your marketing message out to your customers. Advertising, as discussed in Chapter 2, is paid promotion that is intended to support increased sales of your product or service. Examples of advertising include television commercials, billboards, and magazine ads. Publicity is free mention of a company, person, event, product, or service in media such as newspapers and magazines or on radio and television stations.

◀ **Performance Objective 5**
Determine the mix of promotion to use for your business.

If your business is providing an unusual service, you might be able to get a local newspaper to do an article. That article would be publicity for your business—you did not pay for it, yet consumers will learn about your service by reading the article. If you buy an ad in that same newspaper, on the other hand, you're using advertising to promote your business.

Publicity is sometimes referred to as **public relations (PR)**, as discussed in Chapter 2, and is defined by the Institute of Public Relations as, "[T]he planned and sustained effort to establish and maintain goodwill and mutual understanding between an organization and its public." Always save any publicity you receive. Frame and display articles prominently in your place of business (if you do not have an office, carry them in a portfolio that can easily be shown to prospective clients), and make copies to send or hand out, when appropriate. Each item of publicity has enormous value. Consumers give publicity credibility because it was not paid for.

Among the many methods for advertising and promoting your business (in alphabetical order) are:

- *Advertising Specialties:* "Freebies" are always a draw with customers, but do not disappoint them with gifts that look and feel cheap. The best giveaways are those that are useful, such as pens, on which

A billboard in the Bronx, New York City.
(Jochen Tack/DAS FOTOARCHIV., Peter Arnold, Inc.)

prospective customers will see your business name and contact information. Visit a wholesaler to investigate discount prices on quantities of calculators, watches, pens, or other useful items.

- *Banner Ads:* These are the advertisements that run on Web sites.
- *Billboards:* Billboards are often in highly visible locations and use short, punchy copy that motorists can grasp at a glance.
- *Blogs:* A **blog** (short for Web log) is a journal that appears on the Internet periodically (perhaps daily) and is intended for public reading. Businesses provide blogs, often written by their owners, to create a personal connection with the customers.
- *Broadcast Media:* Communication outlets that use airspace, such as radio and television, make up the broadcast media. Advertising often can be purchased or publicity garnered for your business from local, as well as national, media outlets.
- *Brochures:* Place brochures in "take one" boxes around town.
- *Business Cards:* This should include the name, address, and contact information (phone and fax numbers, e-mail address, and Web site) of your business, as well as your own name and title. A card can also include a short catchy phrase or motto, such as *For Sound Advice* if you are operating a stereo-repair business. Always carry some cards with you to hand out to potential clients and contacts.
- *Catalogs:* When you have built a list of 10,000 names, it might be time to pay for a color catalog, because the price of printing per catalog will be sufficiently low. You can produce a two-color catalog with even fewer names.
- *Coupons:* Send out discount (price break) coupons as an incentive to first-time customers, or offer discounts for a limited time. This will encourage people to try your product or service. There are businesses that package coupons from different businesses into a mailer and send them to targeted audiences.
- *Direct Mail:* When you make a sale, get the customer's address, e-mail address, and other information. Once you have developed a

Handing out business cards is one way to advertise yourself, and your product or service.
(© Don Farrall/Getty Images)

mailing list, send out cards or letters regularly, informing customers of sales and special events. You can send e-mail updates, but be sure to always include a sentence such as the following: "If you wish to be removed from this list, please type REMOVE in the subject line of your response." Mailing-list software is easy to use, keep organized, and print labels from. Sophisticated customer-tracking programs are also available.

- *Directories:* Telephone books and lists from professional associations and chambers of commerce are examples of directories. They can be an excellent source of customer leads and good advertising venues. They tend to have a long shelf life and can be used repeatedly.

- *Flyers:* Flyers are one-page ads you can create on a computer or even by hand (if you have artistic talent). Fax your flyer to customers on your mailing list; photocopy and distribute it at church functions, sporting events, under windshield wipers, or hand them out on the street. Flyers can also include discount coupons.

- *Networking:* Networking, as discussed in Chapter 1, is the exchange of information and contacts and, when done efficiently and courteously, can serve as an excellent promotional vehicle.

- *Newsletters:* Company newsletters have become easy to produce for distribution by e-mail and in hard copy. Be certain to include interesting and useful information in an attractive, well-designed format. Remember, it will need to be interesting to your target market in terms they understand.

- *Print Media:* Newspapers, magazines, newsletters (church, community, child care, etc.), the *Yellow Pages*, and other published forms of written communication present advertising opportunities for your business.

- *Promotional Clothing:* T-shirts or caps bearing the name of your business can turn you and your friends into "walking advertisements." You could also put the name of your business on shopping bags.

- *Public Speaking:* Taking advantage of opportunities to address members of your target audience as a guest speaker or paid professional can build your credibility and gain you recognition and customers.

- *Samples or Demonstrations:* Offer samples of your product to potential customers who pass by your business. Or take samples to a high-density location, such as a park or town square. If you are selling a service, consider demonstrating it outdoors or in a mall (get permission first!). When you open your business, you can give away samples of your product to encourage customers to tell their friends about it.

- *Signs:* One of the simplest ways to gain recognition is to use effective signage. Keep it simple and show your brand!

- *Special Events:* Hold contests, throw parties, or put together unusual events to attract attention and customers. Contests and sweepstakes can gather valuable names for your mailing list. Or, participate in special events yourself to gain publicity for your business.

- *Sponsorships:* Sponsoring a local sports team is a great way to involve your business in the community and meet potential customers. Sponsorships are a way of advertising. Just be certain that the audience for the event fits into your target market.

- *Telemarketing:* Once you have an extensive customer list, you can use it to invite people to events or sales. You may also be able to purchase lists. Be careful that you adhere to rules and guidelines with regard to telemarketing and that you respect "Do not call" requests. Sometimes it is worthwhile to hire professional telemarketers.

- **Toll-Free Numbers:** Contact your phone company to find out how to set up an 800 number, so customers can call you for free. Some long-distance providers offer special discounts to small-business owners.
- **Web Sites:** In today's business environment, customers have come to expect quality Web sites. You will have to decide whether customers can order directly from your site.

The following sections highlight key aspects of selected topics in promotion.

Marketing Materials Should Reinforce Your Competitive Advantage

All promotional items for your business should reflect and reinforce your marketing vision, which in turn will reinforce your competitive advantage. They should include the name of your business, your logo, and a slogan, if you have one. All your business materials, in fact, such as order forms, invoices, and receipts, should also reflect and reinforce your business's competitive advantage.

You will have a much stronger impact if all your business materials are tied together with a strong, coordinated image. This should extend beyond your logo into the format, font style, colors, and "look" of your materials. As you create your stationery and business cards (identity set), advertisements, publicity pieces, and brochures, the consistency of your image will help to convey your competitive advantage. If it is done well, your image will be in alignment with your strengths and you will be positioned for success. If this is done poorly, you will lack credibility and it can harm, if not destroy, your chances of success.

Good marketing materials serve three functions:

1. Creating them will organize your business thinking.
2. They will enable you to teach others in your company about the business.
3. They will enable you to go into the marketplace and sell your product or service.

Where to Advertise? Visualize Your Customer

An effective advertisement for a business typically concentrates on the benefit the product or service provides the customer. This is why it is important that you carry through your consumer analysis. You need to know who your customers are and what their lifestyle is in order to know how to effectively reach them. If you are advertising a snowboarding trip, it would be a waste of money to take out an ad in a magazine featuring tropical vacations. By visualizing and knowing your customer, you will avoid wasting money on people who won't be interested in your product or service.

The Media

There are many places to advertise and publicize your business. These are referred to collectively as the **media**, which includes the print and broadcast categories listed previously, as well as the Internet. The trick will be to choose the most effective outlets for your advertising dollars, which may be quite limited. Critical factors to consider when purchasing media are reach and frequency, as well as cost per impression. **Reach** is defined as the number of

A Print Ad Has Five Parts

1. **Headline** (or Title)
2. **Deck** (or Subhead)
3. **Copy** (or Text)
4. **Graphics** (Photos or Drawings)
5. **Logo**

members of your target audience that will be exposed to the advertising. **Frequency** is how often they will be exposed to it. For example, a daily newspaper may reach 500,000 people one time. A directory may reach 2 million people 12 times a year. An important consideration in advertising is the "waste." If you wanted to reach 25- to 35-year-old working women with children in San Francisco, you would consider advertising in the *San Francisco Chronicle*. There may be too much waste, but it may be the best choice available to you. When you calculate the cost per *impression* (cost of the advertising divided by the number of times people see it), you can see if it makes sense. Sometimes it might be more logical to purchase advertising in a smaller, more targeted publication. Other times, the opposite is true.

- *Print Media:* Newspapers, magazines, and newsletters are examples of print media. The *Yellow Pages* of the telephone book are also print advertising. It is not always the largest, most well-recognized newspaper or magazine that is best for your business. In fact, you may find that small community newspapers or lifestyle publications are both better targeted and more economical (consider putting a coupon offer in a neighborhood newspaper). A yearlong study of newspaper advertising determined that a potential customer needs to see an ad at least nine times before the marketing message penetrates.[5] In addition, the study found that, for every three times a consumer sees an ad, he or she ignores it twice. This implies that a consumer will have to see your ad 27 times before actually buying something.

  If you take out a newspaper ad that runs three times a week, therefore, commit to running it for nine weeks at the very least. The most common advertising mistake entrepreneurs make is to give up too soon. One gauge of how effective a given advertising medium will be for your business is to observe it for a while and see whether your competitors use it regularly. If they do, they are probably seeing a good return on their investment, so you should, too.

- *Television:* Even though TV advertising rates are very high, an entrepreneur with a new business can sometimes get them lowered or even get a free mention (publicity) on local cable stations. If you are in a position to purchase commercial TV or radio advertising, consider going with a media-buying service, instead of purchasing it yourself (to avoid paperwork and confusion), or hiring an advertising agency (which will charge quite a bit of money and probably contract with a media-buying service anyway). Media-buying services are granted the same 15 percent discount as advertising agencies, but they generally return 10 percent of the savings to you, keeping 5 percent as their fee. You can find media buyers in the *Yellow Pages.*

---

[5] Jay Conrad Levinson, *Guerrilla Advertising* (Boston: Houghton Mifflin, 1994).

- *Radio:* Advertising on radio is sold in a variety of ways, with prices based upon the length of your ad, the time of day it will run, and the duration and frequency. Radio stations can provide you with sophisticated data regarding their listeners, so that you can more readily determine whether there is a good fit with your target market. University and local community radio stations often do not carry advertising, but may be willing to mention a new business venture that has an interesting or unusual angle.

Print, Audio, and Video Brochures

Advertising can get people interested in your business but, before they buy, prospects will almost certainly want more information. Depending on your business, brochures will enable you to provide that information and turn interest into a sale.

At the bottom of every print ad you run, offer to send a brochure. When you mail the brochure, include a personal letter thanking the prospective customer for requesting it. If you do not hear back in a few weeks, send a follow-up note. You are establishing one-to-one contact with someone you did not know before—the kind of contact that can lead to a sale. The brochure can actually close the sale itself, by providing a toll-free number to call.

Whether you use print, audio, or video brochures will depend on your budget and your business. Some suggestions from Jay Levinson's *Guerrilla Advertising* are:[6]

- Print brochures should fit into a standard envelope, make ordering simple, and connect closely with your advertising.
- Audio brochures work when visuals aren't necessary to sell your product or service, and should run between 10 and 20 minutes. Many U.S. motorists have CD players in their cars and are good candidates for audio brochures.
- Video brochures should run between 5 and 10 minutes and describe your business verbally and visually. If your business has ever been profiled on a television show, you've already got the centerpiece of your video brochure!

Generating Publicity

Publicity is very important for a small business, which often has a negligible advertising budget. To get publicity, you will need to mail or fax a pitch letter and a press release to the magazine, newspaper, TV station, or radio station you hope to interest.

A **pitch letter** "pitches" the story. It tells the person reading it why he or she should be interested in your business. A **press release** is an announcement sent to the media to generate publicity and states the who, what, when, where, and why of a story. A pitch letter allows you to explain the story behind the press release and why it would be interesting and relevant to the media outlet's readers, listeners, or viewers.[7]

Before mailing or faxing a pitch letter and press release, call or e-mail the outlet and ask to whom you should direct the pitch. Say something like, "My name is Jason Hurley and I'm a young entrepreneur with a downtown delivery/messenger service. I'd like to send WKTU a press release about the commitment we have just made to donate 10 hours of free delivery service

---

[6] Levinson, *Guerrilla Advertising*.
[7] Special thanks to Tom Philips of COMPTWP, and Jan Legnitto for the information in this chapter.

per month to Meals on Wheels for Seniors. To whom should I direct a press release?" Sometimes you can find this information on the Internet.

Try to get to know the print, radio, and television journalists pertinent to your business so you can get publicity. The most effective way to get notice for your business is to call the reporters yourself. You might be tempted to hire a professional publicist, but most reporters are bombarded by these people and would rather hear directly from you. Take a whole day to make phone calls pitching your business and explaining why your story is worth writing about. Be totally honest and try to build friendships. Positive reporting develops most often because the writer comes to care about the entrepreneur. Once you establish rapport and credibility with reporters, they may begin to call you for stories, insights, and commentary.

Press releases can generate positive stories about your business in local newspapers and on radio stations. Make sure you send the release about a month before the event you are promoting. Follow up with a phone call 2 weeks later, and then 1 week after that (a week before the occasion). The precise timing will depend on the media outlet and its publication or broadcast schedule.

What's Your Story?

Younger entrepreneurs can have an advantage here, because few young people start their own businesses. The print, radio, and television journalists in your area may want to hear about you.

Bear in mind, however, that reporters are looking for stories. It is fine to send out a press release announcing the opening of your business, but be aware that it would not be a "story" until it is up and running. There is no point sending out a pitch letter and press release until you are actually in business and have a story to tell. The fact that your business is open doesn't necessarily translate into a story for reporters. You have to make the connection!

- What has happened to you or what have you done that would make you and your business an interesting story?
- Did you have to overcome any obstacles in order to start your business?
- Is your product or service unique, or is it something your community really needs?
- How has your business changed you and helped members of your community?

Answers to these questions will help reporters determine whether your story might be of interest to their readers or viewers. Reporters are very busy people, so keep your answers to these questions tight and concise. Try to find one focus or "angle" for your story. What's the "hook"? **Figure 5-1** shows a sample pitch letter.

Sample Press Release

In order to tell your story in a press release or to a reporter, you have to answer six questions: Who, what, when, where, why, and how? Who are you; what did you do; and when, where, why, and how did you do it?

A press release must provide contact information (name, phone, e-mail, and Web site) and answer the six questions (see **Figure 5-2**).

Follow Up a Press Release by Phone

Follow up your press releases with phone calls and e-mail. Try to reach the journalists directly. Be polite but persistent. Do not wait for a newspaper or

Avoid using the phrases "hopes to," "plans to," or "expects to" in your press releases. When reporters see those phrases, they know there is no story yet.

Figure 5-1 *Sample pitch letter.*

January 1, 2004

Joe Smith
100 Main St.
Anytown, NY   12345

Dear _____ :

When Malik Armstead opened his soul food take-out restaurant the Five Spot on Myrtle Avenue in Brooklyn, in 1996, he was taking a risk. He was putting all his savings into the business in a neighborhood that was far from fashionable. On the other hand, Malik came from a less-than-fashionable neighborhood himself, and, when he was still a teenager, an organization called the National Foundation for Teaching Entrepreneurship (NFTE, pronounced "nifty") believed that he could make it as an entrepreneur and gave him the skills to do so.

"NFTE taught me that you do not necessarily have to have a lot of money to start a business," says Malik. "I started my first business in high school with only $50."

- The restaurant is thriving, based entirely on word-of-mouth advertising, and has become a neighborhood staple, providing generous portions of high-quality soul food at reasonable prices.
- Other entrepreneurs have followed the 29-year-old Malik's lead. And as Clinton Hill has now been "discovered" by Manhattanites who can no longer find affordable apartments in Brooklyn Heights or Park Slope, the area is flourishing.
- Malik has hired many young people from the neighborhood. For two current employees, the Five Spot was their first job. One of them has been with the restaurant for over three years and has risen from dishwasher to sous chef.

On February 1st, Malik will expand the Five Spot from its current 800 square feet to 2,500 square feet, including a 60-foot mahogany bar and a 150-foot stage, as well as a full dining room. He will continue to serve great soul food while providing live entertainment by musicians from the neighborhood.

I invite you to meet and interview this young entrepreneur who has helped to transform a neighborhood. You are also invited to join us at the Five Spot for a special VIP party on February 1st at 9 P.M., where there will be free food, drink, and entertainment.

Sincerely,

radio station to return your call; call again (but do not make a pest of yourself); they receive many press releases every day.

As we have said, save all publicity you receive to show potential customers. Publicity has enormous value because it can attract more publicity and more customers. Remember, it has greater credibility for consumers than paid advertising.

The Fifth "P"—Philanthropy

There is a long, proud connection in the United States between entrepreneurs and **philanthropy,** a concern for human and social welfare that is

Figure 5-2 *Sample press release.*

FOR IMMEDIATE RELEASE JANUARY 1, 2004
For More Information Contact:
Malik Armstead — (718) 555-7839

Five Spot Soul Food Restaurant Expands with 60-Foot Bar and 150-Foot Stage
Popular Restaurant Revitalized Myrtle Avenue

On February 1st , Malik Armstead will expand the Five Spot Restaurant at 459 Myrtle Avenue from its current 800 square feet to 2,500 square feet, including a 60-foot mahogany bar and a 150-foot stage, as well as a full dining room. To celebrate, Malik is hosting a special VIP party on February 1st at 9 P.M., where there will be free food, drink, and entertainment.

The Five Spot will continue to serve great soul food while providing live entertainment by musicians from the neighborhood.

- The restaurant is thriving, based entirely on word-of-mouth advertising, and has become a neighborhood staple, providing generous portions of high-quality soul food at reasonable prices.
- Other entrepreneurs have followed the 29-year-old Malik's lead, and as Clinton Hill has now been "discovered" by Manhattanites who can no longer find affordable apartments in Brooklyn Heights or Park Slope, the area is flourishing.
- Malik has hired many young people from the neighborhood. For two current employees, the Five Spot was their first job. One of them has been with the restaurant for over three years and has risen from dishwasher to sous chef.

---

expressed by giving money through charities and foundations. A **foundation** is a *not-for-profit* organization that manages donated funds, which it distributes through grants to individuals, or to other nonprofit organizations that help people and social causes.

Many philanthropic organizations in the United States were established by entrepreneurs. As a business owner, you have a responsibility to help the communities you serve. The people and causes you choose to support should be those that matter to you. Your philanthropy may also generate positive publicity, because you can choose to promote the giving that you do. For this reason, marketing experts sometimes consider philanthropy as the fifth "P."

The Bill and Melinda Gates Foundation is one of the world's largest foundations, with over $33 billion in capital. This money comes from the personal wealth that they earned from Microsoft. As a private foundation, it is required by the federal government to give away 5 percent of the fair market value of its assets every year (this is usually less than the earnings on the fund's investments). The Gates Foundation provides a great deal of money annually (about $1.65 billion, based on a $33 billion fund) to other

◀ **Performance Objective 6**

Find a way to add the fifth "P"—philanthropy—to your business.

Entrepreneurial Wisdom...

Be sure to obtain videotapes of any mention you receive on television. There is no more powerful sales tool than a video that includes a story, however brief, on your business.

charities. These in turn use the money for social and community programs that the Gates Foundation supports, such as those relating to education and health care.

You can be philanthropic even if you have very little money to donate. You can give your time in volunteer work for an organization you believe in. If you know how to paint a house, or if you have some carpentry skills, you could contribute your efforts to help build homes for an organization such as Habitat for Humanity, which provides affordable housing for low-income families. If you love animals, volunteer at your local animal shelter.

To get some ideas on how to make your business socially responsible, check out Standards of Corporate Responsibility at http://www.svn.org/initiatives/standards.html.

Cause-Related Marketing

Cause-related marketing—marketing inspired by a commitment to a social, environmental, or political cause—is an easy way to work philanthropy into your business. You could donate a fixed percentage of your revenue (say, 1 or 2 percent) to a particular charity and then publicize this in your marketing. Or you could donate something from your business. If you own a sporting-goods store, you could donate uniforms to the local Little League team.

Encourage your employees to participate in charitable work, too. Volunteerism is a great way to improve morale and make a difference. AT&T pays its employees to devote one day a month to community service.

Gaining Goodwill

Many entrepreneurs try to make a difference in their communities by giving money and time to organizations that help people. Microsoft, for example, made it possible for the National Foundation for Teaching Entrepreneurship to develop an Internet-based entrepreneurship curriculum, BizTech. Microsoft has donated both money and computer programming expertise to this project.

Why would Microsoft do this?

- First, Bill Gates and other Microsoft executives believe in NFTE's mission and want to help youth learn about business. The Internet-based program makes it easier to teach entrepreneurship to greater numbers of young people around the world.
- Second, Microsoft gains publicity and **goodwill,** which is composed of intangible assets, such as reputation, name recognition, and customer relations. Goodwill can give a company an advantage over its competitors.

Step into the Shoes...

The Body Shop's Campaigns

One of the strongest examples of cause-related marketing by an entrepreneur is Anita Roddick's The Body Shop—a chain of cosmetic and skin-care product stores. The chain pays their employees to volunteer for community service. Roddick's company has run media campaigns on causes ranging from saving whales to preserving the rain forest, and each campaign has had the same result: It has attracted customers in droves.

Roddick (who passed away in 2007) once estimated that The Body Shop gained about $4 million per year in publicity from its various campaigns for solving social and environmental problems.

Nonprofit Organizations

Nonprofit organizations are those whose purpose is to serve a public or mutual benefit rather than to accrue profits for investors. The Internal Revenue Service classifies nonprofits under section 501(c)(3) in the tax code. These corporations are tax-exempt. This means they do not have to pay federal or state taxes, and they are not privately or publicly owned. Essentially, a board of directors controls the operations of a 501(c)(3) nonprofit organization.

Such well-known institutions as the Boys and Girls Clubs of America, the YMCA, the Girl Scouts, the Red Cross, and Big Brothers/Big Sisters are all examples of nonprofits. Their founders were social entrepreneurs and, although they did not earn large sums of money personally and could not sell the organization at a profit, they received great satisfaction and "made a difference." Wendy Kopp of Teach for America and Michael Bronner of UPromise are two examples of social entrepreneurs who founded innovative and successful nonprofit organizations, and are described below.

Teach for America and Upromise

Founded in 1991 by Wendy Kopp, Teach for America recruits recent college graduates to become public school teachers. The organization has trained some 17,000 young teachers, and placed them in 2-year teaching positions in under-resourced schools where they impact approximately 425,000 students annually.

Michael Bronner, a former marketing executive who became a social entrepreneur, started Upromise in 2001. Bronner felt strongly that the cost of sending a child to college had become much too expensive for most families. He believed that there needed to be a better way of helping families save money for college.

Bronner developed the idea that a portion of the money that families already spend on popular goods and services, such as groceries and toys, could go into a college savings account for their children. Upromise works with established corporations, such as AT&T, America Online, and Toys "R" Us. Every time a registered family makes a purchase from one of these companies, a percentage automatically goes into a special college savings account.

What Entrepreneurs Have Built

Many philanthropic organizations in this country were created by entrepreneurs who wanted to do good works with some of the wealth they had earned. Entrepreneurs have financed great museums, libraries, universities, and other important institutions. Some foundations created by famous entrepreneurs include the Rockefeller Foundation, the Coleman Foundation, the Charles G. Koch Foundation, the Ford Foundation, and the Goldman Sachs Foundation.

Some of the most aggressive entrepreneurs in American history, such as Andrew Carnegie, have also been the most generous. In 1901, after a long and sometimes ruthless business career, Carnegie sold his steel company to J. P. Morgan for $420 million. Overnight, Carnegie became one of the very richest men in the world. On retiring, he spent most of his time giving away his wealth to libraries, colleges, museums, and other worthwhile institutions that still benefit people today. By the time of his death, in 1919, Carnegie had given away over $350 million to philanthropic causes.

You Have Something to Contribute

You may not have millions of dollars to give to your community, yet. But there are many ways you can be philanthropic that will help others, get your employees excited, and create goodwill in your community:

- Pledge a percentage of your sales to a nonprofit organization you have researched, believe in, and respect. Send out press releases announcing your pledge.
- Become a mentor to a younger entrepreneur. Help that individual by sharing your contacts and expertise.
- Volunteer for an organization that helps your community. Find out how you can serve on its board of directors or fill another vital role.
- Sell your product to a charity that you support at a discount. The charity can then resell it at full price to raise money.
- When you give it some thought, you will realize that you have a lot to give. Remember, making a contribution does not necessarily mean giving money. You can donate time, advice, and moral support!

These days, customers have access to a lot of information about what companies do with their money. Make sure you are always proud of your business. Choose to support causes that are important to you and make business sense too. Philanthropy will strengthen your relationship with your customers because it goes beyond the sale and into what is truly important in their lives.

Marketing as a Fixed Cost

Let's say you want to launch a new software program. You have researched the consumers, pinpointed your market segment, and determined your marketing mix. You are now ready to implement a marketing plan that will get your vision "out there." There is one more question: Can you afford your marketing plan?

Marketing is part of your business's fixed costs. Marketing should not be budgeted as a percentage of sales, but rather as money that is needed to *drive* sales. As you remember, fixed costs are those that do not vary with sales; they can be remembered as USAIIRD:

- **U**tilities
- **S**alaries
- **A**dvertising
- **I**nsurance
- **I**nterest
- **R**ent
- **D**epreciation

There are also variable costs, such as commissions, that vary with sales. For a business to survive, though, it must be able to cover its fixed costs. Most fixed costs, such as rent, insurance, and utilities, are hard to cut back if your sales are slow.

Marketing costs are more flexible. They fall into the category of advertising and may also show up under salaries, if you hire a marketing consultant or full-time marketing staff. They will be a critical component in determining your company's breakeven point and its viability.

Calculate Your Breakeven Point

◄ Performance Objective 7

Use breakeven analysis to evaluate your marketing plan.

The question is this: Can you sell enough units to pay for your marketing plan? The breakeven point, as discussed in Chapter 2, is the point at which a business sells enough units to equal its fixed costs. If you estimate that your market is roughly 3 million people, but you have to sell 5 million units just to cover the cost of your marketing, the plan is not viable.

This is why calculating the breakeven point tells you if your marketing plan will work. It shows whether or not you can cover your fixed costs with the number of units you plan to sell. If not, the one place you can cut costs is advertising—your marketing plan. However, you should do this with care.

David is an artist who supports his painting career by creating unique tank tops with airbrush designs. The shirts are very popular with the young women in Manhattan's East Village, and David sells the shirts each weekend at a flea market next to Tower Records, on East 4th Street. Let's say he buys eight-dozen (96) tank tops for $576. He airbrushes them and sells them all at the weekend flea market for $1,152. David considers one tank top his unit of sale. Cost of goods sold (COGS) (without labor) would be calculated as $576/96 = $6 with selling price per unit $1152/96 = $12.

- How much did each tank top cost David? $ _____ *This is his cost of goods sold (COGS).*
- How much did he charge for each tank top? $ _____ *This is his selling price per unit.*
- David's unit of sale is one tank top.
- David's cost of goods sold is $6.
- David's selling price is $12.
  $12 (selling price per unit) − $6 (cost of goods sold per unit) = $6 (gross profit per unit)
- David's gross profit per unit is $6 per tank top.

Next, David needs to take a look at his fixed costs. Let's say he spends $150 a month on renting his space at the flea market, and $30 monthly on flyers (advertising). His monthly fixed costs are $150 + $30 = $180. How many tank tops does he have to sell to cover his fixed costs? Use the following formula:

$$\frac{\text{Fixed Cost}}{\text{Gross Profit per Unit}} = \text{Breakeven Units}$$

$$\frac{\text{Fixed Cost: } \$180}{\text{Gross Profit per Unit: } \$6} = 30 \text{ Breakeven Units}$$

David needs to sell 30 tank tops to cover his fixed costs. David typically sells about 20 tank tops each weekend, so in one month he can expect to sell:

$$20 \text{ units} \times 4 \text{ weekends} = 80 \text{ units}$$

David can definitely afford to spend $30 per month on flyers. He could even afford to add another expense to his marketing plan, such as getting business cards printed, or setting up a Web site, where customers could order shirts and find out where he will be selling each weekend.

We do need to recognize that David did not include any labor cost, as he paid himself from the profits. If David were to add in $3 per shirt of labor costs, his COGS would rise to $9 and his gross profit per unit would drop to $3. His new breakeven point would be 60 units. Any payment for the time it took to sell the shirts would come out of the profits.

Breakeven Analysis of a Restaurant

Here is a breakeven analysis from a chicken restaurant in Florida, called Mary Ann's.

Typically, a customer at Mary Ann's buys a bucket of chicken for $8 and a drink for $2, so the average sale per customer is $10. Therefore, a business unit is defined as a $10 sale. The cost of goods sold for each unit is $3.50 for the chicken and $0.50 for the drink, so the cost of goods sold is $4.00 per unit.

Mary Ann's fixed costs for a month are:

Utilities	$1,000
Salaries (indirect labor)	3,000
Ads	1,000
Interest	0
Insurance	1,000
Rent	2,000
	$8,000

The restaurant is open on average 30 days per month.

To figure out how many units Mary Ann's has to sell each month to break even, divide the gross profit per unit into the monthly fixed costs.

Gross Profit per Unit = Unit Price ($10) − COGS ($4.00) = $6.00

$$\text{Breakeven Units} = \frac{\text{Monthly Fixed Costs (\$8,000)}}{\text{Gross Profit per Unit (\$6.00)}} = 1,333 \text{ Units}$$

Since the store is open 30 days per month, to break even Mary Ann's has to make 45 average sales per day:

$$\frac{1,333 \text{ units}}{30 \text{ days}} = 44.33 \text{ (45 units per day)}$$

Breakeven is the point at which fixed costs are recovered by sales but no profit has yet been made. Once you have determined your breakeven point, the next question in the analysis is this: *Can my business reach breakeven in its relevant market?* In the previous example, can Mary Ann's reasonably expect to sell 45 buckets of chicken a day? The answer to this question for you will be in the market research you have conducted to get to this, the last step in creating a marketing plan. You should know the answer to this question. If not, you must conduct further research until you can confidently gauge whether or not you can afford your marketing plan. Revising your plan is another option, of course.

Breakeven analysis is a good tool for looking at all your costs and should be performed frequently. It is especially important after you have completed your marketing plan and before you open your business to see if your plan is realistic.

Chapter Summary

Now that you have studied this chapter, you can do the following:

1. Combine the "Four P's"—product, price, place, and promotion—into a marketing mix.
2. Determine the attributes of your product or service.

3. Strategically set your price.
   - Keystoning
   - Using other pricing strategies
   - Calculating markup
4. Locate your business for maximum effectiveness.
5. Choose where and how to advertise your business.
   - Promotion is the use of advertising and publicity to get your marketing message out to your customers.
   - Publicity is free mention of your business—in newspapers or magazines or on radio or TV.
   - An advertisement is a paid announcement that a product or service is for sale. Examples of advertising include television commercials, billboards, and magazine ads.
6. Use press releases and pitch letters to generate publicity for your business.
   - To get publicity, you will need to mail or fax a pitch letter and/or a press release to the magazine, newspaper, TV or radio station you hope to interest in your business.
   - A pitch letter "pitches" the story. It tells the person reading it why he or she should be interested in your business.
   - In the press release, you are announcing the who, what, when, where, why, and how of your story.
7. Decide how your business will help your community philanthropically.
   - Philanthropy is the giving of money, time, or advice to charities in an effort to help solve a social or environmental problem, such as homelessness, pollution, or cruelty to animals.
   - You can be philanthropic even if you have very little or no money to donate. You can donate your time by volunteering for an organization that is doing work you want to support.
8. Use breakeven analysis to evaluate your marketing plan.
   - Breakeven is the point at which a business sells enough units to cover its costs.
   - Breakeven analysis tells you if your marketing plan is viable. It shows whether or not you can cover your fixed costs with the number of units you plan to sell. If not, the one place you can cut costs is in your marketing plan.

Key Terms

blog	nonprofit organizations
cause-related marketing	not-for-profit
foundation	philanthropy
frequency	pitch letter
goodwill	press release
logo	promotion
keystone	public relations (PR)
markup	publicity
media	reach
mindshare	trademark

Selling Skills Are Essential to Business Success

Direct selling is dealing with a potential customer face to face and trying to convince him or her to make a purchase. Salespeople often become successful entrepreneurs because they hear what the customer needs and wants on a daily and personal basis.

Some great American entrepreneurs (in addition to Durant) who started out in sales:

- Ray Kroc, founder of McDonald's, as we saw in Chapter 1, was selling milkshake machines when he was inspired to turn the McDonald brothers' hamburger restaurant into a national operation.
- Aristotle Onassis was a wholesale tobacco salesman before becoming a multimillionaire in the shipping business.
- King C. Gillette was a traveling salesman when he invented the safety razor.
- W. Clement Stone started out selling newspapers at the age of six before going on to build a great fortune in the insurance industry.

Direct selling experience can be a great foundation for an entrepreneur.
(Digital Vision/Getty Images)

Selling Is a Great Source of Market Research

If a customer is dissatisfied, it is often the salesperson who hears the complaint. In that sense, selling is a constant source of valuable market research. When you start your business, you will probably not be able to hire a sales staff. You will be the sales staff.

Even if you have never sold anything in your life, you can develop into a great salesperson. In fact, you already have a lot of practice selling. Everyone tries to persuade (sell) others to agree to something or to act a certain way. Being face to face with customers, trying to sell your product, may make you nervous at first. But if you think of rejections as learning experiences and opportunities for continuous market analysis, you will look forward to every sales encounter throughout your entrepreneurial career.

The Essence of Selling Is Teaching

Performance Objective 1 ▶

Explain the importance of selling based upon benefits.

The creative art of selling is teaching the customer how the features will become benefits. Inexperienced salespeople make a common mistake: They think telling the customer about the features of a product will sell it. But remember, a customer who buys a drill does not need a drill; she or he needs to make a hole.

BizFacts

Many salespeople earn a *commission*, a percentage paid on each sale. A salesperson making a 10 percent commission selling cars, for example, would earn $1,000 after selling a $10,000 car.

$.10 \times \$10,000 = \$1,000$

Entrepreneurs can use commissions to motivate sales staff. When you are starting out and cannot afford to pay sales representatives full-time salaries, you can offer commissions instead, because they get paid as you get paid.

The essence of selling is teaching how and why the outstanding features of your product or service will benefit your customers. Durant succeeded by showing that a new type of spring (feature) made riding in his buggy carts more comfortable (benefit).

The Principles of Selling

Every entrepreneur has to be able to think through the benefits his or her product can provide, and make an effective sales call. Entrepreneurs *sell* constantly—not just to customers but to potential investors, bankers, and people they want to hire. Commit the following selling principles to memory and you will be on your way to becoming a successful salesperson. These principles apply to any product or service:

◀ **Performance Objective 2**
Use the principles of selling to make effective sales calls.

- *Make a good personal impression:* When selling your product or service, prepare yourself physically. A salesperson must be clean and well dressed—it is important to dress appropriately for your customer base. If you are selling oil to gas station owners, do not wear $800 suits; but you do want to dress professionally. Some suggest that, for sales calls, your business card should not identify you as "president" or "owner," so your prospects can talk with you more easily. This would depend upon who you are meeting, so use common sense.

- *Know your product or service:* Understand its features and the benefits they can create. It is your chance to teach the customer about the product or service. Explain the benefits without overselling. Do not try to share everything you know, however, as that is likely to be too much information. You don't want to alienate the customer, or be boring.

- *Believe in your product or service:* Good salespeople believe in what they are selling. If, during this stage, you begin to feel that your product or service does not measure up to the standards you have set, do not try to sell it. Your business will fail if you do not believe it is the best available in the marketplace for the price. Always be on the lookout for ways to improve your product or develop a better one.

- *Know your field:* Invest in understanding the industry and your competition. Read the trade literature. Learn about your competitors. Buy their products or try their services and compare them with yours. Experience a call from one of your competitor's salespeople. Let this person try to sell to you. This could be a gold mine of information. Study the strengths and weaknesses of your competitor's product or service, because your sales prospects will probably bring them up during your own calls.

- *Know your customers:* Be thorough in your customer analysis. What are their needs? How does your product or service address them? Understand what "makes them tick." Use resources, such as the Internet, to get publicly available background information.

- *Prepare your sales presentation:* Know ahead of time how you want to present your product or service. Identify the key points you believe are important to this particular customer. Jot them down on a note card. Study it. Put it away. Practice the sales call. Role-play. Know how to overcome objections.

- *Think positively:* This will help you deal with rejections you may experience before you make your first sale. Many people do not realize how mentally strong you have to be to conduct sales calls. One entrepreneur went on 400 calls for his import-export firm before he closed a sale of more than $1,000. But this experience made him a much better salesperson.

- **Keep good records:** Have your record-keeping system, including invoices and receipts, set up before you go on your first sales call. Use a database system to keep records of your sales calls and to remind you of appropriate follow-up actions.
- **Make no truly "cold" calls:** Unless you are doing door-to-door sales or retail sales, your prospect meetings should be "warm" calls. You can send an introductory letter, e-mail, or postcard, so that the customer will know why you want to make the call.
- **Make an appointment:** People will be more likely to listen when they have set aside time to hear your sales pitch. They will be less than receptive if you interrupt their day unannounced.
- **Treat everyone you sell to like gold:** Joe Girard is a car salesman who has been dubbed "The World's Greatest Salesman" 12 times by *The Guinness Book of Records.* In his book, *How to Sell Anything to Anybody,* Girard states his Law of 250 as follows: "Everyone knows 250 people in his or her life important enough to invite to the wedding and to the funeral." He goes on to explain, "This means that if I see 50 people in a week, and only two of them are unhappy with the way I treat them, at the end of the year there will be about 5,000 people influenced by just those two a week."[1] Obviously, if each person you sell to influences 250 others, you cannot afford to alienate even one sales prospect! (However, this does not mean that you keep trying to sell beyond rejection.)

The Sales Call

A **sales call** is an appointment with a potential customer to explain or demonstrate your product or service. During the sales call, you will want to do the following:

- Make the customer aware of your product or service.
- Make the customer want to buy that product or service.
- Make the customer want to buy it from *you.*

Electronic Mail, Blogs, and Newsgroups

In today's technology-savvy environment, there are multiple methods for communicating with sales prospects. Among these options are electronic mail, newsgroups, and blogs. Which, if any, is best-suited to your business will require careful consideration on your part. **Electronic mail** (e-mail for short) is defined as correspondence sent via the Internet. **Newsgroups** are online discussion groups focused on specific subjects.

Sending e-mail or posting messages on newsgroups or blogs can help contact sales prospects and keep in touch with customers you already have, but you must use these methods carefully. In the "physical" world you can look for sales prospects by distributing flyers or by calling people on a list. Using e-mail or newsgroups in a similar fashion can result in your e-mail box being jammed with "flames," or hate mail. Most newsgroups do not appreciate receiving unwanted advertisements, called **spam**, and members may respond angrily.

If done correctly, becoming involved in a newsgroup can lead to qualified prospects. Let's say you sell photographic supplies and you hear about

[1] Joe Girard, *How to Sell Anything to Anybody* (New York: Warner Books, 1986), p. 48.

Figure 6-1 *Message to a newsgroup.*

> *This week's discussion on the advantages of the new Nikon mini-camera was very interesting. I'm in the photography supply business and am looking for interesting items to add to my Web site. I have already posted articles from* Advanced Photography *magazine and tips from some of my clients.Does anyone have any other ideas for useful information that I could post? Thanks!*
>
> *Sandra Bowling*
> *PhotoSupply Online*
> *http://www.photosupply.com*
> *E-mail: photosupply@AOL.com*
> *The Photographer's Source for Supplies and Advice*

an interesting newsgroup for photographers. Do not blitz it with ads! Instead, before posting any messages, **lurk** for awhile, meaning that you just read messages and get a feel for the discussions taking place without participating in the discussion. Once you are comfortable, try posting a message. For example, see the text in **Figure 6-1**. Because this is not a sales pitch, no one in the newsgroup should take offense, and your message may attract potential sales prospects to your Web site.

Prequalify Your Sales Calls

Before calling to make an appointment for any sales call, identify and list your **prospects**, the people/organizations that may be receptive to your sales pitch. Include everyone you can imagine, but then go through it carefully and ask:

- Is this individual in my market?
- Does he/she need my product?
- Will my product/service remove a problem or source of "pain" or improve the individual's life?
- Can he/she afford it?

If the answer to any of these questions is "no," making a sales call on that person will probably be a waste of time for both of you. People spend money to buy things they want or need. If your product or service helps, great! If not, do not hesitate to move on to consider the next prospect (sometimes called a "suspect" until they are qualified). Asking such questions is called "prequalifying" a sales call. Invest the time it takes to get your prospect list organized and analyzed. Abe Lincoln's famous saying—"If I had ten hours to chop down a tree, I'd spend nine sharpening my axe"—applies here.

Focus on the Customer

During each call, focus on one thought: What does the customer need? Visualize your product or service fulfilling that need. If you believe in your product or service and there is a good fit, you will be able to see this without any problem. In general, focusing on listening to the potential customer will help you overcome self-consciousness. If you actively listen and probe, the customer will tell you what is important to him or her, either directly or indirectly. A feature that creates a benefit in your mind may be meaningless to one prospect but extremely important to another. Pay attention!

Mental visualization will help you perform better when you are in the actual situation. Practice the sales call in your mind, visualizing how you want it to go, but be prepared to deviate from that vision. Visualization will enlist your subconscious mind in the sales process, instinctively providing you with subtle verbal and body-language cues that can convince a customer to buy from you. You will be better prepared and more comfortable in your role.

The Eight-Step Sales Call

1. ***Preparation:*** Prepare yourself mentally and in your organization. Think about how the product/service will benefit this specific customer. Have the price, discounts, all technical information, and any other details "on the tip of your tongue" or at your fingertips. Be willing to obtain further information if your customer should request it. Visualize the sales call in your mind until it goes smoothly and successfully. Jot down a few key probing questions and points you think will help. Bring the appropriate materials, samples, and data with you.

2. ***Greeting:*** Greet the customer politely and graciously. Do not plunge immediately into business talk. The first few words you say may be the most important. Keep a two-way conversation going. Maintain eye contact and keep the customer's attention. Remember that the customer is first and foremost a human being with whom you would like to make a connection. The more you can learn about his/her family, hobbies, interests—anything to help develop a genuine relationship—the better your chances of eventually securing a sale. However, avoid being perceived as nosy or overly personal. The best salespeople keep files on their customers with all sorts of information, in order to remind them of details for future conversations and to follow up over time. Sales may depend upon the characteristics and benefits of the product or service, but customers buy from people they know and like when they have a choice. They usually have a choice.

3. ***Showing the Product/Service:*** Personalize your product or service by pointing out the benefits for this particular customer. Use props and models (or the real thing) where appropriate. If possible, demonstrate the product or service to showcase its unique selling proposition in a way that will be meaningful for this customer.

4. ***Listen to the Customer:*** After you pitch your product or service once, sit back and let the customer talk about it. This is how you will get your most valuable information. This is how to learn what the customer needs and wants. Neil Rackham, the author of *SPIN Selling*, had his consulting firm, Huthwaite, analyze more than 35,000 sales. He discovered that in successful calls it was the buyer who did most of the talking.[2]

5. ***Dealing with Objections:*** The best, most effective way to deal with objections is to prevent them. Address the known objections in a positive light. However, during the listening phase, you will hear a customer's objections to your product or service. Always acknowledge objections and handle them. Do not pretend you did not hear, or overreact or be afraid to listen. A famous real estate entrepreneur, William Zeckendorf, said, "I never lost money on a sales pitch when I listened to the customer." Do not hesitate to tell the absolute truth about any negative aspect of your product or service. Each time you admit a negative, you gain credibility in the customer's mind. However, be careful to not make a point of each flaw or whine about the product or service.

6. ***Closing the Sale:*** Review the benefits of your product or service. If negatives have come up, point out that, at this price, the product or

---

[2] Neil Rackham, *SPIN Selling* (New York: McGraw-Hill, 1996).

service is still an excellent buy. Narrow the choices the customer has to make. Close the sale, if it is time to do so. Do not overstay your welcome. Stop while you are ahead. An important rule of thumb: If a customer says no three times, you still have a chance. If he/she says it the fourth time, it really means no. If the answer *is* no, take it gracefully. Remember that the sales cycle for your product or service is a critical factor here. Some sales take months or years to close. A "no" today is not necessarily a "no" forever.

7. *Follow-up:* Make regular follow-up calls to find out how he/she liked the product or service. Ask if you can be of any further help. If the customer has a complaint, do not ignore it. Keeping the customer's trust after the sale is the most important part of the whole process.

   A successful business is built on repeat customers. Plus, every time you talk to a customer you are deepening your friendship. Your best sales prospects in the future are people who have already bought something from you. Keep them posted on the progress of your business by sending postcards or flyers.

8. *Ask for References:* Ask your customers to refer you to other potential customers. Try to set up a system that encourages others to send sales prospects your way. Offer discounts, gift certificates, or other incentives to those who refer people to you, for example. Give customers a few business cards to pass on to their friends.

Three Call Behaviors of Successful Salespeople

Neil Rackham, during his research, discovered that successful salespeople exhibit certain "sales-call behaviors."[3] He concluded that there are three steps that lead to more sales:

1. *Let the customer talk more than you do:* According to *SPIN Selling,* "The more your customer talks, the more you will learn about their needs, which puts you in a better position to offer them the most customized and most helpful solutions." Encourage your customers to talk to you about their situations and problems. As they talk, they will begin to understand their own needs better and realize the importance of solving the problem.

2. *Ask the right questions:* How do you get customers to talk to you? Rackham notes that you have to ask the right questions. If your sales calls are leaving you with little information, you're not asking the questions that uncover your customers' needs. Instead of focusing on selling your product, focus on listening to your customer. Try to draw him or her out. Be a friendly listener. You need to fully understand the problem *before* suggesting that your product or service could provide a solution.

3. *Wait to offer products and solutions until later in the call:* First, let your customer talk. Second, once you've got the customer talking, ask the right questions to help uncover the problem. Now you are ready to offer your product or service as a solution to this problem. As Rackham writes, "You cannot know what solution to offer if you do not uncover customer needs and decision criteria first. For example, if you spend your time with the customer talking about how quiet your machine is, and noise is not a factor your customer cares about, you've wasted your time."[4] You cannot offer a valuable solution until you know what problem the customer needs to solve.

---

[3] Rackham, *SPIN Selling,* p. 110.
[4] Rackham, *SPIN Selling,* p. 84.

Analyze Your Sales Calls to Become a Star Salesperson

Performance Objective 3 ▶

Analyze and improve your sales calls.

Every sales call is an opportunity to improve your selling skills—even if you did not make a sale. The star salesperson analyzes each call by asking:

- Was I able to get the customer to open up to me? Why, or why not?
- Did I do or say anything that turned the customer off?
- Which of my questions did the best job of helping the customer zero in on his/her problems? How can I ask better questions?
- Was I able to make an honest case for my product/service being the one that could solve the customer's problem?
- Did I improve my relationship with this person during the call?

Rackham's research shows that, unless you analyze your selling at this level of detail, you will miss important opportunities for learning and improving your selling skills.

Turning Objections into Advantages

Getting the customer to open up may lead to your being told things you may not want to hear about your product or service. These objections, however, will be valuable sources of marketing data. Sales expert Brian Tracy recommends writing down objections and comments that customers make about your product. He believes that all objections fall into one of six categories, and suggests making a list of every objection you've ever heard, and then grouping them under the following headings:

1. Price
2. Performance
3. Follow-up service
4. Competition
5. Support
6. Warranties and assurances[5]

Once you've listed the objections under these headings, take a close look at them. Try to rephrase each set of objections in a single question of 25 words or less.

Work on developing objection-proof answers to each of these questions—answers that are backed by proof, testimonials from customers, research, and data comparing your product with the competition's. If you make the effort to do this, you will learn to appreciate hearing objections. More importantly, you may be able to head off objections before they arise.

- You will have well-prepared responses, backed by written proof.
- If you do hear a new objection for which you have not developed a response, you will be excited to get back to the office so that you can.

Use Technology to Sell

Where appropriate and applicable, use the latest advances in technology to sell your product, help your customers understand and use it, and stay in touch with them. Some examples include:

- A multimedia demonstration or presentation of your product
- A Web site that customers can visit for updates and product facts, to share ideas, and find technical data
- Using e-mail and blogs to stay in touch with customers

---

[5] Brian Tracy, *Be a Sales Superstar: 21 Great Ways to Sell More, Faster, Easier in Tough Market* (San Francisco: Berrett-Koehler Publishers, 2003), p. 84.

Global Impact...

Keep an Open Mind

Your business may be small but do not forget that, via the Internet, you can participate in an exciting global economy. The more you travel and learn about other cultures, the more effective business leader you will become. The best entrepreneurs are tolerant and open-minded. They are curious about other countries, other cultures, other ways of life—because these are all potential sources of business.

Perhaps there is a product you will discover on a backpacking trip in Europe that you can profitably import into the United States. Perhaps there is a consumer need you will find while reading about Panama online that you can meet by exporting your product there. Once you realize you are a citizen of the world, the sky is the limit for your career as an entrepreneur.

To **import** means to bring a product made in another country into your country to sell.

To **export** means to send a product made in your country to another country to be sold.

- "Webinars" and audio conferences to educate and introduce
- Digital planners and calendars, as well as sales software, to keep prospect lists organized and log sales calls
- Personal Digital Assistants (PDAs) and other technology to place orders and secure immediate responses to customer inquiries

All the technological concepts used to identify customers through market research can be instrumental in selling to your segment of the market.

The One-Minute Sales Call

Believe it or not, it is a challenge for most people to pay attention to someone for more than a minute. You will do best if you keep your sales calls under a minute. Write down your sales pitch and practice delivering it to a friend or relative. Have yourself timed. You will be shocked at how fast a minute can go by! You cannot practice your sales calls enough. Spending time planning a call is better than agonizing over why a call failed.

Here is an example to get you started. Let's say you make baby food from organic fruits and vegetables. You are trying to convince the owner of Johnson's General Store to buy your products. Remember, you need to build in places to engage the customer in the conversation.

Hello, Mr. Johnson. Thank you for agreeing to see me today. I'm excited about this product and think you and your customers will be, too.

I brought you a jar of our baby applesauce. It is nicely packaged, don't you think? We hand-decorate each jar. It makes a nice gift for new or expectant parents. The eye-catching ribbons will be sure to attract your customers.

We use only organic fruits and vegetables, no sugar, and very little salt. Our label explains that some babies are sensitive to the additives and dyes found in certain commercial baby foods. These may give sensitive babies headaches or upset stomachs. Our food is very gentle on the baby—and that makes the parents' life much easier!

I understand your concern that our product costs twenty-five cents more per jar than the brands you presently stock. I think your customers will pay more for our high quality and for knowing that their babies are protected from harmful additives or high levels of sugar and salt. Also, because we add very little water to our product, you actually get more food for the money than some of the less expensive brands.

I really think you could start a trend by stocking our baby food, Mr. Johnson. There has been a shift in the market toward healthy food for adults—and those adults are also looking for healthy baby food. Our products combine an eye-catching look with healthy ingredients that new parents and their friends and relatives will not be able to resist. How many jars would you like to order?

software system for your industry. Your database should include every customer you have ever had, as well as potential customers—friends, family, and other contacts. The database should include each person's name, e-mail address, phone and fax numbers, and mailing address. Also include the date of your last contact and a note about what the person bought. Start collecting this information now and you will be ahead of the game when you are actually ready to start making sales calls or sending out marketing material.

As your database grows, you can organize it by region, customer interest, or any number of other variables and send out targeted mailings or e-mails. If you sell gourmet sauces, for example, your notes could tell you whether a customer is interested in hot sauces or dessert sauces. When you add a new hot sauce to your product line, you will know whom to target with an e-mail announcement introducing the sauce, possibly with a special offer.

Make sure that your subject line is effective and interesting. If it is not, your prospect may not even bother to read the message. Remember, most people resent getting e-mail that does not interest them. Always include an offer to drop people from your mailing list at the end of each message. This shows that you are respectful of their privacy.

Exercise

Contact your phone company to find out how to set up an "800" number for your business, so customers can call toll free. Some long-distance providers offer special discounts to small-business owners. AT&T has a program called Small Business Advantage.

How much will an 800 number for your business cost?
Did you find any special discounts?

Ask Customers to Refer You to New Customers

If you feel you established a connection and satisfied your customers, ask them to refer you to others. Offer discounts, gift certificates, and so forth, for referrals. Offer business cards, coupons, or invitations for customers to pass on to their friends.

Chapter Summary

Now that you have studied this chapter, you can do the following:

1. Explain the importance of selling based upon benefits.
   - Features are the qualities of a product or service.
   - Benefits are what the product or service can do to fill customer needs.
   - Customers purchase based upon perceived benefits.
2. Use the principles of selling to make effective sales calls.
   - Make a good personal impression.
   - Know your product or service.
   - Believe in your product or service.
   - Know your field.
   - Know your customers.
   - Prepare your sales presentation.
   - Think positively.
   - Keep good records.

- Make an appointment.
- Treat your customers like gold.

3. Analyze and improve your sales calls.
   - Was I able to get the customer to open up to me? Why, or why not? Did I do or say anything that turned the customer off?
   - Which of my questions did the best job of helping the customer zero in on his/her problem?
   - Was I able to make an honest case for my product/service being the one that could solve the customer's problem?
   - Did I improve my relationship with this individual during the call?

4. Handle customer complaints effectively.
   - A customer complaint is full of valuable information that no one else will tell you.
   - Stay calm when dealing with a customer that is upset. Ask the customer for an explanation of the situation. Do not interrupt. This will give the customer a chance to vent and calm down. If you show that you are willing to listen, you will probably defuse much of the irritation.

5. Provide excellent customer service.
   - Customer service is everything you do to keep your customers happy—especially after the sale. It includes maintaining and repairing the product or service once it has been sold and dealing with customer complaints.
   - A successful business is built on repeat customers.

Key Terms

customer service	lurk
database	newsgroup
electronic mail	prospect
export	sales call
import	spam

Entrepreneurship Portfolio

Critical Thinking Exercises

1. Describe the features of each product listed below and then create a "benefit" statement for each that you would use as selling points.

   Product
   wristwatch with daily events calendar
   milk-free chocolate
   vegetarian dog food
   personal lie detector

2. Create a database for your business. Which five questions will you ask every customer?

3. Describe a business that you deal with as a customer. Describe the customer service at this business. What do you like (or dislike) about it? How could it be improved?

Direct Unit Costs		Jun	Jul	Aug	Sep	Oct	Nov	Dec	Jan	Feb	Mar	Apr	May
Drive-thrus #8, #9, & #10	0.00%	$0.64	$0.64	$0.64	$0.64	$0.64	$0.64	$0.64	$0.64	$0.64	$0.64	$0.64	$0.64
Drive-thrus #11, #12, & #13	0.00%	$0.64	$0.64	$0.64	$0.64	$0.64	$0.64	$0.64	$0.64	$0.64	$0.64	$0.64	$0.64
Mobile Café #1	0.00%	$0.64	$0.64	$0.64	$0.64	$0.64	$0.64	$0.64	$0.64	$0.64	$0.64	$0.64	$0.64
Mobile Café #2	0.00%	$0.64	$0.64	$0.64	$0.64	$0.64	$0.64	$0.64	$0.64	$0.64	$0.64	$0.64	$0.64
Mobile Café #3	0.00%	$0.64	$0.64	$0.64	$0.64	$0.64	$0.64	$0.64	$0.64	$0.64	$0.64	$0.64	$0.64
Mobile Café #4	0.00%	$0.64	$0.64	$0.64	$0.64	$0.64	$0.64	$0.64	$0.64	$0.64	$0.64	$0.64	$0.64
Web Site Sales/Premium Items	0.00%	$6.50	$6.50	$6.50	$6.50	$6.50	$6.50	$6.50	$6.50	$6.50	$6.50	$6.50	$6.50

Direct Cost of Sales	Jun	Jul	Aug	Sep	Oct	Nov	Dec	Jan	Feb	Mar	Apr	May
Drive-thru #1	$0	$0	$0	$11,200	$14,750	$15,488	$14,713	$14,750	$15,488	$14,713	$14,750	$14,013
Drive-thru #2	$0	$0	$0	$0	$0	$0	$0	$0	$11,200	$14,750	$14,013	$14,750
Drive-thru #3	$0	$0	$0	$0	$0	$0	$0	$0	$0	$0	$0	$0
Drive-thru #4	$0	$0	$0	$0	$0	$0	$0	$0	$0	$0	$0	$0
Drive-thru #5	$0	$0	$0	$0	$0	$0	$0	$0	$0	$0	$0	$0
Drive-thrus #6 & #7	$0	$0	$0	$0	$0	$0	$0	$0	$0	$0	$0	$0
Drive-thrus #8, #9, & #10	$0	$0	$0	$0	$0	$0	$0	$0	$0	$0	$0	$0
Drive-thrus #11, #12, & #13	$0	$0	$0	$0	$0	$0	$0	$0	$0	$0	$0	$0
Mobile Café #1	$0	$0	$0	$0	$0	$0	$0	$0	$0	$0	$3,200	$0
Mobile Café #2	$0	$0	$0	$0	$0	$0	$0	$0	$0	$0	$0	$3,200
Mobile Café #3	$0	$0	$0	$0	$0	$0	$0	$0	$0	$0	$0	$0
Mobile Café #4	$0	$0	$0	$0	$0	$0	$0	$0	$0	$0	$0	$0
Web Site Sales/Premium Items	$0	$0	$0	$0	$0	$0	$0	$0	$0	$0	$0	$0
Subtotal Direct Cost of Sales	$0	$0	$0	$11,200	$14,750	$15,488	$14,713	$14,750	$26,688	$29,463	$31,963	$31,963

Show Me the Money!: Finding, Securing, and Managing It

Chapter 7

Understanding and Managing Start-Up, Fixed, and Variable Costs

"All our records had to be hits because we couldn't afford any flops."

—Berry Gordy, founder, Motown Record Company

Anyone can spend unlimited amounts of money and create a good product, but the entrepreneur's goal is to create a product that costs less than the consumer is willing to pay for it. An entrepreneur's ability to find creative ways to manage costs often means the difference between a struggling business and a thriving one.

Entrepreneurs searching for ways to manage their costs have created some of our society's most powerful breakthroughs. When Henry Ford was trying to make his vision of an automobile in front of every home in America a reality, it was the *cost* of building a "horseless carriage" that stood in his way. The motorcar was considered a novelty for rich people. But Ford was determined to build one that almost anyone could afford.

In those days, cars were manufactured one at a time. This was a slow, expensive process that involved a lot of labor. To cut manufacturing costs, Ford had his cars assembled as they moved on a conveyer belt past the workers, with each worker responsible for attaching one item. This **moving assembly line** produced cars quickly with much lower labor costs per unit. The assembly-line concept revolutionized manufacturing and was adopted by many other companies to make products that were previously too expensive to mass-produce. Industrial production exploded in America, as the moving assembly line made it possible for companies to lower their costs enough to sell the average consumer products—from washing machines to refrigerators—that previously only the well-to-do could afford. Ford revolutionized industry by introducing the concept of mass production on a grand scale.

Performance Objectives

1. Describe the variable costs of starting a business.
2. Analyze your fixed operating costs and calculate gross profit.
3. Set up financial record keeping for your business.
4. Create financial statements.

Workers assembling engines on the line at the General Motors plant in Baltimore. (Jim Pickerell, the Stock Connection)

What Does It Cost to Operate a Business?

To run a successful business, you will need to keep track of your costs and have more cash coming into the business than going out. *The bedrock principle of business is that it earns a profit by selling products or services for more than they cost.*

Since everything sold has a related cost (or costs), the business can make a profit only if the selling price per unit is greater than the cost per unit. A litmus test for profitability is the economics of one unit (EOU), as discussed in Chapter 3. It tells an entrepreneur if the business is earning a profit. One step in this process is determining the unit of sale for your type of enterprise. Knowing your EOU will be helpful as you determine your venture's viability.

Many costs are associated with the start-up and growth of a small business. These include start-up purchases, fixed and variable costs, and cash reserves. Each is discussed in turn. All are components of your accounting records, the documents that are used to classify, analyze, and interpret the financial transactions of an organization.

Start-Up Investment

Performance Objective 1 ➤

Describe the variable costs of starting a business.

There is another critical cost to discuss before you can keep good accounting records for your business. We have talked about the costs of producing one unit and the costs of operating a business, but what about the money required to *start* a business? **Start-up investment** is the one-time expense of opening a business. It is also called *seed capital*. In a restaurant, for example, start-up expenses would include stoves, food processors, tables, chairs, silverware, and other items that would not be replaced very often. Also included might be the one-time cost of buying land and constructing a building. Some entrepreneurs also choose to consider the time they put into getting their businesses off the ground part of the start-up investment. To do so, place a value on your time per hour and multiply by the number of hours required to get your business started. You might be shocked at how high the number is!

For a hot dog stand, the start-up investment might look like this:

Hot dog cart	$2,500
License from the city	200
Business cards and flyers	150
Beginning inventory (hot dogs, ketchup, buns, etc.)	50
Change box and receipts	100
Total start-up investment	$3,000

For a more complex business, like a restaurant, the summary start-up sheet might look like this:

Stove	$22,000
Food processors	11,000
Tables and chairs	6,000
Cash register	1,500
Dishes and silverware	8,400
Renovations	15,000
Industrial fans/cooling system	45,000
Industrial dishwashers/dish racks	18,600
Total start-up investment	$127,500

For a manufacturing business, developing a prototype for the item being manufactured would probably be a major start-up cost. A **prototype** is a model or pattern that serves as an example of how a product would look and operate if it were manufactured. Companies that specialize in creating prototypes can be found in the *Thomas Register of American Manufacturers*.

Brainstorm to Avoid Start-Up Surprises

Before starting your business, try to anticipate every possible cost. Talk to other business owners in your industry and ask them what start-up costs they failed to anticipate. Use **Figure 7-1** to estimate your start-up investment.

Once you have brainstormed a list, take it to your advisors or mentors and have them look it over. They will probably find start-up costs you have overlooked. You might not have realized that the electric company may require a $500 deposit to turn on services, for example. Or that you will need licenses and insurance you did not expect. Tack on an additional 10 percent to your estimates for contingencies and emergencies.

Do Your Research on Costs

Better yet, do some research to accurately assess your start-up costs. Look at business plan models in your industry, if possible. Adapt the lists to fit your business and obtain quotations on pricing. Look at available industry data. Do not be caught by surprise on costs that you could have predicted.

Keep a Reserve Equal to One-Half of Start-Up Investment

Start-up investment should include one more thing—a **cash reserve**, or emergency funds, that equals at least half of your start-up costs. For the hot dog cart, therefore, the reserve would be half of $3,000, or $1,500.

Figure 7-1 *Start-up investment checklist.*

Item	Estimated Cost
Beginning inventory	$_____
Your time (valued at $_____ per hour)	$_____
Site improvements (renovation, etc.)	$_____
Furniture and fixtures	$_____
Cash registers	$_____
Computers, software	$_____
Professional consultants	$_____
Supplies	$_____
Deposits	$_____
Registration fees	$_____
Memberships	$_____
Pre-opening salaries	$_____
Training, conventions, seminars	$_____
Pre-opening promotions, advertising	$_____
Contingencies/emergencies (10%)	$_____
Total	$_____

Entrepreneurs must be ready for the unexpected—the only good surprise is no surprise. The reserve will provide a moderate cushion of protection when you need it. When your computer goes down or your biggest supplier raises prices, you will be glad you had this money on hand!

Having a cash reserve will also allow you to take advantage of opportunities. Say you own a vintage clothing store and you hear from a friend whose great-aunt died and left him a great deal of authentic vintage clothing and jewelry. He is willing to sell you the whole lot for $500, which you figure you can resell in your shop for at least $2,000. If you did not have the extra cash on hand, you might have lost this profitable opportunity.

Payback

When compiling and analyzing start-up costs, one consideration will be how long it will take for you to earn back your start-up investment. **Payback** estimates, for you and your investors, how long it will take your business to earn enough to cover the start-up investment. It is measured in months.

$$\text{Payback} = \frac{\text{Start–Up Investment}}{\text{Net Profit per Month}}$$

Example: Ashley's business required a start-up investment of $1,000. The business is projecting a net profit per month of $400. How many months will it take to make back her start-up investment?

$$\text{Payback} = \frac{\$1,000}{\$400} = 2.5 \text{ Months}$$

Fixed and Variable Costs: Essential Building Blocks

Small business owners divide their costs into two categories. **Variable costs** change based on the volume of units sold. **Fixed costs** must be paid regardless of whether or not sales are being generated.

Variable costs change with sales. They fall into two subcategories:

1. Cost of goods sold (COGS), or cost of services sold (COSS), which is associated specifically with each unit of sale, including:
   - The cost of materials used to make the product (or deliver the service)
   - The cost of labor used to make the product (or deliver the service)
2. Other variable costs include:
   - Commissions or other compensation based on sales volume
   - Shipping and handling charges

Fixed costs stay constant whether you sell many units or very few. Examples of fixed costs include rent, salaries, insurance, equipment, and manufacturing plants.

Henry Ford spent money on efficient manufacturing equipment (a fixed cost) but saved a fortune on labor (COGS) by doing so. This reduced his total costs because labor was used in each of the millions of cars Ford produced, but he only had to pay for the plant and equipment once.

For any unit of sale, you can study its Economics of One Unit to figure out what it cost to make that sale. **Figure 7-2** shows an example from a business that sells hand-painted vintage T-shirts.

Figure 7-2 *Manufacturing business: Unit = 1 hand-painted T-shirt.*

Economics of One Unit (EOU) Analysis			
(Define the Unit of Sale)			
Selling Price (per Unit)			$35.00
COGS (Cost of Goods Sold)			
Materials per Unit		$7.00	
Labor per hour	$10.00		
# of Hours per Unit	0.75		
Total Labor per Unit	7.50	7.50	
Total COGS (per Unit)		$14.50 $14.50	14.50
Gross Profit (per Unit)			$20.50
Other Variable Costs			
Commission (10%)		3.50	
Packaging		0.50	
Total Other Variable Costs		$4.00 4.00	4.00
Total Variable Costs (per Unit)		$18.50	
Contribution Margin			$16.50

Calculating Critical Costs

In order to determine the most important factors with respect to costs in your business, you can calculate *critical costs*. This will help you to determine profitability and the factors that can and cannot be easily changed to impact your profits and cash flow.

Calculating Total Gross Profit and Contribution Margin

You can use EOU to calculate whether and by how much you will come out ahead on your per-unit costs for each sale. By using the EOU, you can figure the gross profit per unit (**contribution margin** per unit sold—the selling price minus total variable costs plus other variable costs).

◀ **Performance Objective 2**
Analyze your fixed operating costs and calculate gross profit.

Calculating EOU When You Sell More Than One Product

Most businesses sell more than a single product and they also can use EOU as a value measure of product profitability. A business selling a variety of products has to create a separate EOU for each product to determine whether each one is profitable. When there are many similar products with comparable price and cost structures, a "typical EOU" can be used.

Example: Jamaal sells four kinds of candy bars at school. He sells each bar for $1, but he pays a different wholesale price for each:

Snickers	36¢ each
Almond Joy	38¢ each
Butterfinger	42¢ each
Baby Ruth	44¢ each

Rather than make separate EOUs, Jamaal uses the average cost of his four candy bars (see **Figure 7-3**).

Costs of the four candy bars = (36¢ + 38¢ + 42¢ + 44¢) ÷ 4

Average cost of the four candy bars = $1.60 ÷ 4

Average cost of each bar = 40¢

Economics of One Unit (EOU) Analysis		
One Unit of Sale = One Candy Bar		
Selling Price		$1.00
COGS (direct cost of the product or service)		
Average Cost of Candy Bars (COGS)	0.40	
Average Shipping Cost per Unit	0.06	
Total COGS	0.46	0.46
Gross Profit		0.54
Other Variable Costs (none)	—	—
Contribution Margin		$0.54

Figure 7-3 *Retail business: Unit = 1 candy bar.*

Using an average works if the costs are close, and as long as Jamaal sells roughly the same number of each brand of bar. If he can no longer get Snickers and Almond Joy at some point, for example, he should then change his EOU to reflect the higher price of the other two bars.

What if each unit of sale is made up of a complex mix of materials and labor? The EOU can still help you figure the COGS, other variable costs, and gross profit for the product, although the process will be more complex.

Example: Denise sells turkey sandwiches from her deli cart downtown on Saturdays. She sells each for $5. The materials and labor that go directly into making each sandwich are the COGS. The costs of the materials and direct labor for production are called **inventory costs** until the product is sold. There will also be some other variable costs, such as napkins, a paper wrapping for each sandwich, and plastic bags.

First, make a list of the COGS, and any other variable costs:

COGS

a. Turkey costs $2.60 per lb. Each sandwich uses 4 oz. of turkey meat (16 oz./1 lb.).

b. Bread (large rolls) cost $1.92 per dozen. One roll is used per sandwich.

c. One ounce of mayonnaise is used per sandwich. A 32-ounce jar of mayo costs $1.60.

d. Lettuce costs 80 cents per lb. and 1/16 of a pound (1 ounce) is used on each sandwich.

e. Tomatoes cost $1.16 each. Each sandwich uses a fourth of a tomato.

f. Each sandwich comes with two pickles. Pickles cost 5 cents each.

g. Employees are paid $7 per hour and can make 10 sandwiches per hour (we are assuming no down time and no payroll costs).

Figure 7-4 *Economics of one unit.*

Retail Business: Unit = 1 Turkey Sandwich					Date: 12/1/2008
Selling Price per Unit:					**$5.00**
Cost of Goods Sold	**Price**	**Units**	**Quantity Used**	**Cost Each**	
Turkey (4 oz.):	$2.60	Per lb.	¼ lb.	$0.65	
Bread (roll):	$1.92	Per dozen	¹⁄₁₂ dozen	$0.16	
Mayonnaise (1 oz.):	$1.60	Per 32-oz. jar	¹⁄₃₂ jar	$0.05	
Lettuce (1 oz.):	$0.80	Per lb.	¹⁄₁₆ lb.	$0.05	
Tomato (¼ lb.)	$1.16	Each	¼ each	$0.29	
Pickles (2):	$0.05	Each	2 each	$0.10	
Direct Labor (6 min.):	$7.00	Per hr.	¹⁄₁₀ hr.	$0.70	
Total Cost of Goods Sold per Unit:				**$2.00**	2.00
Gross Profit					**$3.00**
Other Variable Costs					
Napkin:	$3.00	Per 100-pack	¹⁄₁₀₀ pack	$0.03	
Paper Wrapping:	$0.20	Per foot	2 feet	$0.40	
Plastic Bag:	$7.00	Per roll (100)	¹⁄₁₀₀ roll	$0.07	
Total Other Variable Costs per Unit:				$0.50	
Total Variable Costs per Unit:					0.50
Contribution Margin per Unit:					**$2.50**

Other Variable Costs

The following supplies are used every time a sandwich is sold, but are not strictly part of the sandwich's production:

a. Napkins cost $3 per pack of 100. One napkin is included with each sale.

b. Paper wrapping costs 20 cents per foot (on a roll). Each sandwich uses two feet of paper.

c. Plastic carryout bags cost $7 per roll of 100. Each sandwich sold uses one plastic carryout bag. (In reality, more than one sandwich might go into a bag.)

The EOU for the turkey sandwich is shown in **Figure 7-4**.

Fixed Operating Costs

Costs, such as rent or the Internet bill, which do not vary per unit of production or service, are called **fixed operating costs**. Fixed operating costs are not included in COGS (or COSS) because they are not direct costs of creating each product (or service).[1] Fixed operating costs are not included in other variable costs because they do not vary directly with the number of sales made.

Operating costs are also called **overhead**. *This is an informal term for fixed costs. Overhead comes from the literal "over head"—that is, the roof over the business.*

Fixed operating costs do not change based on sales; therefore, they are not included in the EOU. A sandwich shop has to pay the same rent each month whether it sells one turkey sandwich or a hundred. However, the owner of the shop can change the cost of the rent by moving, or can increase or decrease the advertising budget, and the like. These changes are not calculated on a per-unit basis.

---

[1] Cost of goods sold is used for businesses that sell products. Service businesses use the term cost of services sold.

An easy way to remember the seven common fixed operating costs is with the acronym USAIIRD:

Utilities (gas, electric, telephone, Internet service)
Salaries (indirect labor)
Advertising
Insurance
Interest
Rent
Depreciation

Most of these categories are self-explanatory, but depreciation may need clarification. **Depreciation** is the percentage of value of an asset subtracted each year until the value becomes zero, to reflect wear and tear on the asset. It is a method used to "expense" (listed as an expense on the income statement) costly pieces of equipment. Fixed costs are "expensed" during the year the money is spent. When a company pays for advertising, it subtracts that cost from the gross profit for that year. Some items, however, such as a computer, are expected to last for a number of years. A business could choose to expense a computer during the year it was bought, but that would not be accurate. A computer that will be used for 4 years will have been only 25 percent "used up" during the year it was purchased. Expensing the entire cost of the computer during that year makes the accounting records and financial statements inaccurate. If more than 25 percent of the computer's cost is expensed in the first year, the income statement will show a lower profit than it should. Meanwhile, profits in subsequent years will appear to be higher than they should.

This problem is addressed by depreciation, which spreads the cost of an item purchased by a business over the period of time during which it will actually be in use. If the computer will not be replaced for 4 years, then the full price should be shown as an asset and then expensed 25 percent each year. In this way, the cost of the computer and its value to the company will be reflected more accurately.

Fixed Operating Costs Do Change Over Time

If you pay your restaurant manager $3,600 per month in salary, you will have to pay that amount whether the restaurant sells one meal or a thousand. The cost is fixed.

Fixed operating costs do change over time—at some point you may give your restaurant manager a raise. Or, you might hire a new manager at a lower salary. The word *fixed* does not mean the cost *never* changes, just that it does not change in response to units of production or sales. For instance:

- *Advertising:* The cost of advertising will change based on decisions the entrepreneur makes about how much to spend to reach the consumer, not because of current sales.
- *Heating and Cooling Costs:* The price of heating and cooling goes up or down based on the weather and utility prices, not on the amount of revenue the business earns.

Allocate Your Fixed Operating Costs Where Possible

Business owners like to know, whenever they make a sale, how much of that revenue will have to be used to cover cost of goods sold and other variable costs.

Whatever is left over after you pay the COGS and other variable costs is your *contribution margin* (gross profit). You will pay your fixed operating costs out of your contribution margin. Whatever is left over after you pay your fixed operating costs (and taxes) is your **net profit**.

Fixed operating costs can be dangerous because they have to be paid whether or not the business makes a gross profit. The entrepreneur should be careful about taking on fixed costs, but does not have to worry so much about variable costs because, if sales are low, variable costs will be low as well. Wherever possible, the entrepreneur should seek to allocate or distribute as many costs as possible by making them variable.

Here is an example of how to fully allocate your costs, so that you know, each time you sell a unit, how much of your fixed and variable costs the sale covers.

Example: If you sell 300 watches per month at $15 per watch (see **Figure 7-5**), your COGS is $2 per watch and your other variable costs are commissions of $2 per watch and shipping charges of $1 per watch.

Gross profit per unit is $13 ($3,900 in gross profit divided by 300 watches sold). Contribution margin per unit is $10 ($3,000 ÷ 300). Some of this gross profit will have to be used to cover the business's fixed operating costs. It is helpful to determine how much profit will be left over after paying the fixed operating costs, assuming your sales are stable. **Figure 7-6** shows the calculation of the total cost per unit.

For every watch you sell, your total cost, fixed and variable, is $6.50. If you receive $15 for each watch, therefore, your profit before tax is the following:

$15.00 selling price – $6.50 total cost per unit = $8.50 profit before tax.

Figure 7-5 *Retail business: Unit = 1 watch.*

Analysis—300 Watches Sold			
Sales (300 watches x $15 per watch):			$4,500
COGS ($2 per watch x 300 watches):		$600	600
Gross Profit (on 300 watches sold)			3,900
Other Variable Costs			
Commission ($2 per watch)	$600		
Shipping ($1 per watch)	300		
Total Other Variable Costs	$900	900	900
Total Variable Costs (per Unit)		$1,500	
Contribution Margin			$3,000

Figure 7-6 *Retail business: Total cost per unit.*

Total Variable Costs (COGS + Other Variable Costs):		$1,500
Fixed Operating Costs (per month):		
Utilities	$50	
Salaries	100	
Advertising	50	
Insurance	50	
Interest	50	
Rent	100	
Depreciation	50	
Total Fixed Operating Costs:	$450	450
Total Costs (Fixed + Variable) =		$1,950
Total Cost per Unit ($1,950 ÷ 300 watches) =		$6.50 per watch

Step into the Shoes...

Bob's Discount Furniture[2]

Bob Kaufman owns 31 furniture stores in New England. Bob's Discount Furniture is one of the largest TV advertisers in Connecticut. When Bob was starting out in the furniture business in 1992, though, he needed to find creative ways to cut his costs.

Bob found a store to rent for his furniture business, but the landlord wanted him to sign a 1-year lease. Bob knew that rent was a fixed cost. This meant he would have to pay rent every month, whether he could afford to or not, for a full 12 months. He realized that if sales were low he would get into trouble quickly, because he did not have cash in reserve.

What Bob needed was to change his rent from a fixed to a variable cost. He negotiated with the landlord to pay the rent as a percentage of the monthly sales. That way, if sales were low, Bob's rent would also be low. If sales were high, his rent would go up—but he would be able to pay it. Rent was Bob's largest fixed cost. By changing it into a variable cost he cut a lot of the risk out of his new business.

Bob's Discount Furniture became extremely successful. That arrangement helped Bob out when his business was small. Today, Bob and his partners own many of their locations and pay fixed rent on the rest.

---

[2] Thanks to John Harris for this story.

The Dangers of Fixed Costs

If a business does not have enough sales to cover its fixed costs, it will lose money. If losses continue, the business will have to close. As we have discussed, fixed costs are dangerous to a business because they must be paid whether or not the business is making enough sales to cover them. Variable costs, on the other hand, do not threaten a business's survival because they are proportional to sales.

How Inflation Can Hurt Small Business Owners

Inflation is the gradual, continuous increase in the prices of products and services, usually resulting from an increase in the amount of money in circulation in an economy. It can be the enemy of the small business owner. If you save $600 per year to buy new tables and chairs (which cost $3,000) for your restaurant, but find at the end of 5 years that the cost of replacing them has risen—due to inflation—to $5,000, your business could be in trouble if you cannot get the additional $2,000. Savvy entrepreneurs keep up with economic trends by reading the financial section in the newspapers, as well as financial magazines and Web sites. By staying up to date on what is happening, entrepreneurs can plan better for the future and invest wisely.

Using Accounting Records to Track Fixed and Variable Costs

Performance Objective 3

Set up financial record keeping for your business.

Now you are ready to set up your financial records. Nothing that you learn as an entrepreneur will be more important than keeping accurate records of the money flowing in and out of your business. The systematic recording, reporting, and analysis of the financial transactions of a business (keeping numerical records of inflows and outflows) is called **accounting**. It is the primary language businesspeople use to communicate. When you talk to an investor or a supplier about your business, you will need to use this language. He or she will want to see financial statements for your business that describe its performance at a glance.

Before you can create financial statements, however, you must be able to keep track of your daily business transactions. If you develop record keeping into a habit, you will be well ahead of the many businesspeople who tend to stick their heads in the sand when it comes to keeping good records consistently.

Three Reasons to Keep Good Records Every Day

1. ***Keeping good records will show you how to make your business more profitable:*** Perhaps you are making less profit this month than last. Did your expenses go up? Maybe you need to try lowering your costs. Did your sales drop? Maybe you are not spending enough on advertising. Use accurate records to constantly improve your business.

2. ***Keeping good records will document your business profitability:*** If you want people to invest in your business, show them that it is profitable. Keep accurate records to create financial statements and ratios that prove your business is doing well. Remember, you will *always* need to maintain your financial statements so that you will be up to date on your business performance.

3. ***Keeping good records proves that payments have been made:*** Accurate, up-to-date records help prevent arguments because they prove you have paid a bill or that a customer has paid you. Records also prove that you have paid your **taxes**, the fee charged (*levied*) by a government on an income, product, or activity that is imposed on an individual or legal entity (corporation). Sometimes the Internal Revenue Service, the federal agency that collects taxes, will visit a business and check its financial records in a process called an **audit**. If you keep good records and pay your taxes in a timely fashion, you will have nothing to fear from audits.

Keeping good records is simple, as long as you set up an efficient system and follow it every day. When you start skipping days, maintaining accurate and complete financial records will become virtually impossible.

U.S. tax law allows business owners to deduct many expenses from their taxes. These **deductions**, or **tax write-offs**, are reductions in the gross amount on which taxes are calculated, and they will save you money. But you must keep receipts and record check payments to show that you actually had the expenses. A good practice is to write the purpose of the expense on the receipt.

Accounting Software

There are many excellent computer software programs on the market to help the small business owner keep good records and generate financial statements and analytical reports. These include Intuit QuickBooks, Microsoft Office Accounting, and Peachtree Accounting. In addition, companies such as Net Suite offer Web-based accounting for a monthly access fee. There are also programs to help you manage your money. You can use them to write checks, balance your bank account, and track your income. Some software creates project quotes and invoices. There is specialized software for particular types of businesses and for not-for-profit organizations.

The URLs for some of the accounting software companies are:

Microsoft, *http://www.microsoft.com*
QuickBooks, *http://www.quickbooks.com*
Peachtree Software, *http://www.peachtree.com*

Many software companies offer free versions of their products that you can try for a limited period of time or that are free but do not have as many features as the software for sale. This is a great way for you to try out different accounting and other business software before you buy. The costs of these packages have dropped considerably, making them a better value for

Step into the Shoes...
Rockefeller's Record Keeping

John D. Rockefeller, who founded Standard Oil (now ExxonMobil) and built one of the most famous family fortunes in history, reportedly kept track of every penny he spent from age 16 until his death in 1937, at the age of 98. His children said that he never paid a bill without examining it and being certain that he understood it.

Being up to date with your financial records will give you control over your business and a sense of security.

even the smallest businesses. For example, if your business provides services and potential customers expect estimates, they can be generated and tracked by professional services software. Take the time to find the software best suited to your needs.

Receipts and Invoices

For a very small business, it is possible to work with a journal and two files (or boxes) for storing records of your transactions. As your business grows, you can add organizational tools. However, if you are intending to grow the business and you can afford it, you should use a good computer-based system from the start. Whatever system you elect to use, there are certain records to keep.

- A **receipt** is a slip of paper with the date and amount of the purchase on it. *Always get a receipt for every purchase you make.*
- An **invoice**, or bill, shows the product or service sold and the amount the customer is to pay. Once the customer pays the bill, the invoice is marked "PAID." Your invoice becomes the customer's receipt. Keep a copy of each invoice, in numerical order, or organized alphabetically, by customer name.

Buy a carbon-copy receipt book. When you make a sale, give the top copy to the customer as a receipt. Keep the second copy as your invoice or record of the sale. Again, if you can purchase a point-of-sale system, do so.

Keep Two Copies of Your Records

Always keep a copy of your financial records in a location separate from your business. If you are using software, back up your data and keep the media (CD, jump drive, etc.) in a different location. At the end of each day, week, or month, move your new receipts and invoices to this location. How often you will do this depends upon your transaction volume and how much data you are willing to risk losing. By having regular off-site backups, if anything happens to your journal or your business site, you will still have your financial records.

Use Business Checks for Business Expenses

Get a checking account to use only for your business. It is poor business practice to commingle your personal and business funds.

- ***Avoid using cash for business:*** When you pay with cash, there is often no record of your payment. If you must pay in cash, get an itemized receipt.

- *Deposit money from sales right away:* When you make a sale, it will not be complete until the money is in the bank and, if the payment was made by check, until the check has cleared.

"Cash Only" Accounting

This method is called **cash only accounting** because the only time you will make an accounting entry is when you have paid or received cash or checks. If you are using a manual system, every time you pay for something, write it down on the left side of the journal (see **Figure 7-7**). Include the check number. Keep a running balance so you always know how much cash you have on hand.

Each column on the right side of the journal has a heading for a category of income or expense. For each entry on the left side of the journal, make a **matching entry** on the right side. Find the column on the left that describes the entry you made on the right side and enter the same amount in the right-hand column (see **Figure 7-8**). If you use computer software, it will prompt you to make the entries properly.

Cash Journal Categories

- *Variable Costs (VC):* Any cost that changes based on the number of units sold. Includes cost of goods sold (COGS). Multiply COGS by the number of units sold to get total COGS. When you receive revenue, write the total COGS in the COGS column. (COGS is not counted in the "balance" of the two sides of your journal because it is not a "cash" transaction.)
- *Fixed Costs (FC):* Business expenses that must be paid whether or not sales are made (remember USAIIRD).
- *Capital Equipment:* Money you spend on business equipment that you expect to last a year or more.
- *Investment:* Start-up capital plus any money you (or others) have invested in the business. This column is not for loans. This is only for money invested in exchange for part ownership (equity).
- *Loans:* Any money you borrow to start or operate the business is entered in this column.

Figure 7-7 *Journal—Left side.*

Figure 7-8 *Journal—Right side.*

Figure 7-9 *Blank accounting journal—Left side.*

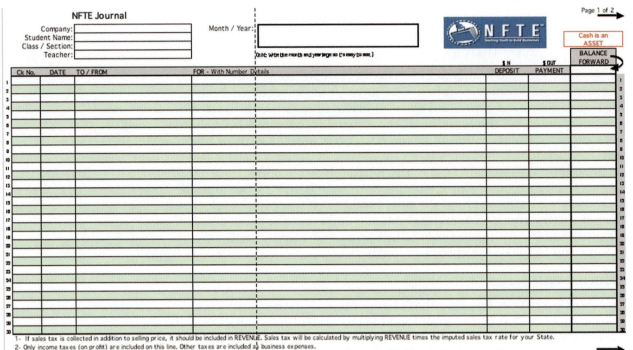

- *Revenue:* Money you receive from sales. *Whenever you write down revenue, declare your COGS in the next column on the same line!*
- *Inventory:* Anything you buy to resell is *inventory.* Include shipping costs from the supplier.
- *Other Costs:* Anything that does not fit into the other expense categories. Include a brief explanation.

Using the Cash Journal

Please see **Figures 7-9** and **7-10** for sample blank accounting journal pages for a manual system.

- Enter only one **transaction** (payment or deposit) per line.
- Use pencil, so you can erase mistakes. Mechanical pencils are best because they make very thin lines, allowing you to write more in a small space.
- Left- and right-hand entries must match and be on the same line. *The only exception is COGS, which is entered with "Revenue" on the right side.*
- Describe each transaction. Details like "how many" and "at what price" can be helpful later.
- Figure the "New Balance" on the left side. This will tell you how much cash you actually have.
- **Reconcile** your journal each month. This means that you will need to go through it and check the right side against the left side to make sure you did not make mistakes. Make adjustments for last month's statement on the next open line of your current journal. Adjustments go in the "Other Costs" column, with an explanatory note.

Figure 7-10 *Blank accounting journal—Right side.*

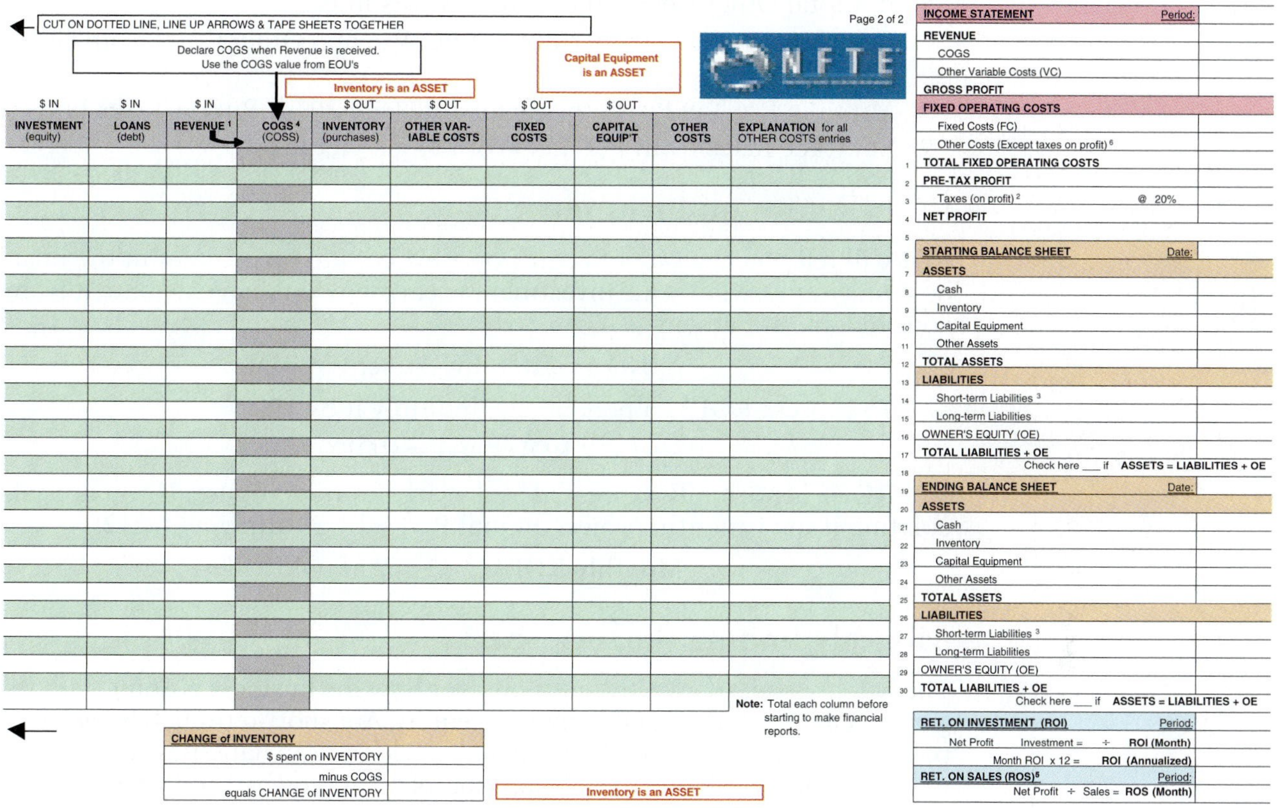

Creating Financial Statements from the Journal

Entrepreneurs use the following financial statements to run their businesses:

- Monthly income statement
- Monthly cash flow statement
- Monthly ending balance sheet

The monthly income statement and monthly ending balance sheet "fall out of" the accounting journal. The journal also shows you your "running cash balance," which you can use to create a cash flow statement and to calculate the return on your investment.

To create a financial statement, simply carry numbers over from the journal to the blank financial statement, as will be explained next.

◀ **Performance Objective 4**
Create financial statements.

Monthly Income Statement

The income statement helps the entrepreneur keep track of sales and costs, and shows whether or not the business made a profit in the previous month (or other time period). If not, the entrepreneur can analyze the income statement to try to figure out how to cut costs or increase revenue or both.

1. Put total from the Revenue column on the line marked Revenue on your Income Statement.
2. Put total from the COGS column on the line marked COGS.
3. Calculate Gross Profit by subtracting COGS from Revenue.
4. Put total Fixed Costs on the FC line.

5. Put total Variable Costs on the VC line.
6. Put total Other Costs on the Other Costs line.
7. Calculate Pre-Tax Profit. Subtract FC, VC, and Other Costs from Gross Profit.
8. Multiply Pre-Tax Profit by the tax rate (use 20%). Put on Taxes line.
9. Subtract Taxes from Pre-Tax Profit to get Net Profit.

ROI (Return on Investment)

ROI will tell you the rate of return on your capital investment in the business or, simply, what your investment is earning. You can calculate it from your income statement.

$$\text{Net Profit} \div \text{Investment} = \text{ROI}$$

To express ROI as a percentage, multiply it by 100.

$$\text{ROI} \times 100 = \text{ROI\%}$$

ROI% is normally expressed as a yearly (annual) figure. If you are calculating it for 1 month, project annual ROI% by multiplying by 12.

$$\text{Monthly ROI\%} \times 12 = \text{Annual ROI\%}$$

Monthly Ending Balance Sheet

The balance sheet shows the entrepreneur how the business is doing with regard to paying off debt and increasing equity. Are short-term liabilities being paid off? Is the business making a dent in its long-term liabilities? Is the business growing? It will provide a "snapshot" of what is owned and what is owed.

(Note: Your Starting Balance Sheet for this month is your Ending Balance Sheet for the previous month.)

1. Put current cash balance on the Cash line.
2. Figure how much Inventory you added this month. Subtract COGS from INV Costs. Add that to the "Inventory" number from the Starting Balance Sheet for this month to get "Inventory" for the Ending Balance Sheet. COGS is really the used-up portion of inventory.
3. Add the Capital Equipment total to "Capital Equipment" from your Starting Balance Sheet. This is Ending "Capital Equipment." (We are not considering depreciation at this point.)
4. (Off the Journal) If you have "Other Assets," add them to the "Other Assets" number from the Starting Balance Sheet. This is Ending "Other Assets."
5. (Off the Journal) If you have "Short-Term Liabilities" at the end of the month, add them to the "Short-Term Liabilities" you still owe from the previous month. Short-Term Liabilities are debts you plan to pay in less than a year. Include taxes you owe on this month's profits in "Short-Term Liabilities."
6. (Off the Journal) If you have "Long-Term Liabilities" at the end of the month, add them to the "Long-Term Liabilities" you owe from the previous month.
7. Calculate Ending Owner's Equity: Add Net Profit from the Income Statement *and* the total of this month's Capital Invest column *and* the Owner's Equity number of your Starting Balance Sheet.
8. Add up Assets. Now add up Liabilities + Owner's Equity. If these two numbers are equal, then you did your Ending Balance Sheet correctly. If not, you made a mistake somewhere.

$$\text{Assets} = \text{Liabilities} + \text{Owner's Equity}$$

Sample Accounting Journal

To illustrate how to use a manual journal and how the financial statements fall out of it, we will complete a journal for a business called Hernando's T-Shirts. Hernando makes custom-printed T-shirts and hoodies. His transactions for October 2008 are described below. As you read about the entries, try to find them in the journal pages (see **Figures 7-11** and **7-12**).

October 1

1. Hernando invests $3,000 of his own money to start his business. On 10/1 he opens his business checking account with a $3,000 deposit.

October 2

2. Hernando buys a silk-screen printing frame and some equipment for $500 from ACME Printing Supply Co. He pays with check #100.
3. Hernando buys ink and supplies from ACE ARTS. He gets enough to make about 300 T-shirts and pays $300 with check #101.
4. He buys six dozen blank shirts from Big Bob's Wholesale. He pays $36 per dozen. The check is #102.

October 5

5. Hernando pays his friend José Rivera $2 each to screen-print 72 shirts. His check #103 to José is for $144.

October 6

6. Hernando pays the monthly $150 registration fee so he can sell at the Grand Flea Market. He pays with check #104.
7. Hernando stops in at the Corner Print Shop and buys 500 business cards for $20.

Figure 7-11 *NFTE journal.*

BizBuilders Journal - 10 ©

Company:	Hernando's T-Shirts	Month / Year:	October, 2008
Student Name:	Hernando LaHideaway		
Class / Section:	Entrepreneurship 101		
Teacher:	Mr. Mariotti		

(hint: Write the month and year large so it's easy to see.)

Cash is an ASSET

	Ck No.	DATE	TO / FROM	FOR - With Number Details	$ IN DEPOSIT	$ OUT PAYMENT	BALANCE FORWARD	
1	deposit	10/1/08	Hernando	Start-up investment in the business. (Since the account is new, there is no forward balance.)	3,000.00		3,000.00	1
2	100	10/2/08	ACME Printing Supply	Startup; Silk Screen equipment		500.00	2,500.00	2
3	101	10/2/08	ACE ARTS	Start up; Silk Screen Ink and Supplies - Enough to make 300 printed T shirts		300.00	2,200.00	3
4	102	10/2/08	Big Bob's Wholesale	Buy 6 Dozen blank T shirts @ $36.00 / doz. ($3.00 each)		216.00	1,984.00	4
5	103	10/5/08	Jose Rivera	Pay to have T shirts printed; Pay Jose $2.00 each for 72 shirts = $144.00		144.00	1,840.00	5
6	104	10/6/08	Grand Flea Market	Monthly Registration Fee		150.00	1,690.00	6
7	105	10/6/08	Corner Print Shop	Business Cards, for 500 cards		20.00	1,670.00	7
8	106	10/8/08	Corner Print Shop	Color Flyers - quan. 200		65.00	1,605.00	8
9	deposit	10/9/08	Deposit Checks from Flea Market	Deposit money from sales of 6 Dozen T Shirts @ $12.00 each (COGS of $6.00 each)	864.00		2,469.00	9
10	107	10/10/08	Big Bob's Wholesale	Buy 15 Dozen blank T shirts (180 T shirts) $36.00 / doz. ($3.00 each)		540.00	1,929.00	10
11	108	10/12/08	Jose Rivera	Pay to have "T" shirts printed; Pay Jose $2.00 each for 180 shirts = $360.00		360.00	1,569.00	11
12	deposit	10/14/08	Deposit Checks from Flea Market	Dep.$ from sales-15 dz. shirts sold; 12 dz. @ $12.00 ea., 3 dz. @ $10.00 ea.(COGS of $6.00 each)	2,088.00		3,657.00	12
13	109	10/16/08	Big Bob's Wholesale	Buy 15 Dozen blank T shirts (180 T shirts) @ $36.00 / doz. ($3.00 each)		540.00	3,117.00	13
14	110	10/16/08	ACE ARTS	More silk screen ink and supplies - Enough to make 450 printed T shirts		450.00	2,667.00	14
15	111	10/18/08	Jose Rivera	Pay to have "T" shirts printed; Pay Jose $2.00 each for 180 shirts = $360.00		360.00	2,307.00	15
16	112	10/19/08	Corner Print Shop	More color Flyers - quan. 200 more		65.00	2,242.00	16
17	deposit	10/21/08	Deposit Checks from Flea Market	Deposit money from sales; Only 9 doz. @ 12.00 ea. (it rained) (COGS of $6.00 each)	1,296.00		3,538.00	17
18	113	10/25/08	Big Bob's Wholesale	Buy 21 Dozen blank T shirts (252 T shirts) @ $36.00 / doz. ($3.00 each)		756.00	2,782.00	18
19	114	10/26/08	Jose Rivera	Pay to have "T" shirts printed; Pay Jose $2.00 each for 21 doz. (252) shirts = $504.00		504.00	2,278.00	19
20	deposit	10/28/08	Deposit Checks from Giselle's Sales	Deposit money from Sales - 24 doz. @ 12.00 ea. (COGS of $6.00 each)	3,456.00		5,734.00	20
21	115	10/30/08	Giselle Rivera	Commission @ 25% of Sales; $3,456.00 x 25% = $864.00		864.00	4,870.00	21
22								22
23								23
24								24
25								25
26								26
27								27
28								28
29								29
30								30

1- If sales tax is collected in addition to selling price, it should be included in REVENUE. Sales tax will be calculated by multiplying REVENUE times the imputed sales tax rate for your State.

2- Only income taxes (on profit) are included on this line. Other taxes are included as business expenses.

3- Taxes owed, but not yet paid should be included in the total of Short Term Liabilities. When they are paid, Short Term Liabilities should be reduced by the amount paid.

4- Cost of Goods Sold (COGS) is the same as Cost of Service Sold (COSS) for a service business. Money spent on direct labor and materials (INVENTORY) is not a "cost" until it's sold, when it becomes COGS.

5- SALES is a synonym for (means the same thing as) REVENUE.

6- The dash symbol " - " stands for " 0 " (zero) in Accounting.

Figure 7-12 *NFTE journal.*

CUT ON DOTTED LINE, LINE UP ARROWS & TAPE SHEETS TOGETHER

Declare COGS when Revenue is received. Use the COGS value from EOU's

Inventory is an ASSET

Capital Equipment is an ASSET

Page 2 of 2

$ IN INVESTMENT (equity)	$ IN LOANS (debt)	$ IN REVENUE[1]	COGS[4] (COSS)	$ OUT INVENTORY (purchases)	$ OUT OTHER VARIABLE COSTS	$ OUT FIXED COSTS	$ OUT CAPITAL EQUIP'T	OTHER COSTS	EXPLANATION for all OTHER COSTS entries
3,000.00									
							500.00		
				300.00					
				216.00					
				144.00					
						150.00			
						20.00			
						65.00			
		864.00	432.00						
				540.00					
				360.00					
		2,088.00	1,080.00						
				540.00					
				450.00					
				360.00					
						65.00			
		1,296.00	648.00						
				756.00					
				504.00					
		3,456.00	1,728.00						
					864.00				
3,000.00	-	7,704.00	3,888.00	4,170.00	864.00	300.00	500.00	-	

Note: Total each column before starting to make financial reports.

CHANGE of INVENTORY

$ spent on INVENTORY	4,170.00
minus COGS	3,888.00
equals CHANGE of INVENTORY	282.00

Inventory is an ASSET

INCOME STATEMENT	Period:	Oct. 2003
REVENUE		7,704.00
COGS		3,888.00
Other Variable Costs (VC)		864.00
CONTRIBUTION MARGIN		2,952.00
FIXED OPERATING COSTS		
Fixed Costs (FC)		300.00
Other Costs (Except taxes on profit)[6]		-
1 TOTAL FIXED OPERATING COSTS		300.00
2 PRE-TAX PROFIT		2,652.00
3 Taxes (on profit)[2]	@ 20%	530.40
4 NET PROFIT		2,121.60
5		
6 STARTING BALANCE SHEET	Date:	10/1/03
7 ASSETS		
8 Cash		-
9 Inventory		-
10 Capital Equipment		-
11 Other Assets		-
12 TOTAL ASSETS		
13 LIABILITIES		
14 Short-term Liabilities[3]		-
15 Long-term Liabilities		-
16 OWNER'S EQUITY (OE)		-
17 TOTAL LIABILITIES + OE		-
18 Check here ___ if ASSETS = LIABILITIES + OE		
19 ENDING BALANCE SHEET	Date:	10/31/03
20 ASSETS		
21 Cash		4,870.00
22 Inventory		282.00
23 Capital Equipment		500.00
24 Other Assets		-
25 TOTAL ASSETS		5,652.00
26 LIABILITIES		
27 Short-term Liabilities[3]		530.40
28 Long-term Liabilities		-
29 OWNER'S EQUITY (OE)		5,121.60
30 TOTAL LIABILITIES + OE		5,652.00
Check here ___ if ASSETS = LIABILITIES + OE		

RET. ON INVESTMENT (ROI)	Period:	Oct. 2003
Net Income ÷ Investment = ROI (Month)		71%
Month ROI x 12 = ROI (Annualized)		849%
RET. ON SALES (ROS)[5]	Period:	Oct. 2003
Net Income ÷ Sales = ROS (Month)		28%

October 8

8. Hernando makes 200 flyers at the Corner Print Shop for $65.

October 9

9. He sells all six dozen T-shirts at $12 each at the Grand Flea Market. He deposits $864 in his bank account. At the same time he "declares" his COGS on the same line as Revenue, as a matching entry. His COGS is $6 per shirt × 72 shirts = $432 ($3 per blank shirt; $2 each, printing; $1 each, ink).

October 10

10. Hernando buys 15 dozen more T-shirts (180 shirts) from Big Bob's Wholesale. They still cost $36 per dozen.

October 12

11. Hernando pays José to print 180 shirts for $360.

October 14

12. Hernando deposits $2,088 from the flea market sales in the bank. He sold 12 dozen T-shirts at $12 each, and 3 dozen for $10 each. He declares his COGS and records that on the same line. COGS is still $6 per shirt.

October 16

13. Hernando buys 15 dozen more T-shirts from Big Bob's at $36 per dozen.

14. Hernando is running out of ink, so he buys enough to print another 450 shirts. The ink costs $450 at ACE ARTS.

October 18

15. Hernando pays José $360 for printing the next order of 180 shirts.

October 19

16. Hernando pays $65 for 200 more flyers.

October 21

17. Hernando deposits $1,296 from sales at the Grand Flea Market into the business bank account. Because it rained, he only sold nine dozen shirts at $12 each.

October 25

18. Hernando buys 21 dozen shirts from Big Bob's for $756.

October 26

19. Hernando pays José $504 for printing 21 dozen shirts.

October 28

20. Hernando deposits $3,456 from sales made by Giselle Rivera, José's little sister. She sold 24 dozen T-shirts at $12. Total COGS is $1,728 (288 units × $6).

October 30

21. Hernando pays Giselle a sales commission of 25 percent. He writes her a check for $864 (.25 × $3,456 = $864).

Three Rules for Managing Your Cash

The accounting journal shows how much cash you have on hand. You can be running a profitable business but still be *insolvent* if your **cash balance**—receipts minus disbursements—becomes negative. In order to avoid getting caught without enough cash to pay your bills, follow these three rules:

1. *Collect cash as soon as possible:* When you make a sale, try to get paid on the spot.
2. *Delay paying bills as long as possible without irritating the supplier:* Most bills come with a due date. The phone bill, for instance, is typically due within 30 days. Never pay a bill after the due date, however, without getting permission from the supplier first.
3. *Always know your cash balance:* Keep a running balance.

Keep Your Accounting Current

If you keep your accounting journal every day, running your business will be a lot easier. At the end of each week, you may want to enter the information from your daily journal into a weekly **ledger**, which is a collection of all the accounts of a business, including sales, cash, accounts receivable, and sales tax due. Posting the information from your daily journals to a ledger once a week will give you a good overview of how your business is doing. If you are using an accounting software program, this step will be unnecessary, as the software automatically creates the ledger.

By keeping good records on a daily basis, you will be able to prepare monthly income statements and ending balance sheets. These will help you make good decisions for your business. Good accounting practices will help you keep track of your cash, too. An entrepreneur should always know the cash balance! Learn how to keep good records now, and it will become second nature after awhile. You will be far ahead of business owners who never know how much cash they have on hand!

Keep at Least Three Months of Fixed Operating Costs in Reserve

During the early days of your business, when you are working hard to attract customers and establish your reputation, you may not be making many sales, but you will still have your fixed operating costs. If you are not prepared for this, you could be forced out of business because you did not pay the rent or utilities. Unfortunately, this happens much more often than you might imagine.

As we noted earlier in the chapter, try to put enough money in the bank to cover at least one-half of your start-up costs *before you open your business*. Such a cash reserve is money you will keep for emergencies—such as not being able to sell your handmade swimsuits because it has been raining for a month! A reserve will keep your business going during tough times, while you think of new ways to attract customers. You can build up a reserve through savings, borrowing, or from investors.

Chapter Summary

Now that you have studied this chapter, you can do the following:

1. Describe the variable costs of starting a business.
   - Start-up investment is the one-time expense of starting a business.
   - Cost of goods sold is the cost of selling "one additional unit."
   - Operating costs are the costs necessary to run the business, not including the cost of goods sold. Operating costs can almost always be divided into seven categories. An easy way to remember these is through the acronym USAIIRD:
     - Utilities (gas, electric, telephone, Internet)
     - Salaries
     - Advertising
     - Insurance
     - Interest
     - Rent
     - Depreciation
2. Divide your costs into two categories: variable and fixed.
   - Variable costs vary (change) with sales. They are broken into two subcategories:
     a. Cost of goods sold, which are the costs associated specifically with each unit of sale, including:
        - The cost of materials used to make the product (or deliver the service)
        - The cost of labor used to make the product (or deliver the service)
     b. Other variable costs, including:
        - Commissions
        - Shipping and handling charges, etc.
   - Fixed costs stay constant whether you sell many units, or very few. Examples of fixed costs include rent, salaries, and insurance.

3. Set up financial record keeping for your business.
   - For "cash only" accounting, the only time you will make a journal entry is when you have paid or received cash or checks.
   - Every time you pay for something, write it down on the left side of the journal. Each column on the right side of the journal has a heading for a category of income or expense. For each entry on the left side of the journal, make a matching entry on the right side. Or, if using software, record each transaction.
4. The accounting journal shows you how much cash you have on hand.
   - You can be running a profitable business but still be insolvent if your cash balance (receipts minus disbursements) becomes negative.
   - In order to avoid getting caught without enough cash to pay your bills, follow these three rules:
     a. Collect cash as soon as possible. When you make a sale, try to get paid on the spot.
     b. Delay paying bills as long as possible without irritating the supplier.
     c. Always know your cash balance.
5. Create financial statements.
   - Use the financial records that you have kept to create financial statements.
   - Monthly income statements track sales and costs.
   - Monthly ending balance sheets show what is owned and what is owed.

Key Terms

accounting	matching entry
audit	moving assembly line
cash balance	net profit
cash only accounting	overhead
cash reserve	payback
contribution margin	prototype
deductions	receipt
depreciation	reconcile
fixed costs	start-up investment
fixed operating costs	taxes
inflation	tax write-off
inventory costs	transaction
invoice	variable costs
ledger	

Entrepreneurship Portfolio

Critical Thinking Exercises

1. Give an example of a business that you have observed lowering the price of a product. How do you think the business was able to lower the price?
2. Describe the record keeping system you intend to set up for your own business.

3. What bank accounts do you intend to set up for your business? Which bank will you use? Why?

4. Imagine that you have invented a guitar strap that goes over both shoulders, thereby reducing shoulder strain for the guitarist. This item could be a big seller, but, before you can apply for a patent or convince investors to back you in producing it, you will need a prototype. Find at least three manufacturers that could create a prototype for you.

5. For a business you would like to start, estimate what you think the fixed and variable costs would be. Choose a category for each cost from USAIIRD: Utilities, Salaries, Advertising, Interest, Insurance, Rent, and Depreciation.

Key Concept Questions

1. Sue, of Sue's Sandwich Shoppe, sells sandwiches and soda from a sidewalk cart in a popular park near her home. She sets up her rented cart in the summers to raise money for college. Last month she sold $3,000 worth of product (sandwiches and sodas) to 300 customers. She spent $600 on the sandwich ingredients and buying the sodas wholesale. Her monthly costs are the following: Utilities = $60, Salary = $1500, Advertising = $0, Insurance = $50, Interest = $0, Rent = $300, Depreciation = $0.

   a. What are Sue's variable costs? Explain.

   b. What is Sue's COGS? Explain.

   c. What are her other variable costs? Explain.

   d. What are her fixed costs? Explain.

   e. What is Sue's EOU?

   f. How much cash reserve should she keep in the bank?

2. Solve the following problems:

Units Sold	Selling Price	Total Revenue
a. 25	$4.64	$116.00
b. 30	$10.99	_____
c. 12	$1,233.00	_____
d. 75	$545.75	_____
e. 20	$45.03	_____

3. Calculate Total Variable Costs for the same items.

Units Sold	Total Variable Costs per Unit	Total Variable Costs
a. 25	$2.00	$50.00
b. 30	$5.50	_____
c. 12	$620.00	_____
d. 75	$280.00	_____
e. 20	$20.00	_____

4. Calculate Total Contribution Margin for the same items.

Total Revenue	Total Variable Costs	Total Contribution Margin
a. $116.00	$50.00	$66.00
b.		
c.		
d.		
e.		

5. Calculate Total Profit for the same items.

Total Contribution Margin	Total Fixed Operating Costs	Total Profit
a. $66.00	$25.00	$41.00
b.	$60.00	
c.	$425.00	
d.	$12,000.00	
e.	$200.00	

6. Calculate Profit per Unit for the same items.

Units Sold	Total Profit	Profit per Unit
a. 25	$41.00	$1.64
b. 30		
c. 12		
d. 75		
e. 20		

Application Exercise

Miriam Lopez makes funky messenger-style bags and knapsacks and sells them to fashionable boutiques in Manhattan. The following are her business transactions for the first five working days of March 2008. Record these transactions in an accounting journal, create an income statement for the first week of March, and figure her return on investment for the week.

1. 3/1/08—Miriam purchases 8 bolts of waterproof canvas cloth from Canal Street Fabrics for $2,000.
2. 3/1/08—A store called The Lab pays its Feb. 20 invoice for $825.04.
3. 3/1/08—Miriam pays the $1,000 monthly rent on her office/workspace.
4. 3/2/08—Miriam buys a used heavy-duty sewing machine for $500. The seller agrees to bill her if she will pay it within 30 days.
5. 3/2/08—Miriam sells 10 bags at a SoHo flea market for $50 each.
6. 3/3/08—Miriam's $120 phone bill was due Feb. 15. To avoid warnings from the phone company, she pays her bill.

7. 3/3/08—Macy's orders 20 of Miriam's bags "on consignment," meaning that the store will only pay if it can sell the bags. If the bags do not sell, the store will return them.

8. 3/4/08—Miriam buys buckles and snaps to make the bags for Macy's for $75.

9. 3/4/08—Miriam decides to hire a publicist to promote her business now that she has a relationship with Macy's. The publicist agrees to work for $250 a week for 6 weeks, with $500 payable in advance to clinch the agreement.

10. 3/5/08—Miriam takes the buyer from The Lab out to lunch: $75.50.

11. 3/5/08—Miriam fills her car's gas tank for $43.29. Since she uses the car almost exclusively for business, she records this as a business expense.

12. 3/5/08—Miriam orders 500 new business cards for $25. She will pay for them when she picks them up next week.

Exploring Your Community

Ask an entrepreneur in your neighborhood to discuss his or her accounting system. Write a one-page essay about the pros and cons of the system and use it to make an oral report to the class.

Exploring Online

Research different accounting software programs online. Choose a program (or programs) for your business and explain your choice in a brief essay.

In Your Opinion

Would you rather keep your financial records in an accounting ledger or on your computer? Why? In each case, how would you protect your records from being lost in a disaster, such as a fire, or, in the case of the computer, a hard-drive crash?

CASE STUDY: The Importance of Cash

Jack Wilson has had a 30-year career in the building and managing of Web pages with two very well-known Web-based marketing companies. During his career, Jack has been in contact with hundreds of people and companies through projects and industry gatherings. For the past 4 years and on his own time, Jack has been developing new ways of making it easier for users to maintain and upgrade Web-page information. Jack is entering the final stages of writing the software that will provide these benefits, and he wants to leave his present position and devote all his time to the project. Jack's employment contract calls for him to honor a non-compete clause for 12 months and he will receive a severance payment of $80,000, which is his approximate annual earnings for the past 2 years.

The new Web-page software will cost about $75,000 in programming fees, and $30,000 in legal fees will be necessary to ready the product for testing and sale. Jack is not experienced in marketing but a consultant that he has met with has predicted that it will take about $30,000 for product packaging and early promotional expenses. The product will probably sell for $2,500 per copy, based on similar software. The market for this type of software will be mainly small-to-medium-sized businesses that maintain their own Web sites. Jack is aware of a handful of existing software companies whose product line would be a good fit for what he is developing. (Some software developers have sold their ideas to larger companies, rather than try to handle the details and expense of launching a product themselves.)

Jack has liquid savings of $18,000 and another $90,000 in an IRA account. He owns a home without a mortgage that is worth about $150,000. Jack is a conservative person and does not lead a lavish lifestyle. He has worked long and hard on his new product idea and feels as though this is his opportunity to make a contribution to his field and be in charge of his own company. Jack also has the opportunity to provide some consulting services to other programming organizations on a project-by-project basis. This work could bring in fees of $40,000, probably from 6 months to a year after completion.

Case Study Analysis

1. Does Jack have enough money to start this business? What strategy would you recommend he pursue over the next year?

2. What strategies would you suggest for this entrepreneur to adopt with respect to his use of cash?

3. Is there enough information given for you to make some early suggestions to Jack about pursuing the product on his own versus selling his idea to an established company?

4. What amount of cash reserve for the business should Jack have in his plan?

CASE STUDY: Futrell Party Promotions[3]

The Problem

The telephone rang. Richard Futrell put on his headset and answered, "Good evening, Boston Teen Hotline. My name is Richard. How can I help you?" The year was 1999. Richard had been working as a hotline counselor at the Mayor's Youth Committee for 3 years. Every night from 6 to 11 P.M. he took calls from teenagers in the Boston area—advising them on many different issues—on relationships, family problems, school, and more. Richard had a natural talent for being a good listener. In fact, he listened so well that over time he started noticing similarities in the types of problems that young people were discussing on the hotline. Specifically, Richard observed that younger teens in the Dorchester and Roxbury communities did not feel safe going out on the weekends in their own neighborhoods. Parents were also worried about the safety of their children and sometimes called to ask whether the Youth Committee ever sponsored teen parties or other events. Richard always felt bad telling parents that the Council did not have the funds to organize these types of events. Richard liked helping people but this was the kind of problem he did not feel he could solve.

Problems Can Lead to Opportunities

But then, one day in October, Richard came up with an idea:

> Everybody was asking, "Is there going to be a Halloween party?" But there was not anyone who was throwing a party, so I said, I'll throw my own party!

I did not know how to DJ, but I had friends who worked as professional DJs. I just contacted everyone I knew who could help out and then made it happen.

Richard decided to use all $700 of his own personal savings to purchase services and supplies for the party. His intention was to earn this money back, and also generate a profit, by charging a $10 admission fee. He thought that $10 was a reasonable price because it was about the same amount that teens would typically spend on a weekend night to go out to a movie or play video games at the arcade. Richard knew that he had to be careful about how he allocated his resources, because a $700 start-up investment was not going to get him very far.

Getting Organized

Richard's first step in planning his party was to brainstorm a list of all the things he would need to purchase and arrange. The list he created follows:

Space Rental _____

DJ _____

Security _____

Insurance _____

Flyers _____

Food _____

Party Decorations _____

[3] This case is based on a real-life example, but selected details have been fictionalized. Thanks to Dr. Stephen Spinelli and Alex Hardy, of Babson College, for granting permission to adapt this case from its original version.

Chapter 8

Using Financial Statements to Guide a Business

> *"The propensity to truck, barter, and exchange one thing for another is common to all men."*
>
> —Adam Smith, Scottish economist

Two partners—Gary and Steve—decided to start an Internet café in Hoboken, New Jersey. Hoboken has a large community of freelance workers, artists, and other types of people who Gary and Steve thought would patronize their business.

The partners used extensive start-up funds to install super-fast "T1" lines, and making the café look up to date. The furniture was custom-designed for the space, as were the metallic ceiling and wall panels. The partners decided to serve gourmet coffees, cakes, and simple sandwiches.

Because so much money was spent on start-up, Steve and Gary tried to cut costs by hiring as staff local kids who would work at minimum wage. It soon became apparent to frustrated customers, however, that the staff could not solve technical problems. Customers who were having trouble printing or accessing documents were often told to wait "until Gary or Steve comes in," which often was not until late in the afternoon.

Neither Gary nor Steve had had previous entrepreneurial experience and most of the financing had come from their respective families. Because neither knew how to prepare an income statement, there was no effective way of keeping track of the money coming in and going out of the business. Within 14 months, the partners had to close their venture because they were not covering their operating costs. If they had been preparing monthly income statements, they could have seen the problems developing and taken action to solve them.

Performance Objectives

1. Read an income statement.
2. Examine a balance sheet to determine a business's financing strategy.
3. Use the balance sheet equation to see the relationship between assets, liabilities, and owner's equity.
4. Perform a financial ratio analysis of an income statement.
5. Calculate return on investment (ROI).
6. Perform "same size" analysis of an income statement.
7. Use quick, current, and debt ratios to analyze a balance sheet.

Scorecards for the Entrepreneur: What Do Financial Statements Show?

In this chapter you will learn how to prepare and use the income statement to guide your business and keep it strong. Entrepreneurs use three basic financial statements to track their businesses.[1]

- Income statement
- Cash flow statement
- Balance sheet

Together, these three statements show at a glance the health of a business.

Entrepreneurs use their financial records to prepare monthly income statements and balance sheets, and then finalize them at the end of the fiscal year. These statements provide concise, easily read and understood financial pictures of organizations. While a journal or check register will provide the cash balance on hand, the income statement and balance sheet give a comprehensive overview of the organization. By performing financial-statement analysis, you can gain a deeper understanding of any enterprise.

Income Statements: Showing Profit and Loss Over Time

Performance Objective 1

Read an income statement.

An older term for the income statement is **profit and loss statement**, but since you cannot have both profit and loss at the same time, the common term today is "income statement." It shows whether the difference between revenues (sales) and expenses (costs) is a profit or a loss. If sales are greater than costs, the income statement balance will be positive, showing that the business is profitable. If costs are greater than sales, the income statement balance will show that the business has lost money.

The income statement is a "scorecard" for the entrepreneur. If the business is not making a profit, examining the statement can show what may be causing the problem. Steps can then be taken to correct the problem before the business becomes insolvent. Profit is a reward for making the right choices. The income statement will enable you to determine whether your decisions have kept you on the right track each month. Learning to prepare an income statement is not difficult, and it is a great business tool.

Parts of an Income Statement

The income statement is composed of the following:

1. **Revenue:** Money (income) received from sales of the company's products or services.
2. **COGS (Cost of Goods Sold)/COSS (Cost of Services Sold):** These are the costs of materials used to make the product (or deliver the service) plus the costs of labor used to make the product (or deliver the service). An income statement reports total COGS for a month.
3. **Gross Profit:** To calculate gross profit, subtract COGS from revenue.
4. **Other Variable Costs (VC):** Costs that vary with sales.
5. **Contribution Margin:** Subtract COGS and other variable costs from revenue.

---
[1] Special thanks to John Harris for many of the ideas in this chapter.

- Alway
  everyc
- Treatin
  setting
  help c

Ideally, you
profit so yo

An Incor

This incon
page, and i
This stater

Sales:

Cost of Goo

Materials

Labor

Total COGS:

Gross Profit

Other Varial

Sales Comm

Less Total V

Contribution

Fixed Opera

Factory Rer

Salaries & /

Depreciatio

Total Fixed (

Profit Befor

Taxes (25%

Net Profit/(

Balan
Liabili

You can qu
sheet (see
shows the
worth of a
abilities a

1. Assets:

6. **Fixed Operating Costs:** Costs of operating a business that do not vary with sales. The most common fixed operating costs are utilities, salaries, advertising, insurance, interest, rent, and depreciation (USAIIRD).
7. **Pre-Tax Profit:** Contribution margin minus fixed operating costs. This is a business's profit after all costs have been deducted, but before taxes have been paid. Pre-tax profit is used to calculate how much tax the business owes.
8. **Taxes:** A business must pay taxes on the income it earns. It may have to make monthly or quarterly estimated tax payments.
9. **Net Profit/(Loss):** This is the business's profit or loss after taxes have been paid. See **Figure 8-1** for an example of an income statement.

Figure 8-1 *Income statement.*

Income Statement — form showing:

Name of Company / Time Period

- Sales/Revenue $
- COGS (Cost of Goods Sold)
  - Total Materials $
  - Total Labor
- Total COGS $ $ $
- Gross Profit $
- Other Variable Costs
  - Commission $
  - Packaging
  - Total Other Variable Costs $ $
- Contribution Margin $
- Fixed Operating Costs (USAIIRD)
  - Utilities $
  - Salaries
  - Advertising
  - Insurance
  - Interest
  - Rent
  - Depreciation
  - Other
  - Total Fixed Operating Costs: $ $
- Pre-Tax Profit $
- Taxes
- Net Profit $

Total Sales/Revenue = Units Sold × Unit Selling Price

Total Cost of Goods or Services Sold = Units Sold × Cost of Goods or Services Sold per Unit

Gross Profit = Sales − COGS

Total Other Variable Costs = Units Sold × Other Variable Costs per Unit

Total Variable Costs = Total Cost of Goods or Services Sold + Total Other Variable Costs

Contribution Margin = Total Sales − Total Variable Costs

Total Fixed Costs = Total of USAIIRDO

Pre-Tax Profit/(Loss) = Contribution Margin − Total Fixed Costs

Taxes = Profit × .20 (Estimated)

Net Profit = Pre-Tax Profit − Taxes

Figure 8-2 *Balance sheet (side-by-side layout).*

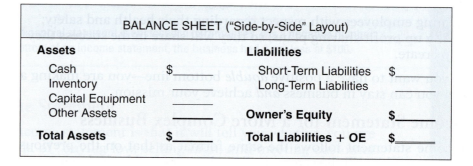

BALANCE SHEET ("Side-by-Side" Layout)			
Assets		**Liabilities**	
Cash	$_____	Short-Term Liabilities	$_____
Inventory		Long-Term Liabilities	_____
Capital Equipment	_____		
Other Assets	_____	**Owner's Equity**	$_____
Total Assets	$_____	**Total Liabilities + OE**	$_____

Figure 8-3 *Balance sheet (vertical layout).*

BALANCE SHEET ("Vertical" Layout)	
Assets	
Cash	$_____
Inventory	
Capital Equipment	_____
Other Assets	_____
Total Assets	$_____
Liabilities	
Short-Term Liabilities	$_____
Long-Term Liabilities	_____
Owner's Equity	$_____
Total Liabilities + OE	$_____

2. **Liabilities:** Debts a company has that must be paid, including unpaid bills.

3. **Owner's Equity (OE):** Also called net worth; this is the difference between assets and liabilities. It shows the amount of capital in the business.

BizFacts

A balance sheet is called a "point-in-time" financial statement because it shows the state of a business at a given moment.

The balance sheet for a big business is typically prepared at the end of the fiscal year, unlike cash flow and income statements, which are prepared monthly. The **fiscal year** is the 12-month accounting period chosen by the business. A fiscal year may differ from the calendar year (January 1 through December 31). A business that uses the calendar year as its fiscal year would prepare its balance sheet in December/January.

Many entrepreneurs, however, also prepare a balance sheet monthly. Business owners use these three financial tools—income statement, cash flow statement (discussed in chapter 4), and balance sheet—to keep the business on track.

Unorganized financial records can lead to chaos in a business.
(A. Chedderros/Getty)

Short- and Long-Term Assets

Assets are all items of worth owned by the business, such as cash, inventory, furniture, machinery, and the like. Assets are divided into short-term (current) and long-term (fixed).

- **Current assets** are cash itself or items that could be quickly turned into cash (liquidated), or will be used by the business within 1 year. Current assets include accounts receivable, inventory, and supplies.
- **Long-term assets** are those that would take more than 1 year for the business to use. Equipment, furniture, machinery, and real estate are examples of long-term assets.

Current and Long-Term Liabilities

Liabilities are all debts owed by the business, such as bank loans, mortgages, lines of credit, and loans from family or friends.

- **Current liabilities** are debts that must be paid within 1 year.
- **Long-term liabilities** are to be paid over a period of more than 1 year.

The Balance Sheet Equation

The terms *owner's equity*, *capital*, and *net worth* all mean the same thing—what's left over after liabilities are subtracted from assets. Owner's equity is the value of the business on the balance sheet to the owner.

> Assets − Liabilities = Net Worth (or Owner's Equity or Capital)

- If assets are greater than liabilities, net worth is positive.
- If liabilities are greater than assets, net worth is negative.

Here is an example: If Dos Compadres Restaurant has $10,000 cash on hand, and also owns $8,000 in equipment, and owes $5,000 in long-term liabilities, what is the restaurant's net worth?

> $18,000 (Assets) − $5,000 (Liabilities) = $13,000 (Net Worth)

> **◀ Performance Objective 3**
>
> Use the balance sheet equation to see the relationship between assets, liabilities, and owner's equity.
>
> *Owner's equity, capital, and net worth are all names for the value of a business to its owner.*

The Balance Sheet Shows Assets and Liabilities Obtained through Debt or Equity

Every item a business owns was obtained through either debt or equity. Therefore, the total of all assets must equal the total of all liabilities and owner's equity.

- If an item was financed with *debt*, the loan is a liability.
- If an item was purchased with the owner's own money, it was financed with *equity*.

If a restaurant owns its tables and chairs (worth $3,000) and its stoves (worth $5,000), and has $10,000 in cash and $4,000 in inventory, the business has a total capital equipment investment of $3,000 + $5,000 = $8,000, and $4,000 in inventory plus the $10,000 in cash. The restaurant also has a $5,000 long-term loan, which was used to buy the stove. Its total assets are $22,000. It has $5,000 in liabilities (the loan for the stove), which leaves $17,000 of owner's equity (OE).

Assuming the restaurant has no other assets and liabilities, **Figure 8-4** shows how its balance sheet would look.

On a balance sheet, assets must equal ("balance") liabilities and owner's equity.

> Total Assets = Total Liabilities + Owner's Equity (OE)

Figure 8-4 *Balance sheet.*

Restaurant			Dec. 31, 2008
Assets		**Liabilities**	
Cash	$10,000	Short-Term Liabilities	$ 0
Inventory	4,000	Long-Term Liabilities	5,000
Capital Equipment	8,000		
Other Assets	—	Owner's Equity	$17,000
Total Assets	**$22,000**	**Total Liabilities + OE**	**$22,000**

The OE is $17,000. It is equal to the total of the cash ($10,000), the stove, tables and chairs ($8,000), plus $4,000 in inventory, minus the $5,000 in liabilities.

The stove is financed with a ($5,000) loan (debt financing). This is a long-term liability. Together, the liabilities and the owner's equity have "paid for" the assets of the business.

The Balance Sheet Shows How a Business Is Financed

The balance sheet is an especially good tool for looking at how a business is financed. It clearly shows the relationship between debt and equity financing. Sometimes businesses make the mistake of relying too heavily on either debt or equity.

- An entrepreneur who relies too much on equity financing can end up losing control of the company, because there will be other owners. If the other owners control more than 50 percent of the business, they may insist on making the decisions.

- An entrepreneur who takes on too much debt can lose the business to banks or other creditors, if unable to meet the loan payments.

All the information you need to analyze a company's financing strategy—total debt, equity, and assets—is in its balance sheet. People who invest in businesses use *ratios* to grasp a company's financial situation quickly. As an entrepreneur, you will want to understand these ratios so you will be able to talk intelligently with investors.

Analyzing a Balance Sheet

A business usually prepares one balance sheet at the beginning of its fiscal year and another at the end. Comparing the two is an excellent way to see whether or not a business has been successful. If it is, the owner's equity (OE) will have increased.

Let's look at the restaurant example again. This time, several other assets and liabilities have been included (see **Figure 8-5**).

The beginning balance sheet was prepared on December 31, 2008. The ending balance sheet was compiled a year later, on December 31, 2009. Compare the two balance sheets (Figure 8-5) to see what has changed over the course of a year.

Assets

- *Cash* has decreased from $10,000 to $8,000. Businesses have cash coming in and going out all the time, so this isn't necessarily a bad thing—as long as the bills are being paid.

Figure 8-5 *Balance sheet.*

Restaurant	Dec. 31, 2008	Dec. 31, 2009
Assets		
Cash	$10,000	$ 8,000
Inventory	4,000	5,000
Capital Equipment	8,000	9,000
Other Assets	—	—
Total Assets	**$22,000**	**$22,000**
Liabilities		
Short-Term Liabilities	0	1,000
Long-Term Liabilities	5,000	4,000
Owner's Equity	**$17,000**	**$17,000**
Total Liabilities + OE	**$22,000**	**$22,000**

- *Inventory* has increased from $4,000 to $5,000. If more inventory will help the restaurant put more items on the menu, it could help increase business. In any case, inventory is an asset because it has a monetary value. Inventory does tie up cash, too.
- *Capital Equipment* has risen from $8,000 to $9,000. The restaurant must have bought more equipment during the year. This is another increase in assets.
- *Other Assets* have not changed.
- *Total Assets* have not changed. The business is keeping less cash, but now has more of what it needs to operate (Inventory and Capital Equipment).

There are no more assets at the end of the year than there were at the beginning. Does this mean it did not have a successful year? (The rest of this analysis will help you figure that out.)

Liabilities

- *Short-Term Liabilities* have increased from $0 to $1,000. That's probably not good, because it means the restaurant owes more money than it did before.
- *Long-Term Liabilities* have declined from $5,000 to $4,000 because the restaurant paid off part of the loan. When you make monthly payments on a loan, part of the payment will go for interest and the rest is paying off the principal. So, part of the payment is an expense and part is reducing a liability.
- *Owner's Equity* has stayed the same. The restaurant owner has no more "value" than at the beginning of the year.

The restaurant does not have more total assets than it had at the beginning of the year, however, and it has less cash. On the other hand, the business has less debt than it did. The balance sheet equation (Assets = Liabilities + OE) shows that the owner's equity in the business has not changed because, although the owner paid down some long-term debt, short-term debt was added.

Figure 8-6 shows another look at the balance sheet, with a "percentage change" column added. This represents how much change took place over the year. (Note that any value set in parentheses is negative.)

Total assets are unchanged, and the restaurant's liabilities (debts) are the same. Short-Term Liabilities are $1,000 greater, and Long-Term Liabilities are 20 percent less than they had been at the start of the year. Owner's Equity is the same.

Figure 8-6 *"Same size" balance sheet analysis.*

Restaurant	Dec. 31, 2008	Dec. 31, 2009	% Change
Assets			
Cash	$10,000	$ 8,000	(20)%
Inventory	4,000	5,000	25%
Capital Equipment	8,000	9,000	13%
Other Assets	—	—	
Total Assets	**$22,000**	**$22,000**	**0%**
Liabilities			
Short-Term Liabilities	$ 0	$ 1,000	N.A.
Long-Term Liabilities	5,000	4,000	(20)%
Owner's Equity	**17,000**	**17,000**	**0%**
Total Liabilities + OE	**$22,000**	**$22,000**	**0%**

The restaurant used its cash to increase its inventory and capital equipment, keeping its debt and equity the same. Reallocating your asset mix can be a smart strategy.

The growth of owner's equity is a good way to measure company success. The following table shows how investors would view different rates of owner's equity growth.

**Annual Rates of Growth in Owner's Equity
of Major U.S. Corporations**

Annual Growth	Assessment of Annual Growth Rate
3%	Very slow, and unsatisfactory in most cases
6%	Slow, but acceptable in some cases
10–11%	Average growth rate
16%	High growth rate
24%	Extremely high growth—not many companies can achieve this, much less keep it up

Depreciation

As we have learned, depreciation is a certain portion of an asset that is subtracted each year until the asset's value reaches zero. Depreciation reflects the wear and tear on an asset over time. This reduces the asset's value. A used car, for instance, is worth less money than a new one.

Balance sheets with significant long-term assets show depreciation as a subtraction from long-term assets. These businesses will keep "depreciation schedules" to track the valuation of each asset that is being depreciated. Businesses with minimal or no depreciation do not need to show it on the balance sheet.

Financial Ratio Analysis: What Is It and What Does It Mean to You?

So far, we have only looked at how an income statement and balance sheet can tell you whether or not your business is making a profit, and whether owner's equity is increasing or decreasing. But you can also create

financial ratios from your income statement and balance sheet that will help you analyze your business further. By making comparisons of performance from period to period and against industry norms, you can adapt your operations and strategies to improve results.

Income Statement Ratios

To create income statement ratios, simply divide sales into each line item and multiply by a hundred. In this way, you are expressing a line item as a percentage, or share, of sales. Expressing an item on the income statement as a percentage of sales makes it easy to see the relationship between items. In the following example, for every dollar of sales, 40 cents went to the Cost of Goods Sold. The Contribution Margin per dollar was 60 cents. The Net Profit, after 30 cents was spent on operating costs and 10 cents on taxes, was 20 cents.

Analyzing income statement items as percentages of sales will make clear how costs are affecting net profit.

Income Statement	Dollars	Math	% of Sales
Sales	$10	$10/$10 × 100 =	100%
Less Total COGS	$4	$4/$10 × 100 =	40%
Less Other Variable Costs	$0		
Contribution Margin	$6	$6/$10 × 100 =	60%
Less Fixed Operating Costs	$3	$3/$10 × 100 =	30%
Profit	$3	$3/$10 × 100 =	30%
Taxes	$1	$1/$10 × 100 =	10%
Net Profit/(Loss)	$2	$2/$10 × 100 =	20%

◀ **Performance Objective 4**
Perform a financial ratio analysis of an income statement.

Analyzing the income statement in this way makes clear how each item is affecting the business's profit. Examining the income statement makes it easy to experiment with ways to improve your business.

To increase contribution margin, you could see if you could cut the cost of goods sold by 10 percent. The next time you analyze your monthly income statement, you will be able to see if this cost cutting increased the contribution margin and by how much.

Return on Investment

An **investment** is something you put time, energy, or money into because you expect to gain profit or satisfaction in return.

When you start your own business, you are investing time and energy into the venture as well as money. You do this because you believe that someday your business will return more than the value of the time, energy, and money you put into it. One way to express this idea mathematically is to calculate the **return on investment (ROI)**, the net profit of a business divided by the start-up investment expressed as a percentage of that start-up investment.

◀ **Performance Objective 5**
Calculate return on investment (ROI).

Investors think in terms of **wealth**—the value of assets owned minus the value of liabilities owed at a particular point in time—rather than money, per se, because a business may own assets (such as equipment or real estate) that have value, but are not in actual cash. Return on investment measures how wealth changes over time. ROI is a rate of growth. To measure ROI you have to know these three things:

1. *Net profit:* The amount the business has earned beyond what it needs to cover its costs.

Global Impact...

Accounting Differences between Countries

Businesses in different countries prepare, present, and even name designated income statements differently. In the United Kingdom, for example, the income statement is called "Group Profit and Loss Account." Topics where global practices differ widely include inventory measurement methods, and ways in which property and equipment are valued. Countries also have varying laws regarding when a sale can be recognized as income and included on an income statement.

In the United States, United Kingdom, Denmark, Norway, Belgium, Brazil, and Japan, for instance, income from a long-term contract can only be included on the income statement as each percentage of the contract is completed. If you have done 10 percent of the work, you can show 10 percent of the income on your statement. In Germany, on the other hand, you cannot include any of the income on your statement until the contract has been 100 percent completed.

2. *Total investment in the business:* This includes Start-Up Investment (the amount of money that was required to open the business, plus all later additional funding).
3. *The period of time for which you are calculating ROI.* This is typically 1 month or 1 year.

$$\text{ROI Formula} = \frac{\text{Net Profit}}{\text{Investment}} = \text{ROI}$$

There is an easy way to remember the ROI formula: *What you made over what you paid, times one hundred.*

If David wants to figure out what his ROI was for the day at the flea market, he must know the following:

1. *Net Profit:* His income statement shows this to be $694.
2. *Investment:* David invests $1,000 in handbags and $25 in flyers, $50 for charms, plus $500 to rent a booth at the flea market. Total = $1,575.
3. *Time Period:* In this case David is calculating his ROI for one day.

He simply divides his investment into the net profit.

> *ROI is normally expressed as a percentage. The ROI formula gives you the answer as a decimal. You can convert the decimal as a percentage by multiplying it by 100 and adding the "%" sign.*

$$\frac{\text{Net Profit (\$694)}}{\text{Investment (\$1,000 + 25 + 50 + \$500)}} = \frac{\$694}{\$1,575} = .4406 \times 100 = 44\%$$

David's ROI was 44 percent for the day. ROI tells you what the rate of return was on your investment.

BizFacts

If you want to project (forecast) your ROI for a year, you will need to convert monthly ROI to annualized ROI. Do this by multiplying by 12.
Monthly ROI % × 12 months = Projected Annual ROI %

ROI is normally "annualized"—expressed by year. If David sells at one flea market per month and earns 44 percent ROI each time, his monthly rate of return will be 44 percent (even though he earns it all in one day). If he keeps this up for the rest of the year, his annual ROI will be: 44% × 12 = 528%.

Return on Sales

Return on sales (ROS) is the percentage created when sales are divided into net income. This is an important measure of the profitability of a business.

$$\text{Return on Sales (ROS)} = \frac{\text{Net Income}}{\text{Sales}}$$

ROS is also called **profit margin**. To express this ratio as a percentage, multiply it by 100 (as you would to express ROI as a percentage).

A high ROS ratio can help a company make money more easily; however, the amount of revenue makes a difference. The size of the sale will also make a difference. Hardware stores sell inexpensive items, so they have to make a higher profit margin on each to make a profit. Auto dealers sell expensive items, so they can afford a smaller ROS on each car they sell.

ROS (Profit Margin) Table

ROS	Margin Range	Typical Product
Very low	2–5%	Very high volume OR very high price
Low	6–10%	High volume OR high price
Moderate	11–20%	Moderate volume AND moderate price
High	20–30%	Low volume OR low price
Very high	30% and up	Very low volume OR very low price

Same Size Analysis

Financial ratio analysis will also allow you to compare the income statements from different months, or years, more easily, even if the sales are different amounts. The percentages let you compare statements as if they were the "same size." For this reason, financial ratio analysis is sometimes called same size analysis.

When the ratio of expenses/sales is used to express expenses as a percentage of sales, it is called an **operating ratio**. The operating ratio expresses what percentage of sales dollars the expense is using up. You can use operating ratios to compare your expenses with those incurred by other businesses in your industry. If your rent is $2,000 per month and your sales in a given month are $10,000, your operating ratio for rent is 20 percent. Is that high or low for your industry? Check trade association data or statement studies to find comparative values. If it is high, you might want to consider moving to another location.

Relating each element of the income statement to sales in this fashion will help you notice changes in your costs from month to month.

◀ Performance Objective 6
Perform "same size" analysis of an income statement.

Example

Compare the "same size" income statements shown in **Figure 8-7**. Rocket Rollerskate did not have as much revenue and did not make as much profit in February as it did in January. The company was able to lower both its COGS and its other variable costs in February, though. Which month was better for Rocket? Can you explain your point of view?

Quick and Current Ratios

In addition to what you can learn from an income statement, a balance sheet will tell you about a business's **liquidity**, that is, its ability to convert assets into cash. Businesspeople use **quick ratios** and **current ratios** to immediately understand what is going on with a business's liquidity. Many entrepreneurs prepare a balance sheet monthly, as well as at the end of the fiscal year, to keep an eye on liquidity.

◀ Performance Objective 7
Use quick, current, and debt ratios to analyze a balance sheet.

$$\text{Quick Ratio: } \frac{\text{Cash} + \text{Marketable Securities}}{\text{Current Liabilities}}$$

Figure 8-7 *"Same size" income statements.*

Rocket Rollerskate Co. "Same Size"			**Date:** January 2008
Revenue	**100%**		**$250,000**
COGS	24%	$60,000	60,000
Gross Profit	**76%**		**$190,000**
Other Variable Costs	14%	35,000	35,000
Total Variable Costs	38%	$95,000	
Contribution Margin	**62%**		**$155,000**
Fixed Costs	34%		85,000
Pre-Tax Profit	**28%**		**$70,000**
Taxes (20%)	5.6%		14,000
Net Profit	**22.4%**		**$56,000**

Rocket Rollerskate Co. "Same Size"			**Date:** February 2008
Revenue	**100%**		**$225,000**
COGS	20%	$45,000	45,000
Gross Profit	**80%**		**$180,000**
Other Variable Costs	12%	27,000	27,000
Total Variable Costs	32%	$72,000	
Contribution Margin	**68%**		**$153,000**
Fixed Costs	38%		85,000
Pre-Tax Profit	**30%**		**$68,000**
Taxes (20%)	6.0%		13,600
Net Profit	**24.2%**		**$54,400**

Step into the Shoes...
Estée Lauder Delivers Beauty

Estée Lauder, born Josephine Esther Mentzer in 1906, parlayed a skin cream formula developed by her uncle into a company selling products in over 100 countries. Lauder started selling the cream in 1946 and introduced "Youth-Dew" fragrance in 1953. The company that she built with her husband found a niche for women's beauty care and evolved from the single beauty cream into multiple complete lines of skin care, makeup, fragrances, and hair care products. Today, the company bearing her name includes numerous brands such as Clinique, Prescriptives, MAC Cosmetics, Coach, and Aveda. The Lauder family continues to control 70 percent of the company.

Named one of *Time* magazine's 20 most influential business geniuses of the twentieth century, Estée Lauder's name is synonymous with beauty and wealth.

This is how entrepreneurs create fortunes. Some establish successful businesses, sell them, and use the resulting wealth to create new enterprises and more wealth. Entrepreneurs also use their wealth to support political, environmental, and social causes. The major philanthropic thrust of the Estée Lauder Company is providing support to the Breast Cancer Research Foundation, addressing a major health concern of its customer base. What will you do with your wealth?

Marketable securities are investments, such as certificates of deposit or Treasury bills, that can be converted to cash within 24 hours. The **quick ratio** tells you whether you have enough cash to cover your current debt. The quick ratio should always be greater than 1. This means that you would have enough cash at your disposal to cover all current short-term debt. In other words, if you had to pay all your bills tomorrow (not loans, just bills), you would have enough cash to do so.

$$\text{Current Ratio:} \frac{\text{Current Assets}}{\text{Current Liabilities}}$$

It is also a good idea to maintain a current ratio greater than 1. This indicates that, if you had to, you could sell some assets to pay off all your debts.

Debt Ratios: Showing the Relationship between Debt and Equity

Many, perhaps most, companies are financed by both debt and equity. The financial strategy of a company will be apparent from certain simple financial ratios. If a company has a **debt-to-equity ratio** of one-to-one (expressed as 1:1), for example, this means that for every one dollar of debt the company has one dollar of assets.

$$\frac{\text{Debt}}{\text{Equity}} = \text{Debt-to-Equity Ratio}$$

All the information you need to analyze a company's financing strategy is there in its balance sheet. It is used to create the following ratio.

$$\text{Debt Ratio:} \frac{\text{Total Debt}}{\text{Total Assets}}$$

The **debt ratio** describes how many of the total dollars in the business have been provided by creditors. A debt ratio of 55 percent means you are in debt for 55 percent of your assets. You will not actually own those assets outright until you pay off the debt. On the other hand, if you need to go to a bank to borrow money, or to a supplier to establish credit, these creditors will want you to have a moderate debt ratio, so you will have to manage your debt based on your objectives.

A debt-to-equity ratio of 100 percent would mean that for every dollar of debt the company has a dollar of equity. Equity is ownership, which is either kept by the entrepreneur or sold in pieces to investors. If the investors hold more than 50 percent of the equity in a business, they could take over control from the entrepreneur—and this sometimes happens.

Entrepreneurs like to have a fairly high debt ratio, because it means they are not financing the business with their own money, but are using that of creditors and suppliers— OPM—other people's money.

Exercise

Using the balance sheet for the restaurant in Figure 8-5, calculate the quick, debt, and debt-to-equity ratios. Write answers on a separate sheet of paper.

Quick ratio: _____

Debt ratio: _____

Debt-to-equity ratio: _____

What do the ratios tell you about how the restaurant is doing?

Operating Efficiency Ratios

Once the income statement and balance sheet have been prepared, you can analyze your business's operating efficiency using the following ratios:

1. Collection Period Ratio:

$$\frac{\text{Average Accounts Receivable (Balance Sheet)}}{\text{Average Daily Sales (Income Statement)}} = \text{\# of days}$$

This ratio measures the average number of days that sales are going uncollected.

2. Receivable Turnover Ratio:

$$\frac{\text{Total Sales (Income Statement)}}{\text{Average Accounts Receivable (Balance Sheet)}} = \text{\# of times}$$

This also measures the efficiency of your company's efforts to collect receivables.

3. Inventory Turnover Ratio:

$$\frac{\text{Cost of Goods Sold (Income Statement)}}{\text{Average Inventory (Balance Sheet)}} = \text{\# of times}$$

This is a measure of how quickly inventory is "moving" (is sold).

By using all of these ratios, you can create an internal scorecard for your business. You will be able to tell at a glance whether you are attaining your goals and where you stand from period to period, and how you compare with your industry. Appendix 6 includes a set of useful formulas and equations to use for such a scorecard.

Chapter Summary

Now that you have studied this chapter, you can do the following:

1. Read an income statement.
   - An income statement shows whether the difference between revenues (sales) and expenses (costs) is a profit or a loss.
   - If sales are greater than costs, the income statement balance will be positive, showing that the business earned a profit. If costs are greater than sales, the balance will be negative, showing a loss.
   - The elements of an income statement are:
     a. *Revenue:* Money a business makes for selling its products.
     b. *Cost of goods sold:* The cost of goods sold for one unit times the number of units sold. Never disclose your cost of goods sold. You want to keep your profit margin private.
     c. *Gross profit:* Revenue less the cost of the product or service.
     d. *Other variable costs:* Costs that vary with sales.
     e. *Contribution margin:* Sales minus variable costs (cost of goods sold + other variable costs).
     f. *Fixed operating costs:* Items that must be paid to operate a business. These items include utilities, salaries, advertising, insurance, interest, rent, and depreciation (referred to as USAIIRD).
     g. *Profit before taxes:* A business's profit after all costs have been deducted but before paying taxes.

Figure 8-9

Angelina	
Assets	
Curren	
Cash	
Inver	
Secu	
Total C	
Long-T	
Total Ass	
Liabilitie	
Short-	
Acco	
Shor	
Total S	
Total L	
Owner's	
Total Liab	

h. ***Taxes:*** A business must pay income tax on its profit. (Sales, property, and other taxes are business expenses and are not included on this line.)

i. ***Net Profit/(Loss):*** A business's profit or loss after taxes.

2. Examine a balance sheet to determine a business's financing strategy.
   - A balance sheet is a financial statement showing the assets (items the business owns), liabilities (debts), and net worth of a business.
   - Every item a business owns was obtained through either debt (bonds, loans) or equity (selling ownership); therefore, the total of all assets must equal the total of all liabilities and owner's equity.

3. Use the balance sheet equation to see the relationship between assets, liabilities, and owner's equity.

$$\text{Assets} - \text{Liabilities} = \text{Net Worth (or Owner's Equity or Capital)}$$

4. Perform a financial ratio analysis of an income statement.
   - Expressing each item on the income statement as a percentage of sales makes it easy to see the relationship between items.
   - Financial ratio analysis will also allow you to compare the income statements from different months or years more easily, even if the sales are for varying amounts.
   - The percentages let you compare statements as if they were the "same size." For this reason, financial ratio analysis is also sometimes called "same size analysis."

$$\frac{\text{Net Income}}{\text{Sales}} = \text{Return on Sales (ROS)}$$

5. Calculate return on investment (ROI).
   - ROI is the net profit of a business divided by the start-up costs, which are the original investment in the business.
   - $\dfrac{\text{Net Profit}}{\text{Investment}} \times 100$

6. Perform "same size" analysis of an income statement.
   - Represent expenses as a percentage of sales or operating ratios.
   - Compare with others in the industry.

7. Use quick, current, and debt ratios to analyze a balance sheet.

$$\text{Quick Ratio} = \frac{\text{Cash Plus Marketable Securities}}{\text{Current Liabilities}}$$

$$\text{Current Ratio} = \frac{\text{Current Assets}}{\text{Current Liabilities}}$$

$$\text{Debt Ratio} = \frac{\text{Total Debt}}{\text{Total Assets}}$$

$$\text{Debt-to-Equity Ratio} = \frac{\text{Total Debt}}{\text{Equity}}$$

d. Th
20
ow

e. Th
yo
pa

7. On a s
sheet
below.

8. Use th

Jean M's Fl

ASSETS

Current Asset

Cash and cas

Accounts rec

Inventory

Total Current

Key Terms

current assets
current liabilities
current ratio
debt ratio
debt-to-equity ratio
financial ratios

fiscal year
investment
liquidity
long-term assets
long-term liabilities
marketable securities

Chapter 9
Cash Flow and Taxes

> *"If you do your job well, the last thing you have to worry about is money, just as if you live right, you will be happy."*
>
> —Edwin Land, founder of Polaroid Corporation

David Kendricks, 28, has started his own label, Kickin' Records. He intends to find and produce hip-hop artists from his hometown of Newark, New Jersey.

David invested $25,000 in his new business. He saved the money by working at 2 jobs for 5 years. He set up a Web site from which he will be able to sell his CDs. He bought an answering machine and created and printed his own stationery and business cards. He has been spending his time from 8 in the evening until 3 A.M. looking for groups to sign to his recording label.

David spends about $100 a night on cover charges, drinks at nightclubs, and tickets for concerts, including transportation. He has been finding, however, that the groups at the better clubs and concerts are already signed and have producers. David has had no sales because he has not yet produced a CD. Now, after 6 months, he's almost $20,000 in debt. One reason David's business may go under is because he is not keeping close watch on his cash flow.

Performance Objectives

1. Use a cash flow statement to guide your business operations.
2. Read a cash flow statement.
3. Manage and forecast cash flow effectively.
4. Understand the future value of money.
5. Calculate the present value of money.
6. File appropriate tax returns for your business.
7. Calculate working capital.

Cash Flow: The Lifeblood of a Business

Cash is the energy that keeps your business flowing, the way electricity powers a lamp. Run out of cash and your business will soon go out like a light. Without cash on hand, you will not be able to pay essentials, even while the income statement says you are earning a profit! If your phone is cut off, it will not matter what the income statement says.

The income statement shows you what the situation is with sales. It tells you how much revenue is coming in and how it relates to the cost of goods sold and operating costs. The balance sheet is a "snapshot" of your business. It shows your assets and liabilities and net worth at a moment in time.[1]

The Income Statement Does Not Show How Much Cash You Really Have

Once you start a business, however, you will notice that sometimes, even when the income statement says you are making a profit, you have no money! There is often a time lag between making a sale and getting paid. If you make a sale and the customer promises to pay you in a week, the sale is recognized on the income statement immediately (if you are using the accrual method), but you will not have the cash until the check clears the bank.

Performance Objective 1 ▷

Use a cash flow statement to guide your business operations.

For all the good information and guidance a monthly income statement can provide, you cannot base your business's daily operation by using the income statement alone. You will also need a monthly **cash flow statement** to track the money coming in and going out of the business.

Author William Stolze calls the cash flow statement "by far the most important financial control in a start-up venture."[2] The cash flow statement records inflows and outflows of money as they occur. If a sale is made in June, but the customer does not pay until August, the cash flow statement will not show the revenue until August, when the cash "flows" into the business. If you are recording transactions on a cash basis, you would not record the sale on the income statement until you received payment.

Step into the Shoes...

King C. Gillette Faces a Cash Crunch

King Gillette was a traveling salesman for 28 years. In his spare time, he tried to invent a successful consumer product. He invented all kinds of gadgets that did not pan out, but, in 1885, when he cut himself shaving with his dull, straight razor, inspiration hit. Gillette thought of a disposable "safety" razor.

Gillette and a partner eventually got financing together and launched their business. The future seemed bright, but soon the company was $12,500 in debt. Even though people were excited about the product, by 1901, "We were backed up

to the wall with our creditors lined up in front waiting for the signal to fire," Gillette wrote later.[3]

Gillette convinced a Boston investor to put money in the company and, by the end of 1904, Gillette was producing a quarter million razor sets per year. This is an example of how crucial an infusion of money can be to a business. A temporary cash crunch nearly destroyed a company that is now more than a century old.

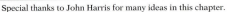

[1] Special thanks to John Harris for many ideas in this chapter.
[2] William Stolze, *Start Up: An Entrepreneur's Guide to Launching and Managing a New Business* (Franklin Lakes, NJ: Career Press, 1994), p. 96.
[3] Russell B. Adams, *King C. Gillette: The Man and His Wonderful Shaving Device* (New York: Little, Brown, 1978).

Exercise

What kind of businesses bring in a lot of cash during part of the year and not much the rest of the time?

Rules to Keep Cash Flowing

In order to avoid getting caught without enough cash to pay your bills, follow these rules:

1. *Collect cash as soon as possible.* When you make a sale, try to get paid immediately.
2. *Pay your bills by the due date, not earlier.* You do not have to pay a bill the day it arrives in your mailbox. Look for the "due date." You will need to mail your payment so it arrives by that date.
3. *Check on your cash available every day.* Always know how much cash you have on hand. Your cash flow will be reflected in your up-to-date accounting journal.
4. *Lease instead of buying equipment where practical.* Leasing distributes the costs over time.
5. *Avoid buying inventory that you do not need.* Unless it is critical to your competitive advantage to offer customers a wide selection, minimize the amount of inventory you stock. Inventory ties up cash—the cash you use to purchase inventory and the cash you spend storing it.

You can calculate your ongoing cash balance by subtracting cash disbursements from cash receipts, as you do when balancing your checkbook. Your goal is *never* to have a negative cash balance. A negative balance means that you are overdrawn in one or more of your bank accounts.

Noncash Expenses Can Distort Your Financial Picture

The income statement also is not an accurate reflection of your cash position when it includes **noncash expenses**, or expenses recorded as adjustments to asset values, such as depreciation. When you depreciate an asset, you are deducting a portion of its cost from your income statement. But you aren't actually spending that cash, you are reducing the value of the asset. You do not pay out money when you record a depreciation expense on your income statement.

Depreciation is a noncash expense because no money actually goes out. When depreciation is deducted from an income statement, therefore, the statement no longer accurately reflects how much cash the business is really holding. By the same token, the cash flow statement does not include depreciation, because it is not actual cash leaving the business.

The Cyclical Nature of Cash Flow

The entrepreneur needs a cash flow statement to depict the cash position of the business at specified points in time. The cash flow statement records inflows and outflows when they occur.

BizFacts

You can calculate your ongoing cash balance by subtracting cash disbursements from cash receipts. You should *never* have a negative cash balance.

In addition, cash flow is cyclical for many businesses, meaning that the amount of cash flowing into a business may depend on where the business is in its fiscal year. A flower store will have a lot of cash coming in around Mother's Day and Valentine's Day, for example, but may have very little during the fall. A college campus bookstore will have to spend a lot of cash before school starts to stock up on books, and will have a lot of cash coming in when students arrive to buy books for their classes. This is why keeping an eye on cash flow at all times will be crucial to the survival of your business. Your utility companies, vendors, and lenders will not care that you won't have money coming in over the next 3 months; they will want their regular monthly payments. When you create your business plan, describe your expectations for seasonal changes in your cash flow and how you will manage your cash to cope with this.

Reading a Cash Flow Statement

Performance Objective 2

Read a cash flow statement.

A simple cash flow statement for a small business follows. The first section records all sources of income. These are cash "inflows," or *cash receipts* (not to be confused with receipts for purchases). The next section reports cash "outflows," or necessary *disbursements* for that month—insurance and interest payments, cost of goods sold, salaries, and so forth.

The last section shows the net change in cash flow. This tells the entrepreneur whether the business had a positive or negative cash flow that month. You can have all the sales in the world and still go out of business if you do not have enough cash flowing in to cover your monthly cash outflows. The cash flow statement is essentially the business's budget.

The Cash Flow Equation

Cash Flow = Cash Receipts − Cash Disbursements

Here is an example of a cash flow statement. Inflows and outflows of cash are divided into three categories:

1. ***Operation:*** Money used to run the business
2. ***Investment:*** Money going into and out of investments in the business, such as equipment, vehicles, or real estate
3. ***Financing:*** Money used to finance the business (debt and equity)

Daniel Crow, an employee in the receiving department of REI's Distribution Center in Sumner, Washington, sorts products during an October inventory.
(Dean J. Koepfler, AP Wide World Photos)

Cash Flow Statement for Lola's Custom Draperies, Inc., March 2008

Cash Flow from Operating:		
Cash Inflows:		
Sales	$65,400	
Total Cash Inflows	**$65,400**	
Cash Outflows:		
Variable Costs		
COGS	$29,360	
Other VC (Sales Commissions)	6,540	
Fixed Costs		
Factory Rent & Utilities	$8,000	
Sales & Administrative	12,000	
Part-Time Tech Support Salary	1,000	
Taxes	2,875	($11,500 × 0.25)
Total cash used in operating activities	**$59,775**	
Net Cash Flow from Operating	**$5,625**	($65,400 − $59,775)
Cash Flow Out from Investing:		
Purchase of Equipment	6,000	
Net Cash Flow from Investing	**$6,000**	
Cash Flow from Financing:		
Loans	$25,000	
Gifts	0	
Equity Investment	0	
Net Cash Flow In from Financing	**$25,000**	
Net Increase/(Decrease) in Cash	**$24,625**	
Cash, Beginning:	**$500**	
Cash, End:	**$25,125**	

Forecasting Cash Flow

As you get your business off the ground, you should prepare monthly cash flow projections to make sure there is enough money to pay the bills.

There are two steps to forecasting cash flow receipts:

1. Project cash receipts from all possible sources. *Remember,* orders are not cash receipts because they may not become cash. Some may be canceled and some customers may not pay. Cash receipts are checks that have cleared, or credit card payments, or cash itself.
2. Subtract expenses that would need to be deducted to meet this level of cash receipts. Cash expenses are *only* those expenses you will actually have to pay during the projected time period.

◀ **Performance Objective 3**
Manage and forecast cash flow effectively.

Global Impact...

Cash Flow Statements Are Not Required in Every Country

In the United States, public corporations are required by law to present cash flow statements. In some countries, however, businesses are not required to present either a statement of cash flow or a statement of "fund flow." This is the case in Germany, Italy, and Denmark. In Germany, many large companies voluntarily provide either a cash flow (or fund flow) statement. The United Kingdom does require cash flow statements, but only for large companies. The international trend, however, is moving toward the U.S. practice of requiring cash flow statements from public corporations, as governments recognize that income statements do not reveal a company's true cash position and can be misleading to investors.

You cannot be completely sure that these projections will be accurate, but you should create them anyway and review and update them constantly. They will be useful to anticipate any shortfalls.

Risking Your Cash on Inventory

As discussed, the entrepreneur takes a **risk** every time he or she spends cash. If you buy inventory, for example, you take the risk that no one will buy it at a price that will give you a profit. (Of course, being in business by itself is taking a risk.)

There are two other risks involved with inventory: storage costs and **pilferage**, or theft of inventory. You will have to be sure you can sell the inventory at a price that will include the cost of storing it, and cover pilfering. Barneys, the famous New York clothing store, eventually had a 7 percent pilferage rate, which helped drive the company out of business (although it made a comeback later).

You should be careful about adding inventory based on the expectation of receiving cash from the customers who owe you money (accounts receivable). However, a percentage of this sum may never be collected. You must keep track of your cash flow statement, or you could get caught in a squeeze between your suppliers—who want you to pay for inventory you have purchased—and customers who haven't yet paid for what they bought. If you cannot pay your creditors, you could lose ownership of your business. That's what happened to Donald Trump and the Taj Mahal, in Atlantic City some years ago. He couldn't pay his loans so he had to turn over 80 percent ownership in the casino to the banks.

Credit Squeeze

Credit is the ability to borrow money. It enables you to buy something without spending cash at the time of purchase. Once you have established a relationship with a supplier, he or she may be willing to extend credit. If you own a store, you might be able to buy Christmas ornaments from a supplier in October and pay for them in 60 days, after your Christmas sales.

If you aren't managing your cash carefully, however, you could get caught in the squeeze discussed above, between your suppliers and your customers. Your suppliers might not extend you credit in the future. If you get into a position where you cannot pay your suppliers, you will have no further inventory and, thus, no business.

The Burn Rate

When you start your business, it is normal to have a negative cash flow from operations for the first few months. You are likely to spend more than you earn in the beginning stages. Some businesses, such as biotechnology companies, that spend a great deal on research and development (R&D)

can have a negative cash flow of as much as $1 million per month! You will need to build these initial cash deficits into your business plan so that they will be covered in start-up costs.

Since a new company will probably spend more money than it earns while it is getting off the ground, the question will be: For how long can you afford to lose cash? The answer will depend on the amount of capital invested and the amount of revenue being earned.

The pace at which your company will need to spend capital to cover overhead costs before generating a positive cash flow is called the **burn rate**. The burn rate is typically expressed in terms of cash spent per month. A burn rate of $10,000 per month means that the company is spending that amount monthly to cover rent and other operating expenses. If the company has, say, $20,000 in cash and is making $2,000 a month in sales, how long could it hold out?

$$\frac{\text{Cash} + \text{Revenue}}{\text{Negative Cash Outflow per Month}}$$
$$= \text{Number of Months before Cash Runs Out}$$

The Value of Money Changes Over Time

When considering cash and cash flow, it is also important to evaluate the changing value of money over time. Cash goes up or down in terms of buying power, depending upon inflation rates. It can also vary in strength relative to foreign currencies. Finally, it can grow as the interest earned previously continues earning additional interest.

The Time Value of Money

Money grows fastest in investments that offer a **compound** rate of return, that is, those that are calculated on interest that has already accumulated. The younger you are when you start saving for a goal, such as retirement, the more compounding will help your money grow. Suppose you put $100 into an investment that pays 10 percent compounded annually. At the end of a year, you will have $110 ($100, plus $10 interest). At the end of the next year, you will have $121 ($110 plus $11 interest). Each year, your money will grow faster because you are earning interest on the interest.

The U.S. government allows you to set up tax-free retirement accounts called IRAs (Individual Retirement Accounts). "Tax-free" means you won't have to pay taxes on the money, including the interest, in your IRA until you reach a specific age. If you do make withdrawals beforehand, however, you will have to pay a *penalty* on that year's income tax.

One type of retirement account, the Roth IRA, can be a good choice for a young person, because it allows a one-time withdrawal of money to buy a house. So, with the Roth, you can save not only for your retirement but for buying a house as well. There is a maximum amount of money allowed for investment in an IRA annually. To encourage people to save, the U.S. government has been gradually increasing that limit.

The Future Value of Money

The **future value** of money is the amount it will *accrue* (gain) over time through investment. You can determine this easily using a Future Value Chart, such as the one on the next page. Look up ten periods at 10 percent on the chart and you will find that $100 invested at 10 percent will grow to $259 in 10 years. Remember, compound interest—money making money—is the essence of investment.

◀ **Performance Objective 4**
Understand the future value of money.

Future Value of $1 after *N* Periods

Periods	1%	2%	3%	4%	5%	6%	7%	8%	9%	10%	11%	12%
1	1.0100	1.0200	1.0300	1.0400	1.0500	1.0600	1.0700	1.0800	1.0900	1.1000	1.1100	1.1200
2	1.0201	1.0404	1.0609	1.0816	1.1025	1.1236	1.1449	1.1664	1.1881	1.2100	1.2321	1.2544
3	1.0303	1.0612	1.0927	1.1249	1.1576	1.1910	1.2250	1.2597	1.2950	1.3310	1.3676	1.4049
4	1.0406	1.0824	1.1255	1.1699	1.2155	1.2625	1.3108	1.3605	1.4116	1.4641	1.5181	1.5735
5	1.0510	1.1041	1.1593	1.2167	1.2763	1.3382	1.4026	1.4693	1.5386	1.6105	1.6851	1.7623
6	1.0615	1.1261	1.1941	1.2653	1.3401	1.4185	1.5007	1.5869	1.6771	1.7716	1.8704	1.9738
7	1.0721	1.1487	1.2299	1.3159	1.4071	1.5036	1.6058	1.7138	1.8280	1.9487	2.0762	2.2107
8	1.0829	1.1717	1.2668	1.3686	1.4775	1.5939	1.1782	1.8509	1.9926	2.1436	2.3045	2.4760
9	1.0937	1.1951	1.3048	1.4233	1.5513	1.6895	1.8385	1.9990	2.1719	2.3580	2.5580	2.7731
10	1.1046	1.2190	1.3439	1.4802	1.6209	1.7909	1.9672	2.1589	2.3674	2.5937	2.8394	3.1059
11	1.1157	1.2434	1.3842	1.5395	1.7103	1.8983	2.1049	2.3316	2.5084	2.8531	3.1518	3.4786
12	1.1268	1.2682	1.4258	1.6010	1.7959	2.0122	2.2522	2.5182	2.8127	3.1384	2.4985	3.8960
13	1.1381	1.2936	1.4685	1.6651	1.8057	2.1329	2.4098	2.7196	3.0658	3.4523	3.8833	4.3635
14	1.1495	1.3195	1.5126	1.7317	1.9799	2.2609	2.5785	2.9372	3.3417	3.7975	4.3104	4.8871
15	1.1610	1.3459	1.5580	1.8009	2.0789	2.3966	2.7590	3.1722	3.6425	4.1773	4.7846	5.4736

The Present Value of Money

Another way to look at investing is summed up by the old saying "A bird in the hand is worth two in the bush." You always want to have your money *now*. If you cannot have it now, you want to be compensated with a return.

Your money is worth more to you when it is "in your hand" for three reasons.

1. *Inflation:* When prices rise, a dollar tomorrow will buy less than a dollar does today.
2. *Risk:* When you put money into an investment, there is always some risk of losing it.
3. *Opportunity:* When you put money into an investment, you are giving up the opportunity to use it for what might be a better investment.

Performance Objective 5 ▶

Calculate the present value of money.

Say a customer promises to pay you, 3 years from now, $10,000 for designing a Web site. Your "next-best opportunity" for investment has an ROI of 10 percent.

Present value is the amount an investment is worth discounted back to the present. Look at the Present Value chart (see **Figure 9-1**) under period 3 (for 3 years) and 10 percent. The present value of $1.00 at 3 years and 10 percent is $0.75. The present value of the promise of $10,000 in 3 years, therefore, is $7,500 ($10,000 × 0.75 = $7,500). Your client's promise is worth only $7,500 in the present. If you accept this arrangement, you should charge interest, because you are essentially providing a $10,000 loan for 3 years. Anytime you are asked to wait for payment, you should be compensated, because money in your hand now is worth significantly more than money promised for the future.

Figure 9-1 *Net present value chart.*

Year	Interest Rate per Year									
	1%	2%	3%	4%	5%	6%	7%	8%	9%	10%
1	0.990	0.980	0.971	0.962	0.952	0.943	0.935	0.926	0.917	0.909
2	0.960	0.961	0.943	0.925	0.907	0.890	0.873	0.857	0.842	0.826
3	0.971	0.942	0.915	0.889	0.864	0.840	0.816	0.794	0.772	0.751
4	0.961	0.924	0.886	0.855	0.823	0.792	0.763	0.735	0.708	0.683
5	0.951	0.906	0.863	0.822	0.784	0.747	0.713	0.681	0.650	0.621
6	0.942	0.888	0.837	0.790	0.746	0.705	0.666	0.630	0.596	0.584
7	0.933	0.871	0.813	0.760	0.711	0.665	0.623	0.583	0.547	0.513
8	0.923	0.853	0.789	0.731	0.677	0.627	0.582	0.540	0.502	0.467
9	0.914	0.837	0.766	0.703	0.645	0.592	0.544	0.500	0.460	0.424
10	0.905	0.820	0.744	0.676	0.614	0.558	0.508	0.463	0.422	0.386
11	0.896	0.804	0.722	0.650	0.585	0.527	0.475	0.429	0.388	0.350
12	0.887	0.788	0.701	0.625	0.557	0.497	0.444	0.397	0.356	0.319
13	0.879	0.773	0.681	0.601	0.530	0.469	0.415	0.368	0.326	0.290
14	0.870	0.758	0.661	0.577	0.505	0.442	0.388	0.340	0.299	0.263
15	0.861	0.743	0.642	0.555	0.481	0.417	0.362	0.315	0.275	0.239

BizFacts

When you sell a business, the price reflects more than the nuts and bolts of the operation. You are also selling the future stream of income that the business will be expected to generate. This income is reflected in the price of the business, which is its *present value*. This is why businesses typically sell for several times their annual net income.

Taxes

Another factor to consider when projecting cash flow for a business is taxes. Like other creditors, tax-levying bodies expect payment in a timely fashion. More importantly, tax payments must be kept current, as some delinquencies can result in business closure and personal penalties.

Cash and Taxes

Once your business begins making a profit, you will have to pay taxes on those profits—and that will also have an impact on your cash flow. Even before you make a profit, self-employed people, such as sole proprietors, by definition, do not have Social Security tax taken out of their income by employers. They must pay their own **self-employment tax**, which is the Social Security tax obligation for those who are self-employed.

    If you have net income from self-employment over a certain annual threshold level, you are required to pay a significant percentage of that income to Social Security as self-employment tax. These taxes must be paid

◀ **Performance Objective 6**
File appropriate tax returns for your business.

quarterly, so you will need to be putting aside cash in order to make the payments and need to note the due dates.

The federal government is financed primarily by personal and corporate income taxes. States usually raise money from **sales tax** on goods (not services). Most states also levy an income tax. City and other local governments are supported primarily by taxes on property.

Filing Tax Returns

Failure to file tax returns at all can lead the IRS to charge penalties and, in extreme cases, seek criminal prosecution for tax evasion.

Corporate, partnership, and individual income tax and self-employment tax returns must be filed (mailed or submitted online) to the U.S. Internal Revenue Service (IRS) by specific dates each year. Corporate returns are due on a different schedule from the traditional April 15 deadline for individual returns. If you file late, you may have to pay penalties and interest. You can check the IRS Web site at *http://www.irs.gov* for deadlines, instructions, and forms.

The tax code is very complex. Check the IRS Web site at *http://www.irs .gov* for information, but if you are still not certain which tax forms to file and when to do so, the IRS also offers booklets and telephone service to help answer questions. Help with the 1040, the most common individual return form is available from 1-800-424-1040. You can also go to the IRS office in your town and meet with an agent who will guide you through the forms for free. It can be worth investing the time and money to ensure your own correct tax filings (rates and forms can change from year to year). As soon as your business starts earning income, you will probably want to seek the services of a tax professional (an *accountant*, or CPA). Remember, in addition to federal taxes, businesses are subject to state and local taxes. Check with state and local revenue departments.

Collecting Sales Tax

If you sell products or services to the public, you will have to charge state sales tax in most states and then (monthly or quarterly) turn the collected money over to the state. Apply to your state's department of taxation for the necessary forms. In New York State, for example, entrepreneurs use the New York State and Local Sales and Use Tax Return to report quarterly sales tax. Some states only charge tax on products; some charge tax on products and services, while a very few do not have a sales tax.

Wage Taxes

If and when you add employees to your company, you will have payroll taxes to withhold from their paychecks and send to the government. You will also have employer taxes to pay. It is impossible to overemphasize the importance of paying these taxes in a timely fashion. As a business owner, you can be held personally liable for these taxes and any penalties. The federal government can take taxes owed directly out of your financial accounts, which will take priority over any other expenses. Failure to manage your employee withholding taxes properly can lead to business closure.

Two ID Numbers You Will Need to Obtain

The legal structure you choose for your business will affect how you handle your taxes, as will be discussed in a later chapter. But certain administrative tasks, including the following, will be the same for all legal structures:

- Obtaining a federal employer identification (EIN) number for the business—this is basically a Social Security number for the company that you will use to identify your business in all interactions with the federal government.

- Obtaining a sales and use tax registration number from the state—you will be required by wholesalers to present this number to prove that you are buying items for resale and are therefore exempt from sales tax.

Corporations, limited liability companies (LLCs), and limited partnerships must, in addition, file an annual report with the state government, along with a tax return, and pay an annual fee. The report must state the business address, and include who the officers, directors, managers, and general partners are, plus other information.

Tax Issues for Different Legal Structures

The legal structure best suited to a business depends upon a number of variables, which will be discussed in Chapter 11. Each legal structure has tax advantages and disadvantages.

- *Sole Proprietorship:* All profit earned by a sole proprietorship belongs to the owner and affects his/her tax liability. The business does not pay taxes on profits separately.
- *Partnership:* The tax issues are basically the same as for the sole proprietorship, except that profits and losses are shared among the partners, who report them on their respective personal income tax returns.
- *Limited Partnership:* This is treated in the same way as a partnership, except that a "limited partner" can use losses as a "tax shelter" without being exposed to personal liability. This can be an incentive for potential investors.
- *Corporation (Subchapter C):* A corporation's profits are taxed whether or not a share of the profits is distributed to the owners. Owners must also pay personal income tax on any profit distribution they receive. This "double taxation" is considered a disadvantage of C corporations.
- *S Corporation:* Small companies can use this structure to avoid the double taxation mentioned above. The S corporation does not pay tax on profits. Profit is taxed only once, as owner income on personal tax returns. This structure requires all partners to take profits and losses in proportion to their ownership (so it does not offer the tax-shelter advantages of the limited partnership).
- *Limited Liability Company (LLC):* This structure separates the owner/partners from personal liability, and provides a more flexible allocation of profits and losses.

Finally, note that dividends paid by a business to stockholders are not tax deductible, but interest payments made to creditors are. This can be an incentive to raise capital via borrowing, depending on the tax issues your business faces.

Make Tax Time Easier by Keeping Good Records

You and your tax preparer will have an easier time if you have been keeping good records throughout the year. You will have to determine your net income. If you have kept accurate and timely accounting records, this should not be difficult.

Mistakes on your tax return or the luck of the draw could cause the IRS to *audit* you. The IRS would send an agent to your business to examine your

Investors Want Their Money to Grow— Can You Make It Happen?

When you ask a banker or friend for money for your business, you are asking for an investment. You should know, therefore, about some of the other options available to your potential investors. After all, they are only going to put money in your venture if you can convince them that it is a more attractive investment than their other options.

There are three categories of financial investments that can provide funds:

1. **Stocks:** Shares of company ownership (equity)
2. **Bonds:** Loans to companies or government entities for more than 1 year
3. **Cash:** Savings accounts, treasury bills, and other investments that can be liquidated (turned into cash) within 24 hours

Real estate—land or buildings—is another important investment. All investments involve some risk, which is the possibility that the money could be lost. There is an interesting relationship between risk and reward:

The greater the potential reward of an investment, the more risky it probably is.

High Reward = High Risk

And so:

If an investment has little risk, the reward will probably not be great.

Low Risk = Low Reward

How Stocks Work

The "stock market" is not in one location. It is made up of a collection of *exchanges* around the world where stocks are traded. The New York Stock Exchange, on Wall Street in Manhattan, is the most well known in the United States.

A trader checks stock prices on his computer. (John Stuart, Creative Eye/MIRA.com)

Per

Cal

A corporation is owned by its stockholders. Each **share** of stock represents a percentage of ownership. A stock certificate indicates how many shares were purchased and how big a piece of the company is owned.

If Street Scooters, Inc., has sold 10 shares of stock, each share to a different individual, that would mean there were 10 stockholders. Each would own 1/10th of the company. If Street Scooters sold 100 shares of stock, each share to a different individual, there would be 100 stockholders. Each would own 1/100th of the company.

Public corporations sell their stock to the general public to raise capital. They use the capital to expand the company, or pay off debts. Once the stock is sold, however, the corporation no longer has control over it. The stock can be bought and sold by anyone. Such trading activity occurs continually on the stock market between brokers. A **stockbroker** has a license that confers the right to make trades for customers.

The price of a stock at any given moment reflects investors' opinions about how well that business is going to perform. If the company does well, the price of the stock is likely to rise. Investors make their returns by selling stock at a higher price than the one at which they bought it.

The daily record of trading activity appears in tables published in *The Wall Street Journal* and in the business sections of many other newspapers. These tables allow investors to track the changing value of their investments.

Let's say you own 10 shares of a stock you bought at $10 per share (a total of $100). You see in the stock table that the price per share has declined to $8.50 that day. Your $100 investment is now worth only $85 (10 shares × $8.50/share = $85). You have three choices:

1. Sell the shares before their value declines further.
2. Keep them, hoping the decline is temporary and that the price will go back up.
3. Buy more shares at the lower price to increase your profit when the price does go back up.

◀ **Performance Objective 5**
Understand stocks and bonds as investment alternatives.

How Bonds Work

Corporations may also use the financial markets to borrow money by issuing bonds. Bonds are interest-bearing certificates that corporations (and governments) issue to raise capital. The federal government, state governments, and even city and town governments use bonds to finance roads, bridges, schools, and other public projects.

Bonds are loans; the original amount borrowed, plus interest, must be paid by the borrower. Bonds are a form of debt financing.

Stockholders never know if they are going to receive dividends or if the value of a stock is going to increase. They may make or lose money on an investment. The risks, and therefore the rewards, can be high. Bondholders, on the other hand, are guaranteed a specific return (the interest rate on the bond) and will get an investment back after a specified time period. Bonds and stocks together are referred to as **securities**.

Bonds are different from other loans because the corporation that issues a bond does not have to pay regular monthly payments on the principal (the amount of a debt before the interest is added). A bond pays interest each year to the purchaser of the bond (the bondholder) until **maturity**, when the investor returns the bond to the corporation for payment and it is **redeemed**, meaning that the investor gets the original investment back on that date.

By financing with bonds instead of a bank loan, a company does not have to make payments on the principal, only the interest. On the other

The risks of holding bonds are lower than those of stock investment but, typically, so are the returns.

hand, the company must manage its money carefully so that it will have the cash available when the bond matures.

If a corporation stops paying interest on a bond, the bondholders can sue the company. A court may force the company to sell assets to pay the bondholders not only interest, but the full amount of the bond.

Until maturity, bonds may be traded publicly, with their price going above or below their **face value**. This is the original amount the purchaser paid ("loaned") to the corporation. The face value of a single bond, also referred to as **par**, is usually $100.

When the bond's market value rises above par, it means it is being traded for more than $100—perhaps someone purchased it at $102. A bond trading above par is trading at a **premium**—in this case, the premium is $2. A bond trading below par is trading at a **discount**. If the above bond were trading at $94, the discount would be $6.

Chapter Summary

Now that you have studied this chapter, you can do the following:

1. Explore your financing preferences.
   - Understand how much risk you are willing to take when financing your business.
   - Know the success rate in your industry.
   - Determine your realistic options.
2. Identify the types of business financing.
   - Gifts and Grants—Money or in-kind gifts given to support the business without a return required.
   - Debt—You borrow the money and promise to pay it back over a set period of time at a set rate of interest. Corporations sell debt in the form of bonds. You could borrow money from family and friends to finance your business.
   - Equity—You give up a percentage of ownership in your business for money. The investor receives a percentage of future profits from the business based on the percentage of ownership. Corporations sell equity in the form of stock. You cannot sell stock unless your business is incorporated, but you *can* sell equity. You could offer ownership and a share of your future profits in exchange for financing.
3. Compare the pros and cons of debt and equity financing.
   Debt Advantages:
   - The lender has no say in the management or direction of the business as long as the loan payments are made.
   - Loan payments are predictable—they do not change with the fortunes of the business.
   Debt Disadvantages:
   - Debt can be an expensive way to finance a business if interest rates are high.
   - If loan payments are not made, the lender can force the business into bankruptcy.
   - The lender may be able to take the home and possessions of the owner of a sole proprietorship or of the partners in a partnership to settle a debt.
   - Loan payments increase fixed costs and decrease profits.
   Equity Advantages:
   - If the business does not make a profit, investors do not get paid. The equity investor cannot force the business into bankruptcy in order to retrieve the investment.

- The equity investor has an interest in seeing the business succeed and may offer helpful advice and obtain valuable contacts.

    Equity Disadvantages:

- Through giving up ownership, the entrepreneur can lose control of the business to the equity holders.
- Equity financing is risky, so the investor frequently wants both to receive a higher rate of return than a lender, and to be able to influence how the company is operated.
- The entrepreneur will share profits with other equity investors.

4. Identify sources of capital for your business.
    - Entrepreneur, friends, and family
    - Financial institutions
    - Community Development Financial Institutions
    - Venture capitalists
    - Angels
    - Vendors
    - Federally supported investment companies

5. Understand stocks and bonds as investing alternatives.
    - Public corporations sell their stock to the general public to raise capital.
    - Bonds are interest-bearing certificates that corporations (and governments) issue to raise capital.

Key Terms

accounts payable	networking
angel	par
bootstrap financing	personal guarantee
charge account	policy loan
credit	premium
credit history	principal
credit reporting agency (CRA)	promissory note
creditor	redeem
debt service	risk tolerance
default	securities
discount	security
face value	share
financing	stockbroker
float	tax abatement
leveraged	tax credit
maturity	venture capitalist

Entrepreneurship Portfolio

Critical Thinking Exercises

1. What type of financing will you seek as start-up capital and why?
2. What steps could you take to improve your creditworthiness?
3. How would you counter the argument from a potential investor that "most small businesses fail?"
4. What challenges do start-up businesses face? Explain.

Key Concept Questions

1. Calculate the annual amount of interest (assuming no principal repayment) for each of the following:

   Term loan of $122,000 over 15 years at 6.5%   _____

   Line of credit for $50,000 drawn 50% all year at 10%   _____

   15 shares of stock purchased at $12.50 per share   _____

   Bonds trading at par for $2,000 with a 7% rate   _____

2. If the owner of Bright Rays Tanning Salon, Inc., invested $200,000 and had an investor pay in $45,000 for 15% of the corporation, what is the valuation of the business?

Application Exercises

1. If you currently subscribe to or use an online service, BBS, or ISP (Internet Service Provider), discuss what you like and dislike about the service and why you chose it.

2. If you accept an equity investment, how could it change your business plans?

Exploring Online

1. Visit *http://www.privacyrights.org/fs/fs6-crdt.htm* to learn about your rights to financial privacy; then answer the following:

   a. Who has access to your credit reports?
   b. What information cannot be legally included in your credit reports?
   c. After how many years is unpaid debt erased from your credit reports?

2. Visit the SBA Web site at *http://www.sba.gov.* Find four possible funding sources for a computer rental and repair company. Describe the pros and cons of each and create a proposed financing mix, assuming a need for $58,000 in start-up funds divided as follows:

Equipment	$27,000
Software	$10,000
Supplies	$ 1,000
Marketing	$ 6,000
Utilities/services	$ 4,000
Working capital	$10,000

Exploring Your Community

1. Find and list three networking opportunities in your community. Describe how you could take advantage of them for your business.

2. Visit a local bank and ask about its commercial lines of credit. Have the banker explain the terms to you and what a small start-up business would have to show to qualify for a line of credit. Report back to the class.

3. Are there any angel investors that might be interested in your business? Who are they and how did you find them?

Unit Three address the core financial issues of an organization through financial statements and ratio analysis. It explains start-up costs and debt repayment. Income statements and balance sheets are illustrated and the methods of analyzing them are articulated.

The specific performance objectives for the unit are:

1. Describe the variable costs of starting a business.
2. Analyze your fixed operating costs and calculate gross profit.
3. Set up financial recordkeeping for your business.
4. Create financial statements.
5. Read an income statement.
6. Examine a balance sheet to determine a business's financing strategy.
7. Use the balance sheet equation to see the relationship between assets, liabilities, and owner's equity.
8. Perform a financial ratio analysis of an income statement.
9. Calculate return on investment (ROI).
10. Perform "same size analysis" of an income statement.
11. Use quick, current, and debt ratios to analyze a balance sheet.
12. Use a cash flow statement to guide your business operations.
13. Read a cash flow statement.
14. Manage and forecast cash flow effectively.
15. Understand the future value of money.
16. Calculate the present value of money.
17. File appropriate tax returns for your business.
18. Calculate working capital.

At the end of this unit, you have an opportunity to see the segments of the sample business plan that have been covered. This covers multiple sections of the complete Daily Perc Plan. You also can go to the Business Plan Worksheet Template on BizBuilder to develop segments of your plan.

These performance objectives translate into the parts of many sections of the business plan, including:

1.0. Executive Summary
    1.1. Objectives
3.0. Company Summary
    3.1. Company Ownership
    3.2. Start-up Summary
5.0. Strategy and Implementation Summary
    5.4.1. Sales Forecast
7.0. Financial Plan
    7.1. Important Assumptions
    7.2. Breakeven Analysis
    7.3. Projected Profit and Loss
    7.4. Projected Cash Flow
    7.5. Projected Balance Sheet
    7.6. Business Ratios
8.0. Funding Request and Exit Strategy
    8.1. Funding Request

1. Executive Summary

Introduce with a favorable initial statement.

The Daily Perc's financial picture is quite promising. Since TDP is operating a cash business, the initial cost is significantly less than many start-ups these days. The process is labor intensive and TDP recognizes that a higher level of talent is required. The financial investment in its employees will be one of the greatest differentiators between it and TDP's competition. For the purpose of this pro-forma plan, the capital expenditures of facilities and equipment are financed. There will be minimum inventory on hand so as to keep the product fresh and to take advantage of price drops, when and if they should occur.

Explanation of differentiation.

Critical financial and operational assumptions.

The Daily-Perc anticipates the initial combination of investments and long-term financing of $515,000 to carry it without the need for any additional equity or debt investment, beyond the purchase of equipment or facilities. This will mean growing a bit more slowly than might be otherwise possible, but it will be a solid, financially sound growth based on customer request and product demand.

Definition of financing need.

Growth strategy defined.

The balance sheet estimates a Net Worth of $1,075,969 for the third year, cash balances of $773,623 and earnings of $860,428, based on 13 Drive-thrus and 4 Mobile Cafés, it is not unrealistic to put a market value of between $4 million and $9 million on the company. At present, such companies are trading in multiples of 4 to 10 times earnings, and it is simple mathematics to multiply the success of TDP by the number of major and smaller metropolitan areas between the mountain ranges of the United States.

Valuation of company based upon earning projections and comparables.

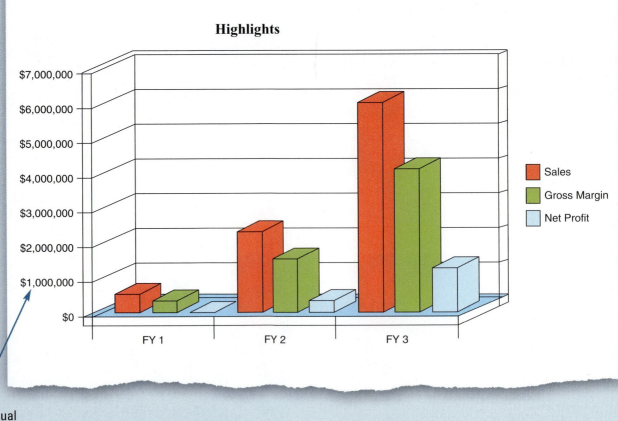

Clear visual representation.

The Daily Perc Business Plan provided by Business Plan Pro® and used by permission of Palo Alto Software.

1.1. Objectives

The Daily Perc has established three firm objectives it wishes to achieve in the next three years:

1. Thirteen Drive-thru locations and four fully booked Mobile Cafés by the end of the third year.

2. Gross Margin of 45% or more.

3. Net After-tax Profit above 15% of Sales.

Statement of performance objectives over 3 years.

3. Company Summary

3.1. Company Ownership

The Daily Perc is a Limited Liability Corporation. All membership shares are currently owned by Bart and Teresa Fisher, with the intent of using a portion of the shares to raise capital.

Legal structure defined.

Owners and their ownership intentions.

The plan calls for the sale of 100 membership units in the company to family members, friends, and Angel Investors. Each membership unit in the company is priced at $4,250, with a minimum of five units per membership certificate, or a minimum investment of $21,250 per investor.

Funding proposal that will need to be reflected in financials.

If all funds are raised, based on the pricing established in the financial section of this plan, Bart and Terri Fisher will maintain ownership of no less than 51% of the company.

Statement shows that owners intend to keep majority interest.

3.2. Start-Up Summary

The Daily Perc's start-up expenses total just $365,670. The majority of these funds—roughly $300,000—will be used to build the first facility, pay deposits, and provide capital for six months of operating expenses. Another $35,000 will be used for the initial inventory and other one-time expenses. The Daily Perc anticipates the need for roughly $25,500 in operating capital for the first few months of operation.

Uses of start-up funds summarized.

The Daily Perc—Start-Up

Table gives a more detailed perspective on the start-up costs by category. Specific detail can be provided in the appendices.

Requirements	
Start-Up Expenses	
Legal	$3,500
Office Equipment	$4,950
Drive-thru Labor (6 months)	$65,000
Drive-thru Finance Payment (6 months)	$12,300
Drive-thru Expenses (6 months)	$8,520
Land Lease (6 months)	$7,200
Vehicle Finance (6 months)	$3,700
Administration Labor (6 months)	$54,000
Web Site Development & Hosting	$5,600
Identity/Logos/Stationary	$4,000
Other	$5,000
Total Start-Up Expenses	**$173,770**

Income statement items.

Start-Up Assets

Cash Required	$25,500
Start-Up Inventory	$35,000
Other Current Assets	$0
Long-term Assets	$131,400
Total Assets	$191,900

Total Requirements	$365,670

The Daily Perc—Start-Up Funding

Start-Up Expenses to Fund	$173,770
Start-Up Assets to Fund	$191,900
Total Funding Required	$365,670

Assets

Non-cash Assets from Start-Up	$166,400
Cash Requirements from Start-Up	$25,500
Additional Cash Raised	$0
Cash Balance on Starting Date	$25,500
Total Assets	$191,900

Liabilities and Capital
Liabilities

Current Borrowing	$9,000
Long-term Liabilities	$131,400
Accounts Payable (Outstanding Bills)	$0
Other Current Liabilities (Interest-free)	$0
Total Liabilities	$140,400

Capital
Planned Investment

Partner 1	$21,250
Partner 2	$21,250
Partner 3	$42,500
Partner 4	$25,500
Partner 5	$29,750
Other	$85,020
Additional Investment Requirement	$0
Total Planned Investment	$225,270
Loss at Start-Up (Start-Up Expenses)	($173,770)
Total Capital	$51,500
Total Capital and Liabilities	$191,900

Total Funding	$365,670

The Daily Perc Business Plan provided by Business Plan Pro® and used by permission of Palo Alto Software.

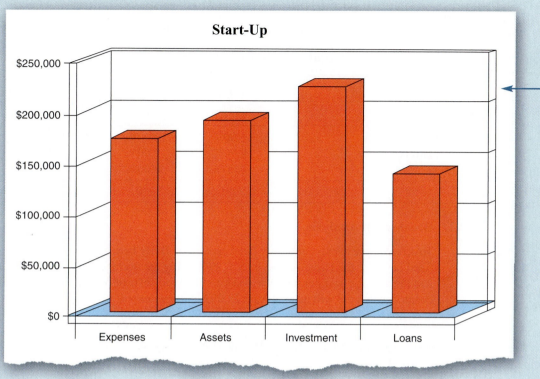

Start-Up

Visual representation of start-up costs in section 3.2.

5.4.1. Sales Forecast

Total first year unit sales should reach 298,402, equating to revenues of $558,043. The second year will see unit sales increase to 1,177,400, or $2,348,900. The third year, with the addition of such a significant number of outlets, will see unit sales increase to 2,992,000, equating to gross sales revenue of $6,022,950.

7. Financial Plan

The Daily Perc's financial picture is quite promising. Since TDP is operating a cash business, the initial cost is significantly less than many start-ups these days. The process is labor intensive and TDP recognizes that a higher level of talent is required. The financial investment in its employees will be one of the greatest differentiators between it and TDP's competition. For the purpose of this pro-forma plan, the facilities and equipment are financed. These items are capital expenditures and will be available for financing. There will be a minimum of inventory on hand so as to keep the product fresh and to take advantage of price drops, when and if they should occur.

Exactly the same language as in the Executive Summary. You may want to make the sections parallel to one another but not be indentical.

The Daily Perc anticipates the initial combination of investments and long-term financing of $515,000 to carry it without the need for any additional equity or debt investment, beyond the purchase of equipment or facilities. This will mean growing a bit more slowly than might be otherwise possible, but it will be a solid, financially sound growth based on customer request and product demand.

7.1. Important Assumptions

The financial plan depends on important assumptions, most of which are shown in the following table. The key underlying assumptions are:

Explanation of major assumptions.

- The Daily Perc assumes a slow-growth economy, without major recession.

- The Daily Perc assumes of course that there are no unforeseen changes in public health perceptions of its general products.

The Daily Perc Business Plan provided by Business Plan Pro® and used by permission of Palo Alto Software.

• The Daily Perc assumes access to equity capital and financing sufficient to maintain its financial plan as shown in the tables.

• Assumptions for the first year appear in Appendix 4-C

The Daily Perc—General Assumptions

	FY1	FY2	FY3
Plan Month	1	2	3
Current Interest Rate	10.00%	10.00%	10.00%
Long-term Interest Rate	9.00%	9.00%	9.00%
Tax Rate	0.00%	0.00%	0.00%
Other	0	0	0

7.2. Break-even Analysis

To arrive at the average monthly fixed costs, The Daily Perc calculated the fixed costs for the Drive-thru to be $28,294. Using the average price per unit, less the average cost per unit, divided into the fixed costs of operation, TDP concludes that we will need at least 23,003 units per month to reach break-even at $43,016 per month.

The Daily Perc—Break-even Analysis

Monthly Units Break-even	23,003
Monthly Revenue Break-even	$43,016
Assumptions:	
Average Per-Unit Revenue	$1.87
Average Per-Unit Variable Cost	$0.64
Estimated Monthly Fixed Cost	$28,294

7.3. Projected Profit and Loss

The Daily Perc is expecting some dramatic growth in the next three years, reaching $558,043 in sales and a 65.5% Gross Profit Margin by the end of the first year. Expenses during the first year leave a Net After-tax Profit of $9,960, or 1.8%. Detailed profit and loss information is included in Appendix 4-D.

Aside from production costs of 34.4%, which include actual production of product and commissions for sales efforts, the single largest expenditures in the first year are in the general and administrative (G&A) area, totaling 54.7% of sales. G&A includes expenses for rents, equipment leases, utilities, and the payroll burden for all employees.

Sales increase by nearly 400% in the second year, due to the addition of two more Drive-thrus and two more Mobile Cafés, reaching a total of $2,348,900. Although operating expenses double in the second year, The Daily Perc will be able to realize a Net After-tax Profit of $368,675 or 15.7% of sales. In that same year, TDP will make charitable contributions of $70,000.

The third year is when The Daily Perc has the opportunity to break into markets outside the metropolitan area. TDP will see nine additional Drive-thru facilities open in the third year, which will drive sales to $6,022,950 and, even with a 200% increase in production costs, help reach a Gross Profit Margin of 68.9%. Several expenses take substantial jumps this year—advertising

---

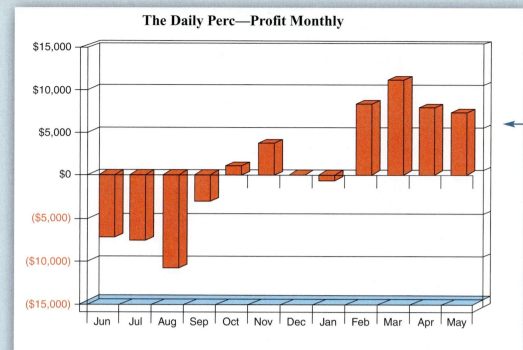

The Daily Perc—Profit Monthly

Visual of monthly projections that are included in the appendices. Could show quarterly or first 3 years to be more effective.

increasing from $36,000 to $72,000 and donations increasing from $72,000 to $180,000—and TDP will be adding several key management team members. These increases, as well as those for increased equipment leases and rents, raise our operating expenses to $2,772,993, leaving a Net After-tax Profit of $1,294,371, or 21.5% of sales.

Increased expenses explained and positive impact still shown.

The Daily Perc—Pro Forma Profit and Loss

Summary of first 3 years. Could add quarterly values for the first year. Monthly and/or quarterly values can be in the appendices. Also called "Projected Income Statement."

	FY 1	FY 2	FY 3
Sales	$558,043	$2,348,900	$6,022,950
Direct Costs of Goods	$190,977	$732,350	$1,783,010
Sales Commissions	$1,416	$35,234	$90,344
Cost of Goods Sold	$192,393	$767,584	$1,873,354
Gross Margin	$365,650	$1,581,317	$4,149,596
Gross Margin %	65.52%	67.32%	68.90%
Expenses			
Payroll	$242,374	$846,050	$2,024,250
Sales, Marketing and Other	$0	$0	$0
Depreciation	$21,785	$92,910	$196,095
Leased Offices and Equipment	$0	$6,000	$18,000
Utilities	$9,640	$19,800	$41,100
Insurance	$12,570	$32,620	$63,910
Rent	$16,800	$50,400	$126,000
Payroll Taxes	$36,356	$126,908	$303,638
Other General and Administrative	$0	$0	$0
Total Operating Expenses	$339,525	$1,174,688	$2,772,993
Profit Before Interest and Taxes	$ 26,125	$406,629	$1,376,603
EBITDA	$47,910	$499,539	$1,572,698
Interest Expense	$16,165	$37,954	$82,232
Taxes Incurred	$0	$0	$0
Net Profit	$9,960	$368,675	$1,294,371
Net Profit/Sales	1.78%	15.70%	21.49%

Clear statement of gross margin in the financial statement is helpful in the business plan.

TDP should show advertising and other marketing expenses explicitly. Charitable contributions also should be shown.

TDP is showing a small net profit in the first year. This is unusual among start-up businesses. Do not be alarmed if you suffer a loss in year 1.

7.4. Projected Cash Flow

Cash flow will have to be carefully monitored, as in any business, but The Daily Perc is also the beneficiary of operating a cash business. After the initial investment and start-up costs are covered, the business will become relatively self-sustaining. With the exception of seasonal dips, which TDP has attempted to account for, through changes in the menu items.

Assuming an initial investment and financing of $515,000, which would include $25,500 of operating capital, The Daily Perc anticipates no cash flow shortfalls for the first year or beyond. March and May are the greatest cash drains, since TDP will be experiencing the cost of a second drive thru and mobile unit start-up. Again, TDP sees heavier than normal drains of cash in December and January, as there will be certain accounts payable coming due. A detailed pro forma cash flow for the first year of operations is included in Appendix 4-E.

The Daily Perc—Cash

Net Cash Flow

Cash Balance

The Daily Perc Business Plan provided by Business Plan Pro® and used by permission of Palo Alto Software.

304

The Daily Perc—Pro Forma Cash Flow

	FY 1	FY 2	FY 3
Cash Received			
Cash from Operations			
Cash Sales	$558,043	$2,348,900	$6,022,950
Subtotal Cash from Operations	$558,043	$2,348,900	$6,022,950
Additional Cash Received			
Sales Tax, VAT, HST/GST Received	$0	$0	$0
New Current Borrowing	$0	$0	$0
New Other Liabilities (Interest-free)	$0	$0	$0
New Long-term Liabilities	$181,463	$253,970	$729,992
Sales of Other Current Assets	$0	$0	$0
Sales of Long-term Assets	$0	$0	$0
New Investment Received	$0	$0	$0
Subtotal Cash Received	$739,506	$2,602,870	$6,752,942

Expenditures	FY I	FY 2	FY 3
Expenditures from Operations			
Cash Spending	$242,374	$846,050	$2,024,250
Bill Payments	$240,175	$1,091,066	$2,573,382
Subtotal Spent on Operations	$482,549	$1,937,116	$4,597,632
Additional Cash Spent			
Sales Tax, VAT, HST/GST Paid Out	$0	$0	$0
Principal Repayment of Current Borrowing	$1,500	$0	$0
Other Liabilities Principal Repayment	$0	$0	$0
Long-term Liabilities Principal Repayment	$26,469	$0	$0
Purchase Other Current Assets	$0	$0	$0
Purchase Long-term Assets	$191,850	$429,700	$1,356,993
Dividends	$0	$0	$0
Subtotal Cash Spent	$702,368	$2,366,816	$5,954,625
Net Cash Flow	$37,139	$236,054	$798,317
Cash Balance	$62,639	$298,693	$1,097,010

Cash from operations and cash sales are the same for this particular business.

TDP is anticipating that no taxes are collected on food or other sales. Some states and certain businesses will have to collect these taxes and reflect them in the cash flow.

Expansion plans include no short-term borrowing.

Borrowing for expansion.

Assuming all investment occurs before the operations begin.

Since no taxes are collected, none are paid out.

Indicates the repayment of principal on current debt. Typically, there will be some each year if there is new debt.

No principal repayment reflected in this cash flow. Normally, a portion of the long-term debt is repaid annually, so that there would be a value in each year.

This number is higher than the new long-term debt and investment total, indicating that a significant portion of the expansion will be paid through operations.

Shows a strong positive cash balance, such that TDP might even be able to reduce debt significantly if desired.

Clear statement of goal.

Investors know not to expect any dividends during this period, because TDP makes it explicit.

7.5. Projected Balance Sheet

The Daily Perc's projected balance sheet shows an increase in net worth to just over $1 million in fiscal year 3, at which point it expects to be making 21.5% after-tax profit on sales of $6.02 million. With the present financial projections, TDP expects to build a company with strong profit potential, and a solid balance sheet that will be asset heavy and flush with cash at the end of the third year. The Daily Perc has no intention of paying out dividends before the end of the third year, using the excess cash for continued growth. The first year projected balance sheet for TDP appears in Appendix 4-G.

The Daily Perc Business Plan provided by Business Plan Pro® and used by permission of Palo Alto Software.

305

Chapter 11

Addressing Legal Issues and Managing Risk

> *"Remember that time is money."*
>
> —Benjamin Franklin, American statesman, inventor, and writer

On May 8, 1886, Dr. John Stith Pemberton, an Atlanta, Georgia, pharmacist, produced the syrup for Coca-Cola, and brought a jug of it to Jacobs' Pharmacy, where it was tasted and sold as a soda fountain drink. The syrup was mixed to create a beverage that was proclaimed to be "Delicious and Refreshing," a theme that Coca-Cola reinforces today.

Dr. Pemberton's partner and bookkeeper, Frank Robinson, thought that "two Cs would look well in advertising," and recommended the name and created the famous trademark "Coca-Cola" in his own script.

Over time, Asa Candler bought rights and acquired complete control of the company. According to the Web site, in May of 1889, Candler published a full-page advertisement in *The Atlanta Journal*, proclaiming his wholesale and retail drug business as "sole proprietors of Coca-Cola . . . Delicious. Refreshing. Exhilarating. Invigorating." By 1892, Candler's flair for merchandising had boosted sales of Coca-Cola syrup nearly tenfold. With his brother, John Candler, Frank Robinson and two other associates, Candler formed a corporation named the Coca-Cola Company. The trademark "Coca-Cola," which had been used 1886, was registered in the United States Patent Office in 1893 and has been renewed periodically.[1]

Performance Objectives

1. Choose a legal structure for your business.
2. Understand the importance of contracts.
3. Protect your intellectual property.
4. Choose the right insurance policies for your business.

---
[1] Information from Coca-Cola Web site at *http://www.Coke.com*

Business Legal Structures

Performance Objective 1 ▶

Choose a legal structure for your business.

Your business, no matter how humble its beginnings, may have the potential to grow into a much larger venture, so it is important that you think through every step of its development. How you organize your company—the legal structure you choose, the relationships with suppliers you develop, the managers you hire—will have a tremendous impact on your ability to grow.

After you pick the kind of business and industry you want to be in, you will know where you fit in the production-distribution chain—you will be able to research markups, markdowns, and discounts in your industry, in order to be competitive. You will also have to choose one of the three basic legal structures:

1. Sole proprietorship
2. Partnership
3. Corporation

Sole Proprietorship

A **sole proprietorship** is owned by one person, who often is the only employee. The owner receives all the profits from the business and is also responsible for all the losses. Most U.S. businesses are sole proprietorships.

The sole proprietor is personally **liable**, or responsible, for any lawsuits that arise from accidents, faulty merchandise, unpaid bills, or other business problems. This means a sole proprietor could lose not only business assets in a lawsuit, but could be forced to sell private possessions to satisfy a court judgment. He or she could lose a house or a car, for example.

Advantages of a Sole Proprietorship

- It is relatively easy to start. A person can become a sole proprietor, albeit not a legal one, simply by selling something to someone else.
- Proper registration does not require much paperwork and it is relatively inexpensive.
- There are fewer government regulations than for the other forms of business.
- Sole proprietors can make quick decisions and act without interference from others.
- A sole proprietor keeps all the profits from the business.

Disadvantages of a Sole Proprietorship

- It can be difficult to raise enough money by oneself to start or expand the business.
- A sole proprietor must often put in long hours, working even 6 or 7 days a week, with no one to share the responsibilities.
- There is no way to limit personal legal liability from lawsuits related to the business.
- There is often no one else in the business to offer encouragement or feedback.
- The odds of failure are high, usually because of a lack of financing or business expertise.

How to Register a Sole Proprietorship

In most states and localities it is easy and relatively inexpensive to register a sole proprietorship. When you do, you will have a legal business!

- If you carry on a business without registering it, you may be liable to civil and even criminal penalties.
- Registered sole proprietorships can use the court system and bring lawsuits.
- Banks like to see business ownership the way employers like to see that you have had previous work experience. If your business is not registered, banks will not even *consider* loaning you money, although some alternative lenders may do so. The time that you operated without registration will be discounted.

Steps to Registering

The registration process varies from state to state and by municipality, but there will be a few common steps:

- Choose a name for your business.
- Fill out a registration form, sometimes requiring a "Doing Business As" (DBA) form with the name of the business and your name, so the state will know the name of the person who owns the business and will be responsible for tax payments.
- An official may then conduct a "name search" to make sure the one you have chosen is not already being used in that jurisdiction. You may even be asked to help research the records yourself.
- Once your registration is completed satisfactorily, you will pay the required fee. This fee can range from under $100 to several hundred, depending upon the type of business and state laws and regulations.
- You may be asked to take the form to a **notary**, a person who has been given the authority by the state to witness the signing of documents, to have it notarized and bring it back to the registration office. You will have to show the notary valid identification to prove who is signing the form. A notary usually charges a modest fee.

Partnership

A **partnership** consists of two or more owners who make the decisions for the business together and share the profits, losses, assets, and liabilities. As in a sole proprietorship, the owners face unlimited liability in any lawsuits. This means that *each* partner can be held responsible for paying debts or judgments, even those incurred by other partners.

The exception is the **limited partnership**. The limited partners have no official say in the daily operation of the business and have, as a result, limited liability. One or more "general partners" manage the company and assume legal liability. There must still be at least one "general partner" who is liable for all partnership debts.

Partners bring different strengths and skills to a business. This can help the venture grow and succeed. In addition, partners can support and advise each other. On the other hand, partnership disagreements can become quite unpleasant and destroy the partnership, the friendship, and the business.

Despite the advantages of partnerships, we suggest being very cautious about entering into one, even with a good friend or relative. A lawyer should be consulted and a Partnership Agreement drawn up that carefully defines the responsibilities of each partner. A Partnership Agreement is absolutely critical.

Corporation

There are several types of **corporations,** but each is considered a legal "person," or *entity,* composed of stockholders under a common name. It has rights and responsibilities under the law and it can buy and sell property, enter into leases and contracts, and be prosecuted. So-called "C corporations" issue stock. The shareholders who purchase the stock then elect a board of directors who manage the company. The shareholders who own the stock own the corporation.

The corporate legal structure offers three key advantages:

1. Corporations may issue stock to raise money. Essentially, the company sells pieces of itself (ownership) to stockholders.

2. The corporation offers limited personal liability to its owners. Unlike sole proprietorships and partnerships, the owners of a corporation cannot have their personal assets taken to pay business lawsuit settlements or debts. Only the assets of the corporation can be used to pay corporate debts. However, most lenders will not lend money to a small, closely held corporation unless the owners personally guarantee the debt—in which case the owners do become personally liable and can have their personal property confiscated to pay it. In addition, it is possible to "pierce the corporate veil" if the business affairs of the corporation and its shareholders are tightly entwined, so that shareholders may be held personally liable in a lawsuit. This is another argument for keeping business and personal finances separate!

3. Corporations can exist indefinitely, so they do not cease to exist when an owner dies or leaves.

> When the abbreviation Inc. (Incorporated), Corp. (Corporation), or Ltd. (Limited) appears after a company's name, it means it has been incorporated.

A disadvantage of corporations is that corporate income is taxed twice. A corporation must pay corporate income tax on its earnings because it is a legal entity. Then, the corporation may distribute earnings as dividends to stockholders. The stockholders must include those dividends as personal income on their tax returns.

Shares of stock represent a percentage of ownership of a corporation. If privately held, the shares are owned by only a few and are not *traded* (bought and sold) publicly, such as on the New York Stock Exchange or that of London or Tokyo (and there are many others). In a "public" corporation, such as Ford or IBM, the company's stock is offered for sale to the general public—anyone may purchase it at the market price. Stockholders may be paid dividends when the company's management considers they are warranted by profits. Dividends are part of the stockholders' return on their investment in the company.

There are several types of corporations:

- *C Corporation:* Most large companies, and many smaller ones, are C corporations. They sell ownership as shares of stock. Stockholders may vote on important company decisions. To raise capital, the C corporation can sell more stock or secure loans.

- *Subchapter S Corporation:* This type of corporation limits the number of stockholders to 75. It offers most of the limited-liability protection of the C corporation, but Subchapter S corporate income is only taxed once—as the personal income of the owners. It is a "pass through" entity for tax purposes. Often, a company will start as an S corporation and change to a C type when it begins to earn profits. The net profits of an S corporation are taxed at the personal income-tax rates of the individual shareholders, whether or not the profits are distributed.

- *Professional Corporation (PC):* Doctors, lawyers, architects, and certain other professionals can form corporations. The initials PC after a doctor or lawyer's name means that individual has incorporated the practice, or belongs to a group practice that has incorporated. Each state decides which professions can form such corporations. Professional corporations are subject to special rules. Professional corpora-

BizFacts

Advantages of Corporations
- Limited personal legal liability for shareholders.
- Money can be raised through the issuance of stock.
- Ownership can be transferred easily, because the new owner will not be personally responsible for the corporation's debts.
- The legal entity survives beyond the life or participation of individuals.

Disadvantages of Corporations
- Corporations are often more heavily taxed than sole proprietorships or partnerships. Their profits are taxed twice: first, as the income of the corporation (except S corporations), and again as personal income when dividends are distributed to stockholders.
- The founder of a corporation may lose control to the stockholders if he or she no longer owns more than half the stock. (This happened to Steve Jobs, cofounder of Apple Computer, who at one point was fired by his own company, though eventually rehired).
- It is more expensive to start a corporation than a sole proprietorship.
- Corporations are subject to many government regulations.

tions cannot protect individual members from malpractice liability, but the other members of a PC are protected from liability arising from the negligence of one individual member.

- *Nonprofit Corporation:* A nonprofit corporation is set up for a purpose other than shareholder financial gain, typically with a specific mission to improve society. Churches, museums, charitable foundations, and trade associations are examples of nonprofit corporations (also called not-for-profits). Nonprofits are *tax-exempt*. Nonprofits may not sell stock or pay dividends. There are no individual shareholders for a nonprofit corporation and any profits that are earned must go toward the advancement of the mission. Nonprofits may have members rather than shareholders.

- *Limited Liability Company (LLC):* The limited liability company (LLC) combines the best features of partnerships and corporations and may be an excellent choice for small businesses with a limited number of owners. In an LLC, income is taxed only as the personal income of the members, and the personal assets of the members are protected from lawsuits, as in a C corporation. In addition, many of the restrictions regarding the number and type of shareholders that apply to the Subchapter S corporation do not apply to LLCs, making them even more attractive. An LLC has a variety of options that make it a flexible type of legal entity. The advice of legal counsel is vital in establishing an LLC.

To compare these legal structures, see **Figure 11-1**.

Tips for Entrepreneurs Who Want to Start Nonprofit Organizations

There are huge needs in society—for food, shelter, education, and more—and there are many people who cannot access these fundamental services and staples. In the United States, there is the 501(c)(3) nonprofit (not-for-profit) corporation to help address this situation. A 501(c)(3) is a tax-exempt legal structure that can receive charitable donations from individuals, businesses, the government, and philanthropic foundations. Examples of well-known nonprofit corporations include the Boys and Girls Clubs, the YMCA, and the Sierra Club. People who donate money to not-for-profits benefit from their generosity by knowing that they are making a gift to a

Figure 11-1 *Comparison of legal structures.*

COMPARISON OF LEGAL STRUCTURES

	Sole Proprietorship	General or Limited Partnership	C Corporation	Subchapter S Corporation	Nonprofit Corporation	Limited Liability Company
Ownership	The proprietor	The partners	The stockholders	The stockholders	No one	The members
Liability	Unlimited	Limited in most cases	Limited	Limited	Limited	Limited
Taxation Issues	Individual* (lowest rate)	Individual* (lowest rate)	Corporate rate; "double taxation"	Individual* (lowest rate)	None	Individual* (lowest rate)
How profits are distributed	Proprietor receives all	Partners receive profits according to partnership agreement	Earnings paid to stockholders as dividends in proportion to the number of shares owned	Earnings attributed to stockholders as in proportion to the number of shares owned	Surplus cannot be distributed	Same as partnership
Voting on policy	Not necessary	The partners	Common voting stockholders	Common voting stockholders	The board of directors/trustees	Per agreed-on operating procedure
Life of legal structure	Terminates on death of owner	Terminates on death of partner	Unlimited	Unlimited	Unlimited	Variable
Capitalization	Difficult	Easier than sole proprietorship	Excellent—ownership is sold as shares of stock	Good—same as partnership	Difficult because there is no ownership to sell as stock	Same as partnership

*When the double taxation of corporations is taken into account.

cause in which they believe. Also, they are able to deduct these contributions from their taxable income.

In the United States, close to one million organizations qualified for 501(c)(3) status in 2003, compared with 600,000 in 1993. Charitable donations rose from $148.4 billion to $240.7 billion in the same 10-year period.[2] While competition for resources has increased, more resources are now available to support the growth of organizations that choose to incorporate as nonprofits.

Like any business, a nonprofit will need to generate revenue to cover its expenses. Failure to meet cash requirements will mean a failure to survive for not-for-profits, too. A nonprofit needs to identify a target market (constituency) and determine how it will deliver its products and services. Some key differences and considerations exist, however, and you should be aware of them before you apply to the IRS for this legal structure:

- *No individual can own a not-for-profit organization.* A nonprofit cannot be bought and sold like other businesses. You would not be able to dissolve and sell it for financial gain. Nor can you issue stock to raise money. These organizations are meant to improve society, not create wealth for individual shareholders.

- *Nonprofits are mission-driven.* Before you can operate as a nonprofit, you will need to be crystal clear about your organization's mission. What problem(s) are you trying to solve? The IRS will not grant tax-exempt status without such a mission. Also, ask yourself if there is likely to be a market of donors who will contribute money to your cause.

- *Define your unit of change.* In a for-profit business, the return on investment is calculated by looking at the corporation's financial records. Not-for-profit entrepreneurs need to think about their ROI a little differently. Not-for-profits do not exist to make money, so the ultimate measure of success will not be financial. Your ROI will be based on how much it will cost you to provide your services as compared with the level of change that was brought about as a result of this investment.

- *Determine how you will evaluate your success.* As a not-for-profit entrepreneur, you will need to set goals regarding the changes you wish to effect. How many homeless people will you feed? How many students will graduate as a result of your dropout prevention program? What changes in knowledge, skills, or attitudes will result from the efforts of your organization? The output and outcome goals that you establish must tie back to your financial and human resource inputs. How much does it cost to provide these services? Given these costs, how many units of change did your organization achieve? How can you document that your organization brought about these changes?

- *Analyze your financing strategy.* Nonprofit corporations can borrow money, as well as earn it. They also have access to a revenue stream that other business structures cannot tap. Not-for-profits generate revenue through grants and gifts from individuals and organizations. They cannot sell stock to raise equity.

Contracts: The Building Blocks of Business

Regardless of the type of legal entity you elect to form, you will need to enter into a variety of legal agreements. A **contract** is a formal, written agreement between two or more parties. When you sign up for mobile telephone service

◀ **Performance Objective 2**

Understand the importance of contracts.

---

[2] Jessica Stannard-Friel, *MBAs at the Crossroads of Corporate and Nonprofit America,* from "On Philanthropy" Web site, *http://www.onphilanthropy.com.* Accessed December 3, 2004.

with a provider, such as Verizon or AT&T, you are signing a contract. You agree to pay for the service at a specified price per month, and in return the company agrees to provide you with access to telephone service, voice mail, data services, text messaging, and the like. Remember that rental leases, any promissory notes and mortgages, advertising agreements, and partnership agreements are all contracts. How they are written (their terms) can often make or break your business.

Contracts are the "building blocks" of business. The relationships between the links in a production-distribution chain are defined by contracts. For example, if a department store wants to sell your hammered-silver necklaces, you might create a 6-month contract specifying how many necklaces you will supply at what price, and how and when the store will pay you.

With that contract in hand you can call your wholesaler. Because you have a large order, you will want to get your supplies in bulk. With the contract as written proof of your relationship with the store, wholesalers may give you credit. You can arrange to buy the silver you need now to fill the order, and pay for it after you sell the necklaces to the store. You can also plan ahead with your advertisers or work out an advertising plan with the store as part of the contract.

The power of a contract is that once the individuals involved have signed it, they must stick to its conditions or risk being sued and penalized in a court of law. If the store fails to buy your necklaces as agreed, you can go to court to force payment. That way, you will be able to honor your contract with your silver supplier. At the same time, the contract obligates you to produce what you have promised and deliver it when you said you would.

Never do business with someone who refuses to put an oral agreement into writing.

See a Lawyer

There are certain times in the life of an organization when investing in the cost of professional services is essential, even though the out-of-pocket cost may seem high. Contract review is one of them.

- Never sign a contract without having an attorney examine it for you.
- Never sign a contract that you have not read completely and carefully, even if your lawyer tells you it is all right.

If you are ever taken to court and argue that "I didn't understand that part of the contract," it will not satisfy the judge. Your signature at the bottom tells the court that you read, understood, and agreed to every word.

Lawyers typically charge by the hour, so be as prepared and organized as possible before visiting one. Many issues can be resolved efficiently and effectively through e-mail and telephone calls, so that costs are minimized. Always read the contract ahead of time and make a copy of it. Mark sections that you do not agree to or understand. Indicate your suggestions for changes. This will help your attorney advise you effectively.

Drafting a Contract

Consult an attorney if you need to **draft**, or write, a version of a contract or agreement, with the understanding that it will probably need to be developed and rewritten. Be certain that you identify and make a list of the key points in advance. Attorneys often have standard formats for specific types of legal agreements, sometimes called **boilerplate language**, which can make the process quicker and less costly.

A Successful Contract Should Achieve "The Four A's":

1. **A**void misunderstanding.
2. **A**ssure work.

3. **A**ssure payment.
4. **A**void liability.

Avoid Misunderstanding

When putting together a contract, clearly state everything that will be done, even what is obvious. Go into full detail (not just how many shirts you will supply to the store and when, but which types, colors, and sizes). If you do not cover all the details, the person with whom you are contracting may add provisions or find "loopholes" you will not like.

Assure Work

For a contract to be legally binding, both parties are required to do one of the following:

- Perform an action or exchange something of value.
- Agree *not* to do something the party was legally entitled to do.

Sometimes one dollar is exchanged as a token payment to legalize a contract. The contract should assure that you or the other party fulfills some kind of obligation. The exact nature of the obligation, and the time frame for accomplishing it, should be specified fully.

Assure Payment

A good contract specifies how payment will be made, and when and for what. It should leave no room for misinterpretation.

Avoid Liability

Because this world is full of surprises, your contract should spell out **contingencies**, unpredictable events beyond your control that could cause delay or failure to fulfill contractual responsibilities. The contract should list contingencies for which you would not be liable. Common contingencies are "acts of God" (earthquake, hurricane, etc.), or illness.

When you share the draft or a list of key topics of your contract with an attorney, ask these two basic questions:

1. Will this agreement fully protect my interests?
2. What would you add, drop, or change?

Letter of Agreement

Sometimes you will not need a contract, because the relationship is going to be brief or the work and money involved are relatively minor. In such cases, a **letter of agreement** that puts an oral understanding in writing, in the form of a business letter, may be enough. The other party must respond to it in writing, either agreeing with it or suggesting changes. However, use this option with care.

Breach of Contract

A contract is broken, or "breached," when a **signatory**, a person who signed the contract, fails to fulfill it. The person injured by the signatory's failure to comply with the contract may then sue for **breach of contract**.

For a contract to be *breached* (broken), it must first be legally binding. Most states require that all signatories be 18 years of age and that the contract represent an "exchange of value." If a contract is breached, a lawsuit must be brought by the injured party within the state's **statute of limitations**, the time period within which legal action may be taken.

A lawsuit is an attempt to recover a right or claim through legal action. Because lawyers are expensive and court cases time-consuming, lawsuits should be avoided whenever possible. Other options are **small claims court** and **arbitration**.

Small Claims Court

Conflicts involving less than a certain sum of money, which varies by state law, can usually be resolved in a small claims court. In Delaware, claims for $15,000 or less can be settled in

(continued)

See a Lawyer (continued)

this manner. In small claims court, each person is allowed to represent him- or herself before a court official. The official hears each side's arguments and makes a decision that is legally binding.

Arbitration

Sometimes contracts specify that conflicts may be settled through *arbitration*, instead of in court. In such cases an arbitrator—someone both sides trust—is chosen to act as the decision maker. The parties agree to abide by the arbitrator's decision.

A Contract Is No Substitute for Trust

A contract is not a substitute for understanding and communication. If you do not like or trust someone, having a contract will not improve the relationship. It could lead, instead, to a lawsuit. Never sign a contract with someone you do not trust.

A good reason never to sign a contract with such a person is that you might need to renegotiate at some point. Running a small business is challenging and unpredictable. In the jewelry example mentioned previously, how will you pay back the silver supplier if the store decides not to buy the necklaces after all? If you have a friendly relationship, you may be able to discuss your situation and renegotiate or cancel the contract.

Protecting What You Have: Intellectual Property

Performance Objective 3

Protect your intellectual property.

A critical process for any entrepreneur is to protect his/her ideas, products, inventions, and designs. Federal and state laws are designed to help individuals and organizations protect these kind of assets from abuse, reputational damage, and theft.

Trademarks and Service Marks

Whether you are advertising your business with flyers at the local laundromat or through a storefront on the Internet, you will need an easily recognizable logo for your product or business (such as McDonald's "golden arches"). A logo is printed on the business's stationery, business cards, and flyers.

As discussed in Chapter 5, a trademark is any word, phrase, symbol, or design, or combination of words, phrases, symbols, or designs that identifies and distinguishes the source of the good (product) of one party from those of others.[3] A **service mark** is the equivalent of a trademark, except that it identifies and distinguishes the source of a service rather than a product.

Exercise

Do each of the tasks identified below and record your information on a separate piece of paper.

Carry out a search online for the name you intend to use for your business. What did you find?

Will you still use this name? Why or why not?

How do you plan to protect the name of your business?

---

[3] U.S. Patent and Trademark Office at *http://www.uspto.gov/go/tac/doc/basic/trade_defin.htm.*

Global Impact...

Protecting Your Trademark Worldwide

If you plan to do business outside the United States, you will need to make sure your trademark is properly registered and protected. The International Trademark Association (*http://www.inta.org*) is an excellent resource. It can help you apply for a Community Trade Mark (CTM), which provides protection for a trademark in the 25 current members of the European Union (Austria, Belgium, the Czech Republic, Cyprus, Denmark, Estonia, Finland, France, Germany, Greece, Hungary, Ireland, Italy, Latvia, Lithuania, Luxembourg, Malta, the Netherlands, Poland, Portugal, Slovakia, Slovenia, Spain, Sweden, and the United Kingdom).

A company uses a trademark so that people will recognize its product instantly, without having to read the company name or even having to think about it. NutraSweet's red swirl and the Nike "swoosh" are examples of trademarks most people recognize. Rights to a trademark are reserved exclusively for its owner. To infringe on a trademark is illegal.

A trademark or service mark does not have to be owned on the U.S. Patent and Trademark Office (USPTO) Principal Register to be legitimate, but there are advantages to listing it:

- Notice to the public of your ownership claim
- Legal presumption of your exclusive right to use the mark as registered
- Ability to bring an action concerning the mark in federal court
- The use of the U.S. registration to obtain registration of your mark in other countries
- The ability to file this mark with the U.S. Customs Service, so that others cannot import foreign goods with your mark on them[4]

You do not need to file an application with the USPTO to use "TM" (trademark) or "SM" (service mark). However, you cannot use "®" until it has been officially registered, and then only for what is listed in the federal registration. To obtain application information, visit the USPTO Web site at *http://www.uspto.gov.*

Copyright

If you are a songwriter, author, or visual artist, you will be creating works that you might sell. If you do not protect your work, however, someone else can appropriate it. A copyright is the form of legal protection offered under U.S. law to the authors of "original works of authorship," including literary, dramatic, musical, and artistic works.[5] Copyright protection is offered for both unpublished and published works. The owner of a copyright has the sole right to print, reprint, sell and distribute, revise, record, and perform the work under copyright. The copyright protects a work for the life of the author/artist plus 70 years. Only the author or someone assigned rights by the author can claim a copyright.

When a work is created, its copyright is automatically secured. According to the Copyright Office, "A work is 'created' when it is fixed in a copy or phonorecord for the first time." The use of a notice of copyright is not required, but is recommended, and official registration of the copyright has certain advantages. The elements of notice for "visually perceptible" copies requires:

- The symbol © (the letter c in a circle) and/or the word "Copyright," or the abbreviation "Copr." and

---

[4] U.S. Patent and Trademark Office.
[5] U.S. Copyright Office at *http://www.copyright.gov.*

- The name of the owner of the copyright, or an abbreviation by which the name can be recognized, or a generally known alternative designation of the owner.[6]

Example: *Copyright © 2008 by Janina Joyce*

There are variations for sound recordings. Legal counsel should be sought for any issues that are unclear. To learn how to register a work, visit the U.S. Copyright Office Web site at *http://www.copyright.gov*.

Electronic Rights

Now that writing, photographs, art, and music can be posted on the Web, entrepreneurs must protect their intellectual property online, as well. The rights to reproduce someone's work online are called **electronic rights**.

Using artwork without permission, even if it is a song or photo or poem posted online, is Internet piracy. President Bill Clinton dealt a blow to Internet piracy in 1998 when he signed the Digital Millennium Copyright Act into law. The act protects copyrighted software, music, and text on the Internet by outlawing the technology used to break copyright protection devices.

There are certain steps that you should take to protect your electronic rights. Beware of contracts that say the following:

- ***"Work-made-for-hire":*** This means you are giving up the rights to your work. Now the buyer can use it anywhere without paying anything beyond the original negotiated fee.
- ***"All Rights":*** This means you are handing over all rights to your work to the buyer.

Here are some strategies for protecting your electronic rights.[7]

- Get the buyer to define exactly what is included in "electronic rights"—online publication? CD-ROMs? Anything else?
- Put a limit on how long the buyer can have the electronic rights—1 year, for instance.
- Ask for an additional fee for each additional set of rights. A good rule of thumb would be to ask for 15 percent of the original fee every time your work is used somewhere electronically. If you sell a drawing to a newspaper for $100, you could ask for $15 if the paper wants to use it on its Web site.

Patents

If you have invented a product or process that you want to turn into a business or to license, you may want to obtain a **patent**, which is an exclusive right, granted by the government, to produce, use, and sell an invention or process. The term of a patent is generally 20 years from its date of filing. A patent grants "the right to exclude others from making, using, offering for sale or selling" the invention in the United States or bringing it into the country via import.[8] Patents come in three forms: *utility* (process or improvement), *design*, and *plant* (varieties of plants). A patent cannot be granted unless it is for something that is "useful," "novel," and "non-obvious."

A patent cannot be obtained on a mere idea or suggestion. An invention should be fully developed and actually viable before you can seek patent protection. You will have to prepare detailed drawings showing exactly how

---

[6] U.S. Copyright Office.
[7] Adapted from the *National Writers Union Guide to Negotiating Electronic Rights*. For more information see *http://www.nwu.org*.
[8] U.S. Patent and Trademark Office at *http://www.uspto.gov*.

Step into the Shoes...
Louis Temple Invents the Harpoon—and Dies Poor

Obtaining a patent can mean the difference between earning millions and living in poverty, as the case of Louis Temple illustrates. Temple was an African American living in New Bedford, Massachusetts, in the first half of the nineteenth century. In those days, whales were hunted for the rich oil derived from their blubber (fat). The oil was used for lighting lamps and making candles. New Bedford was the capital of the whaling industry.

Whales were hunted with spears called *harpoons*. Temple, a blacksmith, invented a "toggle" harpoon, which had a moveable head that prevented the whale from slipping free. Temple gave prototypes of the harpoon to several New Bedford ship captains to try on their whale-hunting voyages.

Whaling voyages took about 2 years. By the time the ships returned and reported the harpoon's great success, Temple's invention had become public domain. He had made no attempt to secure a patent during this time, and other blacksmiths in the town were making their own versions of the harpoon. Although he made some money and opened a larger shop, it was nothing like the fortune he would have earned if he had patented his invention. Temple was injured in a fall at the age of 54 and died soon afterward. His family had to sell everything they owned to pay his debts. If his toggle harpoon had been patented, Temple and his family might have become extremely wealthy. How will you protect *your* intellectual property so you can profit from it?

---

it works. If an invention is put into use by the inventor or discussed publicly for more than 1 year without obtaining a patent, the invention is considered to be in the **public domain**, which means that a patent will no longer be granted—anyone may use or make it without payment. It is important that you not divulge a proprietary invention or concept in meetings or at events without seeking at least preliminary protection.

You do not need to obtain a patent unless you:

- Have invented a product that you intend to market yourself or sell to a manufacturer
- Believe that someone else could successfully sell your invention by copying it

The average patent takes at least 2 years to obtain. A patent search has to be undertaken, to ensure that the idea is new. Getting a patent is a complex legal process. Before starting it, see a registered patent agent or an attorney.

Do not go to the trouble and expense of obtaining a patent unless your invention is unique and you intend to develop it commercially.

The process of obtaining a patent is lengthy, time-consuming, and costly. There are many legitimate sources of assistance, including inventors' groups sponsored by state economic development offices, Small Business Development Centers, and community development venture capital groups. There are also unscrupulous companies and individuals that promise phenomenal success in commercializing ideas at prices that are inappropriate. Be careful to select reputable advisors, including patent attorneys. To learn more about patents, visit the U.S. Patent and Trademark Office Web site at *http://www.uspto.gov.*

Protecting What You Have: Risk Management

In addition to protecting your intellectual property, you should manage risk by protecting your physical property. Imagine if you lost your business property to a fire or flood, and did have the insurance to rebuild and restock. Or, think about an employee being injured and having no insurance for medical care. Risk management goes far beyond insurance. However, understanding business insurance is a good start.

Insurance Protects Your Business from Disaster

Insurance is a system of protection for payment provided by insurance companies to protect people and businesses from having property or wealth damaged or destroyed. There are many kinds of insurance and almost anything can be insured.

If you owned a restaurant, for example, you would need fire insurance. Your insurance agent would help you calculate how much money it would take to rebuild the restaurant and replace everything in it, in case of fire. If you borrowed money from a bank to buy equipment for the restaurant, the bank would require you to carry insurance to cover the loan in case the equipment was destroyed.

Assume rebuilding your restaurant would cost $150,000. You would need an insurance policy that would guarantee you $150,000 in case of fire. You might pay $100 per month for this insurance. This cost of insurance is called a **premium**.

As long as you pay the premiums on your fire insurance policy, you will not have to worry about losing your restaurant to a fire. If it does burn down, your insurance company will pay you to rebuild and restart the business. Insurance helps to prevent random events from destroying you financially.

Basic Coverage for Small Business

Performance Objective 4

Choose the right insurance policies for your business.

You will not necessarily need insurance if you are selling ties on the street or candy at school, but the moment you move your business into a building, or have concerns about people being injured while buying or using your product, you will need it.

A **deductible** is the amount of loss or damage you agree to cover before the insurance pays on a claim. In the restaurant example, the owner might feel confident that he or she could pay $5,000 for damages from a fire. The insurance company would then pay the remaining $145,000. With this higher deductible, the premium would be lower, perhaps $90 per month. The policyholder pays a lower premium in return for a higher deductible. When

Insurance protects your business from disasters like this fire, fought by firefighters in Virginia.
(Joe Sohm/Chromosohm, The Stock Connection)

buying insurance, choose the policy with the highest deductible you can afford to cover. This will give you the lowest possible premium.

Lower deductible = Higher premium

Higher deductible = Lower premium

Although state laws vary, most require business owners who have people working for them to carry:

- *Workers' Compensation Insurance:* Compensates employees for loss of income and medical expenses due to job-related injuries.
- *Disability Insurance:* Compensates employees for loss of income due to a disabling injury or illness.

If you have an automobile or truck that is owned or leased by the business, you must carry the following:

- *Commercial Fleet Insurance:* Covers your liability for personal injuries in an accident, as well as damages to any vehicle involved and injuries to others.

Other useful types of insurance are:

- *Property Insurance:* Provides protection against risks to property such as theft, fire, and weather damage, as specified in the policy. There are specific types of "disaster" insurance, such as flood and earthquake, that also fall under this category.
- *Liability Insurance:* Covers the cost of injuries to a customer or damage to property caused on a business's property—for example, a customer slipping and falling in your store.
- *Product Liability Insurance:* Coverage of risks in case your product harms someone. It is a subset of liability insurance. For example, a caterer may need to be concerned about food poisoning claims.
- *Business Income Insurance:* This is also known as "business interruption" insurance and is the equivalent of disability insurance for your business. It provides coverage if you have a temporary shutdown or significant limitation on your business. Property insurance may replace your facilities and equipment, but it will not compensate for lost business revenue like this form of insurance does.
- *Errors and Omissions Insurance:* This is designed to cover in the event that you make a mistake or fail to do something that causes harm to a customer. It is particularly valuable for service businesses.
- *Life Insurance—Key Person Insurance:* Coverage on the life of the owner or other top manager to assist in the transition and costs of recruitment in the case of death.

Still other types of insurance are available that can be tailored to the needs and resources of your business. When you are ready to take this step, ask other businesspeople to refer you to a good insurance agent.

How Insurance Companies Make Money

By now you may be wondering, "How can an insurance company afford to pay $150,000 to a restaurant owner whose business has burned down, if that individual has only been paying the insurance company $100 a month?"

The answer is that insurance companies employ experts, known as actuaries, who calculate the odds of a particular event actually happening. An insurance company that specializes in fire insurance, for example, will have information about fires in restaurants going back many years. Analysts at

Entrepreneurial Wisdom...

Lying about the Risks of Your Product Is Fraud

Failure to inform a customer of potential danger from your product or service or misrepresenting it in any way is called **fraud**. If a customer proves that you knew your product or service was dangerous but you sold it anyway, you could be directed by a court to pay damages.

The entrepreneur has a moral duty to inform customers of possible danger. It is best not to sell a product or service that could cause harm. Even if you are selling something as "safe" as neckties, make sure they are not made of highly flammable material!

Before you decide to sell a product or offer a service, try to imagine how it might possibly cause injury to someone. If you think it might injure a customer when used according to directions, do not sell it.

the company study this information and determine how often fires tend to occur and how much they cost. Even if some fires do occur, the cost of insurance paid out to one policyholder has been covered by the premiums paid by many others.

Protect Your Computer and Data

Data are critical to any business. Important business data on your computer might include mailing lists, invoices, letters, and financial records. The risk of the loss of this information is a very real one that you will need to address proactively. Since your computer is an electronic device, you should protect it from three things that can wipe out your data:

1. *Power Surges or Outages:* A power blackout can destroy data that you have not yet saved. You can purchase an uninterruptible power supply (UPS) that will keep your computer running when the power goes out. A power surge can damage your computer. Plug all your computer equipment into a multi-outlet surge protector, which can be bought at any hardware store.

2. *Computer Viruses:* A virus is malicious computer software that can attach itself to your software or files and ruin them. Protect your computer with virus protection software like Norton Antivirus or McAfee.

3. *Disk Failure:* Hard drives can crash, destroying valuable data. To prevent this, save everything you do to back up media, such as external drives, CDs, or jump drives. Periodically back up your entire drive.

Disaster Recovery Plans

What will you do in case of fire or any other catastrophe that makes access to your business impossible? Insurance policies may cover many things, but they do not ensure smooth business operations in times of disaster. Whether you operate a home-based business or a large multinational enterprise, you should have a disaster recovery plan for the scale and complexity of your organization. Be sure to write it down and share it with your team. Practice it once or twice a year. Include critical information that team members keep securely off-site. Some issues to address are:

- *Communications:* Who will contact each person in the company, and critical vendors and customers? How will they reach them? Include names, titles, telephone numbers, e-mail addresses, and physical addresses. Update the contact information regularly. Also, know what your message will be.

- *Base of operations:* Where will people go if the normal location is inaccessible? This could be someone's home, another company site, or another business location entirely.
- *Priority activities:* What business activities are most essential/time-sensitive? What activities can be postponed? What is the time frame for reactivation?
- *Return to facilities:* Define a process for regrouping and planning, and designate a leader.

This is a partial list for a disaster recovery plan. While it may seem to be more than is needed, a straightforward plan put in place before a disaster strikes can make the difference between business failure and survival.

Licenses, Permits, and Certificates

There is more to creating a legal business than naming and registering it. Once registered, you will need to comply with federal, state, and local regulations that may apply to your business. You should research these regulations before deciding to start your business, because they may affect what you can do, how you can do it, where you can operate, and when. Such regulations can completely change your potential business operations.

Zoning regulations often prohibit certain types of businesses from operating in specified areas. There may be other regulations, too, such as restrictions on obtaining a liquor license for a bar or restaurant. If your business involves food, you will need to comply with safety and health regulations, conduct food safety training, and probably obtain certain permissions and certificates.

Contact local, county, and state government offices, or your chamber of commerce, to find out which licenses and permits are necessary.

- **Permit**: An official document that gives you the right to carry on a specific activity, such as holding an outdoor concert.
- **License**: An official document that gives you the right to engage in an activity for as long as the license is valid. A driver's license, until it expires, gives you the right to operate a motor vehicle. A child care license permits you to operate a particular size and type of child care facility.
- **Certificate**: Official document that proves something. A certificate of occupancy verifies that a building is safe and ready for use.

If you hire people to work for you, there will be federal, state, and local regulations regarding employees that come into effect.

Chapter Summary

Now that you have studied this chapter, you can do the following:

1. Choose a legal structure for your business.
   - A sole proprietorship is owned by one person who also may be the sole employee.
   - A partnership consists of two or more owners who make the decisions for the business together and share the profits and losses.
   - A corporation is a legal "person" (entity) composed of stockholders under a common name.
   - A Subchapter S corporation limits the number of stockholders to 75. It offers most of the limited liability protection of the C corporation,

but Subchapter S corporate income is only taxed once—as the personal income of the owners.

- A nonprofit (or not-for-profit) corporation is set up with a specific mission to improve society. Churches, museums, charitable foundations, and trade associations are examples of nonprofit corporations. Nonprofit corporations are tax-exempt.
- A limited liability company (LLC) combines the best features of partnerships and corporations and is an excellent choice for many small businesses.

2. Understand the importance of contracts.
   - A contract is a formal, written agreement between two or more parties.
   - The relationships between the links in a production-distribution chain are defined by contracts.
   - Never sign a contract without having an attorney examine it.
   - Never sign a contract that you have not read yourself from top to bottom.
   - A successful contract should:
     - Avoid misunderstanding
     - Assure work
     - Assure payment
     - Avoid liability

3. Protect your intellectual property.
   - Your ideas and creations are your intellectual property.
   - Trademarks and service marks protect your brand identity.
   - Copyrights protect works of authorship.
   - Patents protect invented products and processes.

4. Choose the right insurance policies for your business.
   - Insurance protects people and businesses from the risk of having property or wealth stolen, lost, or destroyed.
   - When buying insurance, choose the policy with the highest deductible you can afford. This will give you the lowest possible premium.
   - Consider the normal and customary types of business insurance.
     - Worker's Compensation
     - Disability
     - Commercial Fleet
     - Property
     - Liability
     - Business Income
     - Errors and Omissions
     - Life

Key Terms

arbitration	draft
boilerplate language	electronic rights
breach of contract	fraud
certificate	insurance
contract	letter of agreement
contingency	liable
corporation	license
deductible	limited partnership

notary
partnership
patent
permit
premium
public domain

service mark
signatory
small claims court
sole proprietorship
statute of limitations

Entrepreneurship Portfolio

Critical Thinking Exercises

1. What can happen to an entrepreneur who is personally liable for the business? How can you protect yourself from personal liability? Say your friend wants to start a business making custom skateboards. Write a memo to your friend, explaining the risks involved and suggestions for limiting liability.

2. With a partner, make a list of the technological tools each of you could personally access. Brainstorm how you might combine your resources to create a successful business. Describe in detail how the partnership would work. For example, would the partner contributing more technology have a larger share of the business, or would profits and expenses be split equally? Draw up a partnership agreement that specifies each partner's duties and how much money and time each will invest.

3. Which legal structure will you choose for your business?
   Sole proprietorship _____
   Partnership _____
   Limited partnership _____
   C corporation _____
   Subchapter S corporation _____
   Limited liability company (LLC) _____
   Nonprofit corporation _____
   a. Why did you choose this structure?
   b. Who will the partners or stockholders for your company be?
   c. Describe the steps you will take to register your business.

4. If your business is incorporated, what percentage of your company is owned by one share of stock? Is your corporation's stock publicly or privately held?

5. Use computer software to create a logo for your business. Do you intend to trademark your logo? Explain.

6. Describe any intellectual property you are developing (without improperly disclosing a potential patent).

7. How do you plan to protect your intellectual property? Explain why it would qualify for protection.

8. Give an example of a business in your community that you think may be infringing on someone else's intellectual property.

9. What types of insurance will your business need and why? What is the highest deductible you feel you can afford? Pick one type of insurance you want to have for your business and find a company online that sells it. List the premium, deductible, and payout.

Chapter 12
Operating for Success

> *"Excellent firms don't believe in excellence—only in constant improvement and constant change."*
>
> —Tom Peters, author and management consultant

Cramer Products, Inc., was founded in Kansas in 1918 by Charles Cramer, a pharmacist. Cramer had created a liniment to treat his own sprained ankle several years earlier. The company was the first devoted to helping athletes prevent injuries and return to action more quickly if injured.[1] Cramer Products sold primarily to interscholastic sports teams and was an industry leader for over a half a century. That changed in the early 1980s, when athletic programs were disappearing, new products appearing, and competition growing.

Cramer decided on a retail strategy to replace its lost revenues. In 1990, management signed super athlete Bo Jackson to a joint venture for a new brand, called Bo Med, and targeted it to recreational athletes. The line debuted in October. In January, after being chosen for both the Major League Baseball All Star Team and the National Football League Pro Bowl, Jackson suffered an injury that ended his football career. Although he continued playing baseball, his star power suffered.

The Bo Med venture was a failure and Cramer products was left deeply in debt, with a great deal of unsaleable inventory. The company's position in its primary market was under assault, its viability as a retailer was damaged, and its management team was demoralized.

Cramer Product's president resigned and was replaced by Thomas Rogge. The new president introduced a style that encouraged a free exchange of ideas. He reorganized the management team and gave individual managers more authority. Cramer liquidated the Bo Med line, salvaging as much of the product as possible for repackaging under the Cramer label, and selling the rest to a distressed-inventory merchant.

To rebuild the core business, Rogge broadened the audience from coaches and trainers to include school nurses and physical therapists, and he set up a team to develop new products. He developed a new retail line, using the Cramer name. Packaging of both the retail and interscholastic products was consolidated into one format, creating a single inventory.

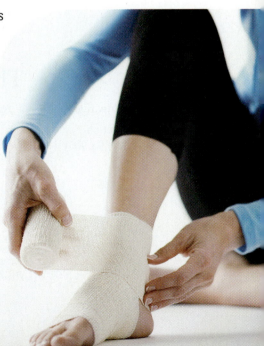

More than 60 new products were added. In 1994, new products accounted for 12% of sales. Rogge re-examined all operational departments, cut the workforce by 25 percent—it now totals 65—and assigned tasks to underused employees, improving productivity.

After 2 years of decline, sales increased 8 percent in 1993 and 12 percent in 1994. Profits set records. Retail growth has improved steadily ever since: Four major sporting goods retailers, with more than 200 outlets, added the Cramer line in 1994 alone. Cramer Products, like so many athletes it has helped, has recovered from its injuries. Years later, Cramer is still going strong.[2]

---

[1] Excerpted from Cramer Products: Treating an Injured Company. *Insights and Inspiration: How Businesses Succeed, the 1995 Blue Chip Enterprise Initiative*. Published by *Nation's Business* magazine on behalf of Connecticut Mutual Life Insurance Company and the U.S. Chamber of Commerce in association with The Blue Chip Enterprise Initiative, 1995, p. 47.
[2] Available at *http://www.cramersportsmed.com*.

Performance Objectives

1. Understand the significance of operations in a business.
2. Develop a production-distribution chain for your business.
3. Manage suppliers and inventory.
4. Ensure product quality.
5. Use technology to benefit your business.

Operations Permit Businesses to Deliver on Their Promises

Performance Objective 1 ▶

Understand the significance of operations in a business.

In order for a company to be successful, it must deliver on its promises to customers. Marketing sets the expectations and makes the promises. Finance and accounting ensure that the financial resources are available to produce the promised products and services. Legal structures and staff are in place to support success. Ultimately, the company must deliver the product or service to the customer as expected, or better. **Operations** is the set of actions that produce goods and services, and its efficiency is critical to business success.

What constitutes operations and the exact steps involved in carrying them out will depend on the nature of your industry and the specific business. As we have discussed, a manufacturing business is one that makes a tangible product and rarely sells its products directly to the consumer. It typically sells large quantities of its product to wholesalers. A wholesale business sells smaller quantities to retailers from warehouses. A retail business typically sells single items directly to consumers; they operate stores that are open to the public. The fourth type of business is service. A service business provides intangibles, such as time, skills, or expertise in exchange for a fee. Your business may fit neatly into this construct or it may be a combination. For example, if you produce jewelry and sell it online and at fairs, you are both manufacturer and retailer. In any case, there is the process of converting inputs to outputs. See **Figure 12-1** for an illustration of the process.

Regardless of what route your business takes, it is important to understand the process of operations. The details of operating all the various kinds of businesses are far too extensive to include here, and are described in publications that pertain to operating a retail store, creating an online business, becoming a wholesale distributor, and so forth. In this chapter, you will learn about operations from the manufacturing perspective, securing suppliers, assuring quality, and delivering the product.

The Production-Distribution Chain

Performance Objective 2 ▶

Develop a production-distribution chain for your business.

The consumer is the final link in a chain that extends from the manufacturer through the wholesaler and retailer. When a consumer buys a pair of athletic shoes in a sporting goods store, for example, the chain would be as follows:

1. Manufacturer produces a great quantity of a particular athletic shoe.
2. Wholesaler buys a large number of these shoes from the manufacturer.
3. Retailer buys a much smaller number of these shoes to stock a store.
4. Consumer walks into the retailer's store and buys one pair of shoes.

At every link in the chain, there are suppliers and customers. For the manufacturer, the suppliers are those who sell the components and raw

Figure 12-1 *Converting inputs to outputs.**

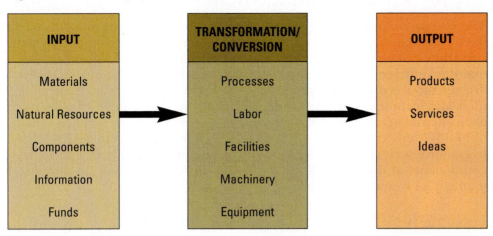

Source: Adapted from Jae K. Shim and Joel G. Siegel, *Operations Management* (Hauppauge, New York: Barron's Educational Series, Inc., 1999), p. 2.

materials that are needed for production, and the customers are the wholesalers. For the wholesaler, the suppliers are the manufacturers and the customers are the retailers or, as in the case of a plumbing wholesaler, the contractors that provide a service using the wholesaler's goods. For the retailer, the suppliers are the wholesalers and the customers are the public: consumers. Consumers are the final customers. Some variations on this chain appear in **Figure 12-2**.

Figure 12-2 *Production-distribution chain variations.*

Supply Chain Management

The management of sourcing, procuring, production, and logistics to go from raw materials to end consumers across multiple intermediate steps constitutes **Supply Chain Management** (SCM). In order to create and maintain efficient material (supply) flows between supply points, SCM addresses models and relations. Various partners must work together to use tools and techniques for increased efficiency and apply their knowledge to decision making. As you find a place for your company in a supply chain, or multiple chains, you can also develop relationships up and down the line to enhance your efficiency and that of your supply-chain partners. Critical components of this process will be identifying and securing suppliers and managing inventory.

Finding Suppliers

The world is literally your market for suppliers. Raw materials, component parts, subassemblies, and completed products may be available to you from around the world. You may be growing and packaging your own fruits and vegetables and have seed, fertilizer, packaging, and machinery and equipment suppliers. Or, you may be creating Web sites and have software and hardware companies, as well as Internet Service Providers, as suppliers. Or, you may own a retail gift store with hundreds of suppliers who themselves each have dozens of suppliers. Regardless of the simplicity or complexity of your supply partners, you will have to find them and work with them. Some places to look:

Your suppliers are partners in your business success.

- Trade shows or conferences
- Trade catalogs or journals
- *Yellow Pages*
- Internet search engines
- Wholesale supply houses and brokers
- Newspapers and magazines
- Competitors
- Firms like yours that are outside of your trading area
- Sales representatives
- Customers

Your suppliers will become partners in your business. Your success depends upon their capacity to deliver what you need when you need it at a price that you are willing to pay. Their success depends on you delivering your product or service and getting paid for it, preferably on a repeat basis, so that they can get paid and be successful, too.

There are many factors to consider when selecting suppliers:

- Conformance of products to your quality standards
- Certification—either from an official organization or via a process that you employ
- Timely delivery
- Lead times
- Minimum-order quantities
- Extension of trade credit
- The value added to your business (i.e., training, promotion, customer leads)
- Flexibility and responsiveness

Inventory Management

Managing inventory is vital to marketing success and to cash flow and there is an ongoing tension between them. If inventory is kept at a maximum, customer satisfaction may be maximized but costs can become too high. If inventory is maintained at very low levels, customers may become dissatisfied (even leaving entirely) but cash tied up in inventory is minimized. In order to balance service and cost management perfectly, factors such as demand, cost, sales price, carrying costs, order or setup costs, and lead times must be known values. In reality, demand projections, lead times, and other variables are generally estimated with varying accuracy. Business owners can use the best information as well as techniques and tools to make inventory management decisions.

Visual Control

A common approach to inventory management in small companies is **visual control**, which simply means that you look at the inventory on hand and when the stock level of an item appears to be low, you reorder. This decidedly unscientific method of choosing when to order will be dependent on you knowing the product usage and reorder time. It is most effective when you sell relatively few items and are actively involved in the business.

Safety Stock and Reorder Points

To avoid running out of materials, businesses frequently establish **safety stock** levels, which are the amounts of inventory or raw materials and work-in-process that are kept to guarantee service levels. The inventory **reorder point (ROP)** is the level at which materials need to be ordered again. A challenge for any business is to find the optimal safety stock and reorder points for all items and supplies that are kept in stock. If too much inventory is on hand, the costs of storage and tying up money may be too great. If too little inventory is available, the costs associated with lost sales and loss of goodwill may be significant. In addition to the holding and stock-out costs, the expenses of ordering may be substantial.

There are a variety of methods for calculating safety stock and reorder points. The calculation of the ROP requires a knowledge or projection of demand, lead time, and the safety stock level, and is calculated as:

ROP = (Average Demand per Unit of Lead Time × Lead Time) + Safety Stock

For example, if the lead time for showerheads is 2 weeks, and you sell 25 showerheads per week and you always want at least 10 showerheads in stock, the

$$ROP = (25 \times 2) + 10 = 60$$

So, whenever inventory falls to 60 showerheads, it is time to reorder. **Figure 12-3** shows this in a graph.

Economic Order Quantity

The **economic order quantity (EOQ)** is the amount of inventory to order that will equal the minimum total ordering and holding costs, and is calculated as:

$$EOQ = \sqrt{\frac{2DO}{C}}$$

Where D = annual demand for the item in units (not dollars), O = ordering cost per order (not units), and C = carrying cost

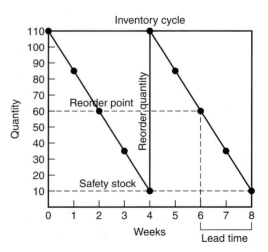

Figure 12-3 *Inventory cycles.*

per unit. For example, Dominique's Bridal Shop buys bridal veils at $80 per unit from its supplier. They sell 640 veils annually, distributed evenly over the months. The holding cost (also known as carrying cost) is 5 percent of the total, or $4 per veil per year. The ordering cost is $20 per order. So,

$$EOQ = \sqrt{\frac{2(640)(\$20)}{\$4}} = \sqrt{6400} = \textbf{80 veils}$$

The total number of orders to place per year = D/ EOQ = 640/80 = **8 orders**

$$\begin{aligned} \text{Total inventory costs} &= \text{Carrying Cost} + \text{Ordering Cost} \\ &= C \times EOQ/2 + O \times D/EOQ \\ &= (\$4)(80/2) + (\$20)(500/80) = \textbf{\$285 per year} \end{aligned}$$

From this example, Dominique's Bridal Shop should have an inventory policy of ordering 80 veils at a time and should place 8 orders per year. This inventory will cost the store $285 per year. **Figure 12-4** illustrates the calculation of economic order quantity in a graph.

If the company manufactured products and wanted to calculate the most economic size for a production run, it would use the same calculation methodology, but O = setup costs rather than order costs.

The Idea-to-Product Process

Taking an idea and turning it into a product can run from a simple to a highly complex process. Some entrepreneurs are excellent "idea people" but have no interest in the nuts and bolts of bringing the concepts to reality. For

Figure 12-4 *Economic order quantity.*

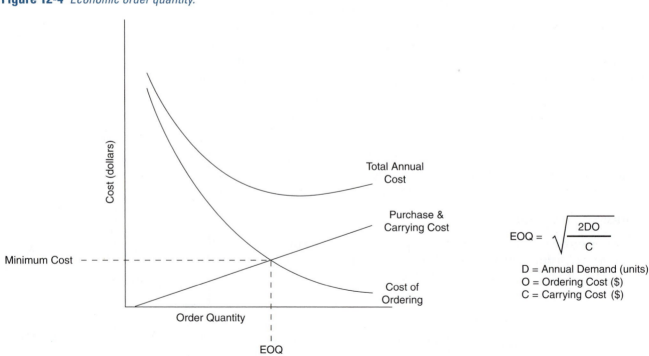

these individuals, securing intellectual property rights and licensing can often be the best option. Other entrepreneurs like to take an idea, whether it is their own or licensed, from the idea stage through production to marketing and sales. If your idea is for a product, rather than a service, understanding the idea-to-product process is critical.

Why Manufacturing Is Unique

Although entrepreneurs have successfully started all types of businesses, manufacturing companies offer some unique advantages. Manufacturers can:

- Make products that do not exist yet
- Fine-tune the design and features of a product in ways that "resale" businesses cannot
- Get a patent on product designs to discourage competitors and provide legal protection

There are disadvantages to starting a manufacturing business, however, including these caveats:

- It can cost a lot to set up and maintain a manufacturing company. Manufacturing equipment can be expensive and so can the costs of purchasing (or leasing) a suitable manufacturing plant.
- It can be costly to hire and train workers.
- Manufacturers have to pay to make the product first, but must then wait for the product to sell before getting their money back. The more processes that are needed, the more costly it can be.

A manufacturer can make every piece of its own product or have parts made by subcontractors. Many companies make the most important or complex parts of their products, but subcontract minor ones. Manufacturers like Ford and General Motors rely on other companies for parts that go into their cars. Many companies do the final assembly, regardless of who makes the parts.

Job Shops

Some manufacturing companies do not actually make a "final" product. Instead, **job shops**, or "jobbers," are subcontractors for other manufacturers. They use their manufacturing plant and equipment to make parts or even entire products for other companies. Job shops usually work with drawings and specifications provided by the product's manufacturer. They commonly get work by submitting and winning a bid. Job shops are useful to manufacturers because they are often able to:

- Produce parts of consistent quality
- Make a part less expensively
- Deliver a part more quickly
- Maintain and provide specialized equipment, so the major manufacturers do not have to purchase or maintain it themselves
- Provide manufacturing facilities to companies that do not have their own

Whether a company makes its own product or has parts or all of it made by subcontractors, what counts is that it controls the design, formula, or specifications of how the product is to be made.

The manufacturer controls the design of the product and provides the following:

- *Drawings and Specifications:* Diagrams and renderings tell others how to make the product and its parts. This includes written information about the materials, dimensions, **tolerances** (ranges of acceptable size variation), and parts to be used.
- *Parts and Materials List:* This list includes all the materials and separate parts needed to make the product.
- *Prototype:* A **prototype** is a model or pattern that serves as an example of how a product would look and operate if it were manufactured. A prototype gives you the opportunity to determine whether it will work correctly. You may also find ways to improve the product or to **value-engineer** it (reduce the cost) while constructing and testing the prototype. Because you are only making one (or a few), prototypes will cost a lot more than the actual product will per unit when it is produced in large quantities.

Whether you do it yourself or have others do it for you, manufacturing involves **tooling costs** and **setup costs**, which are the expenses of creating the specialized equipment and establishing a production run, respectively. Manufacturers calculate these costs before starting to make the product.

- Tooling costs are required to make or adapt the equipment for a product. These costs are also called "one-time" costs because there are no additional costs for additional orders. Manufacturers usually do not include these expenses in their "cost-each" of the product, but they do need to recover their investment in a timely manner. Not all products have significant tooling costs.
- Setup costs have to be paid each time you make a production run, or a "lot," of the product. This covers the time and effort of getting ready to make the product each time. For example, a pattern cutter must be reset for each style and size of a suit jacket. The larger the quantity produced, the smaller the setup costs will be per item manufactured. Almost all products have setup costs.

Manufacturing Tips

1. You may be able to make part or your entire product in your home; however, most cities and towns have zoning laws that limit what you

BizFacts

To find a company to make your prototype, look online at ThomasNet. The Thomas Register of American Manufacturers published its 100th and final print edition in 2006 and went to an online-only version consisting of more than 650,000 manufacturers and distributors. This online database is searchable in various ways and includes drawings of parts and components, as well as resource listings. The global version of the Thomas Register includes international suppliers and product information, and is available in English, German, French, Spanish, Italian, Dutch, Portuguese, Chinese, and Japanese. You can access Thomas online at:

http://www.ThomasNet.com   (national catalog)
http://www.thomasglobal.com   (international catalog)

access to
cated near
cess to a r
retail loca
must be lc
  Facili
ability of
"Will buil
for your b
a particul
ings are c
business
changes t
improver
  What
space tha
based ven
your busi
storage ai
other pro
well as in
cial impo
loading a
space des
ment mai
hesitate t
of a matt
  Layo
fixed-pos
a mass-p
automob
processes
work wel
faucet m
packagin
layout is
difficult t
als and p
residenti
layouts.

Defin
of Ma

The conc
cluding t
tions or
be largel
meal at
diner. In
ducing) t
tomer ex
and the
pectatior
of your c

Global Impact...
Finding Foreign Partners

Large corporations often have foreign operations or have relocated because the costs are lower. Changes in technology have made it easier than ever for small companies to benefit from such cost savings, too. UPS, FedEx, and others are all competing for your international shipping business. You can also ship larger products by boat. Ocean freight is slower but much less expensive. The World Wide Web, electronic mail, and teleconferencing have made the world "smaller" so that entrepreneurs can find opportunities globally. For example, locating an overseas manufacturing partner could turn your idea into a profitable business.

The following resources can help you find foreign partners:

1. The CIA's *World Factbook* at *http://www.cia.gov/cia/ publications/factbook* includes information such as:
   - How much the average worker earns per year
   - How much education the citizens have
   - What languages are spoken

2. Locate foreign companies on foreign search engines. Find "International Search Engines," or "[your country of interest] Search Engines," to get connected.
3. Foreign countries have embassies in Washington, D.C., and consulates in large American cities. They can be good starting points for making international business connections.
4. Request information regarding international trade assistance from a World Trade Center affiliate and your state economic development office.

---

can do in a residential area. Check the zoning requirement *before* basing your business plan on starting a home-based business. If your business involves large trucks making deliveries, you will probably have to find a location in a commercial area.

2. If manufacturing your product requires expensive equipment, consider working with a job shop that can make it for you, at least initially. You can use one job shop, or many, depending on the item. Even if your product is complicated, you may be able to buy the parts and do the final assembly yourself.

3. People who work in job shops know how to make things efficiently. They are seldom asked for design advice, because that's "engineer's work." But see if you can get your jobber to help you improve your design and make it affordable.

4. Look at all aspects of your operation to find ways to maximize your efficiency and minimize waste.

Just-in-Time Manufacturing

Although it is often less costly to manufacture products overseas, many American companies are taking advantage of new manufacturing methods to stay competitive. **Just-in-time manufacturing (JIT)** was developed in Japanese factories, but it can be very effective for an entrepreneur anywhere.

JIT manufacturers eschew traditional concepts, such as increasing the size of lots to take advantage of mass production methods. Instead, JIT focuses on making the smallest amount of product possible while doing it quickly and efficiently. Goals of JIT manufacturing include:

- Running the smallest lots (batches) possible
- Reducing setup time and cost to the bare minimum
- Scheduling production so that products are finished "just in time" to be shipped
- Staying flexible to make the widest range of products, with the smallest setup and changeover costs

Figure 12-5 *Factory layout—mattress factory.*

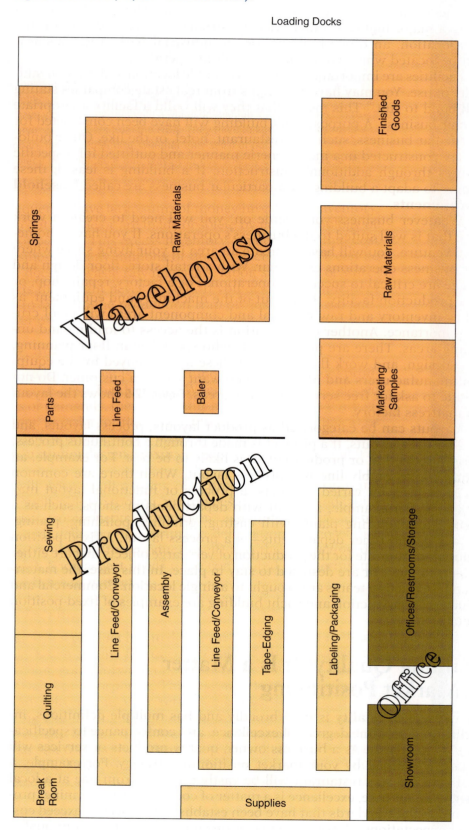

Step into the Shoes...

Positioning Stone Hill Winery through Quality

Jim and Betty Held took over the Stone Hill Winery in 1965, with four young children and a vision of restoring the historic Hermann, Missouri, winery to its pre-Prohibition glory days.[1] They succeeded until the 1970s when high interest rates combined with escalating costs. The winery grew slowly during the 1980s and 1990s and rapidly from the later parts of the 1990s.

Sweet and semi-sweet wines have always been the most popular wines that Stone Hill Winery produces. Jon Held states, "We have provided a wide spectrum of wine styles to satisfy all consumers rather than only the tastes of a select few wine elite. Most importantly, we have listened to our customers rather than to the wine pundits." The Helds analyzed consumer loyalty to wine brands and discovered that one significant factor was first-time consumption of the product, specifically the atmosphere in which it was consumed. They differentiated their advertising message, proclaiming, "Come out to the winery and have a great time."

The Helds knew that if they could invest in new vineyards and equipment they could attain economies of scale.[2] They needed to apply the latest grape and wine production technology so that the winery could consistently produce a range of wine styles with high quality and value. To raise money for this technology they had to grow significantly. The marketing approach and the application of technology worked.

Stone Hill Winery is a three-location tourist destination. They now produce over 255,000 gallons annually with gross revenues of over $9 million per year, while employing the Helds, two of their adult children and more than 100 others. Stone Hill has 170 acres of vineyards and uses grapes from other Missouri vineyards to supplement production.

Jim and Betty Held and their family combined market research, determination, state-of-the-art production equipment and techniques, and quality assurance to create an award-winning enterprise.

[1] Portions of this profile are available at *http://www.stonehillwinery.com/ourWinery/jim_Betty.aspx*.
[2] "Stone Hill Winery: New Tastes, New Approach," *Insights and Inspiration: How Businesses Succeed, The 1995 Blue Chip Enterprise Initiative*®. Published by *Nation's Business* magazine on behalf of Connecticut Mutual Life Insurance Company and the U.S. Chamber of Commerce in association with The Blue Chip Enterprise Initiative, 1995, p. 27.

Profits Follow Quality

For many years, American companies had focused less on quality than on short-term profits. In the early 1950s, however, American economist W. Edwards Deming argued that business should focus on making quality products instead of on maximizing profits—and that profit would follow from that focus. His revolutionary concept was ignored by American corporations, so he went to Japan, which was rebuilding after the devastation of World War II.

In those days, Japan was notorious for the poor quality of its manufactured products. The phrase "Made in Japan" was jokingly used to refer to anything poorly fabricated. Deming gave a series of lectures in Japan, though, that the Japanese took to heart. They began focusing on quality and soon proved that Deming's theory that profits follow quality was correct. The high quality of Japanese cars and stereos won over customers worldwide.

American entrepreneurs and corporate executives traveled to Japan to study why the Japanese had become so successful. They brought Deming's ideas back home, where they finally began to be adopted.

As you develop your business, it will be the consistent quality of your product or service that will lead to profits. If you can develop a way to deliver quality consistently, you will have a business concept that can be profitable, with the potential for generating even greater revenues in the future.

Organization-Wide Quality Initiatives

It is clear that quality management and quality assurance is not solely the job of the production team. As organizations have evolved in our rapidly changing technology- and service-driven environment, quality has come to mean the active involvement of the entire company. A number of efforts and methods have been formed to help businesses ensure quality. Among these are: Lean Manufacturing, Benchmarking, ISO 9000, Six Sigma, Total Quality Management, and the Malcolm Baldrige National Quality Award. Each of these can assist your company in providing the quality that your customers should expect.

Benchmarking

One the most basic organization-wide approaches that you can pursue is the use of **benchmarking**, which is the comparison of your company's performance against that of other companies in your industry—or against best practices, standards, or certification criteria. Benchmarking is what you are doing when you create a competitive comparison for marketing purposes or when you compare your projected or actual financial ratios to industry values. In addition to standard performance measures—such as return on investment, profitability, market share, and the like—individual industries have benchmarks. For example, retail stores measure sales per square foot and restaurants evaluate by customers per labor hour. By using benchmarking, you can identify opportunities for improvement.

A simple method of benchmarking is to create a list of measures that are important to your customers (using primary market research) or to customers in your industry (using secondary research, such as trade journal reports), and comparing your outcomes to them. You can then compare other statistics, if it is helpful. **Figure 12-6** illustrates a portion of such a table for a restaurant.

ISO 9000

The family of standards for quality management systems established by the International Organization for Standardization (ISO) is ISO 9000. These standards are certified by independent companies to document that consistent business procedures are being used and that the organization has been independently audited for compliance. Initially, ISO standards were applied solely to manufacturing. However, service firms have become the predominant recipients of certificates. Organizations will sometimes market their ISO certification, although it is not a guarantee of excellence by itself.

Figure 12-6 *Quality measures for the country diner.*

Measure of Quality	Rating (1 Is Poor, 5 Is Excellent—Based on Industry and Customer Data)				
Customers per labor hour	1	2	3	(4)	5
Average customer wait time for seating	1	2	3	4	(5)
Satisfactory inspection ratings	1	(2)	3	4	5
Number of meals returned to the kitchen	1	2	(3)	4	5
Customer satisfaction ratings	1	2	3	(4)	5
Amount of food wasted	(1)	2	3	4	5
Return on sales	1	2	3	(4)	5

There have been numerous standards employed under varying numbers. Beginning with the ISO 9001:2000 version, **process management** (measuring, monitoring, and optimizing tasks), upper management involvement, continuous improvement, recording customer satisfaction, and utilizing numeric measures of effectiveness became critical to the process. There are industry-specific variations that may apply to your business. There are eight quality management principles for organizational improvement:

1. Customer focus
2. Leadership
3. Involvement of people
4. Process approach
5. System approach to management
6. Continual improvement
7. Factual approach to decision making
8. Mutually beneficial supplier relationships

Regardless of the size of your firm, you can find considerable information on the ISO standards and can build them into your organization from the start. Assistance is available through the American Society for Quality (ASQ) at *http://www.asq.org*, the American National Standards Institute at *http://www.ansi.org*, and ISO at *http://www.iso.ch*.

Six Sigma

Six Sigma is a measurement of quality that was originated in the 1980s by Motorola engineers. It is the use of statistical methods to eliminate defects to a failure rate of 3.4 defects per one million opportunities, or a 99.9997 percent success rate. This is a rigorous process-improvement program that aims to achieve near perfection. The two sub-methodologies employed are DMAIC and DMADV.[5] The DMAIC (define, measure, analyze, improve, and control) system is intended to enhance existing production. The DMADV (define, measure, analyze, design, and verify) process is meant to support new procedures and products.

For most enterprises, this is a very intense program and may be more than is practical in the early stages. However, it may be worthwhile to learn about it and consider whether you can include such methods to build in high standards from the start. Further information is available at:

Six Sigma Academy	*http://www.6-sigma.com*
The Quality Portal	*http://www.thequalityportal.com*
General Electric	*http://www.ge.com/sixsigma.com*
iSixSigma LLC	*http://www.isixsigma.com*
Motorola	*http://www.motorola.com/motorolauniversity.jsp*

Total Quality Management

The quality-assurance methodology of striving for strategic advantage through quality inspired by Deming is called **total quality management (TQM)**. Although it was developed in the 1950s, many of the principles of TQM are still valid and valued. The central notion of **continuous improvement**, or always identifying and implementing changes throughout the organization to focus on the requirements of internal and external customers,

---

[5] Available at *http://www.isixsigma.com*.

is valid for any business. TQM involves constant monitoring and improvement of processing, typically using specific measures of quality, such as compliance with product specifications and operating standards, volume of production, on-time delivery, and return rates.

TQM's success is dependent upon the commitment of all employees toward treating one another as customers and working together to ensure that standards are met at all stages. Each employee accepts responsibility for a role in the production of the products and services.

Malcolm Baldrige National Quality Award

While the previous concepts have focused on quality-management methodologies, the Malcolm Baldrige National Quality Award (MBNQA) is a competitive process established by the United States Congress in 1987 that recognizes quality management. The Baldrige Award is given to businesses, health care, educational, and nonprofit organizations by the president of the United States and is administered by the National Institute of Standards and Technology (NIST).[6] Organizations apply for the award and are judged in the areas of:

- Leadership—organizational leadership and social responsibility
- Strategic planning—strategy development and deployment
- Customer and market focus—market and customer knowledge and customer relationships and satisfaction
- Measurement, analysis, knowledge management—measurement and analysis of organizational performance and information and knowledge management
- Human resources focus—work systems, employee learning and motivation, and employee well-being and satisfaction
- Process management—value creation processes and support processes
- Business results—customer-focused results, product and service results, financial and market results, human resources results, organizational effectiveness results, and governance and social responsibility results

Thousands of organizations use the Baldrige criteria for self-assessment, training, and the creation of business processes. You can obtain the Baldrige criteria and incorporate them into your business at any time. They are more comprehensive than many of the specific production and process measures identified above.

Using Technology to Your Advantage

Performance Objective 5 ▶

Use technology to benefit your business.

Technology can work to your advantage if you use it effectively. Even if your business is not "technological," you can apply technology to make your business operations more efficient and effective. The technology could be as simple as a telephone or as complex as a specialized piece of medical equipment. What is important is that you are aware of the technology available to you and how it might benefit your business. At the same time, you should be wary of adopting technology just for the "wow" factor. A cost/benefit analysis for technology implementation is as important as for any other substantive investment.

---

[6] Available at *http://www.nist.gov/public-affairs/factsheet/baldfaqs.htm*.

Get Your Hands on a Computer

Advances in technology that ordinary people can use have been an important part of the entrepreneurial wave of at least the last decade. With this in mind:

- Every entrepreneur should have access to a computer.
- Every business should have a Web site and electronic mail access.
- Every business should hire employees who are conversant and comfortable with technology.
- Every entrepreneur should be aware of the specialized computer software and equipment that is designed for his/her industry.

The World Wide Web came into being in 1989, when an Englishman named Tim Berners-Lee invented **hyperlinks**—words that, when clicked on, transferred the reader to a new document page anywhere on the Internet. Now pictures, and even video, can be links. Every Web page has an address, called a **URL (uniform resource locator)**, and you can "surf" from one URL to another using hyperlinks. Web pages are **hypertext** documents, meaning they combine text with graphics. Sound and video can also be included.

One of the best investments you can make for your business is to buy a computer. You do not need to have the latest model or even a new one; refurbished computers can be purchased inexpensively. Even the most basic model equipped with basic software can be used to:

- Utilize the Internet
- Create stationery and business cards
- Produce professional letters and check spelling, grammar, and syntax
- Keep financial records
- Maintain an updated mailing list of customers and print mailing labels

If you do not own a computer, consider making arrangements to borrow or use one part time. You can also rent computer time or get it for free at Internet cafés or some office supply stores. Most public libraries and community colleges even offer free Internet access. However, it is best to have your own computer to keep your company's books and records, as well as your other proprietary information, private.

Maximize Your Phone!

Do not forget, however, that "technology" does not have to be new to be useful. The telephone is still one of the businessperson's most important technological tools. You can turn your phone into an answering service for your business by using a voice-mail system, or you can hire an answering service to provide a more personal touch. Either approach is acceptable—until you have staff to answer customer inquiries; although today some companies use automated telephone answering systems even if they have hundreds or thousands of employees.

The telephone is still a key technological tool!

Whether you use voice mail or an answering service, make sure the message that callers hear is clear and professional and gives the name of your business. Change your message often to advertise specials and sales and to keep customers listening. Use mobile phones to stay in touch with customers, employees, and suppliers.

A separate telephone line for your business will provide a number of advantages. Business telephones can be listed in your business name in the phone book, and you will know to always answer with your business name when that phone rings. Also, if you have a home-based business and children, it will be easier to have them resist answering the phone when it is clearly the office line. With text messaging and e-mail sent over mobile phones, the versatility and importance of telephones to today's businesses cannot be overstated.

Identify Market-Specific Software and Technology

In order to increase efficiency and effectiveness in operations, businesses use software and technology designed for their industry or type of business. For example, retail stores often use point of sales (POS) systems that are tailored to their products, and restaurants use ordering systems customized to their menus. Not-for-profits have specialized fund-raising and accounting software. Sports stadiums, concert venues and movie theaters have ticketing systems. Manufacturing plants have materials-planning and inventory systems.

Typically, trade journals feature advertisements for software specific to an industry. The software companies commonly exhibit at trade shows and conferences. Evaluations and comparisons of hardware and software solutions are listed in trade publications and on the Internet.

The investment in industry-specific technology is often many times greater than in generic business equipment and software. However, the up-front investment may lead to both considerable efficiency and savings over the short and/or long term.

Electronic Storefront (Web Site)

No matter what type of business you have, opening an **electronic store-front** will make it more accessible to local customers and can introduce it to potential customers all over the world. An electronic storefront is an online site that customers can visit to view your catalog, price lists, and other information. Today, it is relatively easy to add the option of purchasing your products online, either directly, through a credit-card merchant account, or through a service such as PayPal.

You will need to decide if you want to put your store up with an online service or by yourself. An online service would typically "build" your storefront for you and include promotion and advertisements as part of the deal, to help make its subscribers aware of your store. On the other hand, if you put a site up yourself, you would have more control over what it looked like and where it was located, and your potential customers would not be limited to the subscribers to a particular online service. One of the most cost-efficient ways to set up an electronic storefront is to hire a consultant to help you design it and choose which server to use.

Chapter Summary

Now that you have studied this chapter, you can do the following:

1. Understand the significance of operations in a business.
   - Operations is the delivery on promises.
   - What is required depends on the specific industry and business.
   - Inputs are transformed or converted into outputs through operations.

2. Develop a production-distribution chain for your business.
   - Manufacturers make products in large quantities.
   - Wholesalers buy smaller quantities in bulk from manufacturers.
   - Retailers buy from wholesalers (and sometimes manufacturers).
   - Consumers buy from retailers.
3. Manage suppliers and inventory.
   - Supply Chain Management is used to create and maintain efficient flows of materials between supply partners.
   - Suppliers may be found in a variety of ways and may be located worldwide.
   - Inventory can be managed to minimize cost and maximize customer satisfaction.
4. Ensure product quality.
   - Quality is determined by meeting and exceeding standards, including customer satisfaction.
   - Profits follow quality.
   - Organization-wide approaches to quality include:
     - ISO 9000 certification
     - Six Sigma certification
     - Total Quality Management (TQM)
     - Malcolm Baldrige National Quality Awards
5. Use technology to benefit your business.
   - Technology can provide competitive advantage.
   - Computers are a necessity in today's business world.
   - The telephone continues to be a major asset.
   - Industry-specific software and equipment is frequently beneficial.
   - Electronic storefronts provide additional distribution opportunities.

Key Terms

benchmarking
continuous improvement
economic order quantity (EOQ)
electronic storefront
hyperlink
hypertext
job shop
just-in-time manufacturing (JIT)
leasehold improvement
operations
process management
prototype

quality
reorder point (ROP)
safety stock
setup cost
supply chain management
tolerance
tooling cost
total quality management (TQM)
uniform resource locator (URL)
value-engineer
vertical integration
visual control

Entrepreneurship Portfolio

Critical Thinking Exercises

1. Production-distribution chain

    a. How do you plan to distribute your product to your target market?
    b. What is the estimated delivery time between when you place an order with your supplier and when the product will be available for your customers?

2. A manufacturer makes a line of women's handbags. This company offers 6,000 different styles of handbags in its catalog. It sells almost 25,000 handbags per year, but it is not known which style is going to sell from one week to the next.

    The company has a JIT system and a mass-production system to make the same line of handbags. Both manufacturing systems work well, and both cost about the same to operate. The JIT system can make up to 100 handbags a day; however, it is very flexible. If necessary, it can produce 100 completely different styles in a single day of operation.

    The mass production system takes half a day to set up and can make 1,000 handbags—all the same style—in the second half of the day. It is 10 times as fast as the JIT system.

    Raw materials cost $4 per handbag and are the same whichever system is used to do the work. The company likes to order enough materials to make 2,000 handbags, which is usually enough to cover a month of orders.

    The company has discovered a trick to run more than one style of handbag with the mass-production system. If it sets up in the morning and runs just one handbag until noon, it can use the afternoon to change over to a different style and still have time to run another handbag before closing at 5:00. This gives it two handbags produced in one day, if necessary.

The average day—100 Handbags, Each of a Different Style are Ordered	Mass-Production System: Using the "Regular Method"	Mass-Production System: Using the "2 Setups" Trick	JIT System
Units shipped	1	2	100
Percentage of orders for the day filled	1%	2%	100%
Amount of unsold inventory created	999	0	0
Raw materials available for future work	1,000 units / $4,000 value	1,998 units / $7,992 value	1,900 units / $ 7,600 value

    a. Which system is more efficient? Why?
    b. If the company could only keep one of these manufacturing systems, which one do you think it should keep? Explain.

3. Given an example of a business that is known internationally for the quality of its products, what defines quality for this company?

4. How does the design of a facility affect product quality and production efficiency?

5. Choose a partner in class and make a list of the technology each of you can personally access. Brainstorm how you might combine your technological resources to create a successful business. Describe in

detail how the partnership would work. For example, would the person contributing more technology have a larger share of the business, or would profits and expenses be split equally? Draw up a partnership agreement that specifies each partner's duties and how much money and time each will invest in the business.

6. Examine the labels on the shoes and clothing you are wearing today. Which items were made in foreign countries? How many dollars per hour do you think the people earned who made these articles of clothing? Why do you think the company that manufactured these items had them made abroad?

Key Concept Questions

1. Use your local telephone company's business directory or *The American Wholesalers and Distributors Directory* to locate wholesalers you could visit, or from whom you could order products for resale.

2. Choose one of the quality-assurance methodologies described in this chapter and explain how it might apply to your educational institution.

Application Exercises

1. What might the supply chain look like for one of the following:

   a. Manufacturer of custom rims for automobiles
   b. Car dealership
   c. Building materials wholesaler

2. Suggest at least three quality-assurance measures for the following businesses:

   a. Bank
   b. Residential cleaning service
   c. Commercial HVAC (heating, ventilation, and air conditioning) contractor
   d. Computer manufacturer

Exploring Your Community

Identify two businesses in your community with which you are familiar. Suggest four measures of quality for each business. Rate each business on these quality dimensions. Then, answer the questions below.

Measure of Quality	Rating (1 Is Poor, 5 Is Excellent)				
Company #1					
Measure 1	1	2	3	4	5
Measure 2	1	2	3	4	5
Measure 3	1	2	3	4	5
Measure 4	1	2	3	4	5
Company #2					
Measure 1	1	2	3	4	5
Measure 2	1	2	3	4	5
Measure 3	1	2	3	4	5
Measure 4	1	2	3	4	5

1. What do these measures tell you about the respective businesses?
2. How might they improve on one indicator?
3. Does each business have a customer feedback mechanism? If so, what is it? If not, what would you recommend?

CASE STUDY: Producing Quality Parts— Small Parts Manufacturing

Small Parts Manufacturing Company Inc. (SPM) is a custom fabricated metal parts manufacturing company founded in 1946 by Merton Rockney in Portland, Oregon. This specialty machine shop continues to be operated by his son, Merton Rockney, Jr., and by 2007 had 48 employees and sales of approximately $6.5 million. Steady growth over the decades has been the result of numerous factors, in particular an emphasis on quality.

SPM is a contract manufacturer, a "job shop," that makes metal, machined parts for companies that either use them as components for larger assemblies or resell them. They have a state-of-the-art facility to create the parts and a group of certified subcontractors that provide additional processing—such as plating, painting, and bending—to meet individual orders. Customers provide SPM with their specifications and request price quotes, a service

available through SPM's Web site. Team members work with prospective customers to provide innovative solutions that meet the quality and delivery requirements.

As a job shop, SPM has a variety of equipment for the machining of parts, as well as a staff of skilled tool makers, machinists, and computer technicians. They start with extruded bar stock in round, hexagonal, or square shapes, from which the parts are made. Materials include low-carbon, alloy, or stainless steel; brass; aluminum; plastics, and exotic metals. The company uses traditional machinery—such as screw machines, bench grinders, drill presses, and turret lathes. SPM also employs computer-controlled (CNC) machines and computer-aided design and manufacturing (CAD/CAM), which they house in a climate-controlled room.

Quality assurance is critical to SPM's success. Machining parts to very tight (exact) tolerances is a requirement for their customers. One example of the company's quality-assurance process is its use of Statistical Process Control (SPC), with seven networked data collection stations providing in-process measurements throughout the facility. SPM also uses a machine—a Gage-Master optical comparator with digital readout—to check features that would otherwise be difficult to measure. SPM is ISO 9001:2000 registered and promotes this on its Web site.

SPM has been delivering on its promise to provide high-quality parts to its customers for over 60 years.

Case Analysis

1. How has SPM brought modern technology to the traditional processes of machining custom parts?
2. What is the source of production inputs for SPM?

3. How does SPM assure quality? Do you agree that they chose the right type of quality assurance? Why or why not?

4. What types of regulations are particularly important to SPM and its employees, given the nature of the business?

Case Source

Small Parts Manufacturing Web site: *http://www. smallpartsmfg.com.*

CASE STUDY: Sewing Up Business in New Ways—Sew What? Inc.

Question: What do Maroon 5, Slip Knot, Green Day, Rod Stewart, Elton John, Madonna, and schools near you have in common?

Answer: They are customers of Sew What? Inc., a manufacturer of custom draperies and curtains for theaters, concert tours, exhibitions, and special events.

Megan Duckett, founder of Sew What? has been passionate about theater and concert production since high school. She started her career as a part-time employee at the Arts Centre in Melbourne, Victoria, Australia, before she graduated from a Church of England girls' grammar school (high school). The Arts Centre, the heart of theater in Melbourne, provided her an opportunity to apprentice as a lighting technician with Master Theatre Electrician Jim Paine. There, Megan was exposed to the businesses that serve the theater industry and she discovered that working in the industry was what she was "born to do."

Not long after that, 18-year-old Megan moved into the rock and roll marketplace and continued to work as a lighting technician and on other "back stage" aspects of the business. A critical turning point in her life came unexpectedly one year later. She was assigned to driving Billy Joel's band around while they were in Melbourne. They had an instant rapport and the crew invited her to visit the United States. Much to their surprise, Megan showed up on their doorstep shortly thereafter and soon got a job at a staging company for Rock concerts. Megan knew that she needed to find her niche and stand out from everyone else. As she has noted, "I needed to be invaluable and irreplaceable." Little did she know that sewing would be her ticket to success.

The opportunity to make her mark through sewing essentially came out of nowhere. However, Megan quickly realized that it was the opportunity she sought. Her first sewing job was to reupholster 10 "coffins" for a Haunted Halloween show. She had neither the equipment nor the materials to do the job when she accepted it. Undeterred, Megan rented a sewing machine and went to a local fabric store, where she bought the necessary supplies (at full retail price) and did the work at her kitchen table. The customer could see that it was wonderfully done and called two weeks later with more work. That customer referred others and the business took off. That was in 1992. For five years, Megan says, "The phone kept ringing with orders."

As Megan was preparing her taxes in 1997, she realized that her earnings from the custom projects sewn at her kitchen table matched the pay from her 40-hours-a-week job. She and her husband Adam had just purchased a home, and had transformed the garage into a sewing room. After considerable discussion, Megan left her

Chapter 13

Management, Leadership, and Ethics

> *"Give a man a fish and you feed him for a day. Teach a man to fish and you feed him for a lifetime."*
>
> —Lao Tzu, founder of Taoism

Madam C. J. Walker was born Sarah Breedlove to a poor couple in Louisiana in 1867. Her parents died when Sarah was a child and she was reared in poverty by her married sister. After having overcome incredible difficulties, as Madam C. J. Walker she became, in her forties, the first self-made American female millionaire and one of the first African American millionaires.

Breedlove worked for many years in the cotton fields and as a laundress, moving to St. Louis, Denver, and Indianapolis, before inventing and marketing hair-care products for African American women. Madam Walker (her married name) quickly became successful enough to build a factory to manufacture her line of products. At first she had sold her shampoos and hair-growth merchandise door to door, but soon organized and trained a group of "agent-operators."

At the peak of her career, Walker employed 2,000 agents. One of her successful marketing strategies was to organize the agents into clubs that promoted social and charitable causes in their respective African American communities. She offered cash prizes to the clubs that accomplished the most. She also encouraged her agents to open beauty salons and other corollary businesses. Not only did Madam Walker's methods foreshadow the emphasis we see on socially responsible entrepreneurship, she also created a rich legacy of black female entrepreneurial leadership.

Performance Objectives

1. Explain what makes an effective leader.
2. Recruit, manage, and motivate your employees.
3. Research the laws and tax issues affecting employees.
4. Describe the tasks handled by corporate managers.
5. Make sure your business is run in an ethical manner.

The Entrepreneur Sets the Tone for the Company

No matter who you hire to manage your company, *you* will set the tone for how the business operates. Are you disorganized and chaotic? Chances are your company will be, too. Are you honest and straightforward? Your managers and employees are likely to behave similarly.

Leadership Comes from Self-Esteem

Performance Objective 1

Explain what makes an effective leader.

A **leader** is someone who gets things done through influence by guiding or inspiring others to voluntarily participate in a cause or project. Leadership comes from self-esteem applied to knowledge, skills, and abilities. If you believe in yourself and know what you are doing, you can do things with confidence and will inspire confidence in others. Develop a positive attitude and you can become a leader. Great leaders are optimists—they have trained themselves to think positively. Running a successful business requires leadership.

Manage Your Time Wisely

Leaders learn how to manage their time so they can accomplish more with less. One of the most important things you can do is to learn how to manage your time efficiently. Getting more done in less time can contribute to success.

You may not have employees to manage but you could probably manage your own time better. Here is a tool called a PERT chart (**P**rogram **E**valuation and **R**eview **T**echnique) that you can use to organize the many things you need to do. This one is related to business start-up tasks. As your venture grows, you can use the PERT concept to manage more complex operations. You can also create charts using software such as Microsoft Project.

Sample PERT Chart

Task	Week 1	Week 2	Week 3	Week 4	Week 5	Week 6
Befriend banker	X	X	X	X	X	X
Order letterhead		X				
Select location	X					
Register business	X					
Obtain bulk mail permit			X			
Select ad agency	X					
Meet with lawyer				X		
Meet with accountant				X		
Create vendor statement					X	
Pay utility deposits					X	
Order marketing material					X	
Install phone system			X	X	X	
Have Web site designed						X
Set up database						X
Network computers						X

Managerial Styles That Work

As your business grows, it will develop its own "culture." Companies like Wal-Mart and Home Depot invest significant sums to create a work environment that inspires and motivates their employees. How you or your managers treat one another and the employees will determine the company culture. Adopt the best managerial style for your company and maintain it consistently. According to researcher Daniel Goleman, the principal styles and their advantages and drawbacks are:[1]

- *Coercive:* To *coerce* means to pressure someone into doing what you want. This "commanding" approach can be effective in a disaster scenario or with problem employees who need a forceful manager. In most situations, however, a coercive leadership style damages employee morale and diminishes the flexibility and effectiveness of the company. Employees stop thinking and acting for themselves.

- *Authoritative:* An authoritative leader takes a "come with me" approach, stating the overall goal but giving employees freedom to figure out how best to achieve it. This can work well if the leader is an expert, but may not be so effective if the scenario is one of a nominal leader heading up a group of individuals who have more expertise in the field than he or she does (a team of scientists, for example).

- *Affiliative:* This is a "people come first" method that is effective when the business is in the team-building stage. It can fail when employees are lost and need direction.

- *Democratic:* This style gives employees a strong voice in how the company is run. It can build morale and work if employees are prepared to handle responsibility, but it may result in endless meetings and a sense of leaderlessness and drifting.

- *Pacesetting:* This type of leader sets very high performance standards for him/herself and challenges employees to meet them, too. This can be very good when employees are also self-motivated and highly devoted but can overwhelm those who are not so committed.

- *Coaching:* This style focuses on helping each employee to grow through training and support. This can be a good approach for starting and growing a business, but may not work with employees who have been with the company for a while and may be resistant to change.

How Will You Pay Yourself?

Before you hire employees, figure out how to pay your first employee—yourself. Once your business is breaking even, decide how you will distribute the profit. The decision you make will affect your financial recordkeeping and your taxes, so think it through. The choices are:

- *Commission:* A set percentage of every sale. It is treated as a variable operating cost, because it fluctuates with sales.

- *Salary:* A fixed amount of money paid at set intervals. You could choose to receive your salary once a week or once a month. A salary is a fixed operating cost, because it does not change with sales.

- *Wages:* If you have a service or manufacturing business, you could pay yourself an hourly wage. Wages (yours or those of your employees) are considered a cost of goods sold, because they are factored into the cost of the product or service.

- *Dividend:* A share of the company's profits issued to shareholders.

---

[1] Daniel Goleman, "Leadership That Gets Results," *Harvard Business Review*, March–April 2000.

Pay yourself regularly to reflect your return on investment accurately and to determine whether this business is worth your time.

Entrepreneurs who do not pay themselves regularly tend to overstate their return on investment—they have not taken any pay out of the net profit and treated that pay as a cost. This scenario can also increase the amount of tax the business will owe. Anything that reduces the net profit reduces the tax on net profit. Of course, you will have to pay income tax on the money you pay yourself, but generally you will come out ahead if you treat some of your business profit as self-payment. This will depend upon your legal structure and the tax laws. Recognize that you can only pay yourself (or anyone else) when you have sufficient cash flow or cash reserve to do so.

Another reason to pay yourself is that it enables you to be honest about whether or not the business is really worth your time. Could you be making more money in a different business, or working for someone else? Is the best choice to keep working for yourself? Thinking entrepreneurially includes a realistic consideration of whether you would be happier *not* running a business, at least at the present time.

Adding Employees to Your Business

Performance Objective 2

Recruit, manage, and motivate your employees.

One of the most important things you can do as a business owner is to bring in capable, motivated people. In *Good to Great*, management expert Jim Collins says that great leaders "get the right people on the bus—sometimes even before a company decides exactly what business it will be in."[2] Hiring employees is also called **recruitment**.

Some ways to bring good employees into your business are:

- Bring people in as partners. Partners share the risks and rewards of the venture and will co-own the business with you.
- Hire experts to work on specific tasks on a contractual or hourly basis. For example, you might hire a professional accountant to work one day per month on your recordkeeping.
- Hire someone as a full-time, regular employee. The most common way to do this is through an "at will" arrangement. Typically the "at will" employment relationship continues for an indefinite period, but can be ended by either party without notice or cause, although 2 weeks notice is traditional.

There are specific steps in the recruiting process:

1. *Defining the job.* Think about what you need this employee to do and what kind of skills are needed.
2. *Posting the job.* Determine how people will find out about the position. Will you place an ad in a newspaper? Run online ads? Finding good employees has become much easier with the advent of online job-listing services such as Career Builder (*http://www.careerbuilder.com*) and Monster.com (*http://www.monster.com*).
3. *Screening resumes.* A resume is a concise summary of an individual's education and work experience. When you post the opportunity, ask people who want the job to send their resumes.
4. *Interviewing candidates.* Use the resumes to select several people to interview. Prepare beforehand the questions you want to ask about the individual's knowledge, skills, abilities, and interests.
5. *Checking references.* Ask the candidates who interest you to provide at least three references from previous employers or others who could tell you about their character and work performance. Check them.

Businesswomen conferring. (Color Day Production/Getty Images)

---

[2] Jim Collins, *Good to Great: Why Some Companies Make the Leap . . . and Some Don't* (New York: HarperCollins Publishers, 2001), p. 13.

6. *Negotiating salary.* You and the candidate you choose will have to negotiate how much you intend to pay, and any benefits the job includes, such as health insurance. You should have a clearly defined pay range for each position and stay within it.

7. *Hiring.* Once you decide to hire someone, you will have to complete tax and payroll forms.

8. *Orientation.* This is the process of introducing the employee into the company and teaching him or her about the job. It can save you thousands of dollars to have a printed employee manual that has passed legal review before you begin hiring.

Growing Your Team

Once you decide to add employees to your company, it could take considerable time and effort to identify and hire the talent needed to grow your team. Ways to find the right employees include:

- *Campus Recruiting.* Established companies from all industries visit college campuses every year to meet and scout students about to graduate. Companies in banking, consulting, accounting, consumer products, technology, health care, and others are all big recruiters on college and graduate school campuses.

- *Staffing and Recruiting.* Companies plan and hire according to staffing plans and budgets, and typically use a combination of internal recruiters (employees of the company), outside recruiters (agencies or contingency firms), and Internet job-board postings.

- *Executive Search.* When companies need to hire a senior executive, a CEO, the director of human resources or other leaders, they engage in an "executive search." These top job openings are often not advertised, and the process is often managed by an outside search firm.

Key Hiring Issues

As the business grows and you hire employees, you will have to become familiar with the laws and tax issues affecting employment. These include:

◀ **Performance Objective 3**
Research the laws and tax issues affecting employees.

- **Payroll tax** is a series of wage taxes based on earnings that are deducted from your employees' pay. Your accountant can advise you in more detail when you get to this point, and you can find information on the IRS Web site (*http://www.irs.gov*) and those of state and local revenue departments. For now, it is important that you know you will be responsible for contributing to Social Security, unemployment compensation and other programs on their behalf.

- The **Fair Labor Standards Act** was passed in 1938, and requires you to pay employees at least the federally mandated minimum wage. It also prohibits you from hiring anyone under the age of 16 full time.

- The **Equal Pay Act of 1963** requires employers to pay men and women the same amount for the same work.

- **Antidiscrimination laws** protect employees against discrimination on the basis of age, race, religion, national origin, or because of color, gender, or physical disabilities. Abiding by these laws is both a legal requirement and the right thing to do.

Getting the Best Out of Your Employees

When you do hire people, treat them fairly and with respect. Many companies make their employees part owners by giving shares that entitle them to a portion of the company profits.

Follow these guidelines and you will be a good employer:

- Get the right people. Putting the right people in the right job is at least half the battle. This means getting to know each employee's strengths and weaknesses.
- Provide a fair salary and good working conditions.
- Share your vision for the company.
- Give employees incentives to work effectively—start a profit-sharing plan, for example.
- Give them control over their work.
- Give them definite responsibilities and areas of control.

Encourage Your Employees to Be Socially Responsible

To get more ideas on how to make your business socially responsible, look at the Standards of Corporate Responsibility at http://www.svn.org/initiatives/standards.html.

Early in the twentieth century, Madam Walker motivated her employees by encouraging them to get involved in helping their communities. There are many ways that entrepreneurs can use their businesses to contribute to society. By being an entrepreneur, you have already made an important contribution by providing goods and services to consumers in your area who need them. You can also use your business to support social issues that are important to you. By running your company in a way that is consistent with your ethics and core values, you will develop a **socially responsible business**.

Ways to make your business socially responsible include:

- Recycling paper, glass, or plastic.
- Donating a portion of profits to a charity.
- Refusing to use animal testing on products.
- Offering employees incentives to volunteer in the community.
- Establishing a safe and healthy workplace.

Corporate Management—Building a Team

Performance Objective 4 ▶

Describe the tasks handled by corporate managers.

As a small business grows, it will reach a point where the entrepreneur and a few employees cannot handle operations efficiently. At that stage, the company will probably need professional management to meet its goals efficiently. Adding a management team requires many of the steps noted previously. However, there are additional roles that the team plays, and recruitment differs.

Step into the Shoes...

Charles Schwab Finds His Market Niche

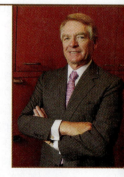

Charles Schwab opened his own brokerage firm in the early 1970s when he was 34. Like Jacoby & Meyers with legal services, Schwab uncovered a market niche when he began offering discount pricing for informed investors who were tired of paying sizable commissions to stockbrokers. These investors did not need anyone else to do their research and make their decisions, and they flocked to take advantage of the cheaper rates. By 1981, Charles Schwab & Company's earnings were $5 million. In 1983, BankAmerica bought the company for $55 million but left Schwab in place as CEO.[3] Just 4 years later, management repurchased the company and offered an IPO as Charles Schwab Corporation. In the 1990s, Schwab became the leading online discount broker and the fastest-growing American company of the decade. As of the end of 2007, Charles Schwab had 13,400 full-time employees, and client assets under management of $1.4 trillion with 7 million brokerage accounts, 1.2 million corporate retirement plans, and 262,000 banking accounts. The Charles Schwab Foundation contributes to over 2,400 not-for-profits with an average of $2.85 million in gifts annually.

---

[3] Available at *http://www.aboutschwab.com*.

Many successful entrepreneurs are creative individuals who tend to get bored with the everyday details of running a business. Wise entrepreneurs recognize this about themselves and hire managers to run the business.

An entrepreneur with a growing corporation can raise capital by selling stock. Some of this capital can be used to hire managers to organize the business. This will free the entrepreneur to spend less time managing and more time thinking up new ideas.

A management organizational chart for a small business might look like **Figure 13-1**.

Figure 13-1 *Management organizational chart.*

```
                    FRED-CITY RECORDS, INC.

                          PRESIDENT
                          Fred Xavier
        ┌───────────────┬───────────────┬───────────────┐
   PRODUCTION        MARKETING         SERVICE          FINANCE
   Vice President,   Vice President,   Vice President,  Vice President,
   Gina Arnold       Chris Morales     Tony Arsenio     Jorge Esteban
```

What Do Managers Do?

Nathan Himmelstein of Rutgers University, breaks management into 10 functions, using the acronym POLDSCCRIM.

1. ***Planning:*** Managers perform three types of planning: strategic, tactical, and operational.
   - *Strategic plans* are typically 3-to-5-year overall strategies for achieving a business's long-term growth, sales, and positioning goals.
   - *Tactical plans* are the short-term implementation plans that bring about strategic goals. Tactical plans are for 1 year or less and have limited, specific objectives.
   - *Operational plans* are short-term methods for achieving tactical goals. These include budgets, regulations, and schedules for day-to-day operation of the business.
2. ***Organizing:*** This function includes everything from hiring people to buying/leasing equipment and resources. It includes setting up an organizational chart and defining each person's responsibilities.
3. ***Leading:*** This function is about the style in which you and your managers lead the company. *Achievement-oriented* managers encourage employee input, share authority and responsibility, and focus on achieving long-term goals. This style is the most appropriate for a small business, although sometimes managers will have to temporarily adopt another style to deal with a crisis or to stabilize operations.
4. ***Directing:*** After you and your managers have made your plans and organized your employees and resources, it is time to direct and motivate employees to perform the work that will move the company toward its strategic goals.
5. ***Staffing:*** This function involves managing the people in the company by making sure they are being placed in the positions that best use their skills and experience. It includes employee training and development, setting up pay and benefits packages, recruiting, and screening.
6. ***Controlling:*** This step involves measuring the business's performance and determining how to improve it. Is the business adhering to its

budget? Are products achieving the level of quality set as a goal? How about customer service? If there are variances between what was planned and what the company actually achieved, controlling will require corrective action to align plans and actions.

7. *Coordinating:* This is the task of combining all management efforts into a unified system. Coordinating includes creating in-house communications and teaching everyone to use them, scheduling regular meetings and updates, and generally making sure all managers are using appropriate styles and are working toward the same goals.

8. *Representing:* Managers represent a company to its people and its people to the company; they also represent the company to the outside world. Managers need to appear and behave in a way that accurately reflects the company culture.

9. *Innovating:* Managers should always be developing new ways to meet strategic, tactical, and operational goals. The entrepreneur may be the guiding creative force behind the company, but managers should also be innovative problem solvers.

10. *Motivating:* Every decision managers make will affect employee motivation and morale positively or negatively. A manager's assumptions about the employees will have an effect. If a manager assumes that people need to be pushed to work, for example, and treats the employees that way, he/she will incur resentment. A manager who assumes that employees want to do their best and embrace responsibility will likely be more successful. Some ways managers can motivate include involving employees in decisions, providing meaningful work, recognizing outstanding contributions, evaluating performance, and rewarding achievement.[4]

Ethical Leadership and Ethical Organizations

Performance Objective 5

Make sure your business is run in an ethical manner.

True leadership is more than the components described previously. It is all of the actions and attributes noted plus the personal values underlying them. **Ethics** are a system of morals or standards of conduct and judgment that help determine right from wrong. The Golden Rule—"Do unto others as you would have others do unto you"—is a well-known ethic. A behavior may be legal and still not be ethical. For example, it is not illegal to be rude to your customers and employees, but it is unethical (and not very smart).

Ethical business behavior is not only moral, but it also makes good business sense. Have you ever bought something from a store and felt you were cheated? How did you react? Did you want to go back? Probably not. You may have even told your friends about the experience. The store lost more than just one customer.

Ethical Employer/Employee Relationships

It is important to treat your employees well. Aside from the fact that it is morally correct to treat people ethically, it is in your best interest to do so. As the entrepreneur, your values will set the ethical tone for your company. If you think it is okay to be rude or cheat a customer, your employees will not only copy your behavior, but they also will probably try to cheat you!

Employees who feel used by their employers will not do their best work. The most successful companies are those in which the employees' interests correspond with what is best for the company.

---

[4] Kathleen R. Allen and Earl C. Meyer, *Entrepreneurship and Small Business Management 3e.* (Blacklick, OH: Glencoe/McGraw-Hill, 2005).

Many large businesses offer their employees company stock at a discount, or give generous bonuses at the end of the year, based on how well the company does. In this way, the employees know that they will profit from the company's success. This will help motivate them to care about the business for which they work.

Corporate Ethical Scandals

The issue of business ethics exploded in 2002, when several huge corporations were found to have published inaccurate financial statements. These false numbers made the companies look so good that they were some of the most highly recommended stock picks on Wall Street.

Top executives at Enron, WorldCom-MCI, Tyco, Global Crossing, and other large firms had inflated corporate earnings so that they would receive huge bonuses, while misleading shareholders and employees. When the truth came out, public confidence in the stock market plummeted, along with stock prices. Investors lost millions.

One of the companies, the energy giant Enron, had strongly encouraged its own employees to invest most or all of their retirement savings in company stock—even while top executives knew the worth of the stock was based on false numbers. These employees had their life savings wiped out by the unethical behavior of the executives.

Enron collapsed and thousands of employees lost their jobs and saw their pension funds reduced to nothing. Tyco was split into four different companies. Its CEO was forced to resign when it was learned that he had used company money to buy an $18 million apartment in Manhattan and furnish it with expensive artwork, among other abuses.

The scandals of 2002 were a failure of **corporate governance**, meaning that these companies did not have rules and safeguards in place to ensure that executives behaved legally and ethically. Even at this early stage in developing your business, you must think about how you will guarantee that your business remains both ethical and legal as it grows.

- *Do Not Treat Company Profits as Personal Funds:* Haphazardly taking business profits for your own use is a bad habit. Decide on a wage or salary you will pay yourself and always document this, as well as your business expenses, and other financial records and statements. You should enjoy the rewards of a successful venture, but you need to be careful to do it ethically and legally.

- *Keep Accurate Records:* Have your business records checked once a year by a professional accountant. By the time your company becomes a multimillion-dollar corporation, you will have established a reputation for honest financial reporting.

- *Use Financial Controls:* Once you have employees, use simple financial controls such as:
  - Always have two people open the mail, so no one is tempted to take company checks.
  - Arrange for yourself and one other person to be required to sign all checks sent out by the business. Using a double signature will assure that no one can use the company money for personal expenses.
  - Implement a cash counting and control system if employees will handle cash.

- *Create an Advisory Board:* Ask businesspeople and other community leaders you respect to be on your **advisory board**—a group of people who will provide you with sound, ethical business advice. Listen to what they have to say.

Human Resources Fundamentals

Human resources is the department of a company that hires, trains, and develops employees. Human resources is also commonly referred to as HR, Human Capital, Casting, or Personnel.

For a business just starting out, it may not be practical to have a director of human resources. The entrepreneur will handle these tasks. A business would probably not need a human resources professional until it has 20 or more employees.

Regardless of the number, once you have employees, there will be human resources functions to be managed. For companies of sufficient size, each of the following areas might represent one or more full-time jobs in the HR department.

Compensation and Payroll

The compensation and payroll area of HR addresses such issues as the level of wages and salary versus bonuses. Along with the entrepreneur and top management, it addresses which employees receive stock in the company and in what amounts and under what terms they do so. It analyzes how compensation ties into the overall finances of the business and how the company's compensation program compares to that of competing companies. HR executives work closely with finance managers to answer questions about compensation and to set company policy accordingly.

Benefits

Full-time employees expect an array of benefits as part of their compensation package. Basics include health insurance (including the employee's family), life insurance, vacation and sick time, and retirement savings plans. HR usually leads the process of selecting the benefits programs that the company makes available. It is common practice to provide employees with benefit options and to have them share in the cost of their benefits.

Organizational Development

The HR team plays a pivotal role in organizational development. The key components of this are:

- *Organizational Structure:* The HR department will help the founder, CEO, management team, and board of directors identify and analyze the pros and cons of possibilities, establish the appropriate organizational structure, and help manage transitions from one framework to another.

- *Employee Retention:* Sometimes compensation alone is not sufficient to prevent an individual from being lured away to work for a competitor. HR develops employee retention programs that help build morale, create mentoring opportunities, and provide professional development and other benefits to keep employees excited about staying. (Note: It is costly to recruit and train new employees.)

- *Succession Planning:* As employees are promoted, retire, or resign, it is important to have plans in place to fill their positions. This is

BizFacts

Many companies staff their human resources units using a ratio of one HR executive per 50 to 200 employees.

particularly true in key leadership roles that are not easily replaced. When you promote your sales manager to vice president of sales, who will fill the vacancy? The HR department will work with managers to find the best successor.

Education and Development

Even senior executives require ongoing professional development education from time to time. HR managers develop employee training in-house and may also use outside training providers for specific situations. Some businesses help companies train their sales teams. Leading universities, such as The Wharton School and Harvard Business School offer executive education curriculums to provide high-level instruction.

Labor Law and HR Compliance

The United States has well-developed laws to protect the rights of workers and employees. Everyone involved in hiring, firing, and managing people needs to be aware of both the letter and the spirit of these laws, which are typically translated into policies by the HR and legal teams at a company. For example, laws forbid companies from hiring or promoting on the basis of age or race. It is illegal for employers to ask candidates how old they are, whether they are married and/or have children, or where they are from—during the interview process. Companies can expose themselves to enormous liability if they do not properly manage the process of hiring, rewarding, and terminating employees.

Human Resources Strategy

Strategic human resources departments will also dedicate resources to identifying ways to maximize the productivity and effectiveness of the overall organization through its HR practices.

- *Diversity:* Many leading companies—with Avon Products being a good example—have found that, by creating a more diverse workforce in terms of gender and ethnicity, they better represent and understand their customer base. This translates into increased sales and greater customer loyalty. Avon is known for having a diverse workforce, from the CEO to the sales representative level, and uses the tagline, "The Company for Women."
- *Benchmarking:* For companies to be competitive, they must understand their own employee base, but they must also understand the skills and motivations of the employees of the companies with which they compete. Benchmarking is a process that lets companies compare themselves with their competitors. As an entrepreneur, you will want to ensure that your employees' skills keep pace with or are ahead of those of your competitors.
- *Retention:* As noted earlier, it is paramount for companies to keep the employees who drive the business. HR strategy puts focuses on programs and benefits that keep employees engaged and motivated to fulfill the company's mission.

Firing and Laying Off Employees

Sometimes you hire someone and it just does not work out, even after repeated attempts to "fix" the problem. If you have to let someone go (fire), you should document the reasons. You can be sued for wrongful termination or breach of contract if an employee believes he or she was fired for no

Global Impact...
Human Resources Firms

Many companies, large and small, are dedicated to providing human resources services to corporate clients around the globe. Here is how some leading firms got started: Adecco provides staffing services to 250,000 clients worldwide. It started in 1957 when Henri-Ferdinand Lavanchy, an accountant at the time, decided to start a recruiting company because a client asked him to help fill a job. In 1969, Lester Korn and Richard Ferry started a recruitment firm with a $10,000 investment. Today, with over $650 million in revenue, Korn/Ferry International specializes in helping clients hire top executives, including CEOs. When companies have thousands of employees, the task of getting paychecks out twice a month can be daunting. Payroll provider Automatic Data Processing Inc. (ADP) cuts checks for over 50 million people on behalf of its clients. ADP was started by Henry Taub in 1949, when he was 22. The company had eight clients and $2,000 in revenue in its first year.

good reason. The rules for termination vary from state to state, so it is best to know your state's law. Generally, you will need to document that an employee acted intentionally ("willfully and wantonly") to damage the best interests of the company.

- Protect your company from wrongful-termination claims by conducting regular employee performance reviews. Have each employee read and sign his/her review (see **Figure 13-2**).

Figure 13-2 *Sample employee performance plan and appraisal.*

Objective #1: _____

Observed Achievements: _____

Objective #2: _____

Observed Achievements: _____

Objective #3: _____

Observed Achievements: _____

Manager Feedback Only:

General Comments: _____

Employee Strengths: _____

Areas for Improvement: _____

Employee Overall Rating (based on numerical scale below): _____

Rating Key:
1. **Outstanding:** Extraordinary performance well beyond the expectations or requirements of the position.
2. **Above Satisfactory:** Excels beyond the basic requirements of the position.
3. **Satisfactory:** Meets requirements of the position. Displays the work of a fully competent employee.
4. **Needs Improvement:** At times, performs at a level that is below that of a competent employee. Improvement is necessary.
5. **Unsatisfactory:** Performance is consistently below the standards set for this position. The employee has clearly failed to complete certain tasks that have been deemed critical to the position. A continued rating at this level may result in the demotion or termination of the employee.

Date: _____

Employee's Signature: _____

Manager's Signature: _____

- If an employee is violating rules, give notification in writing (and keep a copy for your records) and create a performance improvement plan. If performance continues to be unsatisfactory and you have to let the employee go, you will have documentation that there were problems with his/her performance.

Sometimes you might have to lay off employees. They may have performed their jobs well, but you either no longer need their skills or cannot afford to continue employing them. To minimize complications, offer employees **severance**, pay that is continued income for a limited time, and make serious efforts to help them find new employment.

Chapter Summary

Now that you have studied this chapter, you can do the following:

1. Explain what makes someone an effective leader.
   - A leader is someone who has the confidence and energy to do things on his or her own.
   - Leadership comes from self-esteem. If you believe in yourself, you can do things with confidence and you will inspire confidence in others.
   - Leaders learn how to manage their time so they can get more done.
2. Recruit, manage, and motivate your employees.
   - Hiring employees is also called recruitment.
   - Bring people in as partners. Partners share the risks and rewards of the venture and will co-own the business with you.
   - Hire experts to work on specific tasks on a contractual or hourly basis. For example, you might hire a professional accountant to work one day per month on your recordkeeping.
   - Hire someone as a full-time, permanent employee. The most common way to do this is with an "at will" arrangement.
3. Research the laws and tax issues affecting employees.
   - Payroll taxes: If you hire employees, you will have to deduct payroll taxes from their earnings.
   - Fair Labor Standards Act: Passed in 1938, this law requires payment to employees of at least minimum wage. It also prohibits hiring anyone under the age of 16 full time.
   - Equal Pay Act of 1963: This law requires employers to pay men and women the same amount for the same work.
   - Antidiscrimination laws: These protect people against discrimination on the basis of age, race, religion, national origin, or because of color, gender, or physical disability.
4. Describe the tasks handled by corporate managers.
   - Planning
   - Organizing
   - Leading
   - Directing
   - Staffing
   - Controlling
   - Coordinating
   - Representing
   - Innovating
   - Motivating

What You Need to Know to Grow and Go

Chapter 14
Franchising, Licensing, and Harvesting:
Cashing in Your Brand

Franchising, Licensing, and Harvesting: Cashing in Your Brand

Co...
The...
fies...
trep...
of a...
era...
nity...
flov...
goa...
fron...

Gr...

One...
diti...
By...
a bu...
to b...
keti...
"It u...
attr...
stre...

Gı...

One...
hum...
lectu...
busi...

fran...
Stay...
velo...
or e...
that...

beca...
by le...

Foc...

As n...
a coı...
repr...
set o...
cloth...
place...

from...
ter iı...
He c...
own...
stren...

> *"All businesses were launched by entrepreneurs and all were once small."*
>
> —Nat Shulman, family business owner and columnist

Liz Claiborne was a hugely successful entrepreneur who was born in Belgium to American parents in 1929. Women were not expected to work in those days, so when she fell in love with fashion and wanted to become a designer, her family was strongly against it.

Claiborne was determined, though, and at 21 she applied for a job on Seventh Avenue in New York City's garment district. She got employment as a sketcher, model, and "pick-up-pins girl"—and an opportunity to observe her market from the inside. Over the years, she observed that women had begun to join the workforce but few designers were making clothes for them to wear to their jobs. Here was an opportunity to make clothes that women really needed. She founded Liz Claiborne, Inc., with her husband and two partners in 1976.[1] Today, it is a nearly $5 billion public company that provides quality affordable clothing for working women.

This is an example of how one entrepreneur can create a business venture that grows from an idea to a publicly traded international conglomerate. And once the business has a name that stands for something attractive to consumers, the name itself becomes valuable. Liz Claiborne has a number of well-known brand names, such as Kate Spade, Lucky Brand Jeans, Juicy Couture, Liz & Co, and DKNY Jeans.

Liz Claiborne, Inc., sells clothes all over the world, and also licenses its name to other companies—licensing ("renting") the right to use the Claiborne name to sell products that reflect the Claiborne vision. In 2004, for example, Liz Claiborne announced that it would license its name to the Eastman Group (the licensee) to make men's shoes under the Claiborne label. The licensee pays a fee for the license. "Licensing our brands is a key aspect of our growth strategy, enabling us to extend Claiborne's presence in the market," said Barbara Friedman, president of Licensing in a press release. "We are pleased to be teaming with Eastman Group on our Claiborne footwear collection. Their innovative product design and expertise in manufacturing will help us offer superior product and value to the Claiborne customer. The addition of footwear to the Claiborne product mix furthers our goal of making a complete lifestyle statement."[2]

Max Mizrahi, president of Eastman Group, stated: "This is a great opportunity for us to partner with a classic American brand with a reputation for fashion and superb quality. We anticipate that our footwear expertise, coupled with Claiborne's reputation, will open many doors with retailers and make an impact immediately."[3]

[1] Available at http://www.lizclaiborneinc.com.
[2] "Liz Claiborne Inc. Announces Licensing Agreement with Eastman Group," *PR Newswire*, July 1, 2004.
[3] "Liz Claiborne," *PR Newswire*.

4 Al Ries,
5 Ries, F.

The Science of Valuation

There are three primary methods that buyers and sellers use: book value, future earnings, and market-based value. In practice, these three methods are often used concurrently, and all provide helpful perspectives on a company's value. Furthermore, there are many variations on each method. The SBA Web site provides assistance in valuation, and accountants and other professional business advisors can provide assistance as well.[8] Below is a more in-depth description of each.

- *Book Value (Net Worth = Assets – Liabilities):* One of the most common methods for computing a company's valuation, the **book value** technique looks at a company as assets minus liabilities. This way is the most common one used for valuing companies, and also the simplest.
- *Future Earnings:* This method uses a company's estimated future earnings as the main determinant of its value. It is most useful for companies that are growing quickly. In these cases, past earnings are not accurate reflections of future performance. This method of valuation must take into account the time value of money as well as the rate of return.
- *Market-Based (Value = P/E Ratio × Estimated Future Net Earnings):* In the market-based approach, the value of the company is compiled from the price/earnings (P/E) ratio of comparable public companies. The P/E ratio is determined by dividing a company's stock price by its earnings per share. This method is effective because of its simplicity, but may be lacking when there are no similar public companies with which to compare the business.

Despite the sophistication of these three techniques, all of them are ultimately only estimates. Each business will have particular characteristics and special circumstances. In the end, it will be the entrepreneur's job to use negotiation to get the highest price possible.

Once you do decide to sell your business, or pursue some other exit strategy, use the Internet to maximize your prospects. If you decide to sell, you can list your business with databases such as *http://ww.BizBuySell.com* or *http://www.BizQuest.com,* which send registered users who might want to buy your business e-mails alerting them to your offer.

Creating Wealth by Selling a Profitable Business

A successful small business can usually be sold for between three and five times its yearly net profit, because the buyer expects the business to continue to keep generating income. If your net profit for 1 year is $10,000, you should be able to get at least $30,000 (3 × $10,000).

From the buyer's perspective, this represents a 33 percent annual return on the investment required to buy the business ($10,000/$30,000 = 33%), which is a very attractive return.

If you are in business for 3 years, however, and increase your net profit each year, your business will be worth even more. If your start-up company earns $10,000 in year 1, $25,000 in year 2, and $60,000 in year 3, it could be valued at $180,000 by applying the "three times" rule of thumb. How a business grows will affect its value. A business with increasing yearly net profit will be considered more valuable than a business with static earnings.

---

[8] One source of information is the SBA's Small Business Planner section at *http://www.sba.gov/smallbusinessplanner/exit/sellyourbusiness/index.htm.*

This is how entrepreneurs create fortunes. They establish a successful business, sell it, and use the resulting wealth to create new enterprises and more wealth. Entrepreneurs also use their wealth to support political, environmental, and social causes. What will you do with your wealth?

Harvesting Options[9]

Harvesting options for exiting a business fall into five categories:

1. ***Increase the Free Cash Flows:*** For the first 7 to 10 years of the business, you will want to reinvest as much profit as possible into the company in order to grow. Once you are ready to exit, however, you can begin reducing investment and taking cash out. This strategy will require investing only the amount of cash needed to keep the business effective in its current target markets, without attempting to move into new ones.

   ◄ **Performance Objective 5**
   Discuss five ways to harvest a business.

   Advantages

   - You can retain ownership of the firm with this strategy.
   - You do not have to seek a buyer.

   Disadvantages

   - You will need a good accountant to help avoid major taxes.
   - It can take a long time to execute this exit strategy.

2. ***Management Buyout (MBO):*** In this strategy, the entrepreneur sells the firm to its managers, who raise the money to buy it via personal savings and debt.

   Advantages

   - If the business has value, the managers often do want to buy it.
   - The entrepreneur has the emotional satisfaction of selling to people he knows and has trained.

   Disadvantages

   - If the managers use primarily debt to buy the company, they may not be able to finish paying off the deal.
   - If the final payment to the entrepreneur depends on the company's earnings during the last few quarters, the managers may have an incentive to attempt to lower the company's profits.

3. ***Employee Stock Ownership Plan (ESOP):*** This strategy both provides an employee retirement plan and allows the entrepreneur and partners to sell their stock and exit the company. The firm establishes a plan that allows employees to buy company stock as part of their retirement; when the owners are ready to exit, the ESOP borrows money and uses the cash to buy their stock. As the loan is paid off, the stock is added to the employee benefit fund.

   Advantages

   - The ESOP has some special tax advantages; among them: the company can deduct both the principal and interest payments on the loan, and the dividends paid on any stock held in the ESOP are considered a tax-deductible expense.

   Disadvantages

   - This is not a good strategy if the entrepreneur does not want the employees to have control of the company. The ESOP must extend to all employees and requires the entrepreneur to open up the company's books.

---

[9] Special thanks to Jeffry Timmons.

4. *Merging or Being Acquired:* Selling the company to another company can be an exciting exit strategy for an entrepreneur who would like to see his or her creation have an opportunity to grow significantly by using another company's funds.

   Advantages

   - This strategy can finance growth that the company could not achieve on its own; the entrepreneur can either exit the company at the time of the **merger** or acquisition or be part of the growth and exit later.

   Disadvantages

   - This can be an emotionally draining strategy, with a lot of ups and downs during negotiations; the sale can take over a year to finalize.

5. *Initial Public Offering (IPO):* **Initial public offering (IPO)** or "going public" will mean to selling stock in your company in the stock market. It requires choosing an investment banker to develop the IPO, making sales presentations (the "road show") to brokers and institutional investors nationally (and perhaps internationally) and, finally, offering your stock on the market and holding your breath as you watch its price go up—or not.

   Advantages

   - If your business is "hot," this can be a very profitable way to harvest it. The market may place a large premium on your company's value.

   Disadvantages

   - An IPO is a very exciting, but stressful, all-consuming and very expensive way to harvest a company, and it requires a lot of work from the entrepreneur; but ultimately it is the market that will determine the outcome.

This overview of harvesting strategies should help you plan the final stage of your relationship with the company you are starting to create now.

Exit Strategy Options

Simply claiming that your business will "go public" one day will probably get a skeptical reaction from potential investors. Investors understand that you cannot guarantee how you will return their investment or your exact exit strategy, but you can show you understand that for the vast majority of small businesses going public is a fantasy. Demonstrate your understanding of exit strategies by thinking through the four basic possibilities below. Which one do you think best describes what you intend to make happen for your business?

1. *Acquisition:* Do you believe you could create a business that someone would want to buy (*acquire*) one day? Your exit strategy could be creating a business that would be valuable for one of your suppliers or a major competitor. The plan would be that the purchase price will pay you and your equity investors more money than you put into the business. A fair sale price, based on the business's annual net profit, should allow the original investors to realize a good return on their investment. As we have said, a common rule of thumb says that a small business is worth three times its annual net profit.

2. *Earn Out:* To use an earn-out strategy, you will need projected cash flow statements that show the business eventually generating a strong positive cash flow. At that point, you can start offering to buy out your

investors' shares at a price greater than they paid for them. The purchase price usually rises over time.

3. *Debt-Equity Exchange:* If your investors will be lending you money, eventually you can offer to trade equity for portions of the debt. This will slowly reduce the interest due over time (as the face value of the loan decreases). In this way, you can decide at what pace—and at what price—to reduce your debt.

4. *Merge:* This strategy is similar to that of acquisition, but with a *merger* two companies join together to share their strengths. One company might have an extensive customer base, while the other might have a distribution channel the first company needs. Or perhaps each company is doing well in different geographical areas, and a merger would open up these respective markets to the other's products/services. Regardless, cash will change hands and original investors can make their shares available for sale to complete the merger.

Investors Will Care About Your Exit Strategy, Too

As we have said, your exit strategy will be important to your investors. Your business plan should spell out in how many years you expect them to be able to cash out. You will need to include financial data in your plan to project specifics. It will not be enough to mention that someday the company will go public and their share of the business will be worth "a lot of money." Of the thousands of new ventures launched every year in the United States, only a small percentage will ever go public. Yet, according to David Newton, on Entrepreneur.com (January 15, 2001), over 70 percent of formal business plans presented to angel investors and venture capitalists cite "going public" as the primary exit strategy. Most estimate that going public will happen within just 4 years from the launch date. You will need to be more realistic.

Chapter Summary

Now that you have studied this chapter, you can do the following:

1. Determine how you want to grow your business and then exit from it.
   - Decide what your ultimate goals and objectives are.
   - Consider creating a business that will provide employment and wealth for your family.
   - Identify options to broaden product and service offerings through diversification.
   - Evaluate replication strategies.
2. Describe how businesses use licensing to profit from their brands.
   - A brand is a name, term, sign, logo, design, or combination of these that identifies the products or services of a company and differentiates them from those of competitors.
   - The licensee pays a fee for the license and may also pay a royalty (share of the profits) on sales to the licensor.
   - Licensing is only effective when the licensor is confident that his or her company name will not be tarnished by how the licensee uses it.
3. Explain how a business can be franchised.
   - A franchise is a business that markets a product or service in the exact manner prescribed by the founder or successors of the parent company.
   - As an entrepreneur, you could develop a concept and business operation that can be reproduced and sold to other entrepreneurs. They

would pay you a fee for the right to run the business exactly the way that you direct, and pay you a royalty as well.

4. Learn methods of valuing a business.
   - Book value (Net Worth = Assets – Liabilities)
   - Future earnings
   - Market-based (Value = P/E × Estimated Future Net Earnings)
5. Discuss five ways to harvest a business.
   - Increase the free cash flows—Once you are ready to exit, you can begin reducing reinvestment and collecting revenue as cash.
   - Management buyout (MBO)—The entrepreneur sells the firm to the managers, who raise the money to buy it via personal savings and debt.
   - Employee stock ownership plan (ESOP)—This provides an employee retirement plan and allows the entrepreneur and partners to sell their stock to the employees and exit the company.
   - Merging or being acquired—Joining together with another company or being bought by one.
   - Initial public offering (IPO)—"Going public" is getting your company listed on the stock exchange to be traded publicly.

Key Terms

book value	licensing
diversification	line extension
fair market value	liquidation
franchising	merger
harvesting	replication strategy
initial public offering (IPO)	

Entrepreneurship Portfolio

Critical Thinking Exercises

1. Describe the differences between a licensing and a franchising agreement.
2. Give an example of a business that could lead to licensing agreements and a business that could be franchised.
3. Do you plan to franchise your business or license any of your products? Explain.
4. Describe the exit strategy you plan to use to "harvest" your business. Why do you think this exit strategy will be attractive to potential investors?

Key Concept Questions

1. Identify two companies that merged during the past 3 years. Describe the structure of the merger and what has happened to the organization since then.
2. Choose one of the harvesting strategies described in the chapter and research it in depth. Write a one-page report to present to the class.

Application Exercise

Calculate how much each franchisee would owe in royalties.

Franchisee	Royalty Rate	Revenue	Royalty Fee
Franchisee 1	12.5%	$1,000,000	
Franchisee 2	4%	$750,000	
Franchisee 3	6%	$500,000	
Franchisee 4	4%	$1,700,000	

Exploring Online

The American Association of Franchisees and Dealers (AAFD) is a national trade association that represents the rights and interests of franchisees and independent dealers across the country. Visit this association online at *http://www.aafd.org* to learn more about franchises and the resources available. As a potential franchiser, you should know what your prospective customers are reading!

1. Search the site for the article, "AAFD Road Map to Selecting a Franchise." Read the section called "8 Things to Look For in a Franchise." For each of the eight tips in the article, write a one-sentence summary and note how it might apply to your business as the franchiser.
2. Find a franchise online like the one you might want to create. Answer the following:
   a. What is the franchise? What does it sell?
   b. Why are you interested in it?
   c. What is the franchise fee?
   d. What are the start-up costs?
   e. What is the royalty fee?
   f. Describe the training the franchiser offers to franchisees.
   g. Describe the marketing the franchiser provides for franchisees.
3. Find a company online that is similar to the type of business you would like to launch. Assume you would want to sell it. Describe how much you would expect from a buyer and explain your valuation method.

In 1978, when Ben Cohe
cided to sell homemade
verted gas station in B
never imagined that "B
tually grow into an inter
Twenty years later, the b
a homespun Vermont-b
multimillion-dollar con
franchises in locations
Tokyo to Paris. This ups
mous for putting out of
Divinity, Chubby Hubby
for its colorful market
stance, when Ben & Jer
CEO in 1994, it held a "Y
and invited customers t
says for the job. In 19
twenty-first anniversary,
"Coast-to-Coast Free C
550,000 cones to happy

A Commitment to Social Re
Cohen and Greenfield re
gle bottom-line approach
ness. Instead, they cho
responsible causes and b
not always earn maxim
gave something back to s
vironment. For example,
of contributing 7.5 perce
tax earnings to charity. In
a million dollars to help
local Vermont milk supp
tense price fluctuation in
also spent many years p
of an "Eco-Pint" ice crea
unbleached paperboard
These kinds of corporate
& Jerry's a number one n

CASE STUDY: Growth through Franchising—PODS Inc.

In the mid-1990s, Peter Warhurst, a former Largo (Florida) paramedic who had sold a company to Bell Atlantic for $10 million, started a second venture, which became PODS (Portable On Demand Storage). Initially, Warhurst and a partner built a mini-storage center in Clearwater to provide a source of revenue that required little time and few employees. They quickly encountered difficulty in finding a suitable location for a second center, and the idea of bringing storage to customers emerged. "I checked the Internet and nobody was doing it. I couldn't even find somebody to copy."[10] Peter, and two partners from the Largo Fire Department, developed a weather-proof storage unit and a patented hydraulic-lift system ("Podzilla") to transport whatever customers put into their units.

---

[10] Kris Hundley, "Thinking in a Box," *St. Petersburg Times*, March 15, 2004.

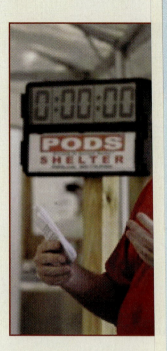

Since the first stor
the business has grov
thought he might be a
business.[11] He quickly
underestimated the de
tomers want PODS fo
business items at a PO
use them for moving.
received numerous in
and franchising.

PODS sold its first
"We want to get the nat
Peter stated.[12] As of A
customers in the Unit
Canada—having made
tions, completed some
cations, and placed mo
in the market.[13] Franc
fered for markets of 20
quired investment of a
up-front fee of $75,0(
10 percent of revenues
PODS maintains consis
and clear communicat

[11] Hundley, "Thinking."
[12] Hundley, "Thinking."
[13] PODS Web site, *http://www.pods.com.*

The Daily Perc—Milestones

Milestone	Start Date	End Date	Budget	Manager	Department
Light Web Site	6/1/YR1	8/15/YR1	$5,600	COO	Mktg.
Open First Drive-thru	7/15/YR1	8/31/YRl	$105,400	COO	Admin.
First Break-even Month	12/1/YR1	12/31/YR1	$0	COO	Finance
Open Second Drive-thru	12/15/YR1	2/1/YR1	$105,400	COO	Admin.
Receive First Mobile Unit	3/1/YRI	3/30/YRl	$86,450	COO	Admin.
Launch Web Site Voting	5/1/YR1	6/1/YRI	$12,500	COO	Mktg.
Open Third Drive-thru	4/15/YR1	6/1/YR1	$105,400	COO	Admin.
Receive Second and Third Mobile Units	7/15/YR2	9/1/YR2	$172,900	COO	Admin.
Open Fourth Drive-thru	12/15/YR2	2/1/YR2	$105,400	COO	Admin.
Install Point-of-Sale System	12/1/YR2	2/1/YR2	$21,000	CIO	MIS
Occupy Headquarters	4/1/YR2	5/15/YR2	$45,000	COO	Admin.
Open Fifth Drive-thru	4/15/YR2	6/1/YR3	$105,400	COO	Admin.
Receive Fourth Mobile Unit	4/15/YR2	6/1/YR3	$86,450	Equip.	Admin.
Open Drive-thrus 6 and 7	7/15/YR3	9/15/YR3	$210,800	COO/Dir.	Mgmt.
Open Drive-thrus 8, 9, and 10	10/15/YR3	12/15/YR3	$316,200	COO/Dir.	Mgmt.
Open Drive-thrus 11, 12, and 13	1/15/YR3	3/1/YR3	$316,200	COO	Admin.
Expand to Kansas City	1/15/YR3	6/1/YR3	$176,943	COO	Mgmt.
Open First Franchise	10/31/YR3	9/1/YR4	$45,000	CFO	Finance
Initiate Exit Strategy	10/1/YR4	1/1/YR4	$100,000	CFO	Mgmt.
Totals			$2,122,043		

Franchise option. ➤ (points to Open First Franchise)
Timing of exit strategy. ➤ (points to Initiate Exit Strategy)

The Daily Perc Business Plan provided by Business Plan Pro® and used by permission of Palo Alto Software.

Appendix 1

100 Business Ideas

What kind of business would you like to start? To jump-start your imagination, look through the following 100 possibilities. We've grouped them so you can find your own interests, hobbies, or skills and see what kind of ventures people with similar interests have started.

Of course, many business ideas fall into more than one category. Writing skills would be needed in "desktop publishing," "writing a cookbook," and "translation," for example. Consider what your friends, family, and neighbors want and need. They are your primary market. In addition, choose a business in which you think you would have a competitive advantage.

You will find the ideas divided into categories. To help you narrow your choice, we've designed the chart below. Read the descriptions on the left and check Yes or No. Where you've answered Yes, look under those headings for suggested businesses that may interest you.

Do You Like To	Yes	No	Look Under These Headings
Work with your hands?			Art, Baking, Cleaning, Cooking, Crafts, Gardening
Play with animals?			Animals, Birds, Fish
Work alone?			Collecting, Computers, Internet, Woodworking, Writing
Work with others?			Advertising, Children, Driving, Bilingual Teaching
Teach people?			Bicycles, Dancing, Music, Teaching
Work with machines?			Bicycles, Computers, Driving
Be creative?			Art, Crafts, Dancing, Holidays, Music, Painting, Silkscreening, Woodworking, Writing
Entertain people?			Entertainment, Dancing, Music
Use computers?			Computers, Internet Web site Design
Use cameras?			Photography, Videography
Buy clothes?			Clothing, Silkscreening
Cook?			Baking, Cooking

Advertising/Publicity

Are you interested in a career in advertising or publicity? These businesses will give you great experience!

Design flyers and posters: Help a local business create its brand!
Distribute flyers, posters, and brochures: Do stores in your neighborhood need people to hand out flyers? These can be distributed on the street,

put on car windshields, or given out at social functions. You could offer this service to shopkeepers on a regular basis. (Just make sure you find out where it is legal to put up posters!)

Publicist: Get hired to write press releases. Help artists, musicians, or entrepreneurs get publicity by sending out releases, e-mails, and calling local newspapers and radio stations.

Image consultant: Help businesses and entertainers market themselves to young people or other targeted populations.

Animals

Do you love animals? Read books to learn how to care for them. Ask a neighborhood veterinarian to be your mentor.

Cat sitter: Get hired to care for cats while their owners are out of town. Be sure to have the owner write down the cat's food and water needs, and an emergency number for the vet.

Dog walker: Take three or four neighborhood dogs at a time out for their walks and make money providing a (very) necessary service for your busy neighbors.

Pet grooming: Give a dog a bath today!

Pet bowls: Create personalized doggie bowls by painting each dog's name on the bowl in nontoxic paint.

Art

Almost any artistic talent can be turned into a business. What can you create that someone else might want?

Artist: Offices decorate with art and so do family members and friends. Create a portfolio of photos of your artwork that you can carry with you to show customers.

Art gallery: Have talented friends? Show their work in your home or at a youth center or other public space. You can take a commission for every piece you sell.

Calligraphy: Learn *calligraphy,* the art of handwriting, in an elegant or unusual style. Calligraphy is in demand for wedding invitations, menus, birth announcements, etc. You can also hand-letter poems or lyrics on fine paper, frame them, and sell them.

Pottery: A hobby like pottery can quickly become a successful business. Sell your pottery at trade fairs. You can put pictures of it online, too. Offer to create special pieces to customers' specifications.

Baking

Some ideas for selling cakes, cookies, brownies, bread, and other products you can bake at home include the following:

Fresh-baked bread for people in need: Set up a nonprofit business that delivers baked goods to people who are too old or sick to bake or to leave their homes to buy fresh bread. You could take donations from people and businesses in your neighborhood, and even apply for grants for your business, because it is helping society.

Bake sales: Hold a bake sale at a flea market, at your church, in your backyard, or at school. (Be sure to get permission.)

Cookie delivery business: Sign families up for your weekly cookie deliveries. You can deliver a batch of a different type of homemade cookie each week.

Bicycles

Just about any skill you have can be turned into a business if you find a way to fill a consumer need. Can you ride a bike? Here are some ideas.

Bicycle repair: Learn to repair flat tires, slipped chains, and worn brakes. You could run a special each spring when people get their bikes out of storage for the warm weather.

Messenger service: Have wheels, will deliver! In New York City, businesses depend on the bike messengers who deliver important documents all over town. Perhaps you could provide a similar service in your area.

Bike design: A graduate of this course, James MacNeil, started Bulldog Bikes, a company that designs and manufactures BMX bikes for urban streets.

Birds

Are you interested in learning about the birds in your area? Do you have a pet bird? Here are some "bird-brained" ideas:

Birdcage service: Offer to clean cages regularly and stock them with food and water. Bird owners can enjoy their pets while you maintain the cages. How do you find bird owners in your area? Try posting flyers at pet stores.

Bird-watching guide: If you teach yourself about the birds in your region, you can organize bird-watching trips to local parks. You can also hire yourself out as a bird guide to people who organize camping trips or hikes.

Raising birds for sale: Popular breeds, like parakeets and finches, are not difficult to raise. Find a mentor to advise you, like a local veterinarian or pet shop owner.

Books

Book selling: Start a business selling books, concentrating on those you like to read yourself. Once you start making money, you can buy in quantity to get lower prices. Although the larger publishers will only give a discount for sizable orders, smaller publishers might be willing to sell you quantities at a discount.

Used book selling: An even cheaper way to get into the book-selling business is to collect used books from friends and family (go through your bookshelf and get rid of books you do not want anymore, too). Set up a table at a flea market or on the street and start selling! (Check local laws before you set up a table on the street.)

Write a book: Another former entrepreneurship student, Michael Simmons, has written *The Student Success Manifesto*, which he sold on his campus at New York University and online at *http://www. successmanifesto.com*. What could you write? A novel? A children's book? A book of advice for other students?

Children

Do you like kids? Are you reliable and responsible? There are a lot of businesses you can create that involve children. Whenever you work with a child, get a letter of reference from the parents so that other parents will know they can trust you.

Babysitting service: Before parents leave their children in your care, make sure they give you cell phone numbers and/or phone numbers where they can be reached, the number of the nearest relative, and the number for the child's doctor. Be sure to ask about bedtimes, food allergies, television and Internet restrictions, and whether the parents want you to answer the phone. Then have fun with the kids!

Mother's helper: A mother's helper keeps children occupied so busy mothers can relax or devote their attention to something else. The mother will still be in the house, but you will take care of the children. This is a safe way to get some babysitting experience.

Teach activities: Teach your specialty (such as crafts, cooking, or exercise) to children one or two afternoons a week, or just have a special playtime with puppets, storytelling, or other activities.

Children's stories: Create a "storytime" at your house for children in the neighborhood. Parents can drop off their children for an hour or two to have you read to them. You could also make tapes of your readings and sell them.

Cleaning

Are you a neatnik? Turn your love of cleanliness into a business!

Car washing: Car washing can be a steady source of income if you put some effort into it. Consider working with a team of friends and advertise speedy service for busy people. Learn to wax and detail cars so you can also offer these services.

House/office cleaning: Houses and offices need to be cleaned. Many people and business owners do not have time to clean and would be happy to hire you.

Laundry and ironing: Do you have access to a good washer and dryer? Doing laundry (like dog walking and house cleaning) is a chore many people cannot find time to do. Laundry and ironing could be combined with another service, such as child care.

Clothing

If you have a passion for clothes, there are many businesses you could start. You can sell old fashions, create new ones, or bring the latest trends to the people in your market.

Clothing design: Create your own line and start out selling to local stores. Two NFTE graduates sold their "skinny jeans" to top stores in New York and Los Angeles.

Vintage clothing: After 20 years or so, fashions often become popular again. Do your parents or other relatives have old clothes they'd like to get rid of? Collect them and start selling "vintage" clothing!

Buying wholesale for resale: A student who took a NFTE course, traveled regularly from her neighborhood to the wholesale district in the nearest city, where she bought trendy fashions that were not yet in the stores in her area. Back home, she resold the clothes in her own store.

Collecting

If you collect baseball cards, sports caps, comics, or other items that are inexpensive now but could gain value in the future, consider a collecting business. You can visit collector fairs to buy and sell your items. Collect things that you genuinely like, because you will have them for a while.

Vinyl records: DJs are always looking for new sounds, so you never know what someone might pay for an old record you bought at a garage sale for 50 cents. Check out *Goldmine* and *Record Collector* magazines for helpful info.

Comics: If you have, say, only $200, you might be able to make more money buying and selling comic books than you could buying and selling stock! Use software like *Comic Collector* to catalog your collection. *Overstreet Comic Book Price Guide* is another good resource.

Computers

Computer repair/software installation: Are you the one your friends (or your parents) call when they have computer trouble? Become a computer consultant and sell your expertise.

Word-processing service: Are you a fast and accurate typist? If you can type well, there are many services you could offer, such as typing papers for other students or typing a manuscript for a busy author.

Desktop publishing: You will need access to a computer, laser printer, and a good word-processing program. You will also need design skills. With these resources, you can create newsletters, menus, and programs, and create and maintain mailing lists.

Web site design: If you are computer literate and comfortable on the Internet, assist others in designing their "home pages" on the World Wide Web. *Dreamweaver* software makes it easy to design Web sites without having to learn HTML.

Graphic arts: Learn how to use programs like Adobe *Photoshop* and *Quark* and you can provide graphic arts services, including photo retouching and the creation of flyers, posters, brochures, and other promotional materials.

Cooking

If you love to cook, you can provide products, services, or both! Let your creativity soar, but always with the customer in mind. What kind of food do the people in your market like? What is difficult to find? Be sure to consider safe food handling!

Catering: A catering business can supply whole menus for parties and other occasions.

Pasta: Create a line of fresh pasta and sauces.

Organic baby food: Parents want their babies to eat healthy, too.

Cookbook: Do you come from a family in which a lot of great recipes have been handed down over the years? Put together a cookbook!

Crafts

Do you like to make jewelry, leather goods, or other handicrafts? Sell your own work and, perhaps, for a percentage, creations by your friends, as well.

Jewelry making: Start with inexpensive supplies, like wire and beads. Maybe one day you will work in gold and diamonds.

Greeting-card design: You can create beautiful greeting cards with rubber stamps, ink, and small silkscreens. If you have a good sense of humor, this is a great place to use it.

Handbags: Decorate vintage handbags or make your own out of felt, fabric, or leather.

Candle making: A crafts store has everything you will need to make decorative candles. You can buy wax or melt down old candles and crayons. Try using empty milk cartons as molds.

Dancing

Dance lessons: Even if you are a beginner, you probably know enough to teach young children.

Hip-hop dance troupe: If you have friends who are also talented dancers, why not get a group together and offer your services to local hip-hop groups?

Driving

Do you like to drive? If you start a business using a car or van, make sure you have up-to-date insurance. Do not borrow a car from a parent or friend for your business without being sure you are covered by the insurance policy.

Errand service: Offer to run errands and make deliveries for small businesspeople and others who do not have the time to do so. Make yourself indispensable and you will soon have a growing business.

Meal delivery: Are there restaurants in your area that do not offer delivery because they do not want to pay for their own staff? You could offer to make deliveries for three or more restaurants so that they can share the cost.

Messenger service: Do you enjoy running around? Try a messenger/small-package delivery service. It is a business with low start-up costs. The service can expand rapidly as you build a reputation for reliability.

Entertainment

Are you a natural performer who enjoys being in front of an audience? Do you know any magic tricks or have theater experience?

Clown: If you love making kids laugh, become a clown and you will be in demand for birthday parties around town.

Magician: Is there a magic club at your school where you could learn tricks? You can also learn from books and practice on your friends. As a magician, you can entertain at birthday parties and other events.

Party DJ: A DJ plays recorded music at parties. You will need one or two turntables and lots of records or CDs and equipment. Some DJs form record pools so they can share their records and equipment. Local record labels might give you free records to promote their artists.

Balloon decorating: Learn how to make balloon animals and how to tie balloons together to make party decorations!

Fish

If fish are a hobby of yours, why not turn it into income?

Aquarium care: You will need to know how to care for both fresh and salt-water tanks. Offer your services to local businesses and restaurants, as well as to individuals.

Fishing: If you live in an area that has good fishing, become a fishing guide. You can organize day trips to nearby lakes and rivers.

Gardening

Chores like mowing the lawn are a lot more fun when you're getting paid. Almost anything you do around the house can be turned into a business.

Fresh herbs and flowers: Is there a room in your house or apartment that gets a lot of sunlight? You can grow fresh herbs and flowers and supply them to restaurants. This can be a good "second" business because plants do not have to be watched every minute of the day.

Yardwork: Do you like working outdoors? From the street, you can often spot lawns and gardens that are not being kept up by their owners as well as they should be. You could also shovel snow in the winter.

Plant care: Offices could hire you to come in once a week to water, clean, and fertilize their plants. As more and more people work outside the home, there is more demand for household plant care, too.

Window boxes: Fill wooden window boxes with flowers. You can make and decorate the boxes yourself.

Hair

Do you love to make your friends' hair look great? Before you start a business styling, cutting or braiding hair, check local regulations for necessary permits.

Holidays

Are you one of those people who gets excited about holidays? Holidays are business opportunities.

Gift baskets: Every holiday is an opportunity to create a different gift basket that you can sell for a profit. You can also offer a custom service and make baskets based on the special interests of the people receiving them.

Seasonal sales: Do you have spare time during the holidays? Try selling seasonal specialties, such as Christmas decorations or Valentine's Day candy, which have short but intense sales seasons. If you are willing to put in the time, you can make a lot of money in a relatively short period.

Internet

People come up with creative new businesses using the Internet every day. What will you invent?

Genealogy: Researching genealogy, which is the history of someone's ancestors, is easy online (but you will have to subscribe to some basic sites to access the genealogical information). Teach yourself how to create family trees. Every family is a potential customer.

Web site: If you come up with a popular idea for a Web site, you can sell advertising space. Got a great comic character? You could create some fun movies. How about electronic greeting cards? What could you put online that other people would want to see?

eBay auctions: Learn how to bid on eBay and you could offer your services to people who have things to sell but do not have the time or skill.

Music

Do you play music? Or just love being around it? Either way, there are a lot of businesses you could start.

Band: Start a rock band and get hired to play at parties, weddings, and corporate events.

Music lessons: Do you play an instrument well enough to teach someone else? Even if you have only intermediate knowledge, you could probably teach beginners.

Stickers and buttons: Rock and rap artists need stickers and buttons imprinted with their logos for promotion. So do stores and sports teams. Why not save them the trouble of contracting with a sticker or button manufacturer? If you establish a relationship with a manufacturer yourself, you can get a good price because you will be bringing that company new business. Turn that price advantage into profit.

String quartet: Do you play in the band or orchestra at school? Get some friends together and start a string quartet to get hired for store openings, weddings, parties, etc.

Painting

Are you good with a brush? Advertise your services on grocery store bulletin boards and with flyers at hardware stores.

Housepainting: You will need to learn about types of paint and how to "cut," so your lines look clean. See if you can find someone experienced who is willing to teach you the basics.

Furniture: Old furniture can be made to look like new with a nice coat of paint. Shop flea markets for bargains you can refinish and sell, or offer refinishing services.

Signage: If you can paint lettering well, you can create signs for local businesses.

People

Are you a "people person"? Try a business that involves getting people together or waking them up!

Dating newsletter: Are you a natural matchmaker? Start an e-mail dating newsletter.

Wake-up service: Are you an early riser? Start a wake-up service for your fellow students.

Photography

Have you ever thought about a career in photography? Get experience and earn money at the same time.

Wedding photography: If you are a skilled photographer, offer to shoot a couple of weddings for free to build your portfolio. Be aware that wedding photography has to be very professional.

Photo journalist: Local newspapers often buy photos of events and parties from freelance photographers.

Sales

If you are in or near a major city, you can go to a wholesale district and buy items in quantity at a discount that you can then sell at retail prices. You can sell almost anything: candy, perfume, headbands, jewelry, ties, watches, etc.

Silkscreening

Silkscreening is easy and relatively inexpensive. All you need are a silkscreen, ink, a "wedge" to press the ink through the screen, and something to silkscreen.

T-shirts: Bands need T-shirts silkscreened with their logos. So do sports teams.

Creative clothing: You can also silkscreen pants, shorts, skirts, and dresses with your own cool designs.

Teaching

Are you always explaining class assignments to your friends? Do you like helping people understand things?

Tutoring: Do you know one of your academic subjects well enough to teach other students? Giving lessons (tutoring) requires patience, but you will discover the rewards and satisfaction of teaching.

Lessons: Anything you can do, from playing guitar to making clothes, you can teach.

Translating

Are you bilingual? Did you grow up speaking another language? Put your language skills to good use!

Translation: Translate ads, flyers, signs, and the like for local shopkeepers who want to reach customers who speak different languages.

Teach English: Teach English as a second language to people in the community who need help.

Teach your second language: Teach your language to people who speak only English.

Video

Do you have a good camera or camcorder?

Videotape events: People like to have their weddings, birthdays, parties, and other events videotaped. You will need samples of your work to show to prospective clients.

Videotape concerts: Bands like to have their shows videotaped so they can see how to improve their performance. You will have to be of legal age, however, to enter a club that serves alcohol.

Digital moviemaking: With digital video, anyone with a camera can make a movie without the expense of buying the film that made moviemaking so expensive. Check out Michael Dean's *$30 Film School* (Course Technology PTR, 2003).

Woodworking

Woodworking skills can be used to create many types of businesses.

Carpentry: If you are skilled at carpentry, sell your services. You can build cabinets and shelves, and help renovate homes.

Birdcages: One student who finished a NFTE course started a successful business by building birdcages out of wood in his uncle's garage.

Decorative carving: If you are artistically talented, try learning scrollwork, which is decorative carving in wood for screens or furniture.

Board games: Create interesting versions of board games, such as chess or checkers.

Writing

Are you a talented writer?

Pennysaver newspaper: Get local businesses to buy ads in your newspaper that customers can cut out and use as coupons. You can write stories about businesses and people in the community, as well.

Fanzine: A *fanzine* is a magazine written specifically for fans of just about anything, from a genre of music to pop stars.

Poetry for special occasions: How about composing poetry for special occasions, like birthdays and graduations? Sell poetry personalized with names, dates, and photos, or lace handkerchiefs embroidered with poetry that guests receive as gifts.

Appendix 2

Sample Student Business Plan

University Parent, Inc.

Fesehaye Abrhaley
Michelle Dorenkamp
Kara Grinnell
Ryan Roth
Sarah Schupp

Table of Contents

Appendix

Executive Summary

University Parent, Inc.
University Parent (UPI) produces institution-specific guides and comprehensive websites for parents of college students. Revenues are generated through the sale of advertising in the local guides and on the websites.

Today, there are 32 million parents of college students
According to surveys and interviews conducted by UPI, parents do not receive the information they need from colleges. They want to know where to have a nice dinner in their student's college town, where to stay, and fun activities to do while visiting. They also want to know how to parent their college student and need to understand the issues their child is facing such as managing money, avoiding credit card debt, and balancing school, a part-time job, and extra-curricular activities.

UPI can help
UPI will produce three free guides per year for each college that will be distributed during summer orientation and August move-in, Fall Parent's Weekend, and in the Spring to prospective parents through the Admissions Office and Campus Tour Office. At the University of Colorado, over 25,000 prospective parents tour the campus. The magazines will be distributed through the university, hotels, and restaurants. The magazine content will include: restaurant reviews, a lodging directory, a shopping guide, calendar of events, graduation requirement Information, map of the city, and a Q&A section.

Proven track record
The first issue of the *Parent's Guide to Boulder* was published in October 2003 and immediately profited from advertising sales. The second edition will be published June 2004, and due to advance advertising sales, will also be profitable. Demand for these first guides have proved that advertisers are committed to purchasing space in the guide and that parents are interested in reading the guide.

Experienced, enthusiastic management team
Sarah Schupp is the founder, CEO, and Chairman of the UPI Board of Directors. She published the initial *Parent's Guide to Boulder* in 2003. A graduate of the University of Colorado with degrees in Business Administration and English Literature, Sarah is capable of expanding the vision of UPI to Colorado and Texas. In Year 3, UPI plans to hire a CEO with national rollout experience.

Other UPI employees include VP Marketing Michelle Dorenkamp, CFO Kara Grinnell, and CTO Ryan Roth. In addition to an excellent management team,

UPI is in the process of developing a board of twelve directors that bring experience in advertising, magazine writing, start-ups, and venture capital.

Plan for expansion
Because of the initial success of the *Parent's Guide to Boulder*, UPI is currently expanding its marketing base to Colorado State University and the University of Denver. A regional office in Boulder will handle advertising sales for the three guides. UPI plans to broaden its base beginning in Year 2, with a goal of being in 44 schools by Year 5.

The offering
UPI is offering 35% of the company for $500,000. This will provide investors with a 60% rate of return, translating to $4.3 million in Year 5 when UPI plans to sell to Hearst Publishing or Conde Nast Publishing. UPI breaks-even in Year 2, generating revenues of $1.8 million. In Year 5, UPI will have revenues of $12 million and a net profit of $4.1 million.

Company Overview

With two successful publications for the University of Colorado and established relationships with over 35 advertisers, UPI is positioned for nation-wide expansion. In October of 2004, UPI plans to produce a total of 9 publications and 3 websites for the University of Colorado, the University of Denver, and Colorado State University. We project UPI will produce 132 publications and high-traffic websites for 44 colleges and universities by Year 5. This will result in net revenues of $12.3 million, net profits of $4.1 million, and a valuation of $70 million. Also in Year 5, UPI plans to market the company to suitable buyers such as Hearst Publishing or Conde Nast Publishing.

4

Product/Service Description

Introduction

You arrive on campus to drop off your freshman student. This is always one of the hardest times of the year for you. Leaving your child miles from home, millions of questions are running through your head. How do they register for classes? How many credits will they need to graduate? What issues will they face being away from home? As you are signing in for orientation, you receive a magazine that specifically answers these questions. Not only does it answer campus life questions, it also offers restaurant reviews, lodging suggestions, and a detailed map of the city. The magazine directs you to a website where you can talk to other parents who have your same concerns. Suddenly you have a sense of relief. Now you have a source of information at your fingertips.

As a Boulder business, you have always wondered how you can directly advertise to CU parents who visit often and spend thousands of dollars while visiting. One day a packet arrives at your business with the first *Parent's Guide to Boulder* from the 2003 Parent's Weekend and a rate card. You are excited that there is now a reasonably priced and direct way to contact CU parents and inform them of your business. You know that purchasing advertising will be well worth every dollar. (Boulder, Colorado served as UPI's test market.)

Description

University Parent produces a comprehensive local guide as well as a website for parents of college students. Through its compilation of articles, pictures, maps, current events, and advertisements, it provides a convenient, thorough source of information for CU parents.

Parent

Guide Feature	Benefit
Distribution through the university, hotels, and restaurants	Convenience
Provides useful information about their student's environment and community	Comfort, Sense of Security
Makes navigating Boulder easier and allows for advance planning	Saves Time
Free! Gives information and coupons for good values in: lodging, eating, shopping, and having a good time	Saves Money

University Parent, Inc.

Advertiser

Guide Feature	Benefit
Targets specific niche	Targeted ROI
Mid-ranged priced advertising	Saves Money
Effective distribution channels	Reaches Target Market, Generates Revenue

Market Comparison
Unlike other publications in college towns, UPI offers its readers focused, relevant information that is unavailable through local newspapers and magazines. It also offers advertisers a targeted, identifiable market.

Stage of Development
UPI produced its first guide in Boulder for Parent's Weekend '03. The profitability of the first guide demonstrated UPI's ability to sell advertising and to produce a useful product. UPI is currently marketing and creating articles for its Summer '04 publication. Our CTO, Ryan Roth, launched the Guide to Boulder's website in April of '04, http://www.guidetoboulder.com. Advertising sales for the website are scheduled to begin in May '04.

Client Base
UPI currently has over 35 clients for the *Parent's Guide to Boulder*. These advertisers include: Wells Fargo, Walnut Realty, McGuckin Hardware, the CU Book Store, the CU Foundation, Greenbriar Inn, Boulder Broker Inn, Boulder Outlook Hotel & Suites, Boulder Express Shuttle, and many more. Of the initial advertisers in the Fall '03 guide, 100% of advertisers solicited purchased advertising for the Summer '04 guide.

Potential Readership Base
Demographic
> 32 million U.S. parents of college students, growing at an annual rate of 6%
> We expect 20% of each college's parent population to read our magazines

Family Income
> Most families sending children to college have a combined household income ranging from $80,000 to $150,000

Cost of Education
> A college education is likely the biggest investment they will make in their student
> A college education costs anywhere from $30,000 to $200,000
> Parents typically provide for their children while in college, paying for expenses such as transportation (car, bike), car insurance, textbooks, clothing, computers and software, food, rent, etc.

2890 Shadow Creek – Boulder, Colorado – 303.579.9871 – info@upi.com

These expenses average between $800–$1,500 per month.

Potential Advertisers

Independent marketing firms that handle national accounts
Local business owners and/or Marketing Managers representing hotels, restaurants, retail stores, travel agencies that must make buying decisions based on distribution and cost.

Industry and Marketplace Analysis

The publication industry has over 17,000 magazines that gross $24 billion in revenue each year. Historically, this industry has grown at a rate of 7 percent, and is expected to grow 6 percent in the future. There is little demand for new titles with the exception of demand for specialty, niche magazines that enable advertisers to reach a well-defined market. Our primary, unexplored niche consists of parents of college students. According to surveys, virtually all CU parents (95%) are uninformed about campus activities, news, and pertinent issues. Currently no other publications are addressing these needs and concerns of CU parents.

In recent years, there has been an increase in online magazines and online versions of print magazines. Major threats in the periodical industry include other advertising mediums such as television, radio, and print. The most competition for publications is in print advertising, which ranges from daily newspapers to monthly magazines. Another threat to the publication industry is the rising cost of paper, which is driving down profits. Some of the internal market changes revolve around a concern over rising paper costs because of deforestation.

Leading advertisers in the magazine industry include: automobile manufacturers, consumer goods companies, entertainment conglomerates, and tobacco firms. Some of the internal market changes revolve around a concern over rising paper costs because of deforestation.

Leading advertisers in the magazine industry include: automobile manufacturers, consumer goods companies, entertainment conglomerates, and tobacco firms. The publication industry is affected by changes in economic conditions since revenue is advertising-dependant.

2890 Shadow Creek – Boulder, Colorado – 303.579.9871 – info@upi.com

University Parent, Inc.

Marketing Strategy

Introduction
UPI's target readership market will include students, parents of present and future students, university faculty and staff, and high school counselors. Aggressive distribution will insure that all sectors of our target market will receive our free guide as well as website information. Our target market for advertising is businesses that want to make parents of college students aware of their products and/or services. We provide these businesses an opportunity to reach a specific, identifiable market at a reasonable cost.

Target Market Advertising Strategy
We will position ourselves as the only publication offering information specifically for parents of CU students and as the only publication offering businesses the opportunity to advertise to these parents.

In Boulder, the primary advertising media are the *Colorado Daily*, *Daily Camera*, *The Onion*, and *Boulder Magazine*. UPI's targeted, niche market strategy offers businesses a superior, more cost-effective media product at a lower cost than these publications. UPI will produce a quarterly mailing to businesses in Boulder that offer a product/service that CU parents may be interested in purchasing. The mailing will be directed to the "businesses' owners" and will include a previous *Parent's Guide to Boulder*, a cover letter specifying why advertising with UPI is effective, testimonials from current advertisers, and a rate card.

As UPI moves into additional markets, this strategy will be replicated and customized as needed.

Pricing Strategy
University Parent will generate revenue from two sources: print advertising in our guides and online advertising on our website.

Print advertising prices (per guide):

Size	Full Color
Eighth Page	$250
Quarter Page	$400
Half Page	$600
Full Page	$800
Back Cover, Inside Cover, Back Inside	$1000

2890 Shadow Creek – Boulder, Colorado – 303.579.9871 – info@upi.com

University Parent, Inc.

Website advertising prices (per month):

Size	Full Color
2" x 1"	$400
2" x 2"	$500
Banner, 1" x 7"	$700
Pop Up	$1000
Ad in email newsletter	$500

Businesses can purchase yearlong magazine and website advertising at a10% discount. The website advertising prices are likely to change based on our website's traffic. The higher the traffic, the higher the price we can charge.

Distribution Strategy
UPI will distribute guides to parents through the university admissions office, parent relations office, and campus tour office. The guide will also be distributed in hotels, restaurants, businesses, and through the Chamber of Commerce. There will be an option on the website to download the guide or have it mailed for a small fee (postage).

Advertising, Sales & Promotion Strategy
UPI will be promoted to advertisers through local networking at Boulder Chamber of Commerce events, press releases in local papers, direct mailings, and referral incentives for current clients. In addition, the website will serve as an effective tool to inform both businesses and parents of our services.

Marketing & Sales Forecasts
UPI's revenue is generated through print and website advertising sales. We project revenues from print advertising at 54% and website advertising sales at 46% of total revenues.

Advertising revenues are calculated by using the print advertising rates multiplied by expected sales for three guides. UPI projects sales of 25 print advertisements per issue at an average cost of $1,000 and 72 website sales per year per institution at an average cost of $750.

Revenue (In thousands $)

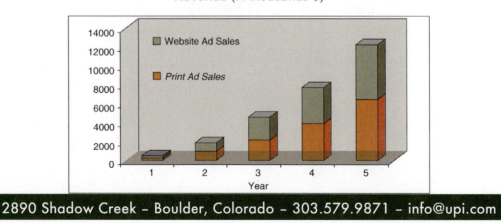

University Parent, Inc.

Revenue Projections

	Year 1	Year 2	Year 3	Year 4	Year 5
Product A—Magazine					
Number of Schools	3	9	22	32	44
Total Issues/Year	9	36	66	96	132
Magazines Printed/Year	90,000	360,000	660,000	960,000	1,320,000
Printing Cost/Per Magazine	0.25	0.23	0.21	0.19	0.17
Number of Units/Ad	225	900	1,800	2,925	4,425
Avg. Price/Ad Page	$1,000	$1,100	$1,210	$1,331	$1,464
Print Adv Total	$225,000	$990,000	$2,178,000	$3,893,175	$6,478,643
Product B—Website					
Advertisements Sold/Yr	360	1,080	2,640	3,840	5,280
Price per unit	$750	$825	$908	$998	$1,098
Web Adv Total	$270,000	$891,000	$2,395,800	$3,833,280	$5,797,836
Net Revenue	$495,000	$1,881,000	$4,573,800	$7,726,455	$12,276,479

Operations Plan

Operations Strategy

Our strategy is to establish a reputation with readers and advertisers that UPI consistently delivers well-received, well-designed, informative magazines and websites. We will develop this reputation by providing products that are professionally designed, error-free, and exceed the expectations of both our readers and our advertisers. We will measure our success through in-person as well as online surveys of our customers.

Our goal is to have highly satisfied customers—our parent readers and our advertisers. To that end, UPI will provide training for all employees that stresses the necessity of exceeding the expectations of our customers in ways such as delivering advertising proofs early or following up with a parent's question promptly and thoroughly.

Scope of Operations

At UPI headquarters, there will be 15 full-time employees. In Year 1, this office will handle advertising sales for the CU, DU, and CSU guides, as well as negotiate next year's Texas expansion.

2890 Shadow Creek – Boulder, Colorado – 303.579.9871 – info@upi.com

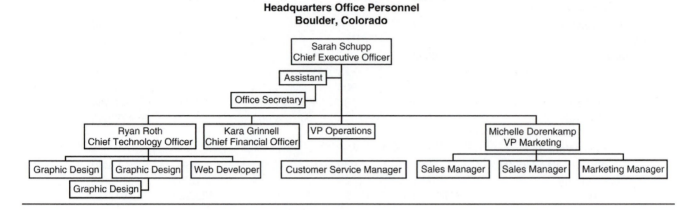

Headquarters Office Personnel
Boulder, Colorado

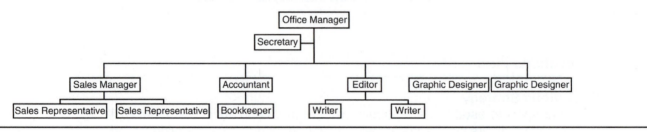

Regional Office Personnel
Locations: Dallas, Atlanta, Boston, Kansas City

Ongoing Operations

UPI headquarters will coordinate with the regional offices to produce a website and three magazines annually for each college. Issues will be published every summer, fall, and spring. The website will be updated as needed, daily if necessary. Advertising sales as well as contact with parents and university faculty and staff will be continuous throughout the year

Operating Expenses

	Year 1	Year 2	Year 3	Year 4	Year 5
Total Operating Expenses	$854,967	$1,547,676	$2,588,328	$3,611,938	$5,083,166
% of Revenue	172.7%	82.3%	56.6%	46.7%	41.4%

2890 Shadow Creek – Boulder, Colorado – 303.579.9871 – info@upi.com

Development Plan

Development Strategy

The first priority for UPI is to establish a strong brand and reputation within each new market. UPI will publish a guide approximately every four months. Our relationship with advertisers will become much stronger with each issue as they realize the value from advertising in our magazine. After three issues (one year), we believe our relationships with advertisers will significantly increase revenues. In year two, returning clients will purchase more advertisements and clients who watched their competitors gain revenue from advertising with us. For the second issue of the *Parent's Guide to Boulder,* advertising sales doubled and every client who purchased an advertisement in the Fall guide purchased an advertisement in the Summer guide.

During the publication cycle for each issue, the first order of business is to brainstorm new ideas and themes. Once the themes are decided, we make those themes available to the advertisers. We then give advertisers a three-month window to purchase advertising space. Contact is made with potential advertiser through "cold-selling," a variant of cold calling.

The "cold-selling" begins with a mass mailing, which is followed up with an e-mail. One week after the e-mailing, our staff follows up with a telephone call. The next seven weeks in the ad purchasing "window" are reserved for meetings with potential advertisers. Through our past experience, we have found that such meetings are vital for closing most deals.

The artwork acceptance window is open from the moment an advertising contract is signed until the artwork acceptance deadline, one week after the close of advertising sales. The first payment for the advertisement is due on the last day of advertisement sales. The second payment is due one week before we send the magazine to the printer.

While ad sales are in full swing, the design of the magazine is developed. Concurrently, article research and story writing for the magazine are performed. Immediately after the design and story writing are finalized, we finalize the layout and update the website; both of these occur over a two-week period.

As soon as the layout is finished, the final copy is sent to the printer. Within 5 days, the printer overnights a digital proof for UPI's approval. Once approved, printing takes approximately one week. Once the copies are received, the magazine is ready for distribution. Distribution takes place over a two-week period. Most magazines are mailed directly from the printer to the distribution point. These distribution points include: the university, hotels, restaurants, and other local businesses.

2890 Shadow Creek – Boulder, Colorado – 303.579.9871 – info@upi.com

Roll-Out Plan

Year 1: Colorado
3 Schools: CU, University of Denver, and Colorado State University

Year 2: Colorado and Texas
9 Schools: *New Regional Office opens in <u>**Dallas**</u>: Southern Methodist University, University of Texas at Austin, A&M, Trinity University, Baylor University, Rice University

Year 3: Colorado, Texas, South
22 Schools: *New Regional Office opens in <u>**Atlanta**</u>: University of Georgia, University of the South, University of North Carolina, University of South Carolina, Duke University, University of Florida, Rollins College, University of Virginia, University of Richmond, University of Louisiana, Louisiana State University

13

University Parent, Inc.

Year 4: Colorado, Texas, South, Northeast
32 Schools: *New Regional Office opens in **Boston**: Harvard, MIT, Tufts, Boston University, Boston College, Princeton, New York University, Columbia University, Barnard College, Villanova University, University of Connecticut

Year 5: Colorado, Texas, South, Northeast, Midwest
44 Schools: *New Regional Office opens in **Kansas City**: University of Kansas, Kansas State University, University of Oklahoma, Oklahoma State University, University of Missouri, Missouri State University, University of Ohio, Ohio State University, Purdue University, University of Michigan, University of Wisconsin, University of Illinois

Year 6: *Continued Expansion*: Northeast, Midwest, West

14

2890 Shadow Creek – Boulder, Colorado – 303.579.9871 – info@upi.com

Management

Sarah Schupp, Chief Executive Officer

Sarah founded *The Parent's Guide to Boulder* in June of 2003.   A graduate of the University of Colorado with degrees in Business Administration and English Literature, Sarah is capable of expanding the vision of UPI across the U.S. In addition, she has developed relationships with the University of Colorado through her 2004 position as the Senior Class President and member of the President's Leadership Class.

Ryan Roth, Chief Technology Officer

Ryan comes to UPI with an extensive background in high-level web technology and information system deployment strategies. As team leader of numerous successful system development projects, Ryan is a valuable addition to UPI as Chief Technology Officer. He joined our team in early 2004 to provide in-depth, focused research on technology issues and solutions to provide University Parent with customized solutions unmatched by any other magazine publisher today. Ryan graduated from the Leeds School of Business at the University of Colorado with a B.S. in Business Administration and an emphasis in Information Systems.

Kara Grinnell, Chief Financial Officer

Kara is equipped with the financial knowledge needed to accomplish all the tasks included in the job of Chief Financial Officer. With a degree in Finance from the University of Colorado, Kara has the appropriate background to help UPI meet its financial goals. Kara has firsthand field experience with financial measurements and is prepared to help UPI become a $100 million venture.

Michelle Dorenkamp, VP Marketing

Michelle will graduate with a Bachelor of Science Degree in Business from the University of Colorado in May 2004. For the past three summers, she has worked in marketing and advertising for a real estate company. She has successfully worked with companies doing a direct mail campaign similar to the one that will be used to attract advertisers for the local guides.

Business Risks

Another company will copy our idea.

Because of a magazine's low start-up costs, it is likely that people will copy our concept. However, we can mitigate this risk by negotiating with national advertisers for annual contracts and with universities for distribution rights. Another way we can mitigate this risk is through strategic growth. By identifying the best regions for expansion, we will capture a new region each year. We are targeting geographically central locations with a high concentration of colleges and universities.

Universities will not cooperate to help us distribute the guide.

When selling advertisements to businesses, our greatest strength is that universities allow us to distribute the guide on campus. This distribution point makes advertisers believe their ROI will be greater because parents pay close attention to materials given to them by the university. However, our guide is an effective public relations tool for universities to give to parents and by maintaining appropriate content, we eliminate this obstacle.

Businesses will not buy advertising.

Our revenue projections are based on selling 25 or more print advertisements per issue and 10 Web ads per month per location. If businesses do not believe that our magazine will serve as an effective marketing tool, they will not purchase advertising. We must prove to advertisers that parents do and will read our magazine and will make buying decisions based on our information.

Each university has a different environment with different demographics.

Because we are producing guides with location-specific information, we must insure that the information we publish is accurate and appropriate for the area. If we miss the target demographic or culture of the area, parents will not read the guide and advertisers will not purchase advertising. To make sure we understand the area, representatives from our regional office will be familiar with every location in their region and will have student interns at each school that will help UPI understand the area and its parent population. In addition, we will use our website to collect marketing data. Weblogs, an online parent chat room, will allow us to track parents' comments and their geographic location, which will enable us to understand the issues at each university.

2890 Shadow Creek – Boulder, Colorado – 303.579.9871 – info@upi.com

Financial Plan

Financial Summary

Revenue for UPI is derived from magazine and website advertising sales. UPI plans to sell advertising to both national and local advertisers. As more people read our magazine and visit our website, the prices we can charge advertisers will increase.

The following table summarizes five years of pro forma financial statements. Assumptions for the financial statements are located in Section G of the Appendix.

	Year 1	Year 2	Year 3	Year 4	Year 5
Operating Revenue	$495,000	$1,881,000	$4,573,800	$7,726,455	$12,276,479
Operating Expenses					
Salaries, Wages, & Benefits	$323,000	$692,230	$1,152,524	$1,526,238	$1,907,539
Depreciation	$6,667	$20,000	$40,000	$60,000	$80,000
Rent & Utilities	$40,000	$85,600	$131,592	$180,803	$233,460
Total Operating Expenses	$854,967	$1,547,676	$2,588,328	$3,611,938	$5,083,166
Income Taxes	$0	$0	-$550,989	-$1,542,198	-$2,749,048
Net Income (Loss)	($401,329)	$197,583	$1,227,012	$2,313,297	$4,123,572

Balance Sheet
Years 0–5 ($)

	Begin	Year 1	Year 2	Year 3	Year 4	Year 5
ASSETS						
CURRENT ASSETS						
Cash	530,000	117,763	281,640	1,616,578	4,006,443	8,252,410
Accounts Receivable		0	0	0	0	0
Inventories		0	0	0	0	0
Other Current Assets		113	3,947	50,228	63,484	75,729
Total Current Assets	530,000	117,875	285,588	1,666,806	4,069,927	8,328,139
PROPERTY & EQUIPMENT	0	16,533	50,133	81,733	109,333	136,133
TOTAL ASSETS	530,000	134,409	335,721	1,748,539	4,179,261	8,464,272
LIABILITIES & SHAREHOLDERS' EQUITY						
CURRENT LIABILITIES						
Short-Term Debt	0	0	0	0	0	0
Accounts Payable & Accrued Expen		5,625	9,281	191,445	306,567	464,840
Other Current Liabilities		113	186	3,829	6,131	9,297
Current Portion of Long-term Debt	0	0	0	0	0	0
Total Current Liabilities	0	5,738	9,467	195,274	312,698	474,137
LONG-TERM DEBT (less current portion)	0	0	0	0	0	0
STOCKHOLDERS' EQUITY						
Common Stock	30,000	30,000	30,000	30,000	30,000	30,000
Preferred Stock	500,000	500,000	500,000	500,000	500,000	500,000
Retained Earnings		(401,329)	(203,746)	1,023,266	3,336,563	7,460,135
Total Equity	530,000	128,671	326,254	1,553,266	3,866,563	7,990,135
TOTAL LIABILITIES & EQUITY	530,000	134,409	335,721	1,748,539	4,179,261	8,464,272

2890 Shadow Creek – Boulder, Colorado – 303.579.9871 – info@upi.com

Offering

Investment Requirements
UPI initially requires $500,000 in seed funding for the first year of operations. This amount will fund the expansion to the University of Denver and Colorado State University as well as funding new employee salaries and the opening of a Colorado regional office in Boulder. Investors will own 35% of the venture.

Valuation
Using the venture capital method, in Year 5, assuming net earnings of $4.1 million, and an industry P/E ratio of 17.3, UPI will have a market value of $70 million.

Financing
UPI seeks $500,000 in seed funding in Year 0. This round will provide the investor with a 35% stake in the venture at a 60% annual rate of return.

Exit Strategy
In Year 5, UPI we be marketed to Hearst Publishing and Condé Nast Publishing. These are logical acquirers because both companies own over 30 niche magazines.

Appendices

    Sarah Schupp, CEO

    Kara Grinnell, CFO

    Ryan Roth, CTO

    Michelle Dorenkamp, VP Marketing

2890 Shadow Creek – Boulder, Colorado – 303.579.9871 – info@upi.com

Appendix A, Income Statement, Years 1–5 ($)

	Year 1	Year 2	Year 3	Year 4	Year 5
NET REVENUES	495,000	1,881,000	4,573,800	7,726,455	12,276,479
COST OF REVENUE	26,362	90,741	152,471	204,023	255,692
% of Revenues	5.3%	4.8%	3.3%	2.6%	2.1%
GROSS PROFIT	468,638	1,790,259	4,421,329	7,522,432	12,020,787
% of Revenues	94.7%	95.2%	96.7%	97.4%	97.9%
OPERATING EXPENSES					
Sales & Marketing	240,750	364,610	674,953	1,023,764	1,734,098
Research & Development	219,800	291,186	360,569	434,809	514,245
General and Administration	394,417	891,880	1,552,806	2,153,364	2,834,823
Total Operating Expenses	854,967	1,547,676	2,588,328	3,611,938	5,083,166
% of Revenues	173%	82%	57%	47%	41%
EARNINGS FROM OPERATIONS	(386,329)	242,583	1,833,001	3,910,495	6,937,620
EXTRAORDINARY INCOME / (EXPENSE)	(15,000)	(45,000)	(55,000)	(55,000)	(65,000)
EARNINGS BEFORE INTEREST & TAXES	(401,329)	197,583	1,778,001	3,855,495	6,872,620
INTEREST INCOME/(EXPENSE)	0	0	0	0	0
NET EARNINGS BEFORE TAXES	(401,329)	197,583	1,778,001	3,855,495	6,872,620
TAXES	0	0	(550,989)	(1,542,198)	(2,749,048)
NET EARNINGS	(401,329)	197,583	1,227,012	2,313,297	4,123,572
% of Revenues	-81.1%	10.5%	26.8%	29.9%	33.6%

21

2890 Shadow Creek – Boulder, Colorado – 303.579.9871 – info@upi.com

Appendix B, Balance Sheet, Years 0–5 ($)

	Begin	Year 1	Year 2	Year 3	Year 4	Year 5
ASSETS						
CURRENT ASSETS						
Cash	530,000	117,763	281,640	1,616,578	4,006,443	8,252,410
Accounts Receivable		0	0	0	0	0
Inventories		0	0	0	0	0
Other Current Assets		113	3,947	50,228	63,484	75,729
Total Current Assets	530,000	117,875	285,588	1,666,806	4,069,927	8,328,139
PROPERTY & EQUIPMENT	0	16,533	50,133	81,733	109,333	136,133
TOTAL ASSETS	530,000	134,409	335,721	1,748,539	4,179,261	8,464,272
LIABILITIES & SHAREHOLDERS' EQUITY						
CURRENT LIABILITIES						
Short-Term Debt	0	0	0	0	0	0
Accounts Payable & Accrued Expen		5,625	9,281	191,445	306,567	464,840
Other Current Liabilities		113	186	3,829	6,131	9,297
Current Portion of Long-Term Debt	0	0	0	0	0	0
Total Current Liabilities	0	5,738	9,467	195,274	312,698	474,137
LONG-TERM DEBT (less current portion)	0	0	0	0	0	0
STOCKHOLDERS' EQUITY						
Common Stock	30,000	30,000	30,000	30,000	30,000	30,000
Preferred Stock	500,000	500,000	500,000	500,000	500,000	500,000
Retained Earnings		(401,329)	(203,746)	1,023,266	3,336,563	7,460,135
Total Equity	530,000	128,671	326,254	1,553,266	3,866,563	7,990,135
TOTAL LIABILITIES & EQUITY	530,000	134,409	335,721	1,748,539	4,179,261	8,464,272

2890 Shadow Creek – Boulder, Colorado – 303.579.9871 – info@upi.com

The Daily Perc—General Assumptions

The Daily Perc
Appendix 4-C

Plan Month	Jun	Jul	Aug	Sep	Oct	Nov	Dec	Jan	Feb	Mar	Apr	May
	1	2	3	4	5	6	7	8	9	10	11	12
Current Interest Rate	10.00%	10.00%	10.00%	10.00%	10.00%	10.00%	10.00%	10.00%	10.00%	10.00%	10.00%	10.00%
Long-term Interest Rate	9.00%	9.00%	9.00%	9.00%	9.00%	9.00%	9.00%	9.00%	9.00%	9.00%	9.00%	9.00%
Tax Rate	0.00%	0.00%	0.00%	0.00%	0.00%	0.00%	0.00%	0.00%	0.00%	0.00%	0.00%	0.00%
Other	0	0	0	0	0	0	0	0	0	0	0	0

The Daily Perc
Appendix 4-D

The Daily Perc—Pro Forma Profit and Loss (Income Statement)

	Jun	Jul	Aug	Sep	Oct	Nov	Dec	Jan	Feb	Mar	Apr	May
Sales	$0	$0	$0	$32,375	$42,637	$44,769	$42,530	$42,637	$77,144	$85,167	$95,392	$95,392
Direct Costs of Goods	$0	$0	$0	$11,200	$14,750	$15,488	$14,713	$14,750	$26,688	$29,463	$31,963	$31,963
Sales Commissions	$0	$0	$0	$0	$0	$0	$0	$0	$0	$0	$708	$708
Cost of Goods Sold	$0	$0	$0	$11,200	$14,750	$15,488	$14,713	$14,750	$26,688	$29,463	$32,671	$32,671
Gross Margin	$0	$0	$0	$21,175	$27,887	$29,281	$27,817	$27,887	$50,456	$55,704	$62,721	$62,721
Gross Margin %	0.00%	0.00%	0.00%	65.41%	65.41%	65.41%	65.41%	65.41%	65.41%	65.41%	65.75%	65.75%
Expenses												
Payroll	$5,500	$5,500	$5,500	$16,000	$18,100	$17,050	$18,800	$19,500	$28,624	$30,700	$38,200	$38,900
Sales and Marketing and Other Expenses	$0	$0	$0	$0	$0	$0	$0	$0	$0	$0	$0	$0
Depreciation	$0	$310	$310	$1,565	$1,565	$1,565	$1,565	$1,565	$2,820	$2,820	$3,850	$3,850
Leased Offices and Equipment	$0	$0	$0	$0	$0	$0	$0	$0	$0	$0	$0	$0
Utilities	$0	$0	$700	$800	$920	$920	$1,050	$1,050	$1,050	$1,050	$1,050	$1,050
Insurance	$0	$0	$1,257	$1,257	$1,257	$1,257	$1,257	$1,257	$1,257	$1,257	$1,257	$1,257
Rent	$0	$0	$1,200	$1,200	$1,200	$1,200	$1,200	$1,200	$2,400	$2,400	$2,400	$2,400
Payroll Taxes (15%)	$825	$825	$825	$2,400	$2,715	$2,558	$2,820	$2,925	$4,294	$4,605	$5,730	$5,835
Other General and Administrative Expenses	$0	$0	$0	$0	$0	$0	$0	$0	$0	$0	$0	$0
Total Operating Expenses	$6,325	$6,635	$9,792	$23,222	$25,757	$24,550	$26,692	$27,497	$40,445	$42,832	$52,487	$53,292
Profit Before Interest and Taxes	($6,325)	($6,635)	($9,792)	($2,047)	$2,130	$4,732	$1,125	$390	$10,012	$12,872	$10,234	$9,429
EBITDA	($6,325)	($6,325)	($9,482)	($482)	$3,695	$6,297	$2,690	$1,955	$12,832	$15,692	$14,084	$13,279
Interest Expense	$1,042	$1,018	$1,058	$1,019	$1,019	$1,019	$1,019	$1,019	$1,756	$1,702	$2,282	$2,210
Taxes Incurred	$0	$0	$0	$0	$0	$0	$0	$0	$0	$0	$0	$0
Net Profit	($7,367)	($7,653)	($10,850)	($3,066)	$1,110	$3,712	$106	($630)	$8,256	$11,170	$7,952	$7,219
Net Profit/Sales	0.00%	0.00%	0.00%	-9.47%	2.60%	8.29%	0.25%	-1.48%	10.70%	13.12%	8.34%	7.57%

The Daily Perc
Appendix 4-E

The Daily Perc—Pro Forma Cash Flow

		Jun	Jul	Aug	Sep	Oct	Nov	Dec	Jan	Feb	Mar	Apr	May
Cash Received													
Cash from Operations													
Cash Sales		$0	$0	$0	$32,375	$42,637	$44,769	$42,530	$42,637	$77,144	$85,167	$95,392	$95,392
Subtotal Cash from Operations		$0	$0	$0	$32,375	$42,637	$44,769	$42,530	$42,637	$77,144	$85,167	$95,392	$95,392
Additional Cash Received													
Sales Tax, VAT, HST/GST Received	0.00%	$0	$0	$0	$0	$0	$0	$0	$0	$0	$0	$0	$0
New Current Borrowing		$0	$0	$0	$0	$0	$0	$0	$0	$0	$0	$0	$0
New Other Liabilities (Interest-free)		$0	$0	$0	$0	$0	$0	$0	$0	$0	$0	$0	$0
New Long-term Liabilities		$0	$0	$5,300	$0	$0	$0	$0	$0	$98,184	$0	$77,979	$0
Sales of Other Current Assets		$0	$0	$0	$0	$0	$0	$0	$0	$0	$0	$0	$0
Sales of Long-term Assets		$0	$0	$0	$0	$0	$0	$0	$0	$0	$0	$0	$0
New Investment Received		$0	$0	$0	$0	$0	$0	$0	$0	$0	$0	$0	$0
Subtotal Cash Received		$0	$0	$5,300	$32,375	$42,637	$44,769	$42,530	$42,637	$175,328	$85,167	$173,371	$95,392
Expenditures		Jun	Jul	Aug	Sep	Oct	Nov	Dec	Jan	Feb	Mar	Apr	May
Expenditures from Operations													
Cash Spending		$5,500	$5,500	$5,500	$16,000	$18,100	$17,050	$18,800	$19,500	$28,624	$30,700	$38,200	$38,900
Bill Payments		$62	$1,866	$1,950	$5,095	$6,930	$14,585	$23,185	$21,242	$23,186	$50,340	$43,684	$48,049
Subtotal Spent on Operations		$5,562	$7,366	$7,450	$21,095	$25,030	$31,635	$41,985	$40,742	$51,810	$81,040	$81,884	$86,949
Additional Cash Spent													
Sales Tax, VAT, HST/GST Paid Out		$0	$0	$0	$0	$0	$0	$0	$0	$0	$0	$0	$0
Principal Repayment of Current Borrowing		$0	$0	$0	$0	$0	$0	$0	$0	$0	$0	$0	$0
Other Liabilities Principal Repayment		$0	$0	$0	$0	$0	$0	$0	$0	$0	$0	$0	$0
Long-term Liabilities Principal Repayment		$2,500	$3,116	$0	$5,166	$0	$0	$0	$0	$0	$7,216	$0	$8,471
Purchase Other Current Assets		$0	$0	$0	$0	$0	$0	$0	$0	$0	$0	$0	$0
Purchase Long-term Assets		$0	$0	$0	$0	$0	$0	$0	$0	$105,400	$0	$86,450	$0
Dividends		$0	$0	$0	$0	$0	$0	$0	$0	$0	$0	$500	$1,000
Subtotal Cash Spent		$8,062	$10,482	$7,450	$26,261	$25,030	$31,635	$41,985	$40,742	$157,210	$88,256	$168,834	$96,420
Net Cash Flow		($8,062)	($10,482)	($2,150)	$6,114	$17,607	$13,133	$546	$1,895	$18,117	($3,089)	$4,537	($1,028)
Cash Balance		$17,438	$6,956	$4,806	$10,920	$28,527	$41,660	$42,206	$44,101	$62,218	$59,129	$63,666	$62,639

The Daily Perc
Appendix 4-F

The Daily Perc—Pro Forma Balance Sheet

Assets	Starting Balances	Jun	Jul	Aug	Sep	Oct	Nov	Dec	Jan	Feb	Mar	Apr	May
Current Assets													
Cash	$25,500	$17,438	$6,956	$4,806	$10,920	$28,527	$41,660	$42,206	$44,101	$62,218	$59,129	$63,666	$62,639
Inventory	$35,000	$35,000	$35,000	$35,000	$23,800	$16,225	$17,036	$16,185	$16,225	$29,356	$32,410	$35,159	$35,159
Other Current Assets	$0	$0	$0	$0	$0	$0	$0	$0	$0	$0	$0	$0	$0
Total Current Assets	$60,500	$52,438	$41,956	$39,806	$34,720	$44,752	$58,697	$58,391	$60,326	$91,575	$91,539	$98,825	$97,798
Long-term Assets													
Long-term Assets	$131,400	$131,400	$131,400	$131,400	$131,400	$131,400	$131,400	$131,400	$131,400	$236,800	$236,800	$323,250	$323,250
Accumulated Depreciation	$0	$0	$310	$620	$2,185	$3,750	$5,315	$6,880	$8,445	$11,265	$14,085	$17,935	$21,785
Total Long-term Assets	$131,400	$131,400	$131,090	$130,780	$129,215	$127,650	$126,085	$124,520	$122,955	$225,535	$222,715	$305,315	$301,465
Total Assets	$191,900	$183,838	$173,046	$170,586	$163,935	$172,402	$184,782	$182,911	$183,281	$317,110	$314,254	$404,140	$399,263

Liabilities and Capital	Starting Balances	Jun	Jul	Aug	Sep	Oct	Nov	Dec	Jan	Feb	Mar	Apr	May
Current Liabilities													
Accounts Payable	$0	$1,805	$1,782	$4,872	$6,454	$13,810	$22,478	$20,501	$21,501	$48,889	$42,079	$46,535	$43,909
Current Borrowing	$9,000	$9,000	$9,000	$9,000	$9,000	$9,000	$9,000	$9,000	$9,000	$9,000	$9,000	$8,500	$7,500
Other Current Liabilities	$0	$0	$0	$0	$0	$0	$0	$0	$0	$0	$0	$0	$0
Subtotal Current Liabilities	$9,000	$10,805	$10,782	$13,872	$15,454	$22,810	$31,478	$29,501	$30,501	$57,889	$51,079	$55,035	$51,409
Long-term Liabilities	$131,400	$128,900	$125,784	$131,084	$125,918	$125,918	$125,918	$125,918	$125,918	$224,102	$216,886	$294,865	$286,394
Total Liabilities	$140,400	$139,705	$136,566	$144,956	$141,372	$148,728	$157,396	$155,419	$156,419	$281,991	$267,965	$349,900	$337,803
Paid-in Capital	$225,270	$225,270	$225,270	$225,270	$225,270	$225,270	$225,270	$225,270	$225,270	$225,270	$225,270	$225,270	$225,270
Retained Earnings	($173,770)	($173,770)	($173,770)	($173,770)	($173,770)	($173,770)	($173,770)	($173,770)	($173,770)	($173,770)	($173,770)	($173,770)	($173,770)
Earnings	$0	($7,367)	($15,020)	($25,870)	($28,937)	($27,826)	($24,114)	($24,008)	($24,638)	($16,382)	($5,211)	$2,741	$9,960
Total Capital	$51,500	$44,133	$36,480	$25,630	$22,563	$23,674	$27,386	$27,492	$26,862	$35,118	$46,289	$54,241	$61,460
Total Liabilities and Capital	$191,900	$183,838	$173,046	$170,586	$163,935	$172,402	$184,782	$182,911	$183,281	$317,110	$314,254	$404,140	$399,263
Net Worth	$51,500	$44,133	$36,480	$25,630	$22,563	$23,674	$27,386	$27,492	$26,862	$35,118	$46,289	$54,241	$61,460

BARTHOLOMEW J. FISHER III
123 Money Lane
Seattle, Washington
bjfisheriii@dailyperc.com
(999) 999-9999

PROFILE

An experienced professional with strong interpersonal, managerial, and problem solving skills. Resourceful, organized, analytical, and versatile.

EDUCATION

STANFORD UNIVERSITY   Master of Business Administration, 1988

Entrepreneurial Management major. Strategic Planning and Marketing concentrations.

UNIVERSITY OF SEATTLE   Bachelor of Science, 1983

Economics major. Marketing minor. Varsity lacrosse player.

PROFESSIONAL EXPERIENCE

WASHINGTON CENTER FOR ENTERPRISE DEVELOPMENT   Seattle, Washington

Director   2000–Present

Directed this Small Business Development Center program that develops human capital among current and prospective entrepreneurs and enterprise managers for the support and growth of sustainable enterprises and wealth in the state of Washington.

FISHER INDUSTRIES, INC.   Seattle, Washington

General Manager   1993–2000

Managed the Sales, Marketing, and Operations of this Krispy Kreme Doughnuts franchise.

FISHER, BAKER AND SCHNIDER   Berkeley, California

President   1988–1993

Operated this advertising and marketing firm, which specialized in the design and implementation of marketing programs. Performed services including strategic and market analyses and advertising campaign creation. Conducted workshops, focus groups, and facilitation services. Wrote articles and press releases for client firms. Marketed FBS services to corporations and organizations.

STARBUCKS CORPORATION   Seattle, Washington

Marketing Manager   1983–1986

Trainee in the Marketing Department. Performed strategic and tactical planning, forecasting, budgeting, financial analysis and modeling, and media and publicity planning.

AWARDS, AFFILIATIONS, & ACTIVITIES

Minority Business Advocate of the Year—Washington Office—U.S. Small Business Administration

Social Venture Partners Seattle—Partner

Urban League of Metropolitan Seattle—Economic Development Advisory Council Member

Rotary Club of Seattle—Member and member of scholarship committee

American Marketing Association—Puget Sound Chapter—Board of Directors

Greenpeace—Member

TERESA ANNE FISHER
123 Money Lane
Seattle, Washington
tafisher@dailyperc.com
(999) 888-8888

WORK EXPERIENCE

STARBUCKS CORPORATION

Senior Financial Analyst   1996–Present

- Lead the development of the business unit's annual operating budget and quarterly forecasts.
- Support the development of strategic and operating plans. Identify and communicate plans' risks and opportunities.
- Conduct decision analyses and communicates results. Build and maintain financial models.
- Perform due diligence for new initiatives.
- Build financial models and provide analytical support for business initiatives and contract negotiations. Identify, analyze, and communicate trends and issues affecting the business.
- Provide analysis and feedback on financial performance and key performance measures.
- Provide financial information and guidance to all levels of management. Ensure financial statements are complete, accurate and timely.

Financial Analyst   1992–1996

- Supported the development of strategic and operating plans.

- Built financial models and provided analytical support for business initiatives and contract negotiations. Identified, analyzed, and communicated trends and issues affecting the business.

- Ensured financial statements were complete, accurate, and timely. Facilitated process development and improvement initiatives.

Store Manager   1990–1992

Assistant Store Manager   1988–1990

Barista   1986–1988

EDUCATION

UNIVERSITY OF SEATTLE   BS, Accounting, 1988

ACTIVITIES

Seattle Area Chamber of Commerce—Retail Alliance member
Cascadia Loan Fund—Loan Review Committee
Rotary Club of Seattle—Member and Chair of Finance Committee
Junior League of Seattle—Life Member
Northwest Sierra Club—Treasurer
Social Venture Partners Seattle—Partner

Appendix 5

Resources for Entrepreneurs[1]

Books

On Starting a Business—and Succeeding

101 Businesses You Can Start on the Internet, by Daniel S. Janal (International Thompson Publishing, Inc., 1996).

The Art of the Start: The Time-Tested, Battle-Hardened Guide for Anyone Starting Anything, by Guy Kawasaki (Portfolio, 2004).

Good to Great: Why Some Companies Make the Leap . . . and Others Do Not, by Jim Collins (HarperBusiness, October 2001).

How to Make 1000 Mistakes in Business and Still Succeed: The Small Business Owner's Guide to Crucial Decisions, by Harold L. Wright (The Wright Track, 1995).

In Search of Excellence: Lessons from America's Best Run Companies, by Thomas J. Peters and Robert H. Waterman (Warner Books; Reissue edition, 1988).

Mancuso's Small Business Resource Guide, by Joseph Mancuso (Sourcebooks, 1996).

Online Success Tactics: 101 Ways to Build Your Small Business, by Jeanette Cates (Twin Towers, 2002).

Start Your Own Business, by Rieva Lesonsky (Entrepreneur Press, 4e, 2007).

What No One Ever Tells You About Starting Your Own Business: Real-Life Start-Up Advice from 101 Successful Entrepreneurs, by Jan Norman (Kaplan Business, 2e, 2004).

The Young Entrepreneur's Guide to Starting and Running a Business, by Steve Mariotti (Three Rivers Press; Compl. Rev. edition, 2000).

On Thinking Like an Entrepreneur

The 48 Laws of Power, by Michael Greene (Penguin Putnam, 2000).

Awakening the Entrepreneur Within: How Ordinary People Can Create Extraordinary Companies, by Michael Gerber (Collins, 2008).

The Entrepreneurial Mindset, by Rita Gunther McGrath and Ian MacMillan (Harvard Business School Press, 2000).

Focus: The Future of Your Company Depends on It, by Al Reis (HarperBusiness, 1997).

Secrets of the Young & Successful: How to Get Everything You Want Without Waiting a Lifetime, by Jennifer Kushell and Scott M. Kaufman (Fireside, 2003).

The 7 Habits of Highly Effective People, by Stephen Covey (Free Press, 1990).

The Student Success Manifesto: How to Create a Life of Passion, Purpose, and Prosperity, by Michael Simmons (Extreme Entrepreneurship Education Co., 2003).

---

[1] Please note that the publisher cannot guarantee that listed URLs will remain active and is not responsible for future changes to the content of the Web sites.

Success Through a Positive Mental Attitude, by W. Clement Stone (Pocket Books, 1991 re-issue). A classic!

Think and Grow Rich, by Napoleon Hill (Ballantine Books, 1990 re-issue). Another classic!

Think and Grow Rich, by Dennis Paul Kimbro (Fawcett Columbine, 1991). An update of Hill's book by an African American.

On How Other Entrepreneurs Succeeded

The Accidental Entrepreneur: The 50 Things I Wish Someone Had Told Me About Starting a Business, by Susan Urquhart-Brown (AMACOM, 2008).

Ben & Jerry's: The Inside Scoop: How Two Real Guys Built a Business with a Social Conscience and a Sense of Humor, by Fred "Chico" Lager. The former CEO of Ben & Jerry's describes the company's remarkable history and activism (Crown Publishers, 1994).

Entrepreneurs in Profile: How 20 of the World's Greatest Entrepreneurs Built Their Business Empires . . . and How You Can Too, by Steve Mariotti and Michael Caslin with Debra DeSalvo (Career Press, 2000).

Kitchen Table Entrepreneurs: How Eleven Women Escaped Poverty and Became Their Own Bosses, by Martha Shirk, Anna Wadia, Marie Wilson, and Sara Gould (Westview Press, 2004).

Life and Def: Sex, Drugs, Money + God, by Russell Simmons (Three Rivers Press, 2002).

Losing My Virginity: How I've Survived, Had Fun, and Made a Fortune Doing Business My Way, by Richard Branson (Three Rivers Press, 1999).

Steve Jobs: Wizard of Apple Computer, by Suzan Willson (Enslow Publishers, 2001).

Student Entrepreneurs: 14 Undergraduate All-Stars Tell Their Stories, by Michael McMyne and Nicole Amare (Premium Press America, 2003).

The Men Behind Def Jam: The Radical Rise of Russell Simmons and Rick Rubin, by Alex Ogg (Omnibus Press, 2002).

Trump: The Way to the Top: The Best Business Advice I Ever Received, by Donald Trump (Crown Business, 2004).

On Negotiating

The Art of Woo: Using Strategic Persuasion to Sell Your Idea, by G. Richard Shell and Mario Moussa (Penguin Group, 2007).

Bargaining for Advantage: Negotiation Strategies for Reasonable People, by G. Richard Shell (Penguin Group, 2006).

Difficult Conversations: How to Discuss What Matters Most, by Douglas Stone, Bruce Patton, Sheila Heen, and Roger Fisher (Penguin Putnam; 1st edition, 2000).

Winning, by Jack Welch (HarperCollins Publishers, 2005).

You Can Negotiate Anything, by Herb Cohen (Bantam Books, 1993).

On Accounting

Accounting Game: Basic Accounting Fresh from the Lemonade Stand, by Darrell Millis (Sourcebooks, 2008).

Accounting Handbook, by Joel G. Siegal (Barron's Educational Series, 2006).

Accounting the Easy Way, by Peter J. Eisen (Barron's Educational Series, 4th edition, 2003).

The Guide to Understanding Financial Statements, by S. B. Costales (McGraw-Hill, 1993).

credit   in bookkeeping, a recording of income. Also, the ability to borrow money.

creditor   person who is owed money.

cyclical   occurring in cycles, periods when things happen in the same pattern.

database   collection of information, such as customer addresses, often stored in a computer.

debit   in bookkeeping, a recording of an expense or an asset.

debt   an obligation to pay back a loan; a "liability."

debt ratio   the ratio of debt (liabilities) to assets.

debt-to-equity ratio   a comparison that expresses financial strategy by showing how much of a company is financed by debt and how much by equity.

deductible   the portion of an insured loss or damage not covered by insurance; the higher the deductible, the lower the insurance premium.

deduction   expense incurred during the course of doing business. A business owner may subtract deductible amounts from income when figuring income tax due.

demand   the willingness and desire for a commodity together with the ability to pay for it; the amount consumers are ready and able to buy at the price offered in the marketplace.

demographics   population statistics.

depreciation   the percentage of value of an asset subtracted each year until the value becomes zero; reflects wear and tear on the asset.

discount   (referring to bonds) the difference between a bond's trading price and par when the trading price is below par.

dividend   each stockholder's portion of the profit per share paid out by a corporation.

donation   a gift or contribution to a charitable organization.

draft   to write a version of a contract or agreement with the understanding that it will probably need to be developed and rewritten further.

economy   the financial structure of a nation or other area that determines how resources and wealth are distributed.

electronic rights   protection of a creator's intellectual property (writing, art, music, etc.) from being used on a Web site without payment to the creator.

electronic storefront   a Web site set up as a store where consumers can see and purchase merchandise.

e-mail   short for electronic mail; messages sent between computers or other devices using the Internet.

employee   a person hired by a business to work for hourly wages salary, or commission.

entrepreneur   a person who organizes and manages a business, assuming the risk for the sake of the potential return.

Equal Pay Act   law passed in 1963 that requires employers to pay men and women the same wage for doing the same job.

equity   ownership in a company received in exchange for money invested. In accounting, equity is equal to assets minus liabilities.

ethics   a system of morals or standards of conduct and judgment.

export   1. *v.* to ship products overseas for sale. 2. *n.* (singular and plural) the products themselves.

external opportunity   an opportunity generated by observing the outside world, as opposed to an internal opportunity, which is generated from an interest or hobby.

face value   the value printed on a bill or bond; not necessarily its market value.

Fair Labor Standards Act   law passed in 1938 requiring employers to pay employees at least minimum wage and prohibiting the hiring of anyone under 16 full-time.

fair market value   the price at which a property or business is valued by the market; the price it would fetch on the open market.

fax   short for facsimile, *n.* a machine that electronically sends printed material over a telephone line; *v.* to use a fax machine.

file   (referring to taxes) to fulfill one's legal obligation by mailing a tax return, and any taxes due, to the Internal Revenue Service or state or local tax authority.

fiscal year   a 12-month period between settling financial recordkeeping.

fixed costs   business expenses that must be paid whether or not any sales are being generated; USAIIRD: utilities, salaries, advertising, insurance, interest, rent, and depreciation.

foundation   an organization that manages money donated to it by philanthropists.

franchise   a business that markets a product or service developed by the franchiser, in the manner specified by the franchiser.

franchisee   owner of a franchise unit or units.

franchiser   person who develops a franchise or a company that sells franchises.

fraud   intentional failure by an individual or organization to disclose the truth about something.

free enterprise system   economic system in which businesses are privately owned and operate relatively free of government interference.

future value   the amount an investment is worth in the future if invested at a specific rate of return.

goodwill   an intangible asset generated when a company does something positive that has value—goodwill can include the company's reputation, brand recognition, and relationships with the community and customers.

gross domestic product (GDP)   the annual estimated market value of all products and services produced within a country.

gross national product (GNP)   the annual estimated market value of all products and services produced by the resources of a country.

gross profit   total sales revenue minus total cost of goods sold.

human resources   segment of a business that hires, trains, and develops the company's employees.

hyperlink   a highlighted or underlined word, phrase, or icon on a Web site that, when clicked on, leads to a new document page anywhere on the Internet.

immigrant   a person who settles in a new country or region, having left his or her country or region of birth.

import   1. *v.* to bring products from overseas into a country to sell. 2. *n.* (singular and plural) the products themselves.

incentive   something that motivates someone to take action—to work, start a business, or study harder, for example.

income statement   a financial statement that summarizes income and expense activity over a specified period and shows net profit or loss.

inflation   the gradual continuous increase in the prices of products and services, usually resulting from an increase in the amount of money in circulation in an economy.

infringe   to violate a copyright, trademark, or patent.

installment   payment on a loan or debt made at regular intervals.

institutional advertising   advertisements placed by large corporations to keep the name of the company in the mind of the public—not to promote a specific product or service.

insurance   a system of protection for payment provided by insurance companies to protect people or businesses from having property or wealth damaged or destroyed.

insurance agent   insurance company employee who sells insurance and helps purchasers determine what insurance they need to protect their assets.

insurance policy   contract between an insurance company and a person or business being insured that describes the premium(s) to be paid and the insurance company's obligations.

intellectual property   intangible property created using the intellect, such as an invention, book, painting, or music.

interest   payment for using someone else's money; payment received for lending money.

interest rate   money paid for the use of money, expressed as a percentage per unit of time.

Internal Revenue Service   the federal government bureau in charge of taxation.

Internet   the world's largest computer network, connecting many millions of users.

interoffice   something sent from one person to another within the same office, or company, using the office distribution system.

inventory   items on hand to be sold.

investment   something into which one puts money, time, or energy with the hope of gaining profit or satisfaction in the future.

invoice   an itemized list of goods delivered or services rendered and the amount due; a bill.

ISP   abbreviation for Internet Service Provider; services that provide access to the Internet for subscribers' computers. Some ISPs, such as Microsoft Network or America Online, also provide software for browsing the Internet and chatting with other subscribers, among other services.

lawsuit   attempt to recover a right or claim through legal action.

layaway   store policy allowing a customer to make a down payment on an item to secure it and then make monthly payments on the balance (the store keeps the item until it is fully paid for).

letter of agreement   written agreement between parties regarding a business arrangement; less formal and detailed than a contract and usually used for arrangements of brief duration.

letterhead   stationery imprinted with the name, address, phone and fax numbers, logo, etc., of a business.

leveraged   financed by debt, as opposed to equity.

liability   an entry on a balance sheet showing a debt of a business.

liability insurance   insurance that covers the cost of injuries to a customer or damage to property caused on a business's premises, or by its product or service.

liable   to be responsible for lawsuits that arise from accidents, unpaid bills, faulty merchandise, or other business problems.

license   *n.* legal authorization to perform some specified thing; *v.* to grant the right to use a licensor's name on a product or service.

licensee   person granted the right to use a licensor's name on a product or service sold by the licensee.

licensor   person who sells the right to use his or her name or company name to a licensee; unlike the franchiser, the licensor does not attempt to dictate exactly how the licensee does business.

limited liability company (LLC)   a form of business ownership offering the tax advantages of a partnership as well as limited legal liability; this structure is not available in all states.

limited partnership   form of partnership in which certain partners have limited investment in a business and therefore limited liability.

logo   short for logotype, a company trademark or sign.

majority interest   ownership of more stock in a corporation than all the other stockholders own together.

management   the art of planning and organizing a business so it can meet its goals.

manufacture   to make or produce a tangible product.

market   a group of people potentially interested in buying a product or service; any scenario or designated location where trade occurs.

market clearing price   the price at which the amount of a product or service demanded by consumers equals the amount the supplier is willing to sell at that price; the price at which the supply and demand lines cross, also called "equilibrium price."

marketing   the development and use of strategies for getting a product or service to consumers and generating interest in it.

marketing mix   the combination of the four factors—product, price, place, and promotion—that communicates a marketing vision.

market segment   a group of consumers who have a similar response to a particular type of product.

markup   an increase in the price of a product to cover expenses and create a profit for the seller.

maturity   the date at which a bond must be redeemed by the company that issued it.

media (pl.)   means of communication (newspapers, radio, television, etc.) that reach the general public, usually including advertising.

memo   short for memorandum, from the Latin word for "to be remembered"; a concise note from one person to another—often "interoffice."

mentor   a person who agrees to volunteer time and expertise, or provide emotional support, to help or support someone else, usually younger.

microloan   a loan of between $100 and $35,000 made to an entrepreneur based not on credit history or collateral, but rather on character, management ability, and business plan. The money can be used to buy machinery, furniture, inventory, and supplies for a new business but may not be used to pay existing debts.

mission statement   a short, written statement that informs customers and employees what a business's goal is and describes the strategy and tactics intended to meet it.

modem   device that connects a computer to a phone or cable line and translates digital information between them.

monopoly   a market with only one producer; the control of the pricing and distribution of a product or service in a given market as a result of lack of competition.

moving assembly line   continuously moving conveyor belt in a factory on which workers assemble cars, appliances, etc.

negotiation   discussion or bargaining in an effort to reach agreement between parties with differing goals.

net   final result; in business, the profit or loss remaining after all costs have been subtracted.

net present value   the net amount an investment is worth discounted back to the present.

network   to exchange information and contacts.

newsgroup   an online discussion group focused on a specific subject.

noncash expenses   expenses a business may incur, such as depreciation, that do not require cash outlay.

operating cost   a cost necessary to operate a business, not including the cost of goods sold. Operating costs almost always fall into USAIIRD: utilities, salaries, advertising, insurance, interest, rent, and depreciation. Operating costs are also called "overhead."

opportunity   a chance or occasion that can be turned to one's advantage.

opportunity cost   the value of what must be given up in order to obtain something else.

optimist   a person who consistently looks on the positive side of situations or outcomes.

overhead   the continuing fixed costs of running a business; the costs a business has to disburse to operate.

owner's equity   net worth; the difference between assets and liabilities.

par   the face value of a bond.

partnership   an association of two or more people in a business enterprise. Should be governed by a legal partnership agreement.

patent   an exclusive right, granted by the government, to produce, use, and sell an invention or process.

payroll tax   employers must deduct this tax from their employees' paychecks and pay it to the designated entity.

percentage   literally, "a given part of a hundred"; a number expressed as part of a whole, with the whole represented as 100 percent.

philanthropy   a concern for human and social welfare that is expressed by giving money through charities and foundations.

pilferage   stealing by employees or customers of a business's inventory.

position   *v.* to distinguish a product or service from similar products or services being offered to the same market. *n.* the place of a product or service in a market.

premium   the amount above par for which a bond is trading on the open market; the cost of insurance, usually expressed as a regular payment by the policyholder to the insurance company.

present value   the amount an investment is worth discounted back to the present.

press release   an announcement sent to the media to generate publicity.

principal   the amount of a debt or loan before interest is added.

product   something that exists in nature, or is made by human industry, usually to be sold.

production-distribution chain   the manufacturer-to-wholesaler-to-retailer-to-consumer process along which a product progresses.

product life cycle   the four stages that a product or service goes through as it matures in the market—introduction, growth, maturity, and decline.

profit   the sum remaining after all costs are deducted from the income of a business.

profit and loss statement   an income statement showing the gain and loss from business transactions and summarizing the net profit or loss.

profit margin   the percentage of each dollar of revenue that is profit; profit divided by revenue times 100.

profit per unit   the selling price minus the cost of goods sold of an item.

progressive tax   a tax that takes a greater percentage of higher incomes than of lower incomes.

projection   a forecast or prediction of financial outcome; business plans include projections of how the entrepreneur expects financial statements to come out.

promissory note   a written promise to pay a certain sum of money on a specified date.

promotion   the development of the popularity and sales of a product or service through advertising and publicity.

proportional tax   a tax that takes the same percentage of all incomes.

prospect   a person who may be receptive to your sales pitch.

prototype   a model or pattern that serves as an example of how a product would look and operate if it were manufactured.

public domain   free of copyright or patent restrictions.

publicity   free promotion, as opposed to advertising, which is purchased.

quality   degree of excellence (of a product or service).

quota   a restriction imposed by the government of a country on the amount of a specified good that can be imported.

rate of return   the return on an investment, expressed as a percentage of the amount invested.

real estate   land or buildings that have value in the marketplace.

recession   an economic downturn; lower than normal employment and business activity.

reconcile   to compare two financial records, item by item, to make sure both have been kept accurately. One may reconcile an accounting journal by comparing the right side to the left, or a checkbook by comparing the entries in the check register to a bank statement.

recruitment   the act of finding and hiring employees.

redeem   to turn in a bond to the issuing corporation at the date of maturity for conversion into cash.

resume (or resumé, or résumé)   a concise summary of a person's education, work experience, and interests.

return on investment   profit on an investment, expressed as a percentage.

risk   with an investment, the chance of losing money.

royalty   a share of the proceeds of the sale of a product paid to a person who owns a copyright; also refers to the fee paid to a franchiser or licensor.

salary   fixed amount of money paid to an employee at regular intervals; treated as a fixed operating cost.

sales tax   consumption tax levied on items that are sold by businesses to consumers. U.S. states raise revenue through sales tax.

savings account   a bank account in which money is deposited and on which the bank pays interest to the depositor.

seasonality scenario   a description of a business's expectations for seasonal changes in cash flow.

self-employment tax   a tax people who work for themselves pay in addition to income tax; includes the Social Security tax obligation for people who are self-employed.

self-esteem   belief in oneself; a good feeling about oneself.

service   intangible work providing time, skills, or expertise in exchange for money.

severance   an extension of salary for a limited time period to an employee who has been let go.

share   a single unit of stock.

shareware free software available on the Internet; shareware is usually the "test" or "light" version of the software.

signatory person signing a contract, thereby legally committing to compliance with it.

small claims court state court where disputes for relatively small amounts of money are settled between complainants who are allowed to represent themselves instead of using attorneys.

socially responsible business a business venture that expresses the entrepreneur's ethics and core values.

Social Security a federal government program that pays benefits to retired people and the families of dead or disabled workers.

sole proprietorship a business owned by one person. The owner receives all profits and is legally liable for all debts or lawsuits arising from the business.

speculative highly uncertain or risky.

start-up cost an expense involved in getting a business going; start-up costs are also called the "original investment" in a business.

statistics facts collected and presented in numerical fashion.

stock an individual's share in the ownership of a corporation, based on the size of the investment.

strategy the plan for how a business intends to go about its own performance and outdo that of its competition.

supply a schedule of the quantities that a business will make available to consumers at different prices.

tactics the specific ways in which a business carries out its strategy.

tariff a tax imposed by a government on an import designed to make the import more expensive than a similar domestic product and, therefore, less attractive to domestic consumers.

tax a percentage of business profits or individual income taken by the government to support public services.

tax evasion deliberate avoidance of the obligation to pay taxes; may lead to penalties or even prison.

tax-exempt the condition of an entity that is allowed to produce income free from taxation.

test market to offer a product or service to a limited, yet representative, segment of consumers in order to receive feedback and improve the product or service, before attempting to place it in a larger market.

trade balance the difference between the value of a country's imports and its exports.

trademark any word, name, symbol, or device used by a manufacturer or merchant to distinguish a product.

trade-off an exchange in which one benefit or advantage is given up in order to gain another.

value pricing a strategy based on finding the balance between price and quality that will attract the most consumers.

variable cost any cost that changes based on the volume of units sold; a term sometimes used instead of "cost of goods sold."

venture capital funds invested in a potentially profitable business enterprise despite risk of loss.

Web site an Internet document that can contain sound and graphics, as well as text.

Index